6/15 $16.77

DEMOCRACY'S EDUCATION

Democracy's EDUCATION

PUBLIC WORK, CITIZENSHIP, & THE FUTURE *of* COLLEGES AND UNIVERSITIES

EDITED BY HARRY C. BOYTE

VANDERBILT UNIVERSITY PRESS   NASHVILLE

This book is printed on acid-free paper.
Manufactured in the United States of America

Library of Congress Cataloging-in-Publication Data
LC control number 2014015261
LC classification number LC173.B69 2014
Dewey class number 379.73—dc23

ISBN 978-0-8265-2035-7 (hardcover)
ISBN 978-0-8265-2036-4 (paperback)
ISBN 978-0-8265-2037-1 (ebook)

I dedicate *Democracy's Education* to the team members, coaches, teachers, faculty, staff, principals, and other participants in Public Achievement, in every country where they are learning to do citizenship as public work and showing its possibilities. They are creating grounded hope for the future, and a new narrative of education.

—Harry C. Boyte

CONTENTS

ACKNOWLEDGMENTS

Democracy's Education grows from the work of the American Commonwealth Partnership (ACP), a year-long alliance of colleges and universities, other associations, and individuals launched at the White House on January 10, 2012, which worked with the administration to revitalize the democratic story of higher education in America, in danger of being replaced with the story that higher education is mainly a ticket to individual success and achievement. I thank Jon Carson, then director of the Office of Public Engagement, who invited me to develop an initiative in partnership with the administration in March 2011, and also Jonathan Greenblatt, and Victoria McCullough at the White House, for their collaboration. I also thank Martha Kanter, Eduardo Ochoa, Phil Martin, Taylor Spanek, Sam Ryan, and Julie Heinz at the Department of Education for being partners in ACP. All were a pleasure to work with as ACP took shape.

My first call after Carson's invitation was to Nancy Cantor, who stands out among American higher education presidents as a bold and visionary architect of "democracy's colleges," to use a concept central to this symposium. Nancy helped put together the Presidents' Advisory Council—Brian Murphy, M. Christopher Brown, Thomas Ehrlich, Freeman Hrabowski, David Mathews, Paul Pribbenow, and Judith Ramaley—and hosted the two planning meetings. I greatly appreciate the sage counsel of the presidents as the American Commonwealth Partnership took shape, and also the support of Paul Pribbenow, who offered to host ACP at Augsburg College.

I express appreciation to the leadership team of Timothy Eatman, Julie Ellison, David Hoffman, Kara Lindaman, Paul Markham, Cecilia Orphan, Scott Peters, Julie Plaut, Blase Scarnati, Lucille Shaw, Stephanie South, and J. Theis. They contributed zeal, intelligence, and strategic insight in helping to plan and organize ACP. I also convey many thanks to George Mehaffy and Jennifer Domagel-Goldman, for all the ways the American Democracy Project contributed; to Jamie Haft, Adam Bush, and Kevin Bott, as well as Tim Eatman and Scott Peters, for the extensive involvements of Imagining America; and to Julie Plaut for Minnesota Campus Compact's contributions.

John Spencer and Karla McGregor at the University of Iowa's Delta Center, Scott Peters of Imagining America and Cornell University, Gwen Ottinger of Drexel University, Sherburne Abbott of Syracuse University, and Nicholas Jordan of the University of Minnesota have been colleagues and collaborators in developing the civic science initiative, which is going strong with support from the National Science Foundation and plans to launch a movement reconceiving the role of science and scientists in society in democratic terms. Julie Ellison has provided outstanding leadership for Citizen Alum. Bill Muse, Jean Johnson, Derek Barker, and John Dedrick were partners in developing the Shaping Our Future national conversations on the public purposes of higher education. The partnership is in a second stage, preparing for a national conversation on what communities should expect from higher education in the context of a dramatically changing world of work, to be launched in 2015. Background meetings with hundreds of citizens across the country have demonstrated that the themes of *Democracy's Education* are much on people's minds.

For feedback on the framing essay as it first took shape in a working paper for the Kettering Foundation, many thanks to Peter Levine, Derek Barker, Luke Bretherton, Lisa Clarke, David Hoffman, David Brown, Lisa Clarke, Garry Hesser, Barbara Crosby, Barry Checkoway, Gerald Taylor, Cynthia Estlund, John Budd, and Doran Schranz.

Special thanks to John Dedrick for encouraging and facilitating this project from the initial Kettering Foundation study through the book. His insights and encouragements in this, as in other projects, are invaluable. I also want to thank my many other colleagues at the Kettering Foundation, over many years, who have created a remarkable intellectual community for exploring these ideas; and to Michael Ames, director of Vanderbilt University Press, for his help throughout the manuscript preparation—and his many years of support for public work.

Finally, I want to express my profound appreciation to Marie-Louise Ström for continuous conversations on all these themes, and for our life partnership in this work.

DEMOCRACY'S EDUCATION

REINVENTING CITIZENSHIP AS PUBLIC WORK

Harry C. Boyte

> To broaden the scope of democracy to include everyone
> and deepen the concept to include every relationship.
> —Septima Clark, on the larger purposes
> of the civil rights movement, circa 1960

The Power of Ideas

The fate of higher education and the larger democracy itself is inextricably tied to the way those of us in higher education understand citizenship, practice civic education, and convey our purposes to the larger society. If we are to navigate successfully the tsunami of changes sweeping over our institutions and society and to claim our own story rather than having it defined by vested interests with more narrow ends in mind, we will have to revisit conventional ideas of citizenship and liberal education. We need to move beyond narrow views of citizenship as voting and voluntarism, and reinvent citizenship as *public work*, work that explicitly and intentionally prepares our students (and ourselves) to be builders of the democracy, not simply helpers, voters, analysts, informers, or critics of democracy.

This means putting *education for work with public qualities* at the center of teaching, learning, and research, for the sake of ourselves as educators, for our students, and for the democracy.

Such civic education and the faith in democratic possibility it embodies have been urged by leaders in higher education such as Martha Kanter, undersecretary of education from 2009 to 2013, who calls for educational experiences that "prepare young people for citizenship that extends across family, community, and work."[1] Kanter's vision about the purpose and story of higher education also challenges conventional wisdom and the public mood.

Today, across the political spectrum, Americans feel powerless to navigate the changes and challenges of our time, from climate change to school reform, from immigration to joblessness and growing poverty. In 1996 the Kettering Foundation commissioned the Harwood Group, a public issues research firm, to conduct focus groups across the country in order to better grasp the "nature and extent of the disconnect between what people see as important concerns and their sense that they can address them." They revealed a nation of people deeply troubled about the direction of society as a whole, even if optimistic about their personal economic prospects after several years of economic expansion. Citizens tied moral concerns to larger dynamics. They saw large institutions, from government to business, as remote and focused on narrow gain. They worried that people were divided by race, ideology, religion, and class. People also felt powerless to address these trends; as a result, they said, they pulled back into smaller circles of private life where they had some control, even if they thought that retreat spelled trouble. "If you look at the whole picture of everything that is wrong, it is so overwhelming," said one woman from Richmond. "You just retreat back and take care of what you know you can take care of—and you make it smaller, make it even down to just you and your unit. You know you can take care of that."[2]

Such feelings have become more pronounced in the opening years of the twenty-first century. Lay citizens, feeling powerless, generally share the view of opinion elites that choosing the right leaders is the way to fix our country's problems—even if it repeatedly fails to do so. In conversations across the country for *Time* magazine before the 2010 and 2012 elections, Joe Klein heard feelings of powerlessness voiced again and again. "Topic A is the growing sense that our best days as a nation are behind us, that our kids won't live as well as we did, that China is in the driver's seat." Citizens voice frustrations that recent elections, in which "insiders" are voted out and "outsiders" voted in, fail to halt national decline.[3]

The sense of powerlessness is acute in higher education, where educators also feel besieged by cost cutting, profit-making colleges, Massive Open Online Courses (or MOOCs, in everyday language) and other distance learning, and demands that higher education be narrowly geared to the needs of today's workplace. All of these dynamics threaten the story of larger purpose, a story that most people in higher education fear is now profoundly endangered.

The dawning realization among the broad population that leaders won't save us—that "we are the ones we've been waiting for," in the words of the old civil rights song and a new book by Peter Levine with this title[4]—has also begun to generate a new movement in which citizens themselves reclaim responsibility for democracy. This idea of democracy animated the civil rights movement: democracy as "including everyone and every relationship," as Septima Clark, a leader in grassroots citizenship education, put it.

Signs of citizens aspiring to be the central agents of democracy are multiplying. "What is today's most significant political movement?" asks David Mathews, president of the Kettering Foundation. "Although it flies below most radar screens, I would pick the quest for a democracy in which citizens have a stronger hand in shaping the future, a strong, citizen-centered democracy."[5]

Mathews is onto something—a quickening in the pace of civically empowering politics, not only in the United States but also around the world. Thus, to cite several examples, the Obama 2008 campaign, with its theme of collective agency, "Yes We Can," showed possibilities for introducing civic politics on a large scale by integrating community organizing methods into its field operation. There was enthusiasm for the message in South Africa, where I live and work several months a year. The Arab Spring for a time generated a "sense of empowerment and civic duty," as the *Financial Times* put it.[6] The growing movement to address the challenge of climate change and global warming adds a sense of "the fierce urgency of now," to recall another phrase from the civil rights movement.

In scholarly terms, signs of hopefulness about democratic possibility include the awarding of the Nobel Prize for Economics to Elinor Ostrom for her work on citizen-centered governance of common-pool resources like fisheries and forests. Citizen democracy is at the heart of the intellectual movement called "civic studies," which Ostrom cofounded in 2007, based on a framing statement, *The New Civic Politics*, organized around concepts of agency and citizens as cocreators.[7]

Other prominent voices calling for attention to democracy and its challenges are appearing. Thus, Thomas Piketty's *Capital in the Twenty-First Century*, documenting in detail growing inequality and its effects on democratic society, rose to the top of best seller lists in 2014. Benjamin Barber's *If Mayors Ruled the World*, a nuanced, sober, and yet also enthusiastic account of cities as laboratories of democratic experiment and innovation, was translated into dozens of languages and became the basis for a planning effort around a global parliament of mayors.[8] In the concluding reflection, I return to these works and show connections to *Democracy's Education*. I argue that higher education's "cultural logic" today is a major factor in the growing inequality that threatens democracy. Claiming higher education's democratic potential is indispensable to a remedy.

Civic agency movements are appearing with growing frequency and also disappearing quickly. What will create foundations for sustaining them? A molecular organizing process that weaves alternative civic and political concepts and their corresponding practices into everyday life is one key. Another is developing a renewed and compelling story of democracy. Concepts include democracy as a society, not simply elections; citizenship as work with public qualities, not simply voting and volunteering; citizens as cocreators and producers of democracy, not mainly consumers of democracy; and politics as the way we work across differences to solve problems and create a democratic way of life, not a polarized partisan spectacle. The story features a narrative of education (K–12 and community-based as well as higher education) as most importantly about educating citizens who can build and sustain democracy, not about education as a private good, a ticket to fame or fortune. The democratic narrative of education, as we will see, has deep roots in American culture. It is danger of being forgotten. Our task is to revitalize it.

Conceptual shifts and a democratic narrative of education point to the power of ideas. They specifically highlight powers in higher education that operate largely without remark. Higher education generates credentialed knowledge, including educational approaches in K–12 schooling. It spreads conceptual frameworks that structure work and social practices of all kinds. It socializes people in professional identities, shapes students' plans for their careers and lives, and helps to define the meaning of "success" in society. Higher education, in short, is a crucial *anchoring institution of citizenship*. In public forums organized as part of a University of Minnesota task force in the early 2000s, exploring ways to strengthen the land-grant mission of public service, the power of higher education was far better understood by ordinary citizens from all walks of life than by faculty within the institution.

I write this essay to challenge those in higher education to recognize, claim, and exercise these powers and their democratic possibilities. We need to move from being largely objects of change, as is the case today, to being agents of change. A story illustrates the possibilities.

Intimations of Possibility

In January 2013, the Center for Democracy and Citizenship (CDC) at Augsburg College partnered with the mayor of the city of Falcon Heights, Minnesota, to organize and run a "citizen town hall" exploring citizen-based approaches to gun violence after the terrible shooting in Newtown, Connecticut, in December 2012. I had written a letter that the *New York Times* used as the basis for a Readers Forum, arguing that government laws alone couldn't fix the problem. Lay citizens need to help quell violence. The audience of twenty-five or so in the citizen town hall included the mayor, the police chief, the city manager, teachers, a local principal, social agency workers, a university professor from the College of Architecture and Design, four students, IT business entrepreneurs—and two elderly residents. The residents expressed regret that "there are so few citizens." No one from any of the work sites in the community raised any questions about their working definition of citizen as volunteer. When CDC staff did raise questions it prompted a lively conversation about how much power there might be in the community to address gun violence if people see their work in civic terms, and their work sites as civic sites. And I imagined the multiplication of civic powers and energies in the United States on questions like climate change, poverty, education reform, or inequality that can occur if higher education educates its students to think of themselves as citizens through their work and equips them to turn their workplaces into empowering civic sites in communities.

These are usefully called "free spaces," in the conceptual language Sara Evans and I have used. Free spaces develop when participants in civic sites have a significant measure of ownership and opportunities to develop public capacities. Free spaces are schools of democracy, created and sustained by public work.[9]

We need education for public work which builds free spaces. Indeed, public work, sustained, largely self-directed, collaborative effort, paid or unpaid, carried out by a diverse mix of people who create things of common value determined by deliberation, is itself a schooling in democracy. Public work is work *by* publics, *for* public purposes, *in* public. Today, public work is both an intellectual and practical challenge. There are obstacles in the way, not only in the ways we organize education but also in conventional ways citizenship is understood and civic and liberal education is practiced, which I believe contribute to the giving-away of our own narrative. Dominant conceptual frameworks oppose work, the everyday activities of constructing the world, and citizenship. But there are also resources to build on, in our history and in today's education.

Sounding Alarms and Proposing Remedies

Calls for revitalization of civic education and civic learning are multiplying. But concepts of work as a site of citizenship and workplaces as civic sites have largely disappeared. I begin with a sketch of the two approaches to citizenship and civic education that are dominant: One is "civics," the study of government and formal politics. The other is called "communitarianism," the term for the school of political theory that has been most responsible for the revival of modern community service and voluntarism. Both have strengths to build on. But neither explicitly sees citizens as cocreators and foundations of democracy, nor work as a site of citizenship. The result is that civic engagement and citizenship are not taken very seriously; public identities such as the "citizen as customer," which undermine robust, productive citizenship, continue to spread; educators' own power and authority are under assault, with insufficient political resources to respond; and the story of education has increasingly become a story of private or individual advancement, not promotion of the general welfare.

CIVICS

Recent statements on civic education and learning strike notes of alarm. "I was dismayed and horribly discouraged when I read that more than 70% of Americans could name all three of the Three Stooges but that barely 20% could name all three of the branches of our Federal government," wrote former senator Bob Kerry, in *Huffington Post* in 2012. "That troubling fact led me to realize that, to an alarming extent, we have entered an era of civic unawareness." Retired Supreme Court justice Sandra Day O'Connor, who has made revitalizing civic education her personal cause, cites studies showing that only about a third of American adults can name all three branches of government. A third can't name any. Less than a third of eighth graders can identify the historical purpose of the Declaration of Independence. "It's very disturbing," said O'Connor. "I want to educate generations of young people so we won't have the lack of public knowledge we have today." O'Connor's efforts have prompted a new civics education law in Florida and pending legislation in Kentucky and Tennessee. Her curriculum, iCivics, emphasizes knowledge about government.[10]

The iCivics curriculum illustrates the form of citizenship education most commonly taught in schools and in programs like Youth in Government, Youth-Vote, Street Law, and others. There are close connections between the civics view of citizenship education, focusing on ignorance about government, and what is called the liberal framework in political theory. Thus, writing in the *New York Review of Books*, Jeremy Waldron touts Alan Ryan's *On Politics*, a recent two-volume history of political thought from Herodotus to the present. "*On Politics* works," he writes, "because of its steadfast focus on government and institutional arrangements for government." The word "citizen" does not appear in Waldron's review, and concepts of citizens as the central actors in politics are nowhere to be found in Ryan's work.[11]

The problem is that the underlying paradigm of citizenship (as voting) and democracy (as government centered) in civics does little to address powerlessness. Its assumption—that citizens are voters who act like customers in choosing from alternative packages of benefits and promises—finds clear parallel in a "school reform" movement, akin to recent efforts to restructure higher education from the top down. Both "school reform" and "restructuring higher education" see citizens—students, parents, communities—largely as customers.

In K–12, the movement calls for accountability through high-stakes, standardized testing and other measures. The effect is to centralize power among managers, experts, and sometimes for-profit corporations, and undermine the power and authority of educators, schools, and local communities. Educational scholar Diane Ravitch, assistant secretary of education during the first Bush administration and once a leading supporter of "No Child Left Behind," has described this dynamic, in the process confounding the educational establishment in which she was once a central figure. In a series of books and articles as well as in her blog, Ravitch has voiced her changing views, which grow from an ongoing conversation with democracy educator Deborah Meier as well as from her reading of the mounting evidence. She switched from being a supporter of high-stakes testing, charter schools, standardized curriculum, external evaluations of teachers, and other approaches in what is called "the accountability movement," to becoming a fierce critic. "The new breed of school reformers consists mainly of Wall Street hedge fund managers, foundation officials, corporate executives, entrepreneurs and policy makers, but few experienced educators," she writes. She notes the irony of the fact that the "reform" movement praises schools in Finland, which has one of the highest performing school systems in the world according to the Programme for International Student Assessment. Yet the reality is that "Finland disproves every part of their agenda." In Finland, "no individual or school learns its score. No one is rewarded or punished because of these tests. No one can prepare for them, nor is there any incentive to cheat." Finnish schools are based on enhancing the power of educators rather than eroding such power, through "improving the teaching force, limiting student testing to a necessary minimum, placing responsibility and trust before accountability, and handing over school- and district-level leadership to educational professionals."[12]

Knowledge of government is useful—when used by citizens who are the central actors of democracy. Otherwise, the focus on democracy as a state-centered system does little to generate the agency, responsibility, and civic imagination needed to transform centralizing dynamics.

COMMUNITARIANISM

The other main framework of civic education comes from the school of political theory called communitarianism. Over the last generation it has been the seedbed for the community service movement and new emphasis on voluntarism. Service and voluntarism have renewed attention to social relationships and civic responsibility, challenging radical individualism and a "me first" culture. These are considerable strengths. But communitarianism neglects the civic possibilities of work, and it gives little attention to power and politics.

Communitarians address what civic educators and scholars see as the unraveling of civic ties and the cultural degradation reflected in "me first" individualism, school shootings, rampant consumerism, incivility in public life, political hyperpolarization, and the like. While solutions for civic ignorance mainly emphasize classroom learning, communitarian remedies like service and voluntarism stress experiences where young people can develop a sense of responsibility and care for others. Thus two widely endorsed reports on America's civic condition, *A Nation of Spectators: How Civic Disengagement Weakens America and What We Can Do about It*, and *A Call to Civil Society: Why Democracy Needs Moral Truths*, both issued in 1998, embody communitarian ideas like social capital, focusing on "norms, networks, and trust," and emphasize strengthening civil society.

A Call to Civil Society, produced by the Council on Civil Society, chaired by political theorist Jean Elshtain, was animated by concern for how students can learn to couple "responsibilities" with "rights." *A Call* had signatories from Cornel West on the left to Dan Coats, Republican senator from Indiana, on the right. "We come together as citizens of diverse beliefs and different political affiliations to issue an appeal for the renewal of the American experiment in self-governance," it begins. The council worked from the premise that "the possibility of American renewal in the next century depends decisively upon the revitalization of our civil society and our rediscovery of the American idea." Citing survey data showing that Americans are "alarmed and overwhelmingly agreed about the problems of moral decline" and "deeply troubled by the character and values exhibited by young people today," the authors of *A Call* propose that "the core challenge facing our nation today is not primarily governmental or economic" but rather the crisis in morality. "As our social morality deteriorates, life becomes harsher and less civic for everyone . . . and we lose the confidence that we as Americans are united by shared values." Moreover, "as we become an increasingly fragmented and polarized society, too many of our fellow citizens are being left behind." The authors hold that "institutions of civil society are nothing less than the seedbeds of civic virtue," and they propose new initiatives to strengthen families and their efforts to resist materialistic pressures, promote moral and character education through faith communities and schools, and strengthen the nonprofit sector.[13]

Yet as a theory of substantial change, communitarianism has major flaws. The focus on individual moral values and helping distorts the relationship between civic engagement and real-world effects. It neglects root causes and cultural dynamics at work in the formation of values. The goals of community service, for instance, typically include self-esteem, a sense of personal worth, and consciousness of personal values, but they omit attention to power, politics, and community impact.[14] In *Educating for Democracy*, Anne Colby, Elizabeth Beaumont, Thomas Ehrlich, and Josh Corngold point out that among the six hundred or so service-learning programs they studied, only 1 percent included "a focus on specifically political concerns and solutions such as working with groups to represent the interests of a community," while more than half provided direct service, such as serving food in shelters and tutoring.[15]

Communitarian citizenship easily masks interests. Enron, after all, was known as a model corporate citizen for its service activities. George W. Bush cloaked bellicose foreign policy in service. After September 11, 2001, President Bush described "American civilization," at war with an evil enemy, as "a nation awakened to service and citizenship and compassion." He called for "all of us [to] become a September 11 volunteer, by making a commitment to service in our communities."[16] Theorists from the state-centered liberal camp criticize communitarianism on just such grounds. Michael Schudson argues that Bush's citizenship substituted "service" for "justice." Schudson says, "There is no acknowledgement that democracy has been enlarged in our lifetimes when individuals have been driven not by a desire to serve but by an effort to overcome indignities."[17]

Traditional civics and communitarian approaches both address real and important issues. But for all their seriousness about bringing civic learning back in, as well as their successes in generating initiatives like iCivics, programs on voluntarism and service learning, civic learning remains an afterthought in education, the standing of those who do civic education continues to decline, and the narrative of higher education increasingly is a story of individual advancement, not collective well-being. According to the 2013 *Survey of College and University Chief Academic Officers*, conducted by the Gallup Poll for *Inside Higher Education*, only 19 percent of the leaders of public institutions believe their schools are "very effective" in "preparing students for engaged citizenship," while a still modest 38 percent of those in private schools see their institutions as "very effective" in such education.[18] Dominant approaches neglect the more general malady, feelings of powerlessness.

Citizen Powerlessness

In the United States, state-centered democracy has generated the major strand of liberalism in the last century, "mass politics," which stresses universal claims, distributive justice, individual rights, and a consumer view of the citizen. Mass politics crystallized in the mobilizing approaches to issue campaigns and elections that emerged in the 1970s, using advanced communications techniques based on a formula: find a target or enemy to demonize, develop a script that defines the issue in good-versus-evil terms and shuts down critical thought, and convey the idea that those who champion the victims will come to the rescue. This formula has origins in progressives' efforts, often successful, to protect advances in environmentalism, consumer protection, affirmative action, and progressive taxation from the 1960s, which they perceived, correctly, were under siege. But it creates unintended collateral damage, feeding into the fragmentations and polarizations in society.[19]

Mobilizing techniques can also be seen as a signature of "mass society" as a whole, which conceives of people as frozen into categories and market niches.

The pattern of one-way, expert interventions, inattentive to the cultures and individual stories of communities, has spread across the sweep of civic life. As early as the 1920s, for instance, YMCAs began to trade in their identity as a movement of citizens served by civic-minded "secretaries" for a new identity—institutions comprised of huge buildings and scientifically trained exercise professionals who provide "programs" for paying members. More generally, schools, colleges, congregations, locally rooted businesses, and labor unions lost civic roots and self-organizing qualities. A multitude of free spaces where people developed a sense of agency in the world, creating relationships across partisan and other differences, have turned into service providers for customers and clients. The result is a mass politics which radically truncates civic interaction.

Mass politics, taking shape over the twentieth century, is based on what historian Steven Fraser called the concept of the "new man," championed by labor intellectuals themselves, among others. The new man was seen as "existentially mobile, more oriented to consumption than production, familiar with the impersonal rights and responsibilities of industrial due process." Mass politics, Fraser observes, "was inconceivable apart from a political elite in command of the state, committed to a program of enlarged government spending, financial reform, and redistributive taxation, presiding over a reconstituted coalition in the realm of mass politics."[20]

It may seem hard to imagine that such deep-rooted trends can be reversed. But it is also increasingly obvious that professionals, including faculty members, need to revitalize civic identities and practices in their own self-interest, forming political relationships with parents, communities, and others. It is also increasingly clear that a large majority of the population has deep if inchoate unease about today's dominant story of higher education—and education more broadly—as mainly a ticket to fame and fortune.[21]

Limits on our civic imagination as well as our actions are also connected with conceptual frameworks that contrast citizenship sites with work.

Citizenship Opposed to Labor and Work

Dominant understandings of citizenship descend from the Greeks. For Aristotle, "a citizen is one who shares in governing and being governed. . . . In the best state he is one who is able and chooses to be governed and to govern with a view to the life of excellence."[22] Aristotle also defined democracy as "the form of government when the free, who are also poor and the majority, govern," calling it a "perversion of constitutional government."[23] Aristotle's skepticism about democracy was tied to his scorn for labor, which he saw as antithetical to citizenship. Labor, in his view, teaches all the wrong lessons. As he put it, "Menial duties . . . are executed by various classes of slaves, such, for example, as handicraftsmen, who as their name signifies live by the labour of their hands—under these the mechanic is included." In his opinion, "the good man and the statesman and the good citizen ought not to learn the crafts of inferiors." Maintaining the distinctions between free citizens concerned with governance, and activities of laborers was crucial. "If [good citizens] habitually practice [such crafts]," Aristotle argued, "there will cease to be a distinction between master and slave."[24] In Sparta, matters were simpler—citizen-warriors were barred from working. Judith Shklar has argued that the Greek philosophers saw "productive and commercial work as so deeply degrading that it made a man unfit for citizenship."[25]

Modern intellectual and political traditions that offered alternatives to the Greek view and championed work as a site of democratic activity and citizenship, from the Knights of Labor and populism to the workplace democracy proposed by intellectuals like John Dewey, Carol Pateman, and others, are now largely forgotten. Today, the traditions of political thought that are most invoked contrast civic activity with labor and work.[26]

This is true even for twentieth-century participatory democratic theorists who haven't shared Aristotle's condescension toward "the people." Thus the great theorist Hannah Arendt viewed work as part of the apolitical world. She saw "manual labor" as an undignified realm of necessity, "herd-like," while "work" was more creative and important, the activity of *homo faber*, or "man, the maker of things," the builder of the world. Yet Arendt still believed that work did not belong in the public arena of "deeds and action," and specifically of politics. She held that the worker's "public realm is the exchange market, where he can show the products of his hand and receive the esteem which is due him." Producers remained "private," or isolated: "*homo faber*, the builder of the world and the producer of things, can find his proper relationship to other people only by exchanging his products with theirs because these products themselves are always produced in isolation." Arendt argued that the thought and manual art that produce craft—the creation of a "model" or idea in one's mind that one then reproduces through shaping materials of the world—necessarily requires isolation. Only apprentices and helpers are needed, she proposed, in relations that are based on inequality.[27]

It is important to note the profound pessimism about the modern condition operating below the surface in Arendt's thinking. Thus, she levels ferocious criticism at the ways in which the modern world deforms and degrades work. Under the forces of *automatism*—her term for the forces that turn human beings into things—"the defining features of *homo faber* are in jeopardy," she writes, as distinctions between ends and means disappear, standards of use and beauty are destroyed, acts of fabrication are swallowed up in consumption, and the driving impulse of work, "the conscious human effort to enlarge material power," evaporates.[28] Richard Sennett begins his recent book *The Craftsman* with a vivid account of how Arendt, his teacher, encountered him on a windy day in New York during the Cuban Missile Crisis in 1962. Shaking him, she insisted he understand the ineluctable instrumentalism of modern institutions, which makes "work" only a means to predetermined ends, stripping it of ethical purposes. Sennett wrote his splendid book as a counter argument.[29]

The devaluation of "work" as a site of citizenship reflects not only intellectuals' ideas but also on-the-ground realities as work has become more scripted and drained of larger meaning. Writing in the *New York Times* Tony Schwartz and Christine Porath note that "just 30 percent of employees in America feel engaged at work," according to Gallup polling. Moreover, the pattern is international. Across 142 countries, "the proportion of employees who feel engaged at work is just 13 percent." They conclude that "for most of us . . . work is a depleting, dispiriting experience, and in some obvious ways it's getting worse."[30]

The separation of work from citizenship is also fed by ideas of civil society, today's dominant map of where citizenship takes place.

Off the Playground of Civil Society

> The world is deluged with panaceas, formulas, proposed
> laws, machineries, ways out, and myriads of solutions.
> It is significant and tragic that almost every one of these
> proposed plans and alleged solutions deals with the
> structure of society, but none concerns the substance—the
> people. This, despite the eternal truth of the democratic
> faith that the solution always lies with the people.[31]
>   —Saul Alinsky, 1946

The idea of civil society vividly illustrates the power of framing theoretical concepts to structure resources and to define civic life. Major foundations have divisions of civil society that allocate hundreds of millions of dollars to volunteer activity. Government agencies give time off to their employees so that they can "do citizenship." In 1998, all living American presidents gathered at a Summit on Volunteerism to praise the idea. The concept of civil society structures civic education and civic learning, which hold civic identities and practices to be activities detached from work.

Civil society in its current usages reflects the experiences from recent social movements such as the democracy movements in the Soviet bloc in 1989. The concept, as now advanced by democratic theorists of such movements, includes a criticism of overweening government. Building on the work of Jürgen Habermas, Jean L. Cohen and Andrew Arato's 1992 book, *Civil Society and Political Theory*, set the pattern of taking work off the civil society map. Cohen and Arato propose a revision of the classical notion of civil society descended from the Scottish Enlightenment and Hegel, where the concept did not include the family, and did include large institutions and commerce. They argue for "a reconstruction [of the concept] involving a three-part model distinguishing civil society from both state and economy" as the way to "underwrite the dramatic oppositional role of this concept under authoritarian regimes and to renew its critical potential under liberal democracies." They define civil society as "a sphere of social interaction between economy and state, composed above all of the intimate sphere (especially the family), the sphere of associations (especially voluntary associations), social movements, and forms of public communication." They "distinguish civil society from both a political society of parties, political organizations, and political publics (in particular, parliaments), and an economic society composed of organizations of production and distribution, usually firms, cooperatives, partnerships, and so on."[32]

Benjamin Barber, the prominent theorist of strong democracy, drew on Cohen and Arato to create the definition used by the Council on Civil Society and more generally in the United States. Civil society, according to Barber, includes "those domains Americans occupy when they are engaged neither in government (voting, serving on juries, paying taxes) nor in commerce (working, producing, shopping, consuming)."[33]

Civil society theory can be seen as an effort to sustain an enclave of free action—what we call free spaces—in an increasingly technocratic world. And many things associated with the concept have merit. Volunteers and service projects often make important civic contributions. Moreover, in broad-based community organizing, civil society perspectives have incubated a pluralist, democratic politics, beyond ideology, with a central focus on citizenship education, or development of people's public skills and leadership capacities. These groups are seen as "universities of public life," in the evocative phrase of the organizer and public intellectual Ernesto Cortes.

But the concept of civil society also creates problems. Most importantly, it consigns citizenship and civic action to the "voluntary sector" separated from government and from work, work routines, and the workplace, in ways that largely remove huge arenas from serious possibilities of democratization—including higher education. The arguments of Barber and Cortes, despite differences, illustrate the point.

Barber is a powerful and effective critic of consumer culture as well as a leading proponent of stronger, more participatory democracy. In his view consumer culture inculcates habits of "choice without consequence." As he put it, "Decades of privatization and marketization have obscured not only what it means to be a public . . . but also what it means to be free."[34] When Barber turns to remedy, however, he eliminates workplaces as sites of citizenship, thus significantly limiting the resources for transforming the threats he identifies. In *A Place for Us: How to Make Society Civil and Democracy Strong*, Barber accepts the argument of Jeremy Rifkin that work is disappearing before the inexorable advance of technology and the market, and that its civic overtones are irretrievably lost. Barber proposes that the voluntary sector is a setting for democracy unhampered by the coercion of government and the commercialism of the market, "a space . . . for common activities that are focused neither on profit nor on a welfare bureaucracy's client services . . . a communicative domain of civility, where political discourse is grounded in mutual respect and the search for common understanding even as it expresses differences and identity conflicts." Barber's location for citizenship is also fatalistic. He believes "work once had the sense of public work and was understood to contribute to strong democratic life. But that has changed. . . . Work [today] is what the rest of us do in the private sector to earn a living."[35]

Fatalism replaces a sense of larger possibilities for institutional change in the writings and practices of Ernesto Cortes, whose central concern is people power. It is important to begin with a sketch of his contributions to the field of community organizing. In the early 1970s, Ernesto Cortes had been trained by community organizing pioneer Saul Alinsky, in his Industrial Areas Foundation (IAF) network. When a group of priests invited Cortes and the IAF to help organize the Mexican community of San Antonio, Cortes's hometown, in 1973, shortly after Alinsky's death, Cortes brought back with him the organizing skills he had learned and a zeal to see his own people gain power and a new dignity. He also brought innovations. Cortes was strongly influenced by a conversation he had had with Cesar Chavez, concerning how organizing among Mexican Americans would be superficial unless it drew explicitly on the religious language and stories of the people. Thus he helped the IAF to broaden its understandings of people's motivations. While organizing in the IAF mold stressed the importance of "self-interest"—beginning with the immediate, visible, and pressing concerns of people—it also began to distinguish between "self-interest" and "selfishness." In this view, people's basic concerns are not only financial or narrowly personal but also embrace such intangibles as the happiness of their families, the well-being of their neighbors and friends, the vitality of their faiths, and their own feelings of dignity and worth. A rich understanding of a populist politics has emerged from such insights, and they have proven centrally important to building what are called "broad-based community organizations" through which poor and middle-income people develop substantial power over time. In San Antonio, the Communities Organized for Public Service (COPS), which Cortes and community leaders organized in 1973, continues today, a leader in bringing literally billions of dollars in infrastructure improvements and economic development into the low-income areas of the city.[36]

Cortes also champions voluntary associations as the only real vehicles for democratic change. Thus in an article in *Kettering Review* in 2006, "Toward a Democratic Culture," Cortes claims the tradition of "associative democracy," based in civil society. "Recent decades have witnessed an erosion of the institutions Tocqueville thought were so important to associative democracy: family, neighborhood organization, political party, congregation, labor union, and mutual-aid society," Cortes argues. He sees community organizations and affiliates as centers of associative democracy.[37]

The focus on associational life is virtually universal among community organizers, despite differences in approach. But associative democracy and civil society theory take substantial institutional transformation off the map, ruling out the possibility of reinvigorating the public cultures and purposes and work practices of institutions such as higher education. Such problems are evident in the above-quoted statement by Saul Alinsky, a key architect of the modern community organizing movement. Alinsky's challenge to "the world deluged with panaceas" shows the strengths of the politics of broad-based community organizing, which has an intense focus on "the people" and their civic learning. But by separating the people from substantial structures of power, such organizing also limits the possibilities for democratic change.

While community organizations descending from COPS have been crucial, there is a defensive quality about them as well. As Cortes has said more than once, he sees such groups "like monasteries of democracy, surviving the dark ages of a degraded culture." This fatalism about broader change is embodied in the theory of power in such organizing. "Power . . . comes in two basic forms, organized people and organized money," argues Mike Gecan, director of New York Metro Industrial Areas Foundation. By putting "organized people" in touch with political leaders and "organized money," citizen groups develop highly interactive patterns of power.[38]

Power has relational aspects in broad-based community organizing, but this theory of power is also largely zero-sum. A few groups have power; most don't. Struggle is required to wrest power from the powerful. Such a power theory is drawn from fights over scarce resources like land or capital, which are finite. This framework neglects to acknowledge power based on control over the flow of information, communications, professional practices, and cultural productions—what might be called knowledge power. The cultural apparatus includes institutions such as higher education and schools, entertainment and communications industries, professional associations, and the intellectual life of a society. These are of enormous power in shaping the larger narratives of society—the purpose of education, the meaning of "a good life," and the direction of our common life as a whole.

In the case of knowledge, power is increased through collaborative work, even if there are large obstacles, later described, created by the ways scientists and other academics have been trained and socialized. Think of the challenges of problem solving about water or dealing with climate change or AIDS or education or creating thriving local economies. Seeing these as "struggles against oppression" is far too narrow.[39]

Theorists and architects of democratic education with a productive, problem-solving quality base their approach on the recognition that a commonwealth of knowledge is not a zero-sum dynamic. This understanding found expression in land-grant colleges, religious schools, community colleges, state colleges and universities, historically black colleges and universities, community colleges, and tribal colleges. The City College of New York, once seen as the nation's intellectual powerhouse, admitted all students from New York high schools—and graduated eleven future Nobel Prize winners. The democratic narrative also found expression in community settings, from Chautauqua movements, religious education, and settlement houses to the Harlem Renaissance and the citizenship schools of the civil rights movement.

The narrative is the democratic genius of American education, based on "cooperative excellence," not "meritocratic excellence." Cooperative excellence is the principle that a mix of people from highly varied backgrounds can achieve remarkable intellectual, social, political, and spiritual growth and can undertake generative public work if they have the right encouragements, resources, challenges, and calls to public purpose.[40]

If the story has been largely forgotten, in the rise of a hypercompetitive, individualist educational system, it is also vital to recover.

Traditions of Citizenship as Public Work

A challenge to conceptions that contrast citizenship with work, common among many of the patrician leaders of the American Revolution, who had little use for work (and condescended toward working people), developed through the colonial experiences and early years of the nation.[41] The labors of settlers who cleared lands, who built towns and villages, wells, meeting halls, and roads, generated what the historian Robert Wiebe has called America's portable democracy.[42] Such experiences cultivated a democratic assertiveness among the people. "Experience proves that the very men whom you entrust with the support and defense of your most sacred liberties are frequently corrupt," wrote a group of artisans in Philadelphia during the Revolution. "If ever therefore your rights are preserved, it must be through the virtue and integrity of the middling sort, as farmers, tradesmen, & etc."[43] Benjamin Franklin spoke and wrote in this vein. The Leather Apron Club, which he founded in Philadelphia in 1727, included tradesmen, artisans, and shopkeepers—those whom he lauded as "the middling people,"—combined hard work and civic commitments. The club discussed civic and political topics of the day, developed plans for self-improvement, and created a network of citizens committed to "doing well by doing good." Members generated a myriad of civic projects, including a street-sweeping corps, volunteer firefighters, tax-supported neighborhood constables, health and life insurance groups, a library, a hospital, an academy for educating young people, a society for sharing scientific discoveries, and a postal system.[44] In a similar vein, Franklin proposed education that combined practical and liberal arts, a union that was to reappear in the country's land-grant colleges.

The connection between work and citizenship further developed in the early years of the new nation. "When [ideals of disinterested civic virtue] proved too idealistic and visionary," writes Gordon Wood, Americans "found new democratic adhesives in the actual behavior of plain, ordinary people."[45] Several interrelated, interacting traditions of citizenship as public work emerged, foundations for making change today:

- community-building, the collective labors of solving public problems and building shared resources;
- vocation and civic professionalism, callings to careers filled with public purpose; and
- democratizing public work, work that deepens and expands democracy.

COMMUNITY-BUILDING

David Mathews has well described the tradition of community-building in his treatment of the emergence of public schools. "Nineteenth-century self-rule . . . was a sweaty, hands-on, problem-solving politics," Mathews writes: "The democracy of self-rule was rooted in collective decision making and acting—especially acting. Settlers on the frontier had to be producers, not just consumers. They had to join forces to build forts, roads, and libraries. They formed associations to combat alcoholism and care for the poor as well as to elect representatives. They also established the first public schools. Their efforts were examples of 'public work,' meaning work done by not just for the public."[46] Such public work drew on traditions of "the commons," lands, streams, and forests for which whole communities had responsibility and in which they had rights of use, and also goods of general benefit built mainly through citizen labors, like schools, libraries, community centers, wells, roads, music festivals, and arts fairs. All were associated with the term "the commonwealth." Indeed, for many immigrants, America represented a chance to recreate the commons privatized by elites in Europe. As the historians Oscar and Mary Handlin observed about the Revolutionary generation of the 1770s, "For the farmers and seamen, for the fishermen, artisans and new merchants, commonwealth repeated the lessons they knew from the organization of churches and towns . . . the value of common action."[47] Such community-building traditions of communal labor can be found around the world. They create rich foundations for a normative ideal of citizenship as collective, self-directed labors, citizenship that is practical and hands-on, and that bridges divisions of status, income, and other differences for the sake of community benefit.[48]

VOCATION AND CIVIC PROFESSIONALISM

Collaborative work that solves public problems and creates common resources for communities is one current of public work citizenship. Work filled with public purpose is another. This concept draws on the rich theological idea of *vocation*. As John Budd observes, "when Martin Luther translated biblical verses such as 'Let each one remain in the same calling in which he was called' from the original Greek into German . . . he used the German word for 'occupation' for 'calling.' Thus, Luther initiated a radically new perspective in which all are called to employ their gifts, 'something that fits how we are made, so that doing it will enable us to glorify God, serve others, and be most richly ourselves.' "[49]

The connection between vocation and education has recently resurfaced in undergraduate education. Liberal arts colleges like Augsburg, the new institutional home of the Center for Democracy and Citizenship, illustrate the recall of vocation and have the potential for significant impact since they are "upstream" centers, shaping the identities and practices of thousands of civic leaders. In its educational vision, *Vocation, Access, and Excellence*, Augsburg highlights the concept of vocation, integrated into its core curriculum, as "a fertile seedbed for the democratic ethos":

> This view of vocation both stresses the importance of education and clarifies its role. One does not seek education for either self-advancement or as a way to reach salvation. Its proper role is in helping persons determine and develop their abilities in preparation for investigating and celebrating God's creation, for probing the mysteries of the human condition, and ultimately for furthering the well-being of society. As Luther said, God doesn't want a

cobbler who puts crosses on shoes; God wants a cobbler who makes good, reliable footwear.[50]

Augsburg's view of vocation has potential for helping to bridge the sharp divide in higher education between professional studies, on the one hand, and liberal arts and civic learning, on the other.

A sense of calling or vocation is associated with the rise of professions. Though professions are often understood in terms of the emergence of a disinterested ethic tied to positivist theories of knowledge and detached from politics and self-interests, an alternative tradition of "citizen-professionalism" contributes especially to American democracy. William Sullivan identifies a central tension in professionalism in the United States since the colonial period, "between a technical emphasis which stresses specialization—broadly linked to a utilitarian conception of society as a project for enhancing efficiency and individual satisfaction—and a sense of professional mission which has insisted upon the prominence of the ethical and civic dimension of the enterprise."[51]

DEMOCRATIZING PUBLIC WORK

The work of making democratic change is a third tradition of citizenship, intertwined with community-building work and civic professionalism. Union and community organizers, civil rights workers, suffragists, and others created a strong tradition of work for democratic social change, mingling with the idea of "work" itself as a wellspring for change. Thus the iconic bookends of Martin Luther King's career were the unforgettable images of thousands of domestic workers walking to their jobs during the Montgomery Bus Boycott in 1955 to protest segregated buses, and the signs of Memphis garbage workers declaring, "I Am a Man," demanding recognition and dignity, in 1968.

The traditions of public work as organizing are important to recall in response to the fatalism of writers like Arendt and Barber about the declining dignity of work and also in response to the fatalism of many people who assume their work and workplaces are unchangeable. For instance, faculty today, like AFL craft unions—for whom the "new industrial order promised the social extermination of a whole social species"—often act in defensive fashion. Yet the better example was in the new industrial unions of the CIO, where skilled workers often made common cause with others. As Fraser describes, "Skilled workers comprised a milieu heterogeneous in background. They included both production and nonproduction workers. Some were quite secular and even anticlerical; others were attracted by liberal currents in Catholic social thought."[52]

Change-making through professional work played a pivotal role in the African American freedom struggle. Gerald Taylor has argued that after the collapse of the Populist Party in the 1890s, the black community turned to "knowledge artisans":

While millions of property owners and artisans sinking into debt peonage, or forced into wage labor, formed the populist movement, the rising professions, what could be called collectives of "knowledge artisans," offers a contrasting story of the search for independence among both whites and blacks, using a different set of strategies in an effort to consolidate control over productive property, work products, tools, and vocational training and accreditation. . . . These intellectual artisans, accountants, doctors, lawyers, engineers among others, gained control over what we now call the professions. The professionalization of these groups provided the ability to negotiate contracts but retain control over their workplaces, their tools and their schedules. They controlled decisions about the learning and application of their knowledge of these intellectual crafts, the formation centers that prepared them and the terms by which they could enter the professions.

Taylor notes that "by the early 20th century, these professional guilds had organized national organizations, stabilized and expanded the income of their members and welded significant economic political and cultural influence."[53] In the African American community, knowledge artisans provided leadership in the continuing freedom struggle by building centers of independent power, ranging from colleges, schools, and congregations to businesses and beauty parlors.

Parallels can be seen among European Americans in the 1920s and 1930s who saw their work as creating sustained foundations for civic change. John Dewey viewed Jane Addams's Hull House settlement in Chicago, which served as a center of immigrant neighborhood life, as an important model for schools as "community centers." As John Rogers, Joseph Kahne, and Ellen Middaugh describe Dewey's work, his "normative vision recasts 'vocation' in democratic terms" in ways that provide resources for contemporary civic education and learning.[54]

Dewey also believed that higher education as well as K–12 schools play a central role in democracy. Indeed, their public function was their essential justification. In response to an editorial in the *New York Times*, which argued the University of Pennsylvania's right to fire the economic reformer Scott Nearing because the trustees disagreed with his views, he argued in a letter:

> You apparently take the ground that a modern university is a personally conducted institution like a factory and that if for any reason the utterances of any teacher, within or without the university walls, are objectionable to the Trustees there is nothing more to be said. . . . [But] the modern university is in every respect, save its legal management, a public institution with public responsibilities. [Professors] have been trained to think of the pursuit and expression of truth as a public function to be exercised on behalf of the interests of their moral employer—society as a whole.[55]

For Dewey, a professor's public function was the justification for tenure and the rationale for the American Association of University Professors (AAUP), which he helped to organize.

I believe Dewey was right: schools at every level have enormous power. Yet Dewey was much too sanguine about professors being trained "to think in terms of their public function." His lapse is part of a wider problem in the way he conceived of politics. While Dewey's theory of schools and colleges as civic centers is of powerful relevance today, he focused on knowledge in too apolitical a fashion, in ways that disregarded the conflicts and negotiations among particular interests, values, power, and viewpoints at the heart of politics. He also neglected the extensive ways in which patterns of professional socialization, justified by the theory (objectivism) that detached scientists are the most important—or even singular—creators of trustworthy knowledge, were spreading quickly.[56] To realize the democratic possibilities that Dewey envisioned for education and the world of work requires a look at ways to democratize the politics of knowledge, as well as examples of public work in educational practice.

The Politics of Knowledge

A sign in the airport in Denver, Colorado, trumpets a message that Colorado State University, located not far away in Fort Collins, wants to communicate to the world: "Local problems, university solutions." This message is operationalized partly in the hundreds of millions of dollars each year spent on translational science, by the National Institutes of Health, based on the idea of translating scientific discoveries into real world "solutions." This also might be called the cult of the expert, which champions the authority of scientific knowledge as the only valid form of knowledge. In this view, elite experts bring solutions to the masses who are viewed as ignorant, passive, and needy. If the masses fail to listen, the remedy is to turn up the volume. A lot of climate science illustrates this pattern. A January 2012 editorial in *Nature*, one of the world's leading scientific journals, calls for scientists to get into the fray. "Where political leadership on climate change is lacking scientists must be prepared to stick their heads above the parapet." The editorial observed that greenhouse gases have continued to rise and "climate change contrarians are multiplying in numbers." Their solution: "Climate scientists must be ever more energetic in taking their message to citizens."[57] Scientists "taking their message to citizens" assumes that the scientists have the answer—and are different than citizens. We need a reconceptualization of the very nature of the relationship between science and society, in which science is understood as mainly a knowledge resource for action *in the world*, not an external description *of* the world, and scientists come to understand themselves as *citizens*, with useful knowledge and perspectives but not all the answers.

Limits of scientific triumphalism are widely discussed in former colonial societies, sometimes with considerable anger. Sabelo Ndlovu-Gatsheni has described colonialism as involving the "imperialism of knowledge which is more dangerous than physical political domination." This meant "control of subjectivity and knowledge which includes epistemological colonization and the re-articulation of African being as inferior and constituted by a series of 'deficits' and a catalogue of 'lacks.'" In his argument, the colonial attitude "enabled the use of race and scientific racism to organise and classify human beings into primitive and modern, civilised and uncivilised, western and non-western, coloniser and colonised, superior and inferior."[58] Similarly, Roy MacLeod summarized recent scholarship about colonial science: "natural sciences, viewed as a product of European rationalism and Enlightenment, were co-opted into a wider cultural project, in the process producing resentments and contradictions that remain part of the post-colonial world."[59]

Yet without politics, the negotiation of meanings, interests, and practices to make and sustain a way of life, there is the danger here of another Manichean binary that holds North Atlantic theories of knowledge to be monolithically oppressive and Africans and other colonized people to be either accomplices in oppression or innocent victims. This overlooks an alternative theory in which different kinds of knowledge and knowledge making interact to create a "commonwealth of knowledge," for the sake of solving the real public problems.

This theory of knowledge can be called civic science, and its practices were once widespread in land-grant colleges and universities. Kenneth Keller, former president of the University of Minnesota, a chemical engineer, in an interview I did with him conveyed the civic science at the heart of the land-grant tradition. "Science is more a civic enterprise than almost anything else," Keller argued. "It requires cooperation. It requires respect. It requires listening. All the things that are virtues in a society are virtues in science."[60] The American Commonwealth Partnership coalition, which the White House invited me to organize to mark the 150th anniversary of the Morrill Act, establishing land-grant colleges, sought to make this history better known.

After 1862, most states established land grant colleges, open but not limited to farmers and mechanics. A second Morrill Act, in 1890, increased funding for land-grant colleges, stipulating that states have "a just and equitable division of the fund to be received under this act between one college for white students and one institution for colored students." Despite the grave injustices inherent in the doctrine of separate but equal, this funding led to the creation of the so-called 1890 Land-Grant Colleges," which trained generations of black leaders in the freedom movement. Land-grant colleges had a strong emphasis on integrating science and technology with liberal arts. They sought to develop professionals with a strong sense of their civic responsibilities, as Scott Peters has documented in rich detail. As John Hannah, president of Michigan State University, put it in 1944, "The first and never-forgotten objective must be that every human product of our educational system must be given the training that will enable him to be an effective citizen, appreciating his opportunities and fully willing to assume his responsibilities in a great democracy."[61] As land-grant schools deepened a commitment to democracy of knowledge, scientists were often leaders. For instance, Liberty Hyde Bailey, dean of agriculture at Cornell and one of the world's leading horticulturalists, stressed practical work with communities to solve public problems and to create civic capacity. Bailey imagined extension as the rural counterparts of urban settlements, and urged extension workers to help create rural civic centers—schools, local businesses, community centers—grounded in community life. Bailey sometimes used the term "public work" to convey the ensemble of reciprocal partnerships, capacity building, and public spaces. His approach at Cornell was to integrate specialized knowledge into a much more comprehensive vision, combining practical arts and liberal arts with a focus on community agency. "Students in agriculture are doing much more than fitting themselves to follow an occupation," he wrote. "They are to take part in a great regeneration. The student in agriculture is fitting himself for a great work." In this way, Bailey challenged practices of narrow, expert-led extension work. Some, he argued, have the idea "that an expert shall go into a community and give advice to the farmers on the running of their farms and on all sorts of agricultural subjects, being teacher, inspector, counselor, confessor, organizer, and guide." Bailey declared this approach was likely to fail on the face of it. Even where it effectively conveyed new information it created dangerous dependencies, not capacities for self-action. "The re-direction of any civilization must rest primarily on the people who comprise it, rather than be imposed from persons in other conditions of life." College-based rural scientists could play key roles if they helped communities develop their own problem-solving capacities, and kept in mind the larger objective, the "commonwealth." Bailey continued, "Real leadership lies in taking hold of the first and commonest problems that present themselves and working them out. I like to say to my students that they should attack the first problem that presents itself when they alight from the train on their return from college. It may be a problem of roads; of a poor school; of tuberculosis; of ugly signs along the highways." The point was not simply or even mainly the specific problem. Rather, it was the fact that the public work of problem solving created opportunities to develop community capacity for self-action and for creating rural democracy.[62]

Civic science is vividly apparent in soil conservation efforts. Soil conservation scientists were constantly reminded that the community's knowledge was prior to their own. Gaining a deep understanding of the community and its history, culture, political life, conflicts, and challenges was essential for their efforts. The result is today's magnificent system of contour farming across the Midwest.

Renewing Public Work

Our civic engagement work through the Center for Democracy and Citizenship (CDC) began in 1987 with an argument that broad-based organizing, growing from a rich tradition of "commonwealth" politics throughout American history, could be translated into institutional change in institutions that had become removed from the life of communities.[63] Four case studies suggest possibilities.

MAKING TEACHING AND LEARNING MORE PUBLIC

As we sought to democratize educational institutions it soon became apparent that institutional organizing requires a shift in framework. Rather than seeing such institutions in conventional ways as fixed and static, defined by structures, procedures, rules, and regulations, we have to reconceive of them as living and dynamic communities, with norms, values, leadership, and cultural identities. Maria Avila, a former Mexican American organizer with the IAF who directed the Center for Community Based Learning at Occidental College, has given a vivid account of what this means. "The medicine for our predicament [in higher education] requires efforts to restructure the way we think, act, behave toward each other, and the way we act as a collective to restructure power and resources." Avila argues that organizing focuses on culture change before structural change. "Culture changes [come] first, leading to structural changes later."[64]

Work is at the heart of self-interest in all institutions, including colleges and universities. Seeing institutions as communities, building public relationships, undertaking intentional changes in their cultures to make them more public, and thinking in political terms about knowledge, as well as other power sources, highlights the dynamics of work routines, incentives, norms, and identities. A public work approach to organizing differs from conventional liberal and communitarian approaches to civic engagement, both of which have strong normative frameworks. Public work avoids exhortations about what teachers, students, staff, or institutions *should* do. Rather, public work connects individual and institutional interests to citizenship and the public good by inviting people to "make work more public," more interactive, collaborative, visible, and filled with public purposes. We saw this early on, for instance, in the efforts of a group that sought to spread active learning practices in higher education, called the Collaboration for the Advancement of Teaching and Learning. Lesley Cafarelli, director of the consortium, explains:

> How can faculty strive to improve their teaching . . . if there are few opportunities to observe and learn from other professionals or to wrestle intellectually with colleagues about ways to cope with both common and surprising difficulties in teaching? How can colleges and universities fulfill their public responsibility if there is little or no collective knowledge of how teaching is practiced, sharing of expertise, or joint exploration of teachers' impact on student learning? An academic culture that preserves the privacy— even secrecy—of the classroom fosters professional isolation and stifles improvement.[65]

Nan Kari and a group of faculty, staff, and students at the College of St. Catherine, working with the CDC, addressed the challenge of "making teaching and learning more public" through adapting community organizing methods like those of Cortes. Their work significantly informed the CDC's general theory of citizenship as public work. Building on such partnerships, public work created the framework of the 1999 *Wingspread Declaration on the Civic Responsibility of Research Universities*, which I coauthored with Elizabeth Hollander on behalf of a group of higher education leaders.

There are other parallel and sometimes allied efforts in education to make work more public. These include the deliberative pedagogies in K–12 schools and higher education supported by the Kettering Foundation and the National Issues Forum Institute. In higher education, such deliberative pedagogies have now a demonstrated track recording for generating agency and action in settings such as Wake Forest University.[66]

CIVIC SCIENCE

William Doherty and his colleagues at the Citizen Professional Center have pioneered in the practices and theory of civic science by translating public work concepts and practices to family and health professions. Their citizen-professional model begins with the premise that solving complex problems requires many sources of knowledge, and "the greatest untapped resource for improving health and social well-being is the knowledge, wisdom, and energy of individuals, families, and communities who face challenging issues in their everyday lives." It has generated multiple partnerships, including suburban movements of families working to untangle overscheduled, consumerist lives; a Citizen Fathers Project among low-income fathers seeking to foster positive fathering models and practices; a new project with Hennepin County to change civil service practices into public work; and a pilot project with Health Partners Como Clinic, called the Citizen Health Care Home, which stresses personal and family responsibility for one's own health and opportunities for patient leadership development and coresponsibility for health.[67]

Shonda Craft, an African American clinical psychologist hired as an assistant professor in Department of Family Social Science at the University of Minnesota, began working with Doherty. She saw "the Citizen Professional model [as] a way of engaging professionals and community members to collaborate without the typical hierarchical relationships." Craft believes that it "addresses issues traditionally defined as individual problems from a more community-focused perspective it also."

Craft sees citizen-professionalism as "a way of life." Craft helped to organize a SMART (Sexually Mature And Responsible Teens) group at South High School on teen pregnancy that embodied many principles of citizen-professional craft. "Today's conversation about teen pregnancy is rife with finger-pointing, she describes. "It emphasizes low self-esteem and uncontrolled hormones, parents with poor monitoring skills, or schools who have usurped the moral duties of families to peddle condoms and eschew abstinence. Recent movies such as *Juno* and television shows such as *Sixteen and Pregnant* have popularized, even idolized teen pregnancy." She worked with a group of teens and professionals to launch a project. In March 2009, the Citizen Teen Pregnancy Prevention Project began at South High School in Minneapolis. They worked carefully to define the group in ways that would not stigmatize or polarize. The "citizen-professionals" were representatives from University of Minnesota, school social workers, and community health advocates who served as facilitators of the process.

> The adults participated alongside the teens in deep conversations about how teen pregnancy impacts girls, boys, children, families, and communities. Initially, the girls group and the boys group had separate conversations. Then the groups joined and began to formulate a set of messages and strategies for sharing their work with others. They dubbed the group SMART (Sexually Mature And Responsible Teens), which set the tone for how these citizen-teens would be described by adults and peers who witnessed their action steps and

heard their messages. The teens appeared on a local radio program focused on health issues, were interviewed for a story that was aired on Minnesota Public Radio, and told their stories for a forthcoming DVD being produced by the University of Minnesota that chronicles their work.

EDUCATING FOR CITIZEN CAREERS WITH JEN NELSON

At Augsburg College, a group of faculty, staff, and students have been working for two years to integrate civic agency, civic politics, and public work into curricular and cocurricular experiences. The transcultural doctoral program (DNP) in nursing has a focus on educating "citizen-nurses," and the new mission statement of the college's education department similarly stresses preparing "citizen-teachers" who will be innovators and leaders in shaping education. The Public Achievement initiative at Fridley Middle School, just north of Minneapolis, offers an example. I founded Public Achievement (PA) in 1990, in association with Jim Scheibel, then mayor of St. Paul, as a contemporary version of the Citizenship Education Program (CEP) of the civil rights era, which had shaped me as a college student. The CEP taught African Americans, and some poor white working people as well, skills and concepts of constructive change. The experiences had often dramatic impact on identity, shifting people from victimhood to being agents of change and civic role models for the nation.

In Public Achievement, young people learn the skills, concepts, and methods of empowering public work. They work as teams guided by coaches, who may be young adults, college students, or teachers. Coaches help guide the work but do not dominate. They also are highly attentive to the development of young people's public skills and capacities. The initiative has spread widely, now used in schools, colleges, and communities in the United States and other societies, including Poland, Northern Ireland, the West Bank and Gaza, Israel Japan and Mexico.

At Fridley Middle School, with Project Star, Michael Ricci and Alissa Blood have changed special education into an empowering learning environment. Kids take the lead in designing their own learning, built around largely self-directed public work projects of their own choosing. In the process, students labeled "EBD," that is, subject to what are called "Emotional and Behavior Disorders," and "OHD," for "Other Health Disabilities," have become community leaders. "In all the other classes, the teachers tell you want to do," says seventh grader Whitney, in a video about Fridley Public Achievement called *Real Power*. "In PA, the teacher says okay, what do you want to do?"[68]

A popular understanding of what special education is appears in the Wikipedia definition, which says that special education is designed for "the education of students with special needs in a way that addresses the students' individual differences and needs." Students with "OHD" are also in Project Star because of behaviors that often interrupt the general education classroom. The problem, as the Wikipedia definition of "EBD" also notes, is that "both general definitions as well as concrete diagnosis of EBD may be controversial as the observed behavior may depend on many factors."[69] Put differently, is the "problem" the kids or their environment? "The kids in our special education classroom weren't successful in mainstream classrooms, where the format has been the same for the last 100 years," explains Ricci in the video. "The world has changed, but the classroom is pretty much the same."

Susan O'Connor, director of the Special Education graduate program at Augsburg College, wanted to try something different. "Special Education generally still uses a medical model, based on how to fix kids," she said. Working with Dennis Donovan, national organizer for Public Achievement with the Center for Democracy and Citizenship, O'Connor and other faculty and graduate students at Augsburg partnered with Ricci and Blood, graduates of their program, to design an alternative.

Both Ricci and Blood believed that an approach that gives students the chance to take leadership in designing their own learning was worth a try. "The idea of trying something different that might give school a purpose for our kids just made sense," Blood explained. Public Achievement offered resources. In the self-contained Project Star classroom, where the primary concern is to teach students strategies that help them manage disruptive behaviors that interfere with learning in school, there is latitude for innovation. "More evidence would be needed [in a mainstream classroom] to allow us to go to the level we did, where we turned Public Achievement into a core part of the curriculum," Blood described.

As a result of the PA experiment, students with challenges that would have removed them from conventional classrooms in many schools have become public leaders in Fridley. They built relationships and received recognition not simply in the school, but also in the larger Fridley community. Their Public Achievement work brought them into contact with school administrators, the school board, elected officials, and other community leaders, and at times media outlets like the local paper and Minnesota Public Radio.[70]

The PA approach also transformed the work of Ricci and Blood by giving such work larger meaning and a new, stronger purpose of empowerment. "My role is not to fix things for the kids but to say, 'this is your class, your mission. How are you going to do the work?' Our main task is to remind them, to guide them, not to tell them what to do," explains Ricci. The video shows how teachers became partners with their students, who choose the issues and learn how to work to address them effectively. Issues this last year included rewriting the school's bullying policy, hosting a district-wide "Kindness Week" to reduce bullying, making murals to motivate peers to get exercise, visiting children in hospital waiting rooms, and educating the public about misconceptions regarding pit bulls. Such work creates multiple opportunities for students to develop academically if teachers are intentional about making the connections. Students compose well-written letters to seek permission from the principal for a project. They use math to figure out what scale their mural will be so they know how much wall space they need. Teachers also change—from "teaching to the test," to working alongside young people as they develop agency. Their curriculum builds citizenship skills, habits, and identities such as negotiation, compromise, initiative, planning, organizing, and public speaking. It also develops what Blood calls "a public professional persona." Both teachers are convinced that these skills, habits, and civic identity will serve the students well throughout life. The change in the young people, eloquently described in their own words in a the *Real Power* video on Facebook, is inspiring.

This is the new model of "citizen-teachers," which Michael Ricci and Alissa Blood are developing. They have changed from "objects" of educational reform to "agents and architects" of reform. In an environment when teachers and faculty across the country feel powerless, they serve as powerful role models for a different future.

LARGE-SCALE INSTITUTIONAL CHANGE WITH BLASE SCARNATI

In 2007, the Center for Democracy and Citizenship began working with George Mehaffy and others at the Association of State Colleges and Universities to create a Civic Agency Initiative. More than a dozen colleges and universities have worked closely together on themes of civic agency and public work, including Lone Star Community College, Western Kentucky University, Georgia State College and University, the University of Colorado at Boulder, Winona State University, Augsburg College, Syracuse University, the University of Washington Bothell, Northern Arizona University, and the University of Maryland, Baltimore County. At NAU and UMBC, organizers translated concepts of civic agency and public work into large-scale institutional change.

Over the last several years at Northern Arizona University (NAU), a group of faculty, working with students, staff, administrators, and community colleagues, has sought to build democratic centers of power—enabling environments—through establishing new coalitions and alliances. The key has been collectively pursuing strategies to reempower faculty, to reverse the tide of faculty despair, to begin to rebuild the university as a civic institution, and to revive a sense of nonhierarchical collective commonwealth through democratic agency.

In the First Year Learning Initiative (FYLI), Blase Scarnati and colleague Michelle D. Miller (a cognitive psychologist) bring faculty together to cocreate, collaborate with one another and their course colleagues, and build new alliances around the curricular spaces that they control. They use community organizing strategies, such as one-on-one meetings off campus to build public relationships with course coordinators. In these meetings, faculty members tell the narrative of their course and their narrative as a teacher. They also explore effective pedagogies and strategies—based on NAU experience and supported by the literature—that can help students increase learning and succeed academically. The conversations are animated by several assumptions: Faculty own the curriculum and can be empowered through curricular work. Curriculum itself can open wildly creative spaces. The organizing uses a cooperative model for course coordination, collaborative not top-down, since top-down mandates are so resisted by faculty. Many faculty have been invigorated by this work. Working cooperatively with their colleagues to achieve curricular ends is a relatively rare experience for many. Many, too, are hopeful about what they can achieve in cooperation with colleagues. Building these interdepartmental coalitions has been quite powerful.

The actual results have also been impressive in conventional assessment terms. Most courses are multisectioned (the largest has seventy-five sections each term), and the reform efforts are approaching some twenty thousand students (not unique enrollments) who have completed FYLI courses at NAU. Michelle Miller has compared the First Year Learning Initiative (FYLI) to more traditional redesign initiatives. For example, state department of education course redesign initiatives conducted between 2006 and 2010 totaled only fifty-five courses, with the mean number of courses per university being only 1.45, and per state only 9.00. In three years, FYLI has completed work with forty-seven courses that have a plurality of first-year students enrolled. These courses have a broad reach across all NAU colleges and disciplines, from biological sciences to business.

A second example is Civic Reengagement for Arizona Families, Transitions, and Sustainability (CRAFTS). Over the last four years through CRAFTS, NAU has built one of the largest programs of action research, civic agency, and public work in the country. It is grounded in collaboration between the Community, Culture and Environment Program (Rom Coles, director), the First Year Seminar Program (Blase Scarnati, director) and the MA in Sustainable Communities Program (Luis Fernandez, director).

The effort includes faculty from departments as diverse as education, biology, philosophy, and criminology. Each year, over 550 new first-year students join previous years' colleagues in experiential opportunities where students are involved in action research with community organizations doing political work on issues identified by the community to create more democratic, just, and sustainable communities.

Key to the success of CRAFTS is NAU faculty, staff, graduate assistant mentors, undergraduate peer teaching assistants, and undergraduate students. They work nonhierarchically and collectively to build new alliances with community-based partners to democratically create intensely dense rhizomatic webs of practice that we call our Action Research Teams (ARTs). ARTs begin with First Year Seminar students organized into course-specific working groups. It includes also a diverse mix: sophomores and juniors who want to continue in the public work of the ARTs and assume leadership and organizing responsibilities for initiatives within each ART, sophomore or junior peer teaching assistants from the First Year Seminar Program who work with the students in each seminar, graduate student mentors assigned to each umbrella ART, and multigenerational community partners, including K–12 students and their parents, community members and organizations, and Navajo elders.

ARTs work with a variety of community organizations, such as the Coconino County Sustainable Economic Development Initiative, Friends of Flagstaff's Future, Northern Arizona Institutions for Community Leadership/Interfaith Council (Industrial Areas Foundation), and key public schools in the Flagstaff Unified School District. Organizers have worked to build fourteen ARTs that

serve as umbrella organizations under which NAU students and faculty collaborate with members of the broader community, working on a variety of environmental, social, educational, economic, and political issues. Many powerful
stories from student and community colleagues come from ARTs work. Each
semester, they organize an ARTs Symposium where ARTs working groups report on their work of the term. Many share that "this work has changed my life."
ARTs have also been effective in increasing retention among key NAU student
populations. Minority students successfully completing First Year Seminars with
ARTs (FYSeminar-ARTs) sections show a significant improvement, 16 percent,
in retention for students earning A, B, or C grades over the NAU average. Female students in FYSeminar-ARTs sections show a significant improvement, 9
percent, in retention. Overall, students successfully completing FYS-ARTs show
a 7 percent improvement in retention. FYSeminar-ARTs participation also significantly increased engagement with course-specific learning activities involving diversity, cultural influences, and multiple perspectives.

Agents of Change, Not Objects of Change: Telling a New Story

As the political theorist and community organizer Rom Coles has observed, it
is hard for many to believe that democratic innovations of public work can add
up to much more than "oases of democracy" in an expanding desert of a technocratic and market-driven culture.[71] A story from *Inside Higher Education* dra-
matizes reasons for discouragement. "North Carolina governor joins chorus of
Republicans critical of liberal arts," read the headline in *Inside Higher Education*.

> Governor McCrory's comments on higher education echo statements made
> by a number of Republican governors—including those in Texas, Florida and
> Wisconsin—who have questioned the value of liberal arts instruction and
> humanities degrees at public colleges and universities. Those criticisms have
> started to coalesce into a potential Republican agenda on higher education,
> emphasizing reduced state funding, low tuition prices, vocational training,
> performance funding for faculty members, state funding tied to job placement
> in "high demand" fields and taking on flagship institutions.[72]

But these criticisms are also wake-up calls. The first populist movement
among small farmers, black and white, grew from the threats to farmers' civic
autonomy. Like farmers "who contested the loss of control over the means of
their work and the intellectual and physical products of that work,"[73] faculty,
staff, students, and others are faced with the prospect that they will either be the
architects of change or they will be its objects.[74]

There is also evidence that the general public will support a new story of
the purpose of higher education, including efforts to make the work of higher
education more public. Thus, the American Commonwealth Partnership and
the National Issues Forums, working with local and state partners like Minnesota Campus Compact, organized more than 120 public discussions across the

country on the purposes of higher education in 2012–2013. These surfaced a sharp disconnection between the discussion among policy makers, focused on cost cutting, efficiency, and a narrow understanding of the science, technology, engineering and mathematics (STEM) disciplines on the one side and the views of the general citizenry on the other. Jean Johnson's report, *Divided We Fail*, contrasts views of policy makers on the purpose—the story—of higher education with views of the general citizenry. "Facing a more competitive international economy and relentlessly rising college costs, leaders say now is the moment for higher education to reinvent itself." In contrast, "forum participants spoke repeatedly about the benefits of a rich, varied college education . . . where, in their view, students have time and space to explore new ideas and diverse fields." Lay citizens emphasized the need to broaden, not narrow, STEM education. As Johnson puts it, "Many stressed that STEM professionals will be more creative if they are more broadly educated." Most to the point, the forums underlined the need for a wide public conversation to enrich curricular and cocurricular education. "The question going forward is whether higher education will be reshaped from the top down, adopting changes and solutions that skip over public concerns, or whether leaders will find ways to co-frame solutions side by side with the citizens they say they want to serve."[75]

We are called to revitalize education as a great civic vocation, a vital form of public work. More broadly, our task is to recall and translate to the twenty-first century a democratic story of higher education and education broadly at the vital center of America.

Both the need and opportunity are present to move from complaint to the constructive work of realizing the democratic possibilities of our powers.

Notes

1. Undersecretary Martha Kanter, "University and State Partnerships to Increase Civic Learning," blog on the Department of Education website, January 24, 2013, *www.ed.gov/edblogs/ous/2013/01/university-and-state-partnerships-to-increase-civic -learning-and-engagement.*

2. Richard Harwood, "The Nation's Looking Glass," *Kettering Review*, Spring 2000, 7–8.

3. See *swampland.time.com/where-in-the-world-is-joe*; quote from Joe Klein, "On the Road," *Time*, October 18, 2010, 38.

4. Peter Levine, *We Are the Ones We've Been Waiting For: The Promise of Civic Renewal in America* (Oxford: Oxford University Press, 2013).

5. David Mathews, "Higher Education and Har Megiddo," *Higher Education Exchange*, 2012, 75.

6. Borzou Daragahi, "Cairo's Voters Shrug at Poll Upheaval," *Financial Times*, April 20, 2012. Daragahi also reports its fading—evident long before the recent bitter clashes between the Marsi government and its opponents.

7. The statement was drafted in 2007 by a group of engaged political and social theorists convened by the journal of political theory the *Good Society*, including Harry C. Boyte, Steve Elkin, Peter Levine, Jane Mansbridge, Elinor Ostrom, Rogers Smith, Karol Soltansoon, cosigned by Archon Fung at Harvard and Xolela Mangcu in South

Africa. Each year there is a Civic Studies Institute for two weeks organized by Levine and Soltan at Tufts. In 2014 Levine and Tufts also published an edited volume of key ideas, *Civic Studies* (Washington, DC: AAC&U, 2014).

8. Thomas Piketty, *Capital in the Twenty-First Century* (Cambridge, MA: Harvard University Press, 2014); Benjamin Barber, *If Mayors Ruled the World: Dysfunctional Nations, Rising Cities* (New Haven, CT: Yale University Press, 2013).

9. Sara M. Evans and Harry C. Boyte, *Free Spaces: The Sources of Democratic Change in America*, 2nd edition (Chicago: University of Chicago Press, 1992).

10. Bob Kerry, "Becoming Aware of Civic Unawareness," *Huffington Post*, May 26, 2012; Howard Blume, "Sandra Day O'Connor promotes civics education," *Los Angeles Times*, December 27, 2011.

11. George Packer, "The New Liberalism," *New Yorker*, November 17, 2009, *www.newyorker.com/magazine/2008/11/17/the-new-liberalism* accessed February 8, 2013; Jeremy Waldron, "How Politics Are Haunted by the Past," *New York Review of Books*, February 21, 2013, 40.

12. See Sam Dillon, "Scholar's School Reform U-Turn Shakes Up Debate," *New York Times*, March 2, 2010; and Diane Ravitch, "The Myth of Charter Schools," *New York Review of Books*, November 11, 2010; and Ravitch, "Schools We Can Envy," *New York Review of Books*, March 8, 2012; quotes from "Schools We Can Envy," online, accessed April 11, 2013, *www.nybooks.com/articles/archives/2012/mar/08/schools-we-can-envy*.

13. The Council on Civil Society, *A Call to Civil Society: Why Democracy Needs Moral Truths* (Washington, DC: Institute for American Values, 1998), 5, 6.

14. Dan Conrad, "Learning Outcomes for Community Service," *Generator*, September 1989, 1–2.

15. Anne Colby, Elisabeth Beaumont, Thomas Ehrlich, and Josh Corngold, *Educating for Democracy: Preparing Undergraduates for Responsible Political Engagement* (Palo Alto: Carnegie Foundation for the Advancement of Teaching, 2007).

16. George W. Bush, "The American Spirit: Meeting the Challenge of September 11," *Life*, September 2002, 4.

17. Michael Schudson, "How People Learn to Be Civic," in *United We Serve: National Service and the Future of Citizenship*, ed. E. J. Dionne Jr., Kayla Meltzer Drogosz, Robert E. Litan (Washington, DC: Brookings Institution Press, 2003), 270.

18. Scott Jaschik and Doug Lederman, eds., *Inside Higher Ed Survey of College and University Chief Academic Officers* (Washington, DC: Inside Higher Education, 2013), 27, *www.insidehighered.com/audio/2013/02/14/2013-inside-higher-ed-survey-chief-academic-officers*.

19. Harry C. Boyte, *Citizenship and the Cult of the Expert* (Dayton, OH: Kettering Foundation, 2009).

20. Steve Fraser, "The Labor Question," in *The Rise and Fall of the New Deal Order: 1930–1980*, ed. Fraser and Gary Gerstle (Princeton, NJ: Princeton University Press, 1989), 70.

21. For a summary of this narrative, see Harry C. Boyte, "To Address the Empowerment Gap We Need to Change the Narrative of Education," *Huffington Post*, June 9, 2014, at *www.huffingtonpost.com/harry-boyte/taking-on-empowerment-gap_b_5470530.html*.

22. Aristotle, *The Politics*, ed. Stephen Everson (Cambridge: Cambridge University Press, 1988), 71.

23. Ibid., 86, 83.

24. Ibid., 57.

25. Judith N. Shklar, *American Citizenship: The Quest for Inclusion* (Cambridge, MA:

Harvard University Press, 1991), 68. John Budd has summarized this ethos for Greek intellectuals, "Free men use things, they do not make them." John W. Budd, *The Thought of Work* (Ithaca, NY: Cornell University Press, 2011), 22.

26. For rich treatment of alternative work-centered intellectual traditions that treat the civic and democratic possibilities and practices of work, see Budd, *The Thought of Work* and Luke Bretherton, *Resurrecting Democracy: Faith, Citizenship, and the Politics of the Common Good* (Cambridge: Cambridge University Press, forthcoming).

27. Hannah Arendt, *The Human Condition* (Chicago: University of Chicago Press, 1958), 161–62.

28. Quoted from Mary Dietz, "'The Slow Boring of Hard Boards': Methodical Thinking and the Work of Politics," *American Political Science Review* 88, no. 4 (1994), 873–86; quotes from 874, 876.

29. Richard Sennett, *The Craftsman* (New Haven: Yale University Press, 2008).

30. Tony Schwartz and Christine Porath, "Why You Hate Work," *New York Times*, May 30, 2014, *www.nytimes.com/2014/06/01/opinion/sunday/why-you-hate-work.html* accessed June 11, 2014.

31. Saul Alinsky, *Reveille for Radicals* (New York: Random House, 1946), 40.

32. Jean L. Cohen and Andrew Arato, *Civil Society and Political Theory* (Cambridge, MA: MIT Press, 1992), ix.

33. Benjamin Barber, "The Search for Civil Society," *New Democrat*, no. 7 (March/April, 1995), 4. Jean Elshtain used Barber's definition in framing the work, which produced *A Call to Civil Society*. See Elshtain, quoted in "Institute, University of Chicago to Form Council on Civil Society," *Family Affairs* 7, no. 1–2 (Spring 1996), 3.

34. Benjamin R. Barber, "Civic Schizophrenia," *Kettering Review*, Summer 2006, 10.

35. Benjamin R. Barber, *A Place for Us: How to Make Society Civil and Democracy Strong* (New York: Hill and Wang, 1998), 41, 42, 44.

36. This history of Cortes's innovations is adapted from Harry C. Boyte, *Community Is Possible: Repairing America's Roots* (New York: Harper and Row, 1984), ch. 5, "Empowerment."

37. Ernesto Cortes Jr., "Toward a Democratic Culture," *Kettering Review*, Summer 2006, 48.

38. Michael Gecan, *Going Public: An Organizers' Guide to Citizen Action* (Boston: Beacon Press, 2004), 35.

39. I develop this argument in detail in my 2002 Dewey lecture at the University of Michigan. See "A Different Kind of Politics: John Dewey an d the Meaning of Citizenship in the 21st Century," *Good Society* 12, no. 2 (2003), 1–15.

40. See Boyte, "To Address the Empowerment Gap."

41. See Harry C. Boyte and Nan Kari, *Building America: The Democratic Promise of Public Work* (Philadelphia: Temple University Press, 1996).

42. Robert H. Wiebe, *Self-Rule: A Cultural History of American Democracy* (Chicago: University of Chicago Press, 1995).

43. Quoted from Michael Kazin, *The Populist Persuasion: An American History* (New York: Basic Books, 1995), 9.

44. See Walter Isaacson, "The America Ben Franklin Saw," *Washington Post*, November 21, 2012.

45. Gordon Wood, *The Radicalism of the American Revolution* (New York: Vintage, 1991), ix.

46. David Mathews, *Reclaiming Public Education by Reclaiming Our Democracy* (Dayton, OH: Kettering Foundation Press, 2006), vii.

47. Oscar Handlin and Mary Handlin, *Commonwealth: A Study of the Role of Government in the American Economy, Massachusetts, 1774–1861* (Cambridge, MA: Harvard University Press, 1969), 30.

48. See Boyte, "Constructive Politics as Public Work," *Political Theory* 39, no. 5 (2011), 630–60.

49. Budd, *Thought of Work*, 167.

50. *Vocation, Access, and Excellence: The Educational Vision of Augsburg College* (Minneapolis: Augsburg College, 2012), *web.augsburg.edu/president/educational-vision/EducationalVision12-2012.pdf*, accessed January 30, 2013.

51. William Sullivan, *Work and Integrity: The Crisis and Promise of Professionalism in America* (San Francisco: Jossey-Bass, 1995), 28.

52. Fraser, "Labor Question," 65.

53. Gerald Taylor, "Prometheus Unbound: Populism, the Property Question, and Social Invention," *Good Society* 21, no. 2 (2012), 224–25.

54. John Rogers, Joseph Kahne, and Ellen Middaugh, "Multiple Pathways and the Future of Democracy," in *Beyond Tracking: Multiple Pathways to College, Career, and Civic Participation*, ed. Jeannie Oakes and Marisa Saunders (Cambridge, MA: Harvard Education Press, 2008), 164.

55. Dewey quoted in Harry C. Boyte, "A Different Kind of Politics: John Dewey and the Meaning of Citizenship in the 21st Century," *Good Society* 12, no. 2 (2003), 7.

56. Dewey's definitional mistake can be found in his address "Social as Social Centre." Despite its luminous vision—and its consequences, helping to spawn a movement for schools to become centers of community life across the nation—he articulated a faulty distinction between "politics" and "society." "I mean by 'society' the less definite and freer play of the forces of the community which goes on in the daily intercourse and contact of men in an endless variety of ways that have nothing to do with politics or government," Dewey argued. Dewey proposed that citizenship needed to be defined more broadly, "to mean all the relationships of all sorts that are involved in membership in a community," and that the range of school activities related to citizenship education was wide. But his definition took the political edge off of citizenship. Quoted from Harry C. Boyte, "A Different Kind of Politics: John Dewey and the Meaning of Citizenship in the 21st Century" (Dewey Lecture, University of Michigan, November 1, 2002), on Academia.org, 12, *www.academia.edu/6881659/Harry_Boyte_A_Different_Kind_of_Politics_—_John_Dewey_and_the_Meaning_of_Citizenship_in_the_21st_Century.*

57. "Reach Out about Climate," editorial, *Nature*, no. 481 (2012), 5.

58. Sabelo Ndlovu-Gatsheni, "Decolonising the University of Africa," *Thinker*, May 2013, 47.

59. Roy MacLeod, "Reading the Discourse of Colonial Science," *Les Sciences Coloniales* 2 (Paris: L'Institut Français de Recherche Scientifique pour le Développement en Coopération, 1996), 90; see *horizon.documentation.ird.fr/exl-doc/pleins_textes/pleins_textes_7/carton07/010008834.pdf.*

60. Keller quoted from Boyte, *Going Public: Academics and Public Life* (Dayton, OH: Kettering Foundation Press, 2004), 5.

61. Peters furnished the quote from Ruby Smith. Hannah quoted in Scott J. Peters, "Educating the Civic Professional: Reconfigurations and Resistances," *Michigan Journal of Community Service Learning* 11, no. 1 (Fall 2004), 47.

62. Liberty Hyde Bailey, *New York State Rural Problems* (Albany: Lyon, 1913), 11–12, 133, 29–30.

63. See Harry C. Boyte, *CommonWealth: A Return to Citizen Politics* (New York: Free Press, 1989), *www.thefreelibrary.com/CommonWealth%3a+A+Return+to+Citizen+Politics.-a08310217.*

64. Maria Avila, "Transforming the Culture of Academia: An Organizing Based Model of Civic Engagement," draft in author's possession, August 11, 2003.

65. Lesley Cafarelli, *Dilemmas in Teaching: Cases for Faculty Reflection* (Minneapolis: Collaboration, 1998), excerpts in author's possession, 3.

66. For evidence in higher education, see John Dedrick with Laura Grattan and Harris Dienstfrey, *Deliberation and the Work of Higher Education: Innovations for the Classroom, the Campus, and the Community* (Dayton, OH: Kettering Foundation, 2008); Stacey Molnar Main's report is forthcoming from the Kettering Foundation.

67. William J. Doherty, Tai J. Mendenhall, and Jerica M. Berge, "The Families and Democracy and Citizen Health Care Project," *Journal of Marital and Family Therapy* 36, no. 4 (October 2010), 389–402.

68. "Public Achievement in Fridley: Transforming Special Education," *youtu.be/VaRimtavig8.*

69. Wikipedia entrees on Special Education and EBD, accessed June 15, 2013.

70. "Fridley Middle Schoolers Take on District's Bullying Policy," at *minnesota.publicradio.org/display/web/2012/05/31/fridley-middle-schoolers-take-on-districts-bullying-policy.*

71. Rom Coles, "Of Tensions and Tricksters: Grassroots Democracy between Theory and Practice," *Perspectives on Politics* 4, no. 3 (Fall 2006), 547–61.

72. Read more: *www.insidehighered.com/news/2013/01/30/north-carolina-governor-joins-chorus-republicans-critical-liberal-arts.*

73. Taylor, "Prometheus Unbound," 226.

74. For the summary of the *Good Society* special issue "Reclaiming Democratic Populism" (2012), which includes Taylor's article and others making the case that an information age populist movement is beginning to appear, see Harry C. Boyte, "Reclaiming Democratic Populism," *Basic Facts*, Scholars Strategy Network, March 2013, *www.scholarsstrategynetwork.org/sites/default/files/ssn_basic_facts_boyte_on_reclaiming_populism.pdf.*

75. Jean Johnson, *Divided We Fail: Our Leaders and Citizens Talking Past Each Other on Higher Education?* (Washington: National Issues Forums Institute, 2013), 2, 3.

PART I

Democratic Narratives

In his work on moral philosophy, *After Virtue*, Alasdair MacIntyre challenges the forgetfulness about our common narratives that pervades the modern world. "I can only answer the question 'What am I to do?' if I can answer the prior question, 'Of what story or stories do I find myself a part?'"[1]

Contributors to this section are great storytellers of higher education, helping us to remember its democratic story, of which we are a part. Remembering this story and its many expressions is crucial for deciding and acting on "what we should do."

---

[1] Alasdair MacIntyre, *After Virtue: A Study in Moral Theory* (Notre Dame, IN: University of Notre Dame Press, 1981), 216.

1

HAR MEGIDDO: A BATTLE FOR THE SOUL OF HIGHER EDUCATION

David Mathews

What's the connection between American higher education and a town (Megiddo) on a mountain (*har*) in the ancient Middle East? Any connection may seem unlikely. But bear with me.

In January 2012, the White House hosted a meeting called "For Democracy's Future: Education Reclaims Our Civic Mission." Later in March, we discussed what had happened in Washington at the Kettering Foundation. (Kettering, by the way, is a nonprofit, nonpartisan, nongovernmental research foundation rooted in the American tradition of inventive research.)

We were talking to Caryn Musil and Elizabeth Minnich, both from the Association of American Colleges and Universities (AAC&U), about a report that had been made at the Washington meeting, which was prepared by a committee that included Derek Barker, a Kettering program officer. The report proposed a number of steps that academic institutions could take to benefit American democracy.[1]

At some point in our conversation, Derek noted that an eight-hundred-pound gorilla had been in the room when the Washington committee drafted its report. The "gorilla" had an agenda quite different from the one the committee was considering; the objective was to make colleges and universities more productive and efficient in order to stem the growing cost of a college education, which has significantly outpaced inflation. No one introduced the gorilla, but everyone knew he was there.

Elizabeth Minnich recalled other meetings where these external pressures and higher education's own concerns were being discussed. The tension between the two agendas is significant. Colleges and universities are being asked to cut expenses and do more with less while at the same time reach out and do more for external constituencies. The tension was so great in one of these meetings that an academic participant said she felt like pulling out her hair!

Struck by how powerful this tension is, I was reminded of the fateful battle at Megiddo in 1479 BCE when Thutmose III attacked and eventually drove out the prince of Kadesh. The clash was prominent in Middle East history and appears to be the basis for the biblical "Armageddon."

Today, a great battle appears to be looming on the plains below the mountaintop citadels of higher education. The attacking forces want to put more productivity requirements on academe. These forces draw their strength from public concerns about the high cost of college and the lack of jobs for graduates. This attack is already having effects, such as more reliance on less expensive adjunct faculty.

Making the case that higher education doesn't have responsibility for graduating young people with job skills at an affordable cost would be difficult. I certainly wouldn't try to do it. After all, from the time of the colonial colleges (which trained ministers) to the present, institutions of higher learning have recognized that students need to be prepared for their careers. And it would make no sense at all to argue against cost effectiveness. I've heard of campuses where students live in their cars and skimp on meals in order to make ends meet. Still, there is reason to be concerned about the implicit assumption in the attacks that higher education is largely for the benefit of individuals and that any social benefit is the sum of these individual gains. The counterargument is well put in a chapter in *What Is College For?*, where Ellen Condliffe Lagemann and Harry Lewis argue that "higher education has vital purposes beyond aggregated individual economic benefits." Lagemann and Lewis fear that such purposes have "fallen by the wayside."[2]

In the fortress at modern Megiddo where these citadels of academe are located, the defense is divided. One camp consists of academic traditionalists who champion the cultivation of the mind and fly the banner of excellence. The other camp is a polyglot array of the new legions of outreach: civic engagement, public scholarship, and community development. A richly heterogeneous lot, they have no common banner.

I admit that using the battle at Megiddo as an analogy is shamelessly overdramatic and potentially misleading. The attacking forces today aren't trying to destroy colleges and universities. Nonetheless, the stakes are high; in the current clash, the mission and role of higher education are at issue. While the destruction of higher education's Megiddo is unlikely, colleges and universities could be severely damaged by slow starvation from want of outside resources.

Could this clash be avoided or even made constructive? Some see constructive change coming through a greater use of technology, as in massive open online courses (MOOCs). Yet, while appreciative of technology, I hesitate to give up on face-to-face instruction and the educational value it brings.

I would suggest a defense that is really an offense. Get off the mountain and form a new compact with the public, an alliance based on making a closer fit between both institutions of higher education and their missions and the public and its problems.

In this new offensive, higher education would make use of its history as a movement in support of the great democratic movements in America. These movements gave higher education a soul, an animating spirit. Beginning with turning colonial colleges into "seminaries of sedition" during the American Revolution and continuing with the creation of the state universities to provide leadership for a new nation, American higher education has been shaped by public purposes.[3] These purposes are reflected in the founding of the agricultural and mechanical colleges, in creating colleges for African Americans and Native Americans, and in establishing community colleges. In every case, higher education has been enriched by an alliance with citizens who have a great cause. That is exactly what I am proposing now when I suggest that the democratically inclined in academe might find much in common with a citizenry concerned with having a stronger hand in shaping the future.

Unfortunately, this history has been fading from higher education's memory. I recall an observation from a report, *The Changing Agenda for American Higher Education*, on a 1976 Airlie House conference, which was sponsored by the then Department of Health, Education, and Welfare. The report includes a quote from Earl Cheit, dean of the business school at the University of California, Berkeley, who said, "review procedures, regulation, litigation now command so much attention from college and university officials, it is easy to forget that for most of its history higher education in the U.S. was a movement, not a bureaucracy."[4] Why is recapturing academe's history as a movement essential? Because the movement reflects a public mission.

What public concerns today might bear on the mission of colleges and universities? Americans are anxious about the future. Some are worried that the country has lost its moral compass as news of another ethical lapse is reported. People fear that even communities have lost much of their sense of community, of responsibility for the common good. Many Americans long for a return of prosperity, but that involves more than having a well-paying job. They want meaningful work for themselves and for their children. They want our nation to be a nation of producers, not just consumers. And most Americans want to have a stronger role than they have now in a political system that seems to push them to the sidelines, unable to make a significant difference.

Using a phrase coined by Ben Barber, I would call this a struggle for "strong democracy." That is a democracy where, in Harry Boyte's terms, citizens are producers of public goods rather than just consumers of services, constituents of politicians, or simply voters.[5]

What is higher education's relationship to this quest for a strong, citizen-centered democracy? Unfortunately, that question is being overshadowed by cost and productivity issues. As I've said, ignoring these issues or demonizing their advocates isn't going to be effective. After all, reducing costs is key to realizing two values higher education holds dear: greater access and greater diversity. The trouble is that the preoccupation with costs and career readiness is obscuring the equally valid concern with higher education's role in democracy.

The good news is that academe has been trying to reach outside its walls for some time. There have been efforts to legitimize the scholarship that has public relevance and to give students opportunities to serve worthy causes. Having studied the relationship between higher education and the public for more than thirty years, the Kettering Foundation hasn't before seen anything like the current interest in civic engagement.

This civic initiative is widespread. Most of the energy is coming from faculty members who want to integrate their scholarly interests with their public lives.[6] And nearly all types of institutions are involved. The initiatives reach down into academic disciplines, into the professional schools—even into the nature of knowledge itself. Some academics are looking into the civic roots of disciplines from political science to speech communication, and others advocate restoring the liberal arts to their role as civic arts.[7] Recent conferences recall what Aristotle said on moral reasoning and what Isocrates wrote on the importance of public deliberation.[8] And some professions are moving beyond technical skill and expertise to look at the social and political dimensions of their work. (See Bill Sullivan's pioneering study of civic professionalism.[9])

For all of its promise, however, the civic engagement initiative in academe faces some serious challenges. One is to give greater intellectual integrity to the initiatives. Nearly everyone involved would say they serve democracy, yet what they mean by democracy varies considerably. That isn't the problem, however. The problem is that there is too little analysis of those meanings, which opens civic engagement to the charge that it is largely rhetorical, a public relations Potemkin village with good intentions but little substance.

Ideally, advocates of public scholarship, service learning, and similar ventures would explain what they think democracy is and what it requires—and then critique what they are doing by these standards. This would be an open, shared analysis. Scholars interested in community economic development may already be moving in this direction by looking into the relationship between their concepts of community and development, on the one hand, and concepts of democracy, on the other.[10]

This kind of internal critique could put the work citizens do as citizens alongside the work of scholars and professionals to see if they are aligned and supportive, or, if they aren't, how they might become mutually beneficial. Journalists have come closest to doing this when some have compared the way they name problems with the way citizens give names to problems. Journalists tend to describe problems in professional terms; people name problems in terms of what is deeply valuable to them.

Other challenges to engagement initiatives on campus include the almost total absence of trustee participation. For years now, the Kettering Foundation has tried in vain to locate a conversation among trustees about their own relationship to a citizenry that wants to get off the sidelines. Although trustees ostensibly represent these citizens, we've only met a handful who have wanted to address people's concerns about the future of our democracy. Recently there has been an effort to see if civically minded alumni might fill this vacuum.

The need for tenure standards that recognize public scholarship is an obvious challenge. Another is creating spaces within the institutions for initiatives in strong democracy, spaces that provide structure without the constraints that come from the typical academic silos. Fortunately, there are some new centers dedicated to strengthening public life that are trying to create this space. Of course, there are many kinds of institutes that make useful contributions, but the ones in the best position to turn civic engagement into democratic engagement are those that focus on building a greater capacity for citizens to do their work, work such as the collective decision making that is the key to collective action. We have found more than seventy such centers or institutes so far, and the number is growing.[11]

Still another on-campus challenge—and opportunity—is in the way students come to see themselves as political actors. Strategically, students are critical as a source of energy for civic engagement, particularly when their idealism is instructed by mentoring faculty members. On some campuses, faculty and students have come together in classes where the faculty introduce students to a deliberative politics they can practice every day—a politics of shared problem solving.

There are also campuses with promising experiments to push beyond service and service learning (both are valuable) to embed students in ongoing community problem solving. Auburn University students are spending their summers in towns across Alabama as part of a civic engagement program called Living Democracy. The students don't just drop into the communities; they live there long enough to see the consequences of their work.[12]

The ultimate test of the civic engagement initiatives on campus is whether they connect with the struggle for stronger democracy off campus. Restoring a sense of mission and public purpose to colleges and universities can't be done without engaging the citizenry—*on its own terms.*

In an essay entitled "Ships Passing in the Night?," I reported on Kettering research that found a significant difference between the questions citizens pose as they struggle to solve the problems of their communities and the responses of academic institutions that want to assist them.[13] In communities hit by some type of disaster—a hurricane, a collapsed economy, a rash of crime and violence—people want to know how *they* can come together as a community, despite their differences, to rebuild their communities. Academic institutions are less likely to engage this question and more likely to offer what they can—expert advice and services or technical assistance.

This lack of alignment undermines what the Megiddo analogy suggests is critical: a solid connection between efforts to strengthen democracy off campus and the civic initiatives on campus. To meet this challenge, academics will have to find roles off campus that go beyond providing expert knowledge—perhaps even beyond being a "coach" for communities, or a "guide-on-the-side." More appropriate roles may have to do with fostering the public or collective learning that produces practical wisdom, which communities need to solve their problems. Academics have different ways of knowing to produce the expertise that they provide. That expertise is certainly valuable, but it tends to dominate or dislodge the practical wisdom citizens must create. The two epistemologies need to be reconciled. Maybe academics could learn in tandem with communities—as colearners—by aligning these different ways of knowing.

Another possibility for connecting efforts to strengthen democracy off campus with the civic engagement initiatives in academe would be to revisit the mission of higher education as seen from the public's perspective rather than the perspective of colleges and universities. Asking people what they want from colleges and universities usually prompts predictable answers: lower costs and jobs for graduates. However, if people were first asked a broader question about their concerns for the future—and then what academic institutions should be doing about those concerns—the responses might be surprising and more authentic. A number of institutions in the Shaping Our Future project have been engaging citizens through deliberative forums on the mission of higher education and the role it should play in our social, political, and economic progress.[14] If this becomes a new way of hearing the public, it could bring higher education into a closer alignment with the democratic aspirations of citizens.

Returning to today's clash at academe's Megiddo, costs have to be reined in because some type of postsecondary education is the key to most high-paying jobs today. Access to higher education is critical. At the same time, the soul of America's colleges and universities has been shaped by the social, economic, and political movements that spawned these institutions. Take that history away, and academic institutions become what Earl Cheit feared—bureaucracies whose goals are merely efficiency. Public purposes, the animating spirits of our colleges and universities, would be lost. That can't be allowed to happen, even with an eight-hundred-pound gorilla in the room.

Notes

1. The National Task Force on Civic Learning and Democratic Engagement, *A Crucible Moment: College Learning and Democracy's Future* (Washington, DC: Association of American Colleges and Universities, 2012).
2. Ellen Condliffe Lagemann and Harry Lewis, "Renewing the Civic Mission of Higher Education," in *What Is College For? The Public Purpose of Higher Education*, ed. Ellen Condliffe Lagemann and Harry Lewis (New York: Teachers College Press, 2012), 9–45.
3. Louis Leonard Tucker, *Connecticut's Seminary of Sedition: Yale College* (Chester, CT: Pequot Press, 1974).
4. David Mathews et al., *The Changing Agenda for American Higher Education* (Washington, DC: US Government Printing Office, 1977), 31.
5. Benjamin Barber, *Strong Democracy: Participatory Politics for a New Age* (Berkeley: University of California Press, 1984) and Harry C. Boyte, *The Backyard Revolution: Understanding the New Citizen Movement* (Philadelphia: Temple University Press, 1980).
6. Claire Snyder-Hall, "Beyond the Ivory Tower: The Civic Aspirations of Faculty," *Connections*, 2012, 34–36.
7. R. Claire Snyder, *Shutting the Public Out of Politics: Civic Republicanism, Professional Politics, and the Eclipse of Civil Society* (Dayton, OH: Kettering Foundation, 1999). Also see the *Civic Arts Review*, which is published by the Arneson Institute for Practical Politics and Public Affairs at Ohio Wesleyan University. Edited by Bernard Murchland, the journal is "dedicated to the proposition that education, liberally conceived, is the basis of a free society."
8. Isocrates, "Antidosis," in *Isocrates*, trans. George Norlin, vol. 2 (1929; reprint, New York: G. P. Putnam's Sons, 2000), 179–365; and Aristotle, *The Ethics of Aristotle: The Nicomachean Ethics*, trans. J. A. K. Thomson (London: Penguin Books, reprinted 1956), 84–87, 176–84.
9. William M. Sullivan, *Work and Integrity: The Crisis and Promise of Professionalism in America* (New York: HarperBusiness, 1995).

10. Theodore R. Alter, "Achieving the Promise of Public Scholarship, in *Engaging Campus and Community: The Practice of Public Scholarship in the State and Land-Grant University System*, ed. Scott J. Peters et al. (Dayton, OH: Kettering Foundation Press, 2005), 461–87.

11. Scott London, *Doing Democracy: How a Network of Grassroots Organizations Is Strengthening Community, Building Capacity, and Shaping a New Kind of Civic Education* (Dayton, OH: Kettering Foundation, 2010); and Alice Diebel and Randall Nielsen, "Learning Exchanges with Centers for Public Life," *Connections*, 2013, 18–21.

12. Libby Sander, "Auburn Students Become Small-Town Citizens for the Summer," *Chronicle of Higher Education*, July 9, 2012, *chronicle.com/article/article-content/132769*, accessed November 20, 2013.

13. David Mathews, "Afterword: Ships Passing in the Night?," in *A Different Kind of Politics: Readings on the Role of Higher Education in Democracy*, ed. Derek W. M. Barker and David W. Brown (Dayton, OH: Kettering Foundation Press, 2009), 93–104.

14. Jean Johnson, *Divided We Fail: Are Leaders and Citizens Talking Past Each Other on Higher Education? An Interim Report on the 2013 National Issues Forums* (Dayton, OH: Kettering Foundation, 2013).

2

A DEMOCRACY'S COLLEGE TRADITION

Scott J. Peters

The land-grant college, established and supported through the Morrill Acts of 1862 and 1890 and the Equity in Education Land-Grant Status Act of 1994, was once viewed as "democracy's college." Historians of American higher education have mainly characterized this designation in ways that are centered on access. A land-grant college was "democracy's college" because it provided a diverse range of women and men, from all classes and walks of life, with access to three things: degree-granting programs in common vocations, a means of social and economic mobility, and technical information and services.[1]

Access was and still is an important dimension of the democratic meaning and significance of land-grant colleges. But there is another dimension that has received relatively little attention. A land-grant college was also "democracy's college" because it engaged people in public work in everyday places—work that at its best was not only *for* but also *of and by* the people, embodying the democratic spirit of an often-quoted line from President Lincoln's Gettysburg Address.

For many women and men during the late nineteenth and early twentieth centuries, a public-work-centered way of interpreting the democratic meaning and significance of land-grant colleges wasn't a secondary afterthought. It was a primary conviction. We see this in something Isabel Bevier, a leader in the field of home economics, wrote in 1920: "And so another great door of opportunity was opened for human betterment; another chance was given for men and women, hand in hand, to work at the world's problems. That, to me, has always been one of the very great benefits that the land-grant college has given to our daily life—the fact that the men and women have worked together at the world's problems."[2] A democratic tradition that engages men and women in off-campus public work survives into the present in the land-grant system. But it's in decline, as powerful forces diminish its strength and threaten its survival. And it's most often understood in narrow, instrumental ways that miss its broader civic and cultural significance. For example, it's understood as "service."

Service, institutionalized through extension work, has long been seen as a key element in what has made and still makes land-grant colleges distinctive. Reflecting this view, Patricia Crosson has written that land-grant colleges provide the "most celebrated and successful example of the articulation and fulfillment of the service ideal" in the entire history of American higher education.[3]

Crosson's claim may well be true. But the democracy's college tradition that I focus on in this essay is not about service. It's about politics. It's a tradition that engages faculty members, staff, and students in collaborative off-campus work with others that is political in nature, even though it's almost never understood or named as such. It's not political in a state-centered sense, with a focus on policy making and elections. Rather, it's political in a local community- and neighborhood-centered sense, with a focus on social as well as technical problems, and on cultural ideals and aspirations as well as material and economic interests and needs. In practice this tradition has of course been imperfect. It's been more or less democratic, and more or less productive. But at its best it has engaged the common people as productive *agents* of public work, in ways that align with a democratic, populist variety of everyday politics in everyday places.[4] As such, the tradition both flows from and contributes to a still unfolding history of change and debate about not only the theory and philosophy but also the location and practice of politics and citizenship in a democratic society. This gives it a broad significance, with implications that reach beyond higher education to our larger society.

As a scholar, I've spent much of my time pursuing the task of unearthing and documenting a democratic, public work tradition in land-grant colleges, both through historical research and through narrative inquiry and analysis of stories about the work and experiences of contemporary land-grant faculty, staff, and students.[5] So far I've spent relatively little time pursuing a more important—and much more difficult—task: the task of reclaiming and rebuilding this tradition in our time. While this task involves and requires intellectual work, including historical research that unearths and examines the tradition's origins, development, and decline, little lasting progress can or will be made in pursuing it without skilled and tenacious organizing.

The democracy's college tradition we need to reclaim and rebuild is, in contemporary language, a tradition of civic or public engagement. It's pursued and embodied in off-campus practice, through public work that addresses gritty, real-world problems in ways that advance not only people's economic and material needs and interests but also their cultural and political ideals and their agency as citizens. We see this expressed as a core principle in a passage from a book that was authored by one of the tradition's most important practitioners and philosophers—a horticultural scientist from Cornell University named Liberty Hyde Bailey. In his 1915 book, *The Holy Earth*, Bailey wrote: "It is not sufficient to train technically in the trades and crafts and arts to the end of securing greater economic efficiency—this may be accomplished in a despotism and result in no self-action on the part of the people. Every democracy must reach far beyond what is commonly known as economic efficiency, and do everything it can to enable those in the backgrounds to maintain their standing and their pride and to partake in the making of political affairs."[6] This passage can be read as an interpretation of the key charge to land-grant colleges that is included in the Morrill Act of 1862: "to promote the liberal and practical education of the industrial classes in the several pursuits and professions in life."[7] To "train technically in the trades and arts and crafts" represents the "practical" component, while the liberal component is represented by efforts to "enable" the common people to "maintain their standing and their pride and to partake in the making of political affairs." The operative word here is the word "and." Not liberal *or* practical education, but liberal *and* practical education, interwoven in ways that support the development of a civic or democratic professionalism.[8]

In practice the pursuit of the liberal and practical education charge hasn't been limited to campus classrooms. It has included education that is provided in off-campus "extension" work in people's neighborhoods and communities, on their farms, and even in their homes. It also hasn't been limited to scholars from social science and humanities fields. In fact, the best examples of practice I've found in my research are of scholars who, like Liberty Hyde Bailey, come from fields in the agricultural, biological, and natural sciences.

Practitioners of the tradition that took and still take Bailey's interpretation of the "liberal and practical education" charge seriously have had to contend with pushback, and a frustrating lack of understanding and support. To illustrate this, I'd like to relate a story a professor at a land-grant college (I'll refer to her as "Professor X") told me during a focus group discussion that I facilitated in early 2011 about the public purposes of land-grant colleges. Professor X is an associate professor in an agricultural science field. Her expertise is in nutrient management. She works closely with dairy farmers on the challenge they face of complying with environmental regulations, and more expansively of making their farms more sustainable. During the focus group she told the following story, taken verbatim from a transcript of the discussion (the transcript excerpt also includes my voice as facilitator, and the voice of an associate professor of nutrition I'll call "Professor Y"):

> PROFESSOR X: Yesterday I was in a meeting and I asked somebody high up in the administration in our college a point blank question. The question was, "In your interaction with our stakeholders, what do they want from us?" And the response was the same as always. And that I don't buy.
> FACILITATOR: Same as always being what?
> PROFESSOR Y: The best scientific knowledge on X? (Y asked this in a sarcastic voice)
> PROFESSOR X: No. The response that came after that was, "Somebody on the other end of the phone line that tells them what to do." My experience is so opposite of that, that I was floored by that response. I work with dairy farmers. And what the farmers want from us is not an answer. They want us to partner with them to find solutions. There is certainly a fraction of the farming community that wants to pick up the phone, ask me a question, get an answer and implement it. But the ones that are progressive, the ones that we should be working with to move forward, are the ones that say, "What do you think of this? Can we put something in place to get some answers?" They're working towards networks of on-farm research. They want us to be partners in finding answers. They don't want us to give them the answer.

To elevate our interpretation of the significance of this story, we need to read it alongside a passage from "A Farm Bureau Creed," which was published in a book by M. C. Burritt in 1922:

> We believe in self-help for ourselves, our community, our country; in our own abilities well developed and properly supported to solve our own problems; and in local and voluntary leadership. . . . We believe in a program, a definite, carefully considered plan of work, local in conception and in character, which looks toward the solution of the problems which are vital to the welfare of the farm and the home. This plan of action for the organization should be made at home by those most concerned, but with the best expert advice and assistance. We believe in a partnership between farmers and the public agricultural agencies—between practice and science—for the working out of this program.[9]

Reading Professor X's story alongside this passage helps us to see the democracy's college tradition as a *living* tradition, however much it might also be in decline, against the grain, and at the margins. Her story is remarkably well aligned with the elements of a nearly century-old "creed" that names—better than anything else I've ever uncovered in my historical research—the grounding principles of the democracy's college tradition. While neither the creed nor Professor X's story include the words "democracy," "politics," or "citizenship," they can—and I believe should—be read as expressions of a populist philosophy of democratic politics, a philosophy that centers on a view of citizenship as public work that is taken up in everyday, ordinary places, of and by the people. Just as Professor X did in the story she told in 2011, the creed positions farmers and public agricultural agencies—including especially land-grant colleges—as partners. Like Professor X's story, it doesn't strip academic experts of their civic agency. But it places primary agency for public work in farmers' hands.

A second reason why Professor X's story is significant has to do with something else it reveals: disagreement over core issues of identity and work. There is no way to overestimate the significance of such disagreement. The ways land-grant faculty, staff, and administrators answer the questions of who they are and what they should do—or not do—have dramatic consequences. It makes a big difference whether faculty members understand their identity as detached experts who tell people what to do from a distance, or as engaged partners who work face-to-face with people in their own neighborhoods and communities.

A third reason why Professor X's story is significant has to do with what it reveals about the way some academic professionals understand what their "stakeholders" want. The administrator in Professor X's story offers a cynical, minimalist view that positions stakeholders as customers or clients of expert advice and services. Based on the authority of her own experience, Professor X offers a sharply different view. Her view has no trace of cynicism, or of minimalist expectations about the willingness of people to contribute to and be engaged in difficult public work. While it will surely sound implausible to cynics, it reveals promising possibilities we should take seriously.

I want to make two additional points here, inspired by Professor X's story and "A Farm Bureau Creed." First, the democracy's college tradition in the land-grant system isn't just about the pursuit of political ideals and principles. It's about problem solving. It reflects a commonsense bet about what it takes to understand and address complex problems, especially "wicked" problems about which people have reason to disagree. What it takes, in the words of the creed, is a "partnership between practice and science," a partnership that honors and incorporates different kinds of knowledge, experience, and expertise. When such a partnership results not only in effective problem solving but also in "self-action on the part of the people," as Liberty Hyde Bailey put it, when it produces programs and plans that are "local in conception and in character," that are "made at home by those most concerned," then it reflects and advances the democracy's college tradition at its best.

The second additional point I want to make is simply that the historical record is mixed. The democracy's college tradition hasn't always been pursued at its best. What it demands is difficult and time consuming. Its practitioners had and have flaws and shortcomings. They're not always democratic in their behaviors and attitudes, and they have often exhibited racial, gender, cultural, and other forms of bias and prejudice. Their work has also often contributed to ecological destruction, or to the interests and power of corporations and the state. And they were and still are—as we see in Professor X's story—up against different traditions, views, and practices that are more technocratic than democratic in nature, and often times more powerful. As a historical example, consider Gladys Baker's account of what happened in the 1930s when US Department of Agriculture administrators attempted to recruit extension agents to organize and facilitate deliberative forums about pressing policy issues: "The training and experience of the agents did not fit them with the necessary tolerance and objectivity for this task; for they were accustomed to parceling out a continuous supply of 'right answers' to immediately pressing farm problems and consequently often found it difficult to see the practical value of philosophical discussion groups. Leaders in some states reported that it was difficult to keep the country agent from monopolizing the discussion and insisting that the group accept his viewpoint and judgment."[10]

Here it is useful to step back and raise what were and still are among the largest and most challenging questions we can raise about land-grant colleges—or any other college for that matter. What are their public purposes? What ends and which interests should they seek to advance? What are their roles in a democratic society?

These questions are normative rather than empirical in nature. They are inescapably political. And they are rarely asked and pursued in public settings and ways.

In a diverse society composed of different interests and viewpoints, different public philosophies, different cultures and races, different genders, and different kinds and levels of power, we might expect histories of the land-grant system to reveal a great deal of disagreement and even conflict over questions of public purposes and ends. Yet until quite recently, historians of the land-grant system have downplayed disagreement and conflict over public purposes and ends, or left it out entirely. This includes the accomplished historian Earle D. Ross. In the final sentence of his 1942 book, *Democracy's College: The Land-Grant Movement in the Formative Stage*, Ross offered the following summary of what land-grant institutions faced and accomplished during the first thirty or so years of their existence: "the real test of all the land-grant institutions was their ability and disposition to fulfill their peculiar mission in the new era, and it was in ministering to the technical, social, and political needs of the nation come of age that they attained measurably to the vision of the true prophets of the industrial movement in becoming real people's colleges—with all their limitations a distinct native product and the fullest expression of democracy in higher education."[11] As a concluding sentence, this is quite troubling. There's no hint in it of debate and disagreement over public purposes and ends. In fact, it implies the opposite. It also implies that the early work of land-grant institutions was an unambiguous success.

Ross's study suffers from a failure that he shares with several other historians of the land-grant system. As Roger L. Williams has recently written, Ross and other scholars failed to attend in their works to complex realities in land-grant history of "paradox, inconsistency, and ambiguity," the "clash of competing ideas and interests," and "rough-and-tumble politics."[12]

There is another failure in land-grant historiography, one that Williams's own work suffers from. While he notes in his book that "the idea of democracy" was a "powerful causal agent in the land-grant movement," he flattens its meaning to one dimension: the provision to all classes of people of an equal opportunity to pursue a higher education for any and all occupations. And he characterizes and effectively dismisses other historians' attention to democracy in their studies of land-grant history as being "romantic."[13]

Whether attention to democracy is "romantic" or not turns on how we understand what democracy is, and how we attend to it (see David Mathews's contribution to this book). In his organizing essay in this book, Harry Boyte invites us to see democracy and democratic citizenship as public work. Studying and viewing land-grant history with this conceptual framework, a great deal becomes visible that is otherwise hidden from view. And it becomes possible to interpret what we see in ways that are connected to a larger history of debate and change about the meaning, location, and practice of democracy, and of higher education's roles in it.

Instead of viewing attention to democracy in land-grant history as something that is "romantic," we need to see it as something that is necessary to provoke and inform a much-needed conversation about higher education's public purposes, work, and roles in a democratic society. Just as importantly, we need to see it as a way of countering a different kind of romanticism that has reemerged in recent years. I'm speaking here of the romanticism that we find in the view that we can best understand and address complex technical and social problems through detached, disinterested, and positivist forms of research and science; that all we (by "we" I mean academic professionals) have to do is tell people—over the phone or by text message, blog entry, or other digital means—what we know and what they should therefore do; or, now all the rage in many places, that all we have to do is develop "evidence-based programs," constructed from the findings of random controlled trials and implemented *to the letter* using fixed, predetermined scripts. Despite the fact that little progress in the real world is ever achieved by implementing anything "to the letter," people appear to be taking this view seriously—thanks in part to the demands by funders and government agencies for quantitative "proof" of a program's effectiveness, and the incentive of hundreds of millions of dollars of National Institutes of Health (NIH) funding for "translational research."[14]

The view I've just characterized, perhaps a little too harshly in order to make a point, is not just romantic. It's also tragic. It leaves no room for civic agency for anyone except scientists who conduct random controlled trials. It diminishes rather than enhances "self-action on the part of the people." As such, it marks an abandonment of a set of democratic principles and ideals that were articulated in 1915 by Liberty Hyde Bailey, in 1922 in "A Farm Bureau Creed," and at many other times by many others. It overlooks the view and promise of science as an ethical and social process to be practiced rather than a body of expert knowledge to be applied.[15] Along with other forces and trends, it fuels and accelerates the decline of the democracy's college tradition that embodies such principles and ideals in practice. And it challenges all those who care about it to ask how, if at all, it can be reclaimed and rebuilt.

The short answer to this question, as I said at the outset of this essay, is through skilled and tenacious organizing. Not organizing as protest. Rather, the kind of organizing that Maria Avila and Harry Boyte write about in their contributions to this book: deeply relational, attentive to self-interests, critical but also prophetic and hopeful in tone, highly strategic in ways that are based on a rigorous analysis and mapping of realities and dynamics of power, and grounded in productive public work. Grounded also in stories, including the stories that are told, examined, and refined though the application of Marshall Ganz's public narrative framework: the story of self, the story of us, and the story of now.[16]

Stories and storytelling might sound like weak tools to use in the tough work of organizing. In reality, few tools can be more powerful. I know of no better way of showing how indispensable they are than to quote Alisdair MacIntyre. "I can only answer the question 'What am I to do?'" MacIntyre writes, "if I can answer the prior question 'Of what story or stories do I find myself a part?'"[17]

A chapter in a larger story of the building of democracy's education, the origins, development, and decline of the democracy's college tradition in the land-grant system is a story that I find myself a part. I aim also, with many others, to not only find but also make myself a part of the story of its rebuilding.

Notes

1.   Earle D. Ross characterized a land-grant college as a "democracy's college" in the title of his history of the origins and early development of the land-grant system, *Democracy's College: The Land-Grant Movement in the Formative Stage* (Ames: Iowa State College Press, 1942). For examples of works that center the land-grant college's "democratic" meaning and significance on access, see Ross's book, as well as Edward

Danforth Eddy Jr., *Colleges for Our Land and Time: The Land-Grant Idea in American Education* (New York: Harper and Brothers, 1957); Alan Nevins, *The State Universities and Democracy* (Urbana: University of Illinois Press, 1962); James B. Edmond, *The Magnificent Charter: The Origin and Role of the Morrill Land-Grant Colleges and Universities* (Hicksville, NY: Exposition Press, 1978); Wayne D. Rasmussen, *Taking the University to the People: Seventy-Five Years of Cooperative Extension* (Ames: Iowa State University Press, 1989); Roger L. Williams, *The Origins of Federal Support for Higher Education: George W. Atherton and the Land-Grant College Movement* (University Park: Pennsylvania State University Press, 1991); John R. Campbell, *Reclaiming a Lost Heritage: Land-Grant and Other Higher Education Initiatives for the Twenty-First Century* (Ames: Iowa State University Press, 1995); and National Research Council, *Colleges of Agriculture at the Land-Grant Universities: Public Service and Public Policy* (Washington, DC: National Academy Press, 1996).

2.   Isabel Bevier, "The Land-Grant Colleges and the Education of Women." In *The Story of Isabel Bevier*, ed. Lita Bane (Peoria, IL: Chas. A. Bennett, 1955), 139–40.

3.   Patricia H. Crosson, *Public Service in Higher Education: Practices and Priorities* (Washington, DC: Association for the Study of Higher Education, 1983), 22.

4.   For a perspective on this kind of politics, see Harry C. Boyte, *Everyday Politics: Reconnecting Citizens and Public Life* (Philadelphia: University of Pennsylvania Press, 2004).

5.   See, for example, Scott J. Peters, Nicholas R. Jordan, Margaret Adamek, and Theodore R. Alter, eds., *Engaging Campus and Community: The Practice of Public Scholarship in the State and Land-Grant University System* (Dayton, OH: Kettering Foundation Press, 2005); Scott J. Peters, "Every Farmer Should be Awakened: Liberty Hyde Bailey's Vision of Agricultural Extension Work," *Agricultural History* 80, no. 2 (Spring 2006), 190–219; Scott J. Peters, Daniel J. O'Connell, Theodore R. Alter, and Allison Jack, eds., *Catalyzing Change: Profiles of Cornell Cooperative Extension Educators from Greene, Tompkins, and Erie Counties, New York* (Ithaca, NY: Cornell Cooperative Extension, 2006); Scott J. Peters, "Reconstructing a Democratic Tradition of Public Scholarship in the Land-Grant System," in *Agent of Democracy: Higher Education and the HEX Journey*, ed. D. Brown and D. Witte (Dayton, OH: Kettering Foundation Press, 2008), 121–48; Scott J. Peters (with Theodore R. Alter and Neil Schwartzbach), *Democracy and Higher Education: Traditions and Stories of Civic Engagement* (East Lansing: Michigan State University Press, 2010); Scott J. Peters, "Storying and Restorying the Land-Grant Mission," in *The Land-Grant Colleges and the Reshaping of American Higher Education*, ed. Roger L. Geiger and Nathan M. Sorber. Perspectives on the History of Higher Education 30 (New Brunswick, NJ: Transaction Publishers, 2013), 335–53; Scott J. Peters, "The Pursuit of Happiness, Public and Private," preface to *The People's Colleges*, by Ruby Green Smith (Ithaca, NY: Cornell University Press, 2013), xiii–xxv.

6.   Liberty Hyde Bailey, *The Holy Earth* (New York: Charles Scribner's Sons, 1915), 41.

7.   Morrill Act quoted in Eddy, *Colleges for Our Land and* Time, 33.

8.   On the history and theory of civic or democratic professionalism, see William M. Sullivan, *Work and Integrity: The Crisis and Promise of Professionalism in America* (San Francisco: Jossey-Bass, 2005), and Albert W. Dzur, *Democratic Professionalism: Citizen Participation and the Reconstruction of Professional Ethics, Identity, and Practice.* (University Park: Pennsylvania State University Press, 2008).

9.   M. C. Burritt, *The County Agent and the Farm Bureau* (New York: Harcourt, Brace and Company, 1922), 265–66.

10. Gladys L. Baker, *The County Agent* (Chicago: University of Chicago Press, 1939), 85.

11. Ross, *Democracy's College*, 181–82.

12. Roger L. Williams, *The Origins of Federal Support for Higher* Education*: George W. Atherton and the Land-Grant College Movement* (University Park: Pennsylvania State University Press, 1991), 9. For an account of the kind of "rough and tumble politics" in land-grant history that Williams is referring to, see Scott M. Gelber, *The University and the People: Envisioning American Higher Education in an Era of Populist Protest* (Madison: University of Wisconsin Press, 2011).

13. Williams, *The Origins of Federal Support*, 19.

14. For critiques of the logic and politics of random controlled trials, see Michael Scriven, "A Summative Evaluation of RCT Methodology: An Alternative Approach to Causal Research," *Journal of Multidisciplinary Evaluation* 5, no. 9 (2008), 11–24; Gert Biesta, "Why 'What Works' Won't Work: Evidence-Based Practice and the Democratic Deficit in Educational Research," *Educational Theory*, 57 no. 1 (2007), 1–22; Gert Biesta, "Why 'What Works' Still Won't Work: From Evidence-Based Education to Value-Based Education," *Studies in Philosophy and Education* 29, no. 5 (2010), 491–503; and Dave Holmes, Stuart J. Murray, Amélie Perron, and Geneviève Rail, "Deconstructing the Evidence-Based Discourse in Health Sciences: Truth, Power and Fascism," *International Journal of Evidence-Based Healthcare*, 4 no. 3 (2006), 180–86. For positive views of random controlled trials and the promise of translational research, see Elaine Wethington and Rachel E. Dunifon, eds., *Research for the Public Good: Applying Methods of Translational Research to Improve Human Health and Well-Being* (Washington, DC: American Psychological Association, 2012).

15. On the theme of science as an ethical and social process and how it has been developed and practiced by "scientific democrats" in the American university, see Andrew Jewett, *Science, Democracy, and the American University: From the Civil War to the Cold War* (New York: Cambridge University Press, 2012). Also see my review of Jewett's book in *History of Education Quarterly* 53, no. 3 (August 2013), 316–19.

16. See Marshall Ganz, "Public Narrative, Collective Action, and Power." In Sina Odugbemi and Taeku Lee, eds., *Accountability through Public Opinion: From Inertia to Public Action* (Washington, DC: World Bank, 2011), 273–89.

17. Alasdair MacIntyre, *After Virtue: A Study in Moral Theory* (Notre Dame, IN: University of Notre Dame Press, 1981; reprint 1984), 216.

3

THE DEMOCRATIC ROOTS
OF ACADEMIC PROFESSIONALISM

Albert W. Dzur

Harry Boyte threads four topics together in his wise and provocative essay: education, power, work, and democracy. Higher education, Boyte argues, has the power—through its traditional credentialing, socializing, and concept-building functions—to *anchor* a participatory, public-work-oriented form of citizenship that American democracy needs to thrive. Boyte challenges academics "to recognize, claim, and exercise this power and its democratic possibilities," and he provides promising examples from a number of campuses of how it can be done. When, he writes, "higher education educates its students to think of themselves as citizens through their work, and equips them to turn their workplaces into empowering civic sites, in their communities and in society," then it can address one of the most significant threats to contemporary democracy: persistent and deep feelings of citizen powerlessness.

This is an attractive conception of higher education and one I endorse, but, as I will argue below, it swims against the current of how most American universities now operate; democracy is counternormative on today's campus. Public work calls for a different mode of being an academic and a more democratic conception of professionalism. Those who move in this direction will find much support, but they will also meet active resistance from colleagues who see nothing wrong with the status quo, and, perhaps even more difficult for long-term culture change, we will encounter the equally forceful passive resistance of those sympathetic to the critique but simply unwilling to move away from academic business as usual. While Boyte's examples help show *how* it can be done, some people may need more to appreciate *why* it should be done. In response, especially to the complacent, we need to think more deeply about a topic less mentioned in Boyte's essay, but central to his social and political theory more generally: freedom.[1] In thinking through the *why* that can motivate change, we also need to help our academic centers, institutes, and disciplines pay attention to the creative energy produced through new forms of democratic action happening all around the university.

A Democratic Culture in Eclipse

An intellectual ancestor of Boyte's essay is the "Port Huron Statement," written by Tom Hayden and others in the Students for a Democratic Society.[2] Hayden advocates participatory workplaces, social relations, and governing institutions in the face of dominant bureaucratic and market-oriented bodies. He urges students to see and use the university as a site of transformative change: as both a model of participatory democracy inside and as an agency for transmitting it outside. Committed to traditional norms of horizontal collegiality and truth seeking, faculty take good reasons seriously, and their seminars are places of critical dialogue in which students can challenge repressive, hierarchical, and self-interested organizational norms, thus sensitizing and activating their fellows. As graduates receive credentials and pass through the gates of the corporate and public worlds, they will incrementally remake these in a participatory democratic fashion.

Hayden's narrative offers the flattering idea that deep down the university is more egalitarian, dialogical, and free-spirited than it appears on the surface. Yet when students read his manifesto today, it fails to persuade. They care about reforming institutions, and they are not apathetic, so the problem is not with the goals or the readers. The trouble with reading "Port Huron" today is students recognize that their university is *less* democratic than it seems on the surface and therefore provides an unsteady platform for transformative change.

Universities prize their self-image as collegial organizations, yet they now have highly unaccountable vertical management structures. Relying on private search firms, boards of trustees and regents choose presidents and provosts with no authentic input from faculty, students, or community members. Once ensconced, top administrators are evaluated using procedures less transparent and public than in business firms. Faculty and student opinion is rarely seriously consulted on major administrative measures.

The absence of a vibrant democratic culture is evident, too, in the classroom and in daily faculty-student noninteraction. Though research and disciplinary specialization are commonly blamed, the deeper problem is *social distance*: faculty members' inability to see and act with students as fellow citizens, collaborators—if only neophytes—in a common public project of understanding and improving shared social, political, and economic structures.

To serve as a site of democratic renewal, universities must convey *through their own practices* that institutions are not external, alien, and impervious to change, but are composed of real people with discernment and agency. What are the core ingredients of this more democratic academic culture? In his 1937 essay "Democracy and Educational Administration," John Dewey argued that without power sharing between members of an institution, "there is correspondingly little sense of positive responsibility."[3] "The democratic idea itself demands that the thinking and activity proceed cooperatively."[4] Power sharing requires free speech, collegial respect, reciprocity, absence of unnecessary hierarchy, suspicion of lock-step proceduralism, and commitment to collective decision making. Truth be told, most contemporary American colleges and universities systemically fail to live up to these norms, which are overpowered by forces present in all modern organization—bureaucracy, routinization, legal accountability, risk management, and market definitions of efficiency and productivity.

Administrators who accept Boyte's invitation to do public work have a significant role to play in fostering real dialogue with real faculty and student committees with real responsibilities. For their part, faculty who accept the invitation can do much more, as well, to recognize students as cocreators. Beyond receptivity to student voice and influence in seminars and in the shaping of curricula, there is the fundamental issue of how little time there is for research, student interaction, campus obligations, and work with community organizations. There is never enough time. To model democratic practice, faculty and administrators need to work together to find the time—fewer students per class, fewer classes per faculty member, fewer credits necessary to graduate—through some kind of calculus outside the current crude "quantity over quality" efficiency metrics; something that will permit respect for research, students, and community.

Rethinking Professionalism: Freedom, Power, and Public Work

The public work approach, Boyte writes, invites faculty to "'make work more public,' more interactive, collaborative, visible, and filled with public purposes." No moralistic stance, the call to public work ties in directly to faculty interests in conducting meaningful research and effective teaching. What faculty engaged in public work might lose in disciplinary standing they gain back in efficacy, at least at a local level, regarding the issues and problems their disciplines were established to address.

Boyte's invitation can be made more compelling, I think, especially for those currently complacent about academic business as usual, by articulating the connections between public work and something perhaps more important than power and significance: freedom. We need to look closely at freedom in academic professionalism so we can reflect in a critical and catalytic way on how being professionals—and training people to become professionals and skilled workers—can be done in ways that enhance rather than shrink people's freedom.

Many of us become academics because of the freedom university life affords. No merely abstract ideal, academic freedom is manifest every day in the workplace autonomy that allows control over curricula, course topics, and readings. It is exercised every day too in exploring, reflecting on, and engaging problems on one's own terms, in one's own way, as one sees and defines them. It is what gets scholars up in the morning and keeps them going on projects that can take a quarter or half or all of a person's lifetime to successfully complete.

Academic freedom is not given, of course; it is fought for every day on campuses across the country in meeting after meeting after meeting. The claim attributed to Henry Kissinger, "academic politics are so bitter because the stakes are so low," is true only if one thinks the stakes are increments of formal power or money. In fact, the claim is false—and it betrays an ignorance of scholarly motivations—because the stakes are freedom: within the workplaces, collective projects, and common spaces that make colleges and universities what they are.

Now one way to think about public work and freedom is to say that in return for this freedom academics need to be more engaged, collaborative, visible, and filled with public purposes. Public work is the price to be paid for freedom.[5] To see social relations as a hypothetical contract that sets prices and rewards strains credulity, however, because nobody has ever signed such a contract.[6] I think it misses the mark as well because it tacitly assumes that freedom and public purposes are at odds when in fact they can be congruent and reinforcing. Setting aside the contract model, we need to ask a few questions instead: Why do we academics cherish this freedom? Why do we choose this life over the life outside the university, if not because we have found the life outside the university to be unfree in many respects: mainstream workplaces are all too commonly constrained, cabined, scrutinized, measured, invasively monitored, and hierarchically managed. The question is not whether we academics should trade off our freedom to make a difference in our communities; it is, rather, what have we done with our freedom to promote that of others?

What I am suggesting is not for academics to become meta–social workers or community organizers; there are others better equipped for those necessary jobs. I am suggesting, instead, that we look more carefully into the ways we think about and train people for professional and skilled work. Are we contributing—through our conceptual models, our disciplinary knowledge, and our training programs—to other people's self-definition and self-determination, or are we mostly cultivating our own? There are some very basic choices to be made here:

- We can train doctors, nurses, and public health workers to see and treat people primarily as patients, or we can train them to listen to and respect people's knowledge and agency in the process of working on health and well-being together.[7]
- We can teach legal professionals to represent clients, deliver justice, and provide security to a largely passive populace, or we can teach them to include citizens and neighborhoods in cocreating a just social order.[8]
- We can prompt policy analysts and public administrators to devise cheaper and faster means of serving citizens as clients, or we can encourage them to involve citizens as equals in the planning process and in collaborative governance.[9]
- We can continue to pass along tried and true curricula fitting for largely passive classrooms, or we can help teachers encounter students as people with a voice and choice in their education.[10]

The list above can go on, and the first alternatives, for the status quo positions, will persist if those currently complacent continue to do nothing. There will be no "tipping point" toward a more democratic professionalism unless people recognize the real costs of business as usual, paid out in others' unfreedom. This is likely to be a long, trying, and unglamorous disciplinary struggle. Taking public work seriously means digging in and engaging the abstract world of concept building, testing, and evaluation.

There are other costs to the status quo, of course, and it is important to note a few very briefly. There are the political difficulties of the world academics have helped shape populated by providers and clients, producers and consumers, a world with profoundly undemocratic institutions that every day assert without even having to say it: "lay citizens cannot do justice, cannot do public safety, cannot do planning, or a proper education, or community health because we the professionals do that work for you." There are internal problems with status quo professionalism too, for institutions that treat people primarily as patients, clients, and consumers rather than active agents, partners, and collaborators *do not adequately deliver the goods* of justice, public safety, planning, education, and community health, and are *unfulfilling to work in* because they separate professionals from important social sources of emotional nourishment and practical local knowledge.

"We must stop using our academic freedom to take other people's freedom away" is an admittedly moralistic admonition. It might serve, nonetheless, to rouse the complacent. We who love our work in the natural and social sciences, the arts, and the humanities, in the schools of law, education, and engineering, can reflect on why our work is so desirable. By collaborating with students, community members, and people in industry, we can learn what can be done to create similar opportunities for others to have the kind of good work we value when they graduate. Even more important, we academics need to listen more, to take up the knowledge of people outside our normal disciplinary channels, to learn about the different modes of task sharing, collaboration, co-ownership, and democratic divisions of labor that brilliant nonacademic innovators in a range of fields and institutions are making manifest in daily life. I have to confess that I have seen more democratic creativity outside the university than inside.

Sparks of Democratic Energy within Contemporary Institutions

For a number of years now I have met and interviewed people I call democratic professionals working in a range of fields and institutions.[11] They are quietly, subtly, and without much academic attention or media fanfare reconstructing schools, clinics, city governments, criminal justice programs, and many other established practices all around us every day. What is fascinating to me is that many of their personal histories with this work originate in intense pessimism and disaffection with contemporary institutions. The schools, hospitals, newspapers, government offices, and programs for which they received work training and certification appeared to be controlled by untouchable and unfathomable forces—of bureaucracy, rationalization, and abstract managerial systems, not to mention market measures of efficiency. Moreover, they seemed to be failing to produce the high-quality services and outcomes they promised; even worse, they were not treating people well or bringing out our best.

This sober realism about institutional dysfunction led some to realize that their traditional professional training had set them up to be successful failures. Being the best professional they could be, understood in traditional terms, was insufficient to rectify the problems plaguing these domains. And while the palpable sense of being out of control could have easily led to apathy, quietism, and conventionalism, it did not for them. The fighting creed of the democratic professional is the absolute refusal to reproduce the currently dominant institutional environment. I have heard this same sentiment put in numerous ways: "I refuse to reproduce schools, hospitals, newspapers, administrative offices, government programs that do things *to* rather than *with* people, that disempower, that devalue or discourage lay contributions, that frustrate collaboration, that hinder collective work. I have one life, and with it I will make my school, my hospital, my newspaper, my office, my program a place of agency, of sharing, of dignity."

What this has meant, in practice is that democratic professionals:

- are alert to the ways their organizations and institutions reflexively disempower the agency and trivialize the knowledge of lay people;
- consider how normatively central—not minor or symbolic—tasks can be altered so that lay people can take part or become more aware;
- establish regular self-sustaining opportunities for load-bearing public participation and dialogue.

Consider a story we can call "Basketball Blowup," which takes place in Forest Grove Community School, a public charter school located in a coastal agricultural community in Oregon. During recess a few months ago, some seventh-grade students were playing basketball. Tensions from inside the classroom were coming out in the game. Two boys were closely guarding another boy, trying to steal the ball and reaching in aggressively. This boy got really mad and lashed out, punching one of his opponents.

When the victim's father heard about what had happened, he came to Principal Vanessa Gray with an ultimatum: "Either the offender gets suspended or I am going to call the police and ask them to charge that boy with assault." Principal Gray had a different plan.

After calming the parent down, she sought out the basketball players and a group of students who were on the playground and pulled them into her office one by one to talk about what happened. As she asked each individually to tell her about what had happened on the court, they all said the same thing. The facts surrounding the basketball blowup were not in dispute.

Principal Gray allowed the victim to go home, sent his teammate back to class, and kept the perpetrator in her office for a while to talk. Over the course of their conversation, she came to realize that communication was something he needed to work on. Being able to use his voice when things are mounting and he is feeling stressed and frustrated was an underdeveloped skill. Telling him she understood his frustration, she also made it clear that it was not acceptable to communicate with his fists. Moreover, Gray took responsibility for her own role in the conflict, acknowledging to the perpetrator that he had come to her earlier in the year to say that basketball was really tense sometimes.

This is really helpful for me to do a better job of trying to understand what a kid is communicating to me and for you, kid, to learn a little more about how to use your voice. The way you expressed the tensions on the basketball court earlier this school year was in the same tone you use when you tell me that school is boring or you are going skiing this weekend. What you said did not make me concerned that you were angry. And I'm wondering if your way of expressing your frustration with your classmates has also been similarly flat and that you need to work on feeling more comfortable with saying "Hey I'm upset!" "I'm mad!" "I want someone to do something about it!" "I want someone to work with me on this."

Before sending him home for the day, she tells him that there are going to be some further conversations when he comes back to school.

The next day the conferencing begins, and Principal Gray tells the three students that they cannot play basketball until they have a congress with all the basketball players about what the rules are going to be and how they are going to go forward with the game. "I really wanted these three to understand: they messed up the basketball game. And I wanted the other basketball players to understand they were bystanders. They knew these tensions were going on a long time before it erupted and before I knew about it. I wanted them to understand they had a responsibility to right a wrong and there are lots of ways for them to do it."

So what is interesting about this story? Rather than sealing off a problem, attributing blame to a specific central actor, and taking ownership of it as simple disciplinary matter for the administration to take care of, Principal Gray did four things: she made the problem public; she had conversations with everyone involved; she spread out responsibility for the conflict, herself included; and she empowered everyone involved—including bystanders and others in the school—to figure out ways of creating more peaceful basketball games at recess.

Was there an offense that happened that should not have? Yes. Was there an offender? Yes. Was there a victim? Yes. But the democratic process Gray used focused on the relationships that were causing tension rather than the individuals, and that focus allowed her to help the individuals work on the skills they need to have better relationships in the future.

The kind of school this principal is running offers an amazing kind of civic education: Forest Grove Community School students are learning—by doing—important lessons in how to govern themselves. I have come to see people like Gray as democratic geniuses—drawing on the Latin root of "genius"—"to bring forth." They are bringing forth more deliberative and more collaborative modes of being together.

Democratic energy is being generated *inside* this school through *everyday* routines performed by students, teachers, and administrators who refuse to let themselves be captured by conventional assumptions about disciplinary order and institutional hierarchies. Civic engagement is not a class or a subject area in this school, nor is it an extracurricular activity; it pervades the culture of the playground, the library, the hallways, the assembly rooms, the school garden, and the principal's office.

With this story in mind we can turn back to the question of the role for American colleges and universities in democracy's education. What can we, as academics, offer democratic innovators? The first thing is humility: we can offer our ears and pens and keyboards, for there is a lot for us to learn. Second, we can be colleagues, in a way, when we draw out lessons from their work, delve deeply into context, compare cases, and build and rebuild conceptual models, in as collaborative a way as possible. Third, we can form networks to share information and build platforms for problem solving. And fourth, we can incorporate some of the lessons of new democratic practice into our own institutions, modeling what we have learned.

Dewey described educational institutions hopefully, but also with some edge, as "dangerous outposts of a humane civilization."[12] There is so much to be done to resurrect our fading collegial norms and to nurture new, stronger democratic bodies on campus; so much to be done in the lab and classroom; and so much to be done in the free spaces of imagination, while we read, write, and contribute to the democratic republic of ideas. Let's accept Boyte's invitation and get to work.

Notes

1. See, e.g., Sara M. Evans and Harry C. Boyte, *Free Spaces: The Sources of Democratic Change in America* (New York: Harper and Row, 1986); and "A Commonwealth of Freedom," in *Building America: the Democratic Promise of Public Work*, ed. Harry C. Boyte and Nancy N. Kari (Philadelphia: Temple University Press, 1996), ch. 10.

2. James Miller, *"Democracy Is in the Streets": From Port Huron to the Siege of Chicago* (New York: Simon and Schuster, 1987).

3. John Dewey, "Democracy and Educational Administration" (1937), in *John Dewey: The Later Works, 1925–1953*, vol. 11, ed. J. A. Boydston (Carbondale: Southern Illinois University Press, 1987), 223.

4. Ibid., 225.

5. To be clear, this is not Boyte's argument, but it is an argument I have frequently heard about why "civic engagement" is a legitimate request to make of academics.

6. As Hume's followers keep pointing out to Locke's.

7. Bill Doherty's work on citizen health care is exemplary here. See, e.g., William J. Doherty, Tai J. Mendenhall, and Jerica M. Berge, "The Families and Democracy and Citizen Health Care Project," *Journal of Marital and Family Therapy* 36, no. 4 (2010): 389–402.

8. A democratic professional approach would introduce students to community policing, restorative justice programs, and other ways of bringing the public back in to the work of criminal justice. See, e.g., Lauren Abramson and D. B. Moore, "Transforming Conflict in the Inner City: Community Conferencing in Baltimore," *Contemporary Justice Review* 4, nos. 3 and 4 (2001): 321–40; Wesley Skogan, *Police and Community in Chicago: A Tale of Three Cities* (New York: Oxford University Press, 2006).

9. See, e.g., Carmen Sirianni, *Investing in Democracy: Engaging Citizens in Collaborative Governance* (Washington, DC: Brookings Institution Press, 2009); Harry Boyte, "Reframing Democracy: Governance, Civic Agency, and Politics," *Public Administration Review* 65, no. 5 (2005): 536–46.

10. See, e.g., Cristina Alfaro, "Reinventing Teacher Education: The Role of Deliberative Pedagogy in the K–6 Classroom," in *Deliberation and the Work of Higher Education: Innovations for the Classroom, the Campus, and the Community*, ed. J. Dedrick, H. Dienstfrey, and L. Grattan (Dayton, OH: Kettering Foundation Press, 2008), 143–64;

Dana L. Mitra, *Student Voice in School Reform: Building Youth-Adult Partnerships that Strengthen Schools and Empower Youth* (Albany: State University of New York Press, 2008).

11. For background, see Albert W. Dzur, *Democratic Professionalism: Citizen Participation and the Reconstruction of Professional Ethics, Identity, and Practice* (University Park: Penn State University Press, 2008). For more on contemporary democratic innovators, see my ongoing Trench Democracy series in *Boston Review*. Albert W. Dzur, "Trench Democracy: Participatory Innovation in Unlikely Places," *Boston Review*, October 11, 2013. *www.bostonreview.net/blog/dzur-trench-democracy-1*. A companion series, Conversations on Participatory Democracy, can be found in the *Good Society* journal. Albert W. Dzur, "Democracy in Schools: A Conversation with Donnan Stoicovy," *Good Society*, January 27, 2014. *goodsocietyjournal.org/democracy-in-schools-donnan-stoicovy/*.

12. John Dewey, "Education as Politics" (1922), in *John Dewey: The Middle Works, 1899–1924*, vol. 13, ed. J. A. Boydston (Carbondale: Southern Illinois University Press, 1986), 334.

PART II

Policy Makers and Presidents as Architects of Change

Substantial efforts for deep change need philosophers as well as storytellers. In *Blood Struggle*, Charles Wilkinson describes how Indian philosophers like Charles Eastman and Black Elk, who articulate core philosophy of native cultures and the way it differed from dominant European-American values and practices, played crucial roles in the survival and revitalization of the Indian tribes.[1] The authors in this section play analogous roles in the higher education engagement movement. They are reviving the tradition of college and university presidents as public philosophers, today all too rare in the turn toward narrow managerialism and fundraising that has taken over in many places.

---

[1]Charles Wilkinson, *Blood Struggle: The Rise of the Modern Indian Nations* (New York: W. W. Norton, 2005).

4

DEMOCRACY'S FUTURE— THE FEDERAL PERSPECTIVE

Martha Kanter

> The name of American, which belongs to you, in your national capacity, must always exalt the just pride of Patriotism. . . . It should be the highest ambition of every American to extend his views beyond himself, and to bear in mind that his conduct will not only affect himself, his country, and his immediate posterity; but that its influence may be co-extensive with the world, and stamp political happiness or misery on ages yet unborn.
> —George Washington, Farewell Address, September 19, 1796

> The patriots of 1776 . . . gave to us a republic: a government of, and by, and for the people, entrusting each generation to keep safe our founding creed. . . . You and I, as citizens, have the power to set this country's course. You and I, as citizens, have the obligation to shape the debates of our time—not only with the votes we cast, but with the voices we lift in defense of our most ancient values and enduring ideals. . . . With common effort and common purpose, with passion and dedication, let us answer the call of history and carry into an uncertain future that precious light of freedom.
> —Barack Obama, Second Inaugural Address, January 21, 2013

Educating for Citizenship and National Character in Today's America

The above two quotations—separated by more than two hundred years, by momentous changes in domestic and world events and incalculable advances in technology—nonetheless convey an equal sense of urgency in declaring that the fate and future of the American experiment will always rest with the American people. Whether under our first president, or our forty-fourth, the preservation of America's highest ideals is entrusted to each new generation of *citizens*. As long we remain a representative democracy, that responsibility will never shift—and the stakes will never lessen.

Will our education system—and especially, our postsecondary institutions—make it their mission to prepare every American to fulfill the role of citizen, in the twenty-first century? Do today's institutions of higher education consider it their moral purpose to build an informed, engaged, public-minded citizenry—one that can act to protect the rights of the individual and increase the common good?

The answer to these questions will determine the health and persistence of our centuries-old experiment as a constitutional republic.

Right now, the United States is facing strong headwinds. Public distrust and frustration with government are a roadblock to creating change. Our nation is more diverse than ever, offering us opportunities to embrace new ideas, yet we have Washington gridlock, a broken immigration system, and too many Americans worried about what to do if they face a health care crisis. And—perhaps most alarming for our democracy—the path to the middle class is threatened as the gap between the rich and poor grows at an alarming rate.

Society's most powerful engine to create access to the middle class and vibrant participation in our democracy is education. Yet pervasive achievement gaps and opportunity gaps threaten that access. An alarming number of adult Americans struggle with basic reading, writing, and math; an estimated one-third of our nation's children are not prepared for kindergarten; and a fifth of high school students drop out along the pathway to graduation, postsecondary education, and the skilled workforce. Despite our national ethos as a land of opportunity, social mobility in the United States actually ranks below several other leading countries.

To address these challenges, we must strive to reach the national goal President Obama set forth soon after taking office: that by 2020, the United States will once again have the world's highest proportion of college graduates. And, consistent with this goal, we must also ensure that every American, of every age, is "citizenship ready."

We need to invest in an educated citizenry by renewing our call for revitalized public engagement; by promoting civic knowledge, skills, and dispositions that are more robust and widespread; and by ensuring that these are more deeply enmeshed in every aspect of American life—from the personal to political to the professional—than ever before.

Much has been said and written about the danger that the United States will become a "citizenless democracy." In fact, we have every reason to believe that we are in a "civic recession" based on countless signs of anemic civic health.[1] For example, few Americans can name all three branches of government, or one Supreme Court justice, or the current vice president. Few can explain why we waged the Cold War.[2]

Our high school students don't fare much better. Just 24 percent of high school seniors demonstrated skills and knowledge of at least a "proficient" level in civics and American history, in the recent report card of the National Assessment of Education Progress (NAEP). Only 27 percent of seniors could identify two privileges US citizens have that noncitizens don't, while just 8 percent were able to provide two responsibilities of US citizens. Moreover, when polled about specific topics they had studied, less than half of those surveyed reported studying other nations' systems of government, or international organizations like the United Nations[3]—perspectives that have never mattered more than in our current era of globalization.

We don't get much better results from college students. In one study of fourteen thousand college seniors, the average score on a test of civics knowledge was an F. Most colleges don't require preparation in civic learning; at many institutions, history is optional as well.[4]

What do these indicators tell us? They demonstrate that civic learning and democratic engagement are not the staples of every American's education. In far too many schools and on too many college campuses, civic learning and democratic engagement are add-ons, rather than an essential part of the core academic mission.

They tell us that our education system must do more to combat the civic recession; that much needs to be done to help students become informed and engaged members of our society. While there is no single answer, we know that in order to prepare youth and adults for intelligent, active participation in the civic and democratic life of our communities, states, and nation, we must reinvigorate and elevate the quality of civic learning in America.

Still, the picture isn't all bleak. Studies also suggest that students who are provided with effective, robust civic-learning experiences are more likely to develop stronger critical thinking skills as well as earn better grades, graduate from high school, enroll in college, and complete college on time—all while gaining a commitment to civic problem solving.[5]

Indeed, we can see signs of progress and hope as we chart our course for a new era of civic learning and engagement. Students educated in civic learning are more likely to vote and discuss politics at home; are four times more likely to volunteer and work on community issues; and are more likely to be more confident in their ability to speak publicly and communicate with their elected representatives.

Research shows that civic learning not only promotes civic skills and attitudes but also builds twenty-first-century competencies like solving complex problems, thinking critically, analyzing information, working creatively in collaboration with others, participating in civic life, and cultivating an ongoing commitment to learning.[6]

Indeed, we're seeing promising examples emerge that confirm more and more schools, colleges, and universities are using experiential service learning and civic preparation to hone students' core subject knowledge and to cultivate deep ties with their communities.

For example, iCivics, a nonprofit, web-based education project founded by former Supreme Court justice Sandra Day O'Connor, is making gains in its mission of empowering K–12 students with a deeper knowledge of their government.

The iCivics organization is committed to reinvigorating civic learning through interactive and engaging learning resources, and to using these resources to empower teachers and prepare students with the tools they need to become the next generation of active citizens. iCivics has already reached a wide audience: more than forty thousand educators and three million students use iCivics to provide or receive civics instruction every year, and this number continues to grow.[7] This suggests that iCivics and projects like it can have marked success in empowering educators and encouraging civic participation among students.

There are exciting efforts underway in institutions of higher education, as well. Oregon's Portland State University (PSU) is encouraging civic participation in the communities that surround the campus. PSU is committed to its identity as an engaged university: one that promotes a reciprocal relationship between itself and the community. This is a mission that reflects its motto of "Let Knowledge Serve the City." For nearly twenty years, the university has focused teaching, research, and outreach on resolving community issues. They are achieving their mission through multiyear efforts, including a project to protect an urban watershed. Successive PSU classes collected environmental and social data, educated local children and developed high school curricula, created videos, facilitated public discussions of the watershed, and directly cleaned up wetlands and constructed facilities.[8] This community collaboration is a direct example of putting theory into practice for the benefit of the community at large.

At De Anza College, where I served as president, we engaged in a similar project with students learning and applying skills in citizenship and biology, while tagging fish in partnership with our region's office of the US Fish and Wildlife Service agency. Like PSU and the city of Portland, we realized that we "share a fate" as a community, and that the university must share a commitment to working with the city and with civic organizations to resolve common issues. Of particular note in recent years is the creation of De Anza College's Institute for Community and Civic Engagement, established through the leadership of President Brian Murphy. With a mission of empowering students to become agents of change in their communities and beyond; fostering postsecondary education that meets the needs of the communities the college serves; and helping develop pathways to meaningful participation in local, state, and federal government decision-making processes, the institute's offerings are numerous. They now range from open educational resources to an eighteen-unit Certificate of Achievement in Leadership and Social Change program, to the "Mentors for Youth Empowerment" project, which places De Anza College volunteers at area high school sites, where they facilitate civic engagement projects and help students plan a roadmap to college.[9]

In Illinois, the mission of Governors State University (GSU) is to create "an intellectually stimulating public square" and serve as "a model of diversity and responsible citizenship." This institution, through the dynamic vision of President Elaine Maimon, is offering another example of best practices in civic learning.

The freshman class follows a core curriculum focusing on civic engagement, sustainability, or global citizenship. The university works to create a model in which informed citizenry and democratic responsibility are woven into academic studies. For example, GSU hosted a forum last February for the candidates running in the congressional district's special primary. It provided students the opportunity to connect their studies to civic engagement and ask targeted questions related to their fields of interest.[10]

Last year, in Massachusetts, the state Board of Higher Education voted to add a civic engagement goal to the state's strategic "Vision Project." In essence, the board has now charged the state Department of Higher Education to "develop a plan for incorporating a civic education and engagement key outcome" into the Vision Project, which already commits the state to track progress toward becoming a national leader in measures like college participation, college completion, student learning, workforce alignment, closing achievement gaps, and university research.[11] It is important to note that the idea for adding citizenship as a measure originated with faculty members in institutions across the commonwealth.

Here, too, a strong base of visionary leadership has been essential to supporting civic engagement and, in this case, making it central to the higher education agenda of an entire state. The commonwealth's commissioner of higher education, Richard Freeland, has rightly called the duty to educate students for citizenship "one of the most fundamental—and often neglected—responsibilities of colleges and universities in the United States." He characterizes this latest step as one in which "Massachusetts public higher education is affirming its role in nurturing a responsible democracy."

Massachusetts's action means that it is the first state to add student civic engagement to its collection of commonly tracked statistics such as graduation rates and performance on licensure exams, according to the Association of American Colleges and Universities (AAC&U).

It's also worth praising the College, Career, and Civic Life (C3) Framework for Social Studies State Standards released in September by the National Council for the Social Studies. The C3 Social Studies Framework—developed by over twenty states and fifteen social studies content organizations—was designed to help states as they develop specific requirements for geography, civics, economics, and history. The C3 Framework encourages civic engagement through building critical thinking, developing problem-solving skills, and participating in activities that require drawing conclusions and taking informed action—all essential skills to becoming an engaged citizen.[12]

These examples all show that the education community and its partners are gaining momentum in building a stronger culture of student engagement, in expanding civic learning across the curriculum and through service, and in forming broader partnerships between our schools, our campuses, and our communities—exactly the type of education system our democracy needs to face the challenges and seize the opportunities of the present day.

But, is there a role for the federal government in promoting the nation's return to civic health? I would contend that there is.

The Federal Role—Creating a Climate for Civic Learning

Clearly, the federal government cannot and should not be the prime mover in renewing our nation's civic health. The government cannot and should not presume to act alone in attempting to shape the way schools and colleges prepare students for deep engagement with the issues that face our democracy. To succeed in educating our citizens for democracy, we need strong leadership from educators, policy leaders, and key stakeholders from business, philanthropy, labor, and government. Educators themselves must champion this cause—and, encouragingly, tens of thousands of them already are mobilizing to reinvent the way we prepare students for effective democratic citizenship.

But because this is an issue of such great importance, the federal government must use its powers of policy and persuasion. And during my time in the Obama Administration we worked hard to show strong support for raising civic learning to prominence throughout our college-going and career-preparation initiatives.

Furthermore, over the past three years, the Department of Education supported a major national dialogue and study—organized by the AAC&U and the Global Perspectives Institute—to determine the level of and set goals for the renewal of students' civic learning and preparation in schools and colleges. In a national convening, "Civic Learning and Engagement for Democracy's Future," held at the White House on January 10, 2012, over sixty colleges, universities, community colleges, and national organizations made commitments to help move civic learning from the margins to the center of the education reform agenda, at all levels.

The White House convening released and discussed two national reports that chart a path forward. The first, commissioned by the Department of Education, entitled *A Crucible Moment: College Learning and Democracy's Future*, provides an organizing framework for civic learning from school through college, including many examples of curricula, pedagogy, and community-based partnerships that exemplify what it means to make civic learning an intrinsic part of school and college learning.[13]

The second report, *Advancing Civic Learning and Engagement in Democracy: A Road Map and Call to Action*, encourages schools and postsecondary institutions to increase high-quality civic learning and engagement and supports the inclusion of civic learning in K–12 curriculum. It also supports the identification of best practices and indicators to understand students' civic strengths and weaknesses. Most importantly, it identifies nine specific actions that the US Department of Education is undertaking to provide leadership and support for civic learning as a national priority.[14]

Most recently, to advance the efforts of the US Department of Education over the past three years, the White House has tapped Tufts University to address the value and assessment of civic engagement to chart the activities and outcomes of educational institutions. The White House Civic Learning and National Service Summit was held on October 16, 2014, and marks another step forward to raise the public discourse about America's identity as a nation and its role in shaping an educated citizenry.[15]

THE OBAMA ADMINISTRATION'S COMMITMENT TO CIVIC LEARNING

Each action outlined in the Road Map represents just one small piece of the national agenda, but taken together they have become a driving force behind the department's ongoing work to fulfill the president's vision of "cradle-to-career" education reform and achieving the 2020 postsecondary completion goal.

The first objective promotes ways for schools and postsecondary institutions to increase and enhance high-quality civic learning and engagement opportunities. Going forward, the department plans to continue to encourage institutions from grade school to graduate school, to increase their role in developing informed and engaged citizens.

This could include expanding their efforts to encourage states, schools, and postsecondary institutions to conduct civic audits, develop plans to prepare students to lead engaged civic lives, and publish their results. The department can also support efforts by school and postsecondary leaders and teachers to cultivate civic-learning partnerships and to adopt recommendations from leading national efforts.

The department has set as its second objective to identify and support the development of improved indicators of students' civic strengths and weaknesses and help the field craft appropriate responses to them. For example, to amplify tools such as the National Assessment of Educational Progress civics exams, the National Center for Education Evaluation and Regional Assistance will add questions to an upcoming national survey of high school students, the National Longitudinal Transition Study, about their transitions to postsecondary education. These findings and other relevant data will help educators and the public become more aware of the state of civics education and provide opportunities for them to react with programs and practices that may increase civic-learning opportunities in all sectors of education.

Does research really confirm the benefits of civic learning? To know whether or not there are tangible outcomes, this third objective aims to identify promising practices in civic learning and engagement and encourage efforts to improve data and capture research about what works.

As its fourth objective, the department is considering ways to leverage federal investments and public-private partnerships in support of civic learning—for example, by encouraging grantees and grant applicants to include civic-learning and engagement initiatives in federally funded education programs.

As recently as last summer, the department announced the release of a Dear Colleague Letter to the nearly seven thousand institutions of higher education that participate in the Federal Student Aid program, reminding them of their duty to support civic engagement on their campuses. The Higher Education Act, the law that authorizes institutions to join federal programs and receive federal aid, in fact includes a provision that requires institutions to foster a culture on their campuses that actively encourages citizenship.

The department must support civic learning in schools and on campuses across the country by looking to all the programs that it sponsors.

That is why the fifth objective in the Road Map commits the agency to encouraging the expansion of community-based work-study placements under the

Federal Work-Study (FWS) program. Currently, the FWS mandates that institutions of higher education use at least 7 percent of the total amount of funds awarded to provide community-service jobs for students. In the 2009–2010 award year, federal funding for these jobs topped $220 million—a sum augmented by a much larger pool of nonfederal matching funds from states, local communities, foundations, and individual donors excited by civic learning as an intergenerational investment in our nation's future.

In the years ahead, the department should encourage expanded efforts to place FWS students in assignments tailored to their interests in federal, state, or local public agencies—or in private nonprofits. The agency should also encourage postsecondary institutions to track outcomes for students and the community, give credit for service and civic learning, and share promising evidence-based practices nationally. The commitment made by Tufts University at the White House Summit on Civic Education to follow up on this strand of work is heartening.

The sixth objective encourages public-service careers among college students and graduates—and especially to attract top talent to teaching, public safety, and related fields. The administration is taking significant steps to make it easier for many borrowers, including those who devote their time and talent to public service, to repay their federal student loans through the Public Service Loan Forgiveness program, the Income-Based Repayment plan, and other tools.

Recognizing the importance of civic learning to students of all ages, the seventh objective supports civic learning as part of a well-rounded K–12 curriculum. The department's Blueprint for Reauthorizing the Elementary and Secondary Education Act (ESEA) has proposed a new competitive program: Effective Teaching and Learning for a Well-Rounded Education. And this administration stands ready to implement it as we continue calling on Congress to reauthorize the ESEA. The funding would assist states, local education agencies, and nonprofits in developing, implementing, evaluating, and replicating programs that demonstrably contribute to a well-rounded education—including civics, government, economics, and history.

The Road Map's eighth objective asks historically black colleges and universities (HBCUs), Hispanic-serving institutions (HSIs), and other minority-serving institutions (MSIs) to identify high-impact, evidence-based civic-learning practices that increase student success. The MSIs—especially HBCUs—have a proud record of preparing students to be national and community leaders in civil rights, the sciences, engineering, and medicine. The department will encourage MSIs to maintain their focus on developing civic leadership and to identify best practices that might benefit all of America's colleges and universities.

The ninth objective outlined in the Road Map seeks to increase student and family participation in education programs and policies at the federal and local levels. President Obama's first executive order was a memo to federal agencies about making government more transparent, participatory, and collaborative. Consistent with that call, the Department of Education has begun to identify and promote opportunities for students and families to participate as collaborators and problem solvers in education reform.

As *A Crucible Moment* states, "It is time to bring two national priorities—career preparation and increased access and completion rates—together in a more comprehensive vision with a third national priority: fostering informed, engaged, responsible citizens." An integral part of that charge is the federal government's Road Map. While it cannot be the sole driving force behind the work that must be done, it can serve and support that work.

Delivering the Next Generation of Citizens Is a Shared Responsibility

Preparing all students to be twenty-first-century leaders—equipped to fulfill their civic and democratic responsibilities—is a challenge. We can strive to prepare them to succeed in a world of unprecedented complexity and interconnectivity, yet while we as stakeholders remain passionate and committed, we know that we cannot do this work alone.

President Obama noted the importance of recognizing our individual and collective civic duty in his 2013 State of the Union Address. He reflected that "as Americans, we all share the same proud title—we are citizens. It's a word that doesn't just describe our nationality or legal status. It describes the way we're made. It describes what we believe. It captures the enduring idea that this country works only when we accept certain obligations to one another and to future generations, that our rights are wrapped up in the rights of others; and that—well into our third century as a nation—it remains the task of us all, as citizens of these United States, to be the authors of the next great chapter of our American story."

While cultivating a nation of educated citizens is a shared responsibility for us all, it must always be the explicit mission and moral purpose of higher education, K–12 schools, and their many partners—including the federal government. It is the great charge of our generation, no less than of those before us, to work together to advance our society toward that more perfect union enshrined in our Constitution. We can do no less as Americans for the future of our nation!

Notes

1. Jonathan Gould, Kathleen Hall Jamieson, Peter Levine, Ted McConnell, and David B. Smith, eds. 2011. *Guardian of Democracy: The Civic Mission of Schools*. Philadelphia: The Leonore Annenberg Institute for Civics of the Annenberg Public Policy Center at the University of Pennsylvania and the Campaign for the Civic Mission of Schools, *www.civicmissionofschools.org*.

2. Andrew Romano. 2011. "How Dumb Are We?," *Newsweek*, March 20, *www.newsweek.com/2011/03/20/how-dumb-are-we.html*.

3. National Center for Education Statistics. May 2011. *The Nation's Report Card: Civics 2010*, Institute of Education Sciences, Washington, DC, retrieved from *nces.ed.gov/nationsreportcard/pubs/main2010/2011466.asp*.

4. Intercollegiate Studies Institute, National Civic Literacy Board. 2007. *Failing Our Students, Failing America: Holding Colleges Accountable for Teaching America's History and Institutions*, Wilmington, DE: Intercollegiate Studies Institute, *www.americancivicliteracy.org/2007/summary_summary.html*.

5.   A. Dávila and M. Mora. January 21, 2007. "Working Paper 52: Civic Engagement and High School Academic Progress: An Analysis Using NELS Data." CIRCLE: The Center for Information and Research on Civic Learning and Engagement, retrieved from *www.civicyouth.org.*

6.   Jayne E. Brownell and Lynn E. Swaner. 2010. *Five High-Impact Practices: Research on Learning Outcomes, Completion, and Quality.* Washington, DC: Association of American Colleges and Universities.

7.   *iCivics.org.* 2014. Teachers Guide to *iCivics.org,* retrieved from *www.icivics.org/ teachers.*

8.   Portland State University. 2013. Let Knowledge Serve the City, retrieved from *www. pdx.edu/sites/www.pdx.edu.oaa/files/oaa_missionvision.pdf.*

9.   De Anza College. Institute for Community and Civic Engagement, retrieved from *www.deanza.edu/communityengagement.*

10.   Governors State University. 2013. ECHO, Educating Citizens to Help Others, *Service Learning Programs, www.govst.edu/echo/default.aspx?id=38572.*

11.   Massachusetts Department of Higher Education, Vision Project. 2012. *Time to Lead: The Need for Excellence in Public Higher Education,* retrieved from *www.mass.edu/ visionproject/timetolead.asp.*

12.   National Council for Social Studies. 2013. *College, Career, and Civic Life (C3) Framework for Social Studies State Standards: Guidance for Enhancing the Rigor of K–12 Civics, Economics, Geography, and History,* retrieved from *www.socialstudies.org/ system/files/c3/C3-Framework-for-Social-Studies.pdf.*

13.   National Task Force on Civic Learning and Democratic Engagement. 2012. *A Crucible Moment: College Learning and Democracy's Future.* Washington, DC: Association of American Colleges and Universities.

14.   US Department of Education, Office of the Under Secretary and Office of Postsecondary Education. January 2012. *Advancing Civic Learning and Engagement in Democracy: A Road Map and Call to Action,* retrieved from *www.ed.gov/sites/default/ files/road-map-call-to-action.pdf.*

15.   Harry Boyte, "White House Civic Summit on Education," *The Blog* (blog), *Huffington Post,* October 20, 2014, *www.huffingtonpost.com/harry-boyte/ white-house-civic-summit-_b_6006642.html;* "The White House and Tufts University's Tisch College to Convene Civic Learning and National Service Summit in October," *Tufts Now,* September 15, 2014, *now.tufts.edu/news-releases/ tisch_college_civic_learning_national_service_summit.*

5

REINVENTING SCHOLAR-EDUCATORS AS CITIZENS AND PUBLIC WORKERS

Nancy Cantor and Peter Englot

At its core, the organizing essay for this volume reflects a desire to broaden and make more inclusive many of our most cherished conceptions—of citizenship, liberal education, public work, civic sites—in ways that fundamentally challenge how we as scholars, educators, and educational leaders do our best work for and in democratic settings, be they communities or universities, or better yet in the third spaces between them where boundaries evaporate. Boyte starts with broader conceptions of: citizenship, as more than the exercise of property and voting rights, work as more than a job, and workplaces as civic sites where collaboration is empowered and collective efforts to make progress on communal challenges can flourish. Drawing, as he does, on the civil rights lyric "we are the ones we've been waiting for," Boyte requests that we envision ourselves as citizens of a place, not on the sidelines studying and working next to it, but deeply and actively embedded in it, doing *public work*—that is, "work *by* publics, *for* public purposes, *in* public."

While this is a vision as uplifting as the lyric, we want to suggest that it implies some hard reworking, or at the least, broadening, of the fundamentals of faculty roles and responsibilities as scholars and educators, to expand to embrace the umbrella of citizenship and public work, to be citizen-faculty, akin to Julie Ellison's concept of citizen-alums.[1] Just as the "civics" and the "communitarian" movements, while important contributors to a reawakening about our frayed polity, may too frequently pit work against citizenship and skirt questions of power and powerlessness, so too will we bump up hard against university cultural norms and values that contrast scholarship and service, excellence and diversity, the "cult of the expert" versus the "community of experts" within which citizen-scholar-educators might enact public work.

This does not mean that faculty can't be successful citizens of a place, doing public scholarship and publicly engaged teaching in public, by publics, and for public purposes, and we will give some illustrations here of just such efforts, but it does suggest that we conceive of this as transformational work, pushing up against some strong norms and practices prevalent in our ivory towers (even our engaged institutions) and the disciplines that undergird them.[2] In particular, scholar-educators who do public work not *on the side* of their "regular" work, but *as* their regular work, are more likely to collaborate, often with nonacademics, even with other "citizens" (without pedigrees) or with colleagues from other disciplines, making it harder to assess their personal productivity, and perhaps distancing them from their own disciplinary colleagues. Ironically, they may even face the criticism of not doing enough university "service," because their work is *in* public not just *in* their departments and disciplines. Moreover, to the extent that their public work (whether as publicly engaged scholarship or teaching or both) really takes place in public, embedded in both the messiness and the vibrant diversity of "real life," they may acquire a humility about what they do or do not know and a respect for the expertise of others (especially of "ordinary people") that runs quite counter to the "cult of the expert" and to the push for accountability of "clear results," as Boyte well describes. This can become its own version of an academic nightmare when it comes time for promotion and tenure.

While it is critically important, therefore, that we focus on broadening the rewards and reducing the obstacles for individual faculty doing public scholarship and engaged teaching, it is also critical that we think more broadly about the culture of work in the academy—that is, about where and with whom and for what purposes we do this work, not to mention who we are as a community of scholars and students and professional staff. In other words, what is the best ecosystem for whole communities of "academics" to become citizens of a place, collaborating for public purposes as they produce scholarship and educate future generations? To consider this question directly, we will turn now to lessons learned from our prior work in Syracuse, pursuing the university's vision of Scholarship in Action over the last decade, but also from similar work in other communities and institutions.

Scholarship in Action: Work in Public, Citizens of a Place

We begin with the notion, at once simple to articulate and complicated to enact, that the creation of an *ecosystem* is required for scholar-educator-citizens to accomplish work "in public, with publics, for public purposes." Building that ecosystem begins with the recognition that this kind of work must be made a real part of the institution's mission, not something that is nice to do if time permits. At Syracuse, that meant defining the university as a public good through its vision of Scholarship in Action—a commitment to forging bold, imaginative, reciprocal, and sustained engagements with our many constituent communities, local as well as global. We drew on well-honed traditions of public and collaborative work in our professional schools, from architecture and design to the "iSchool," journalism, and education, and encouraged the spread of engaged, reciprocal partnerships across many disciplines, sectors, and communities. By naming what we were already doing in this public way, scientists and engineers designing technologies to remediate Lake Onondaga, a superfund site once a sacred site in Syracuse, or to revolutionize biomaterials, came into this wider scholarly tent, allowing at the same time the work of the "community geographer" using geographic information systems to map patterns of hunger in Syracuse to be seen as cutting edge scholarship.

Just as it is critical to find ways, repeatedly, to assure faculty that this public work represents a broad and inclusive tent, so too is there a strong and ever-present need to allay the suspicions of the many publics with whom we collaborate. Too often there is a sense (and perhaps a reality) that academics are "talkers not listeners," and that we are exclusionary in our practices of collaboration. A powerful counterpoint to this message is to be found readily in the work of the arts and cultural disciplines, as the national consortium Imagining America reminds us. At Syracuse, for example, theatrical productions, such as Ping Chong's *Tales from the Salt City* (based on narratives from Syracuse citizens) and gallery exhibitions, including from Stephen Mahan's Photography and Literacy classes with middle school and high school students and poster projects based on interviews with residents of the Near Westside from Julia Czerniak's architecture studio, served as strong testimony of our belief in the wisdom of our broadly diverse, multigenerational community.

Drawing on the power of the arts and cultural disciplines to amplify community voices and build the critical bridges crossing boundaries, real and imagined, of campus and community, works powerfully to allay long-held perceptions of exclusion. So too can the deliberate commitment to "third spaces" of collaboration, where public work can take place in public and be sustained over time and across projects, go a long way. We have seen the wonder of how this kind of space—that is, real shared civil infrastructure—can generate long-lasting collaborations and trust. By turning an abandoned furniture warehouse in downtown Syracuse into not only a center for academic teaching, learning, and creative work, locating SU's design programs and center for design, research, and real estate—upstate—there, but also the home of our Office of Community Engagement and Economic Development, we signaled that we were there for the long haul. Soon, a 501c3 community-university-business-government collaborative was born and housed there—the Near Westside Initiative—focused on the adjoining neighborhood, which was the ninth poorest census tract in the country, and that floor in the Warehouse as the safe and trusted third space. Here, hot, contested, and ever-so-productive discussions take place, continuously spawning project after project, with over \$70 million in private-public investments in this long-forgotten but richly talented and diverse neighborhood. And key to promoting the social infrastructure of collaboration that came from this commitment to shared space and discussion was the presence day in and day out in the Warehouse not only of faculty and students, but, just as importantly, professional staff nurturing this ecosystem and keeping it going by feeding new people into new projects all the time. This happened in "Just Lunch" gatherings or specially tailored meetings to bring all the relevant expertise to the table at once to make progress on some complex neighborhood challenge (such as creating a "movement on main street" public art/streetscape to encourage exercise and social gatherings or engaging new market tax credits for structural renovations).

The commitment not only to space and professional staff but to continuously engaging a broadly inclusive "community of experts" is absolutely essential to the on-the-ground success of these projects, programs, and generative partnerships, as it is on the Near Westside of Syracuse, where it includes the revered neighborhood parish priest, the third-generation grocer, and the wisest grandmother, as well as SU architects and engineers and health communication "experts." Building on decades of work in intergroup dialogue and mounting evidence about the value of diversity in public problem solving,[3] these vibrant, multisector, multigenerational, multidisciplinary communities of experts epitomize what Boyte describes as groups that do work in public for public purposes. At the same time, this ecosystem of engagement draws in a wonderful mix of university citizens—deans and faculty, professors of practice, professional staff, publicly engaged graduate students, undergraduates committed to integrating social justice and their curricular majors, recent graduates (whom we call engagement fellows) funded by Imagining America and Syracuse University to work with local nonprofits and take graduate courses, and more. And from the energy of these diverse communities of experts come the long-lasting generative partnerships that continuously produce unexpected but high-impact projects, such as the collaboration between that third-generation grocer, the local hospital, SU public health faculty, the Central New York Regional Economic Development Council, and so many others, that will bring a state-of-the-art health center right into the deeply trusted and much-beloved, albeit always stressed, Nojaim's food market in the heart of the Near Westside neighborhood.

As diverse as the ecosystem for successful public work is in these communities of experts, nothing matters more to sustaining hope for the future than weaving a strong commitment to educational opportunity right into the projects and programs on the ground in the neighborhoods. We draw the analogy here to the farm teams that Major League Baseball spawns, and in Syracuse this has meant identifying neighborhoods like the Near Westside as Say Yes to Education neighborhoods, drawing on the services and supports of our district-wide school improvement movement, to cultivate the often left-behind talent of this remarkable city.[4] For higher education to really embrace our roles as public goods, and to fulfill the promise of publicly engaged scholarship and pedagogy, we must be partners in creating educational opportunity writ large in our communities, even as the students may go on to a variety of institutions near and far—just as players in a farm system do. In the midst of changing the educational odds citywide, strong programs on the ground in neighborhoods like the Near Westside have made a substantial difference in galvanizing support and connecting our faculty and students to the lives and aspirations of Syracuse's next generation. For example, several faculty in the College of Visual and Performing Arts run a "talent agency" in the neighborhood, working with talented youth to prepare portfolios of work to cement their road to college. And that road becomes a vibrant two-way street with SU students and faculty creating studios in the neighborhood, and expanding their vision and the sites for their creative work along the way. Everyone wins in this rich a public ecosystem.

Speaking of creating two-way streets brings us back to the central questions of how to transform our campuses to embrace the diverse interests and experiences of students and faculty and staff who want to be citizen-scholars. Institutional transformation, as Susan Sturm suggests, requires building an "architecture of inclusion," brick by brick.[5] This includes recruiting efforts for students in "geographies of opportunity" across the country and world where students see and experience the pressing issues in their home communities and strive to bring that knowledge to bear in their new places. It includes embracing a range of faculty who value the connections between their disciplinary knowledge and those issues of the world, as rendered in local contexts, as well as drawing in a range of faculty across the disciplines whose work might not immediately seem "relevant" but actually is often very applicable. Clearly finding ways to reward "work in public" in the construction of curricula and the assessment of scholarly productivity and departmental service is critical, as is the articulation of "just academic spaces" (as the Democratizing Knowledge faculty consortium at Syracuse calls them), where identities don't need to be checked at the door in order to talk across differences in experience, background, and disciplinary expertise. And ever-so-critical is the recognition that none of us knows automatically how to talk across difference, as the extensive work on intergroup dialogue by Patricia Gurin and her colleagues across nine institutions documents.[6]

Yet, when we deliberately work to put those differences on the table in structured conversation, the skills are honed that make it possible to become successful scholar-educator-citizens and to do the public work that Boyte calls for in the framing essay of this volume. Doing this work is never going to be easy, but acknowledging that we too have to change for the world to change is a major step forward, and worthy of all the efforts, as the work holds so many rewards for so many of us, within and outside the academy. And, as he says, "we are the ones we've been waiting for."

Notes

The authors drew in this essay on their decade-long work at Syracuse University.

1. See Julie Ellison's work on Citizen Alums, University of Michigan, Ann Arbor, MI.
2. Julie Ellison and Timothy K. Eatman, *Scholarship in Public: Knowledge Creation and Tenure Policy in the Engaged University* (Syracuse, NY: Imagining America, 2008).
3. Patricia Gurin, Biren (Ranesh) A. Nagda, and Ximena Zúñiga, *Dialogue across Difference: Practice, Theory, and Research on Intergroup Dialogue* (New York: Russell Sage Foundation, 2013); Susan Sturm, Timothy Eatman, John Saltmarsh, and Adam Bush, *Full Participation: Building the Architecture for Diversity and Public Engagement in Higher Education*, white paper (New York: Columbia University Law School, Center for Institutional and Social Change, 2011), 4.
4. Nancy Cantor, "Diversity and Higher Education: Our Communities Need More Than 'Narrowly Tailored' Solutions," *Huffington Post*, August 2, 2013; also see Say Yes to Education, Inc., *www.sayyessyracuse.org*.
5. Susan P. Sturm, "The Architecture of Inclusion: Interdisciplinary Insights on Pursuing Institutional Citizenship." *Harvard Journal of Law and Gender* 29 (2006), 247, 248–334.
6. Gurin et al., *Dialogue across Difference*.

6

INSTITUTIONALIZING CIVIC ENGAGEMENT AT THE UNIVERSITY OF MINNESOTA

Robert Bruininks, Andy Furco, Robert Jones, Jayne K. Sommers, and Erin A. Konkle

> I'm concerned that in recent years higher education's historic commitment to service seems to have diminished. I'm troubled that many now view the campus as a place where professors get tenured and students get credentialed; the overall efforts of the academy are not considered to be at the vital center of the nation's work. And what I find most disturbing is the growing feeling in this country that higher education is a private benefit, not a public good.
> —Ernest Boyer (1994)

Twenty years ago, Ernest Boyer warned that universities were turning a corner, away from the public purposes defined by a century of visionary policy and leadership.[1] He expressed concern that higher education might retreat to an earlier era, in which the first universities catered primarily to young men of wealth and privilege and were considered inferior to their European predecessors. While it is true that leaders of the nation's foremost private institutions began the early work of transforming higher education, the emergence of an explicit public mission, which connected the creation and distribution of new knowledge with economic development, the cultivation of human capital, and the solving of real-world problems, created a uniquely American system of higher education that quickly became the envy of the world.[2]

As early as the seventeenth century, the value of higher education extended beyond the individual. The earliest universities were established in North America so that the colonies would have educated clergy for the guidance and benefit of the society. Beginning with the Morrill Act of 1862, US higher education policy began a conscious shift toward more explicit public purposes, promoting higher education as a means of economic development, encouraging broader access, and emphasizing research with public application. This and subsequent legislative initiatives expanded access and strengthened the connections between institutions and issues of economy, democracy, and national advancement, creating an undeniable place for higher education in the public sphere. These policies stimulated a national partnership between government, universities, and the private sector that has elevated US universities to global preeminence. The resulting *multiversity* was not universally embraced.[3] However, its impact is evident. According to the 2012 Academic Ranking of World Universities, seventeen of the top twenty universities in the world are US institutions—including six public institutions.[4]

The start of the new millennium brought with it not only a renewed civic commitment among the nation's colleges and universities, but also a new approach to public engagement in higher education. This new approach had four features that distinguished it from how colleges and universities conducted civic work previously. The first distinction is that civic engagement was not just about fulfilling the institution's public service or outreach mission but, rather, was seen as an important strategy for fulfilling the institution's research and education missions. In this regard, for public, land-grant universities, community-engaged work is as much about advancing the institution's identity as an internationally recognized research university or its identity as a world-class institution of higher learning as it is about fulfilling its land-grant identity.

The second distinction of the contemporary approach to public engagement has to do with how engagement work is conducted with external entities. Typically, community-partnered work meant having institutions of higher education doing work *for* or *in* the community. In contrast, the standards for today's public engagement work are centered on securing a more participatory approach that emphasizes working *with* the community. This suggests that external partners are not just sites for research studies or placements for student learning, but also that they are entities that have knowledge and expertise that can inform and even enhance the quality of the academy's work.

A third distinction of public engagement in the new millennium has to do with the focus of the work. Traditionally, civic engagement has been driven by community-based projects, most of which have a short shelf life dictated by time-limited grants or other temporary support. Too often, when the funding period ended, so did the project. Too few projects realized their ambitious goals. For example, despite hundreds of millions of taxpayer dollars awarded to higher education to develop projects to improve K–12 education, the K–12 education system is in much disrepair. Today's public engagement work seeks to tackle these more challenging and complex issues by emphasizing partnerships over projects. This newer approach to public engagement is about having institutions of higher education work together with community entities to identify a set of projects that operate synergistically and through broad participation so that all are working toward a common set of goals. This approach moves away from the long-standing piecemeal approach to higher education civic engagement.

The fourth distinction has to do with the goals and purposes of public engagement. In the past, an important goal of higher education was to have civic engagement programs. Throughout the history of American higher education, civic engagement programs have been in place at nearly every US institution. However, today's public engagement work is not about developing civic engagement programs. The goal is not to simply *do* public engagement. Rather, the goal is to see public engagement as a *strategy* for accomplishing important institutional priorities and facilitating institutional transformation and advancement. Public engagement is a strategy for advancing interdisciplinary work, building multicultural understanding, internationalizing the curriculum, deepening student engagement in learning, enhancing graduation rates, enhancing faculty scholarship, and advancing a host of other important institutional priorities. Public engagement is one of many approaches used to enhance and strengthen an institution's priorities. Indeed, institutions that approach public engagement through this lens have the greatest success in furthering the institutionalization of their public engagement agendas.

Today's public engagement focus requires that our colleges and universities move beyond rhetoric and individual projects to implement systemic institutional commitment linking the promises of research and education to partnerships that address the needs of our nation and communities. As John Muir stated, "when we try to pick out anything by itself, we find it hitched to everything else in the universe."[5] The more typical approach to increasing public engagement in higher education frequently emphasizes the implementation of high-profile committees or projects. Such strategies often ignore the deeper requirements of public engagement that include creating broad and deep understanding of critical philosophical principles and values, the importance of cultural celebration and recognition, the alignment of civic commitment with institutional culture policies and resources, the launching of strategic initiatives that link the human resources of higher education to community challenges and needs, and the inclusion of civic engagement commitments into institutional systems of governance and accountability.

Advancing and institutionalizing a contemporary approach to civic engagement requires visionary thinking and strategic planning designed to transform the academic culture and broader institutional norms of practice. For the University of Minnesota, long-range strategic thinking and administrative planning proved critical to ensuring that institutionalizing this new kind of engagement would not turn this initiative into yet another short-lived educational reform effort.

Building a Public Engagement Agenda

In the first years of the new millennium, the University of Minnesota embraced this new approach to civic engagement and put in place a systematic effort to strengthen and rebuild the University of Minnesota's connections with a broader citizenry. The effort was launched in 1998 with the creation of a high-level Civic Engagement Task Force. Over the next two years, the task force worked with key institutional leaders on strategies for strengthening public engagement and recommending practical measures across the full range of university activities, including scholarship, teaching, and work with communities.

The task force sponsored an inventory of civic engagement activities at the university and made connections with other higher education institutions and groups across the country. Through new funds, it sponsored a number of initiatives and organized public forums and discussions with stakeholders within and outside the university. Finally, its working groups gave sustained attention to the meaning of civic engagement for scholarly activities individually and in disciplines and fields, for teaching, and for connections of the university with communities. These changes came with an enormous set of intellectual and practical challenges. To continue such work, the task force proposed a university-wide Council on Public Engagement.

Leadership, Governance, and Institutional Priorities

The early efforts in strengthening the foundation for public engagement to thrive led to sustained changes in the university's policies and leadership strategies. Some of the key milestones related to strengthening policies, governance, and leadership were the creation of a standing system-wide Council on Public Engagement (COPE) to establish and monitor progress for the university, the creation of a senior-level leadership position, and the inclusion of emphasis for community-engaged scholarship and teaching in promotion and tenure guidelines. Each of these foundational components set into motion a series of efforts that helped deepen public engagement within the institutional culture and professional work.

To promote a broader, more focused agenda, COPE approved the following definition of public engagement: "Public engagement is the partnership of university knowledge and resources with those of the public and private sectors to enrich scholarship, research, and creative activity; enhance curriculum, teaching and learning; prepare educated, engaged citizens; strengthen democratic values and civic responsibility; address critical societal issues; and contribute to the public good."[6] Following the recommendations set forth by COPE, the Office of Public Engagement (OPE) was established in 2006 to build a university-wide agenda to advance the contemporary approach to public engagement, which includes deepening community engagement practices within and across the university's research, teaching, and outreach functions. OPE's work also focuses on expanding the role of public and community engagement in ways that advance the university's capacity to produce research of significance, to ensure the delivery of quality teaching, and to perform outreach that maximizes benefits to local, state, national, and international communities. OPE works across the five campuses of the university system to help build and strengthen each campus's capacity to conduct community-engaged research, teaching, and/or outreach. Also at this time, the university agreed to step forward and serve as a pilot institution for the newly developed Carnegie Community Engagement Classification. The university received the designation in 2006 and was one of only six research universities to be honored with the recognition during that year.

In June 2008, OPE set in motion a Ten-Point Plan for Advancing and Institutionalizing Public Engagement at the University of Minnesota to deepen quality community engagement practices across the system as well as to make public engagement a more explicit and integral component of the university's work. This plan guides the strategic initiatives that are in play to make community engagement a more integral component of the university's research, teaching, and outreach activities.

Recognition and Celebrations

Celebrating excellence and high achievement is important for sustaining and renewing priorities of healthy organizations. At the University of Minnesota, we celebrate excellence in teaching and service to students and the university, and we also celebrate service to the community through the Outstanding Community Service Award. Through action by the university's Board of Regents, the provost established the Outstanding Community Service Awards in 2001 to recognize remarkable examples of community service. This award honors the accomplishments of faculty, staff, and members of the greater university community who give of their time and talent to make substantial and enduring contributions to the community and to improving public life and the well-being of society. In 2012, the university established the President's Community Engagement Scholar Award, which is given to one faculty member who produces high-quality scholarship in partnership with community members. Similar to the university's Distinguished Teaching Award and other university-wide awards, each college and each system campus nominates one faculty member as an award finalist. From the list of finalists, one faculty member is selected to receive a $15,000 award.

Implementing the Agenda

To move from institutional tinkering to institutional transformation, it is important to implement and support key initiatives that can help realize the goals of a university-wide public engagement agenda. These initiatives also signal to key stakeholders that the agenda will have staying power rather than the short life spans of most educational reform efforts. Institutional commitment to public engagement requires alignment strategies, resources, and metrics to assess progress, learning, and impact. At the University of Minnesota, we sought to implement and support initiatives that would help remove some of the barriers and overcome some of the challenges that hindered the advancement of public engagement. A few of the initiatives that the University of Minnesota has implemented and supported are highlighted in this section.

Engaged department grant program. One of the challenges the university faced in sustaining community engagement efforts was the fact that much of the engagement work was reliant on individuals. That is, public engagement efforts, for the most part, were initiated, cultivated, and nurtured by particular individuals (faculty, staff, students, unit directors, and so on) who conducted the engagement work. If an individual left the university or decided to work on another issue, the engagement work would usually end. We realized that for engagement work to be fully sustained and embedded into the academic culture, it needed to be owned by the academic programs. The Engaged Department Grant Program was established to move the ownership of public engagement from individuals to the academic programs. This initiative provides grants of up to $10,000 to department teams to develop and implement action plans that deepen the integration of community engagement into the departmental research and/or teaching initiatives. Of the forty-four departments/academic units that have applied to the program, twenty have received grants and have been designated as Engaged Departments. Through this program, departments have: developed or redesigned their faculty activity reporting to provide more space for faculty to report on their community-engaged scholarship; established a civic strand within a major by building articulation among existing courses that have a community engagement component; and redesigned their undergraduate curriculum to include more community-based experiential learning experiences, among other developments.

Metrics initiatives. An accurate account of the scale and scope of the public engagement activities taking place across the institution is essential for being able to tell the institution's public engagement story, as well as to identify gaps in the engagement work. To address this issue, OPE established a Public Engagement Accounting and Assessment Task Force in 2008, which ultimately recommended that the university infuse public engagement within the university's existing data collection and measurement systems. In 2010, OPE formed the university's Public Engagement Metrics Committee, which established the university's public engagement metrics framework. Because public engagement is viewed not as a program, but rather a strategy for accomplishing key university priorities, this framework was built to align with the university's overarching (non-public-engagement) metrics and strategic goals. The Public Engagement Metrics Committee identified ways to qualify and quantify the range and scope of public engagement activities across the more than two hundred centers and units at the university that conduct community-engaged research, teaching, and outreach. Based on this framework, the university is now able to:

- provide an annual report on undergraduate students' civic and community engagement experiences from the Student Experience at the Research University (SERU) survey;
- systematically account for courses that have a community engagement component through the incorporation of a "community engagement" course attribute, which is recorded in the registrar's official course offering data;
- more fully capture faculty community-engaged scholarship through more incorporation of community-engaged work in the research and teaching sections of faculty activity reports; and
- account for the size and nature of research grants that have a community engagement component through the incorporation of a community engagement checkbox on the research proposal routing form that all principal investigators complete when submitting a grant proposal.

These and other mechanisms to collect data on the nature, scale, scope, and impact of the university's public engagement work were not available prior to the work of the Public Engagement Metrics Committee.

Engaged faculty learning communities. Faculty need safe spaces to explore and experiment with community-engaged work. These spaces seem to be most effective when they allow faculty to make mistakes, learn from their peers, and receive feedback and ongoing support. Several units received funds to implement faculty learning communities for engaged scholars, which bring together faculty members from different disciplines to develop their individual capacities to do high-quality community-engaged teaching and learning. In some of these efforts, participating faculty receive mentorship from more seasoned engaged scholars at the university.

Linking strategic initiatives. These sets of initiatives focus on supporting work that uses public engagement as a means to accomplish institutional priorities such as enhancing interdisciplinary work, meeting the "broader impacts" requirements of National Institute Health (NIH), the National Science Foundation (NSF), the Department of Education (DOE), and other federal funding agencies, advancing the university's student learning and development outcomes, facilitating liberal education requirements, internationalizing the curriculum, achieving diversity and equity goals, and other initiatives. These initiatives include several grant programs that provide incentives for units and individuals involved in community-engaged work to more explicitly link their work to one or more university-wide strategic goals (for example, advancing interdisciplinary work, internationalizing the curriculum, incorporating e-learning, and so on).

Engagement staff and leader networks. Public engagement's becoming fully institutionalized into an institution's culture is predicated on having high-quality community engagement practices, and programming. This means that the directors and managers of units that conduct community-engaged work must have the tools, preparation, and experiences they need to be successful and thrive. The university has underway a set of strategic initiatives to strengthen the internal networking among staff and academic leaders who have responsibility for advancing various aspects of the community engagement agenda. For example, in 2010, OPE established the Associate Deans Public Engagement Network (a group of associate deans who are responsible for advancing public engagement in their colleges) and the Public Engagement Leaders Network (a group of managers, directors, and coordinators who oversee units that have community engagement as part of their work).

Engagement zones. Because of the decentralized nature of the institution and prevailing entrepreneurial spirit that permeates the academic culture, it not easy to know where all the engagement work is taking place or what the nature of the work is. In fact, in certain neighborhoods near the university, there might be several university-sponsored community engagement activities underway that might not be linked or connected in any way. The Engagement Zone Initiative focuses on bringing together and building synergy among existing projects within a community that are addressing the same issue but are otherwise working independently. The goals are to avoid duplication of efforts, maximize resource efficiency, and build collaborative partnerships to leverage capacity and maximize societal impact.

National and international networking. The University of Minnesota prioritizes representation at important national and international meetings and gatherings pertaining to the advancement of research universities and higher education in order to learn from other higher education institutions about their public engagement agendas as well as to spotlight some of the university's work and agenda in this area. These include membership on the Research Universities Network for Community Engagement, National Review Board for the Scholarship of Engagement, the Association of Public and Land-Grant Universities' (APLU) Council on Engagement and Outreach (CEO) and the Committee on Innovation and Community Economic Prosperity (CICEP), International Talloires Network of Community Engaged Universities, Engagement Scholarship Consortium, International Association for Research on Service-Learning and Community Engagement, Imagining America, Campus Compact, and others. The first such campus-wide initiative for public engagement was spearheaded through the Career and Community Learning Center.

Academic and curricular integration. In 2002, the Career and Community Learning Center (CCLC) assumed responsibility for the Twin Cities campus-wide service-learning infrastructures. Now named the Community Service-Learning Center, the center supports faculty members in their work to incorporate community-based learning experiences into their curricula. To facilitate credit-bearing service-learning courses, the center develops and maintains reciprocal relationships with over one hundred community partners and supports several other programs that engage students in advanced, academically based community involvement experiences. During the 2012–2013 academic year, over 203 service-learning courses were offered across fifty-one academic departments on the Twin Cities campus. Through these service-learning courses, students contributed 114,150 hours of volunteer service to Twin Cities–area nonprofit and public agencies as part of their academic coursework. In 2002, the center introduced the Outstanding Community Partner Award to highlight the work of organizations and their staff representatives. The center also provides other recognition to faculty and students who participate in service-learning efforts.

Student leadership in community-based work is also a core value of the Community Service-Learning Center's work. This leadership focus is embodied in the center's Community Engagement Scholars Program, which was launched in 1998 by students with support of staff and community partners. The program recognizes students who integrate more than four hundred hours of community volunteering into their academic majors and other educational experiences. Students in the program also complete eight credits of academic coursework that includes service-learning experiences and structured reflection. Students who complete the program receive a university medal, official recognition at graduation, and a notation on their academic transcripts. Since its inception in

2005, student enrollment in the Community Engagement Scholars Program has grown fivefold, with more than five hundred students having participated during the 2012–2013 academic year.

Community integration. A primary goal of the university's new approach to public engagement is to move from an "expert outreach" approach (whereby communities are problematized and the university is the expert expected to solve the community's issues) to an approach that values the knowledge, expertise, and experience of the community and relies on that community knowledge to coconstruct, codiscover, and codevelop high quality and impactful campus-community engagement initiatives. This shift in approach focuses on establishing partnerships in which the university is working *with* the community, rather than working *in* or doing *to* the community. This approach also requires that the university become more embedded and integrated in the community. While the university has had a long history of community embedded through its comprehensive extension service across the state, this embeddedness has been less deep and pervasive outside of the extension programming. Indeed, despite being one of the few land-grant research universities situated in a urban, metropolitan area, the university's integration into the local urban communities was, for the most part, sporadic and episodic. The focus of the engagement work tended to be on individualized, opportunistic projects rather than a more comprehensive, multifaceted and strategic partnership with the community.

One important step the university took to move toward a more community integrated approach to civic engagement was to collaborate with the community of North Minneapolis in establishing the Urban Research and Outreach/Engagement Center (UROC) in 2008. Housed in a renovated building in North Minneapolis in the heart of a highly diverse community, UROC embodies an embedded and integrated approach for university-community engagement and urban problem solving. Since its inception, UROC has become home to a dozen University-sponsored programs committed to connecting members in Northside communities with faculty, students, and others (businesses, faith-based institutions, and so on) working on research and problem-solving (through authentic and engaged partnerships) related to the issues that are most relevant and important to the community. Today, UROC serves as a space in which the community members and university members meet to explore joint research and outreach programming as well as to build long-term partnership agendas that can tackle critical local issues, such as foreclosures, sex trafficking, violence prevention, broadband access, food security and nutrition, youth development and student achievement, job creation, and host of other issues. One of the major outcomes from this approach to engagement has been the building of greater trust between the university and the Northside community. This deeper trust has opened the door to providing opportunities for deeper and more intensive research-based engagement work that leads to real impact in the community.

Promoting and organizing public work. The university provided considerable leadership in organizing people and resources to address significant and ongoing community challenges. Much of the work is organized into interdisciplinary centers, situated within and between institutions of higher education and other organizations. These structures create opportunities to work across fields, to leverage resources through external funding and partnerships, and to move resources more and more rapidly in relationship to emerging and persistent community needs. The flexibility of such structures enables more agile organization and renews the priorities of units that have lost their competitive standing, largely in terms of need, impact, or access to growth of external resources. Today, pushing the boundaries of knowledge in one field often means crossing into other disciplines. And interdisciplinary work often has mutual reward; often the tools required to build new knowledge in one field create innovation in another.

Learning and renewal. One of the more challenging aspects of public engagement is the development of metrics that promote and assess value and progress of learning and impact. The university uses its primary planning document, the University Plan, Performance, and Accountability Report, to identify areas in which it intends to excel, to define strategic actions and investments to accomplish its goals, and to measure the impact of these initiatives. This accountability document focuses on the three core missions of the university—research and faculty excellence, student experience, and engagement—together with three supporting areas—human resources, facilities, and institutional efficiently and effectiveness. The prominence of engagement in this plan and in the university's accountability reporting reflects the institution's commitment to measuring and improving performance in this area.

Our goal of becoming an "engaged university" is translated into a diverse array of access and civic engagement activities that, taken together, benefit Minnesotans across every community in the state. Public engagement is about more than bringing the university into communities or using its resources to meet needs and solve problems. Beyond these important contributions, the university intends to act more as an active citizen, along with our fellow Minnesota citizens, considering and taking action on issues of mutual interest and importance. At the same time, it faces the pressing issue of financing civic engagement as sources of public support decrease, and as it moves toward a hybrid financing model.

Conclusion

The commitment to civic and community engagement is often accompanied by concerns that it will erode the central focus and purposes of our colleges and universities. The more common concerns are that:

- public engagement will take away from conducting high quality scholarship and teaching;
- public engagement is too costly and drains resources from teaching and education;
- public engagement erodes investment in academic disciplines; and
- public engagement is not funded, recognized, or rewarded by institutions.

However, with a new approach to public engagement, which focuses on using community engagement as a strategy for advancing the research, teaching, and education missions, more targeted and strategic focus on public engagement and civic involvement can be a source of new vitality, resources, and renewal of American higher education.

The last fifteen years of public engagement efforts at the University of Minnesota have not completely changed the traditional norms of academic practice. However, a public and civic engagement focus raised questions and prompted debate and conversation about the value and importance of public value in securing the future of the university. Programs described here exemplify the numerous ways in which the university is already deeply connected in two-way engagement with communities throughout the state of Minnesota and beyond its borders. As it looks to the future, the university recognizes that it must: continue to state the values of engagement as a cornerstone of its public, land-grant mission; seek creative approaches to investing in these activities; measure and reward success in strengthening and expanding its engagement-related initiatives; include community voices in the development of the engagement initiatives; and develop effective communication tools to inform the entire community about the wealth and impact of these activities.

Notes

1.   The epigraph is from Ernest Boyer, "Creating the New American College," *Chronicle of Higher Education*, March 9, 1994, A48.
2.   Jonathan R. Cole, *The Great American University, Its Rise to Preeminence, Why It Must Be Protected* (New York: Public Affairs, 2009).
3.   Cole, *Great American* University.
4.   Academic Ranking of World Universities 2012, *www.shanghairanking.com/ARWU2012.html*.
5.   John Muir, *My First Summer in the Sierra* (Cambridge: Riverside Press, 1911), 110.
6.   Office of Public Engagement 2013, *www.engagement.umn.edu*.

7

EDUCATION FOR A RAPIDLY CHANGING WORLD

Judith A. Ramaley

This symposium volume is built on a foundation of long-standing reflections about the roles and responsibilities of our nation's colleges and universities as vital resources for nation building and hubs for the exercise of public work. In his lead essay, Harry Boyte argues that the fate of higher education is inextricably linked to our system of government and to the working of democracy. He calls for colleges and universities to embrace the task of educating our students for active citizenship both on campus and beyond.

In this essay, I will explore ways to understand and address the current gaps between our approach to liberal education and our ideas about the world of work and the workplace and the changing nature of professional practice. How can we infuse our curriculum with both in-depth study of the human condition and the world around us and practical experiences that prepare our graduates to address the challenging problems that arise in today's world? How can we prepare thoughtful and responsible scholars, practitioners, and citizens whose work both "pays and matters," to quote one of our authors, Julie Ellison? (See page 162.)

In a recent report, the Commission on the Humanities and Social Sciences asked, "Who will lead America into a bright future?" The report answered the question succinctly and issued a challenge to all of us who seek both to educate our students and to live responsible, creative, and productive lives ourselves. Our overall goal as educators in the twenty-first century should be to prepare

> citizens who are educated in the broadest possible sense, so that they can participate in their own governance and engage with the world. An adaptable and creative workforce. Experts in national security, equipped with the cultural understanding, knowledge of social dynamics and language proficiency to lead our foreign service and military through complex global conflicts. Elected officials and a broader public who exercise civil political discourse, founded on an appreciation of the ways our differences and commonalities have shaped our rich history. We must prepare the next generation to be these future leaders.[1]

While this rich vision of a future shaped by informed and wise leaders and an engaged citizenry should guide our efforts, we cannot hope to create educational environments and collaborations that offer the opportunity to practice these virtues and acquire the habits of mind and heart that can guide the wise application of knowledge to the world's complex problems unless we ourselves create a working democracy and a culture of collaboration on our own campuses and in our relationships with the broader society of which we are an integral part.

The path ahead of us will be shaped by an understanding that the meaning of an education is changing as we go deeper into the twenty-first century. Among the expectations that have emerged about how we should approach curriculum in today's context are (a) the necessity to integrate material across fields; (b) the importance of learning more deeply; (c) the importance of bringing together how we think and act (knowledge and skills) with what we know about ourselves (values and motivation) and how we relate to other people and (d) the practice of a sense of moral responsibility. These concepts underlie recent formulations of what it means to be educated and the components that must be addressed in order to prepare creative, productive, and responsible citizens for a changing world order.[2]

These ideas are explored in great depth by Palmer and Zajonc, who pose a question at the heart of their text that can inform our efforts to contribute to the emergence of a democratic way of life suited to the needs of a new era. How can higher education become a more multidimensional enterprise; one that draws on the full range of human capacities for knowing, teaching, and learning; that bridges the gaps between the disciplines; and that forges stronger links between knowing the world and living creatively in it, in solitude and in community?[3]

In bringing together these four elements we can support learning that has more meaningful consequences for both ourselves and our students and for the people affected by how we apply our knowledge and skills to understanding and responding to pressing world problems. Through a curriculum of this kind, we can interpret and act on the ideas so clearly articulated by John Dewey nearly a century ago in his signature text *Democracy and Education*, in which he defined democracy as "primarily a mode of associated living, of conjoint communicated experience."[4]

Martha Nussbaum points out that when we explore the relationship of a liberal education to citizenship, we are joining a long tradition of thoughtful philosophical reflection that argues that "an education is 'liberal' in that it liberates the mind from the bondage of habit and custom, producing people who can function with sensitivity and alertness as citizens of the whole world," people who, in other words, have a moral imagination. She goes on to say that "becoming a citizen of the world is often a lonely business. It is, in effect, a kind of exile—from the comfort of assured truths, from the warm nestling feeling of being surrounded by people who share one's convictions and passions. . . . It is up to us, as educators, to show our students the beauty and interest of a life that is open to the whole world, to show them that there is after all more joy in the kind of citizenship that questions than in the kind that simply applauds, more fascination in the study of human beings in all their real variety and complexity than in zealous pursuit of superficial stereotypes, more genuine love and friendship in the life of questioning and self-government than in submission to authority. We had better show them this, or the future of democracy in this nation and in the world is bleak."[5]

So, having defined the problem, it is time to move to a consideration of how we can build an educational environment that can offer the kinds of experiences that will foster the qualities of informed and engaged citizens who "participate in their own governance and engage with the world."

Education in the Twenty-First Century:
Learning to Deal with Wicked Problems

What kind of education makes sense in today's world, and how might we go about educating in ways that truly prepare the kind of educated citizenry that we need? The answers are surprisingly simple in the abstract, but it is not as easy to work out how best to design a pathway to the kind of education that most observers think will serve each of us well.

One of the best descriptions of what it means to be educated was produced by William Cronon.[6] Educated people can be described as fully by how they interact with other people as by what they know.[7] In Cronon's list of traits, a clear portrait emerges of educated people who (1) listen and pay attention to the ideas of others; (2) read and understand; (3) can talk with anyone; (4) can write clearly, persuasively, and movingly; (5) can look at something complicated, and figure out how it works and how to respond to complex and changing problems; (7) focus on other people's ideas, dreams, and even nightmares, not just their own mental landscape, and practice humility, understanding, and self-criticism; (8) know how to get things done in the world and leave the world a better place; (9) enjoy nurturing and encouraging other people and appreciate the value of being a member of a community; and (10) above all, follow E. M. Forster's injunction from *Howards End*—"Only connect"—by which Cronon means the ability to see the connections that allow us to make sense of the world and to act within it in creative and responsible ways.

Kim Stafford, in his reflections on the writer's craft, summed up these ideas in his own way. He wrote, "a new connection among a constellation of dispersed facts is always original. There lies the pleasure of discovery and creation." Reading the world in this way, according to Stafford, "honors an old paradox about reading, for the verb 'to read' originally meant both to decipher a text and to explain a mystery."[8]

Stafford's approach to reading the environment brings to mind the concept of wicked problems, the kind that permeate our lives today both in our own communities and across the globe. It is these kinds of problems that we must address through the public problem solving that takes place in a healthy democracy. The concept of a wicked problem was developed in the early 1970s by Rittel and Webber.[9] According to Camillus, a wicked problem can be identified by studying its characteristics.

> Wicked problems often crop up when organizations (or communities) have to face constant change or unprecedented challenges. They occur in a social context; the greater the disagreement among stakeholders, the more wicked the

problem. In fact, it's the social complexity of wicked problems as much as their technical difficulties that make them tough to manage. Not all problems are wicked; confusion, discord and lack of progress are telltale signs that an issue might be wicked.[10]

The features of a wicked problem sound very much like our concerns about the workings of democracy in our nation today. To quote Camillus again, any wicked problem "involves many stakeholders with different values and priorities." The problem itself is a tangled knot, like the multiple roots of an impacted wisdom tooth. These problems are "difficult to come to grips with" as they "change with every attempt to address them."[11] If that were not enough, these challenges have no obvious precedent, and there is no well-practiced or simple way to solve them.

Today's global challenges range from democratization to sustainable development and the response to climate change, to the availability of clean air and water, public health issues, alternative energy usage and several other agreed-on wicked problems.[12] This realization leads us to consider how we can engage our students, faculty, staff, and community partners in the task of working on a problem that changes as we study it, defies easy solutions, and requires us to work with people we have never met before who may or may not share similar values and who most certainly enjoy very different perspectives and expertise. The leaders of today's world must have had experience with these kinds of questions and some opportunity to come up with workable ways to manage them in a collaborative, open, and respectful way at home, abroad, or both.

Our nation's colleges and universities have always sought to prepare their graduates for life and work in their own era. The pressures we face today, both from outside the academy and from within the higher education community, are complex, interlocking, and hard to manage. These challenges require us to rethink what it means to be educated in today's world and to explore ways to provide a coherent and meaningful educational experience in the face of the turbulence, uncertainty, and fragmentation that characterize much of higher education today.

One useful formulation of what it means to be educated in today's world was proposed by Paul Lingenfelter, who wrote, "the most valuable 'products' of education are the ability to use knowledge and skill to solve unscripted problems, to explore the frontiers of knowledge and understanding, and to experience life in a deeper way."[13] To complete the portrait, consider the overview of a baccalaureate education first offered by *Greater Expectations* in 2002 and then developed into a prospectus by the Association of American Colleges and Universities in their Liberal Education and America's Promise (LEAP) initiative and captured in a set of Essential Learning Outcomes. The path of an education that addresses these goals can be documented and assessed using a set of VALUE Rubrics.[14]

The Essential Learning Outcomes closely align with the Cronon (1999) expectations for the outcomes of a liberal education and with the changing expectations of how higher education will contribute to the well-being of society.

AAC&U (2007) outlines the four components of an education for the twenty-first century.

- Knowledge of human cultures and the physical and natural world through study in the sciences and mathematics, social sciences, humanities, histories, languages, and the arts, focused by engagement with big questions, both contemporary and enduring.
- Intellectual and practical skills, including inquiry and analysis, critical and creative thinking, written and oral communication, quantitative literacy, information literacy and teamwork, and problem solving practiced extensively, across the curriculum, in the context of progressively more challenging problems, projects, and standards for performance.
- Personal and social responsibility, including civic knowledge and engagement—local and global, intercultural knowledge and competence, ethical reasoning and action, and the capacity for lifelong learning, anchored through active involvement with diverse communities and real-world challenges.
- Integrative and applied learning, including synthesis and advanced accomplishment across general and specialized studies demonstrated through the application of knowledge, skills, and responsibilities to new settings and complex problems.

The elements proposed initially in *Greater Expectations* (2002), expanded in Liberal Education and America's Promise (2007), and supported by a number of effective approaches to education referred to as High Impact Practices,[15] offer a clear and effective way to design pathways to advanced study and to meaningful degrees. These ideas also form the elements of the framework called the Degree Qualifications Profile (DQP) that provides a way to define what we should expect of someone who holds an associate's, bachelor's, or master's degree.[16]

The components that form the logic of an undergraduate education suitable for the early twenty-first century are interlocking, and the interactions between them can best be expressed by learning in the context of local, regional, or global challenges that will shape our future. In order to collaborate with leaders outside the academy (for example, lawmakers, business leaders, members of nonprofit agencies, and so on), it is essential that we all agree about what it means to be educated. Unfortunately, too few individuals outside the academy have thought about a twenty-first-century vision of quality, never mind the importance of coherence, intentionality, and integration to making such a vision a reality.[17]

How Is the Higher Education Community Changing?

The simple answer to this question is that we are moving away from a focus on individual achievement and rewards and toward a culture of mutual responsibility, intentionality, and a habit of collaboration. In fact, the elements that define community engagement as a concept also apply to the behavior of a campus community. Although the formal definition of community engagement developed by the Carnegie Foundation for the Advancement of Teaching is meant to describe the character of effective university/community collaboration, the same elements can apply equally well to the ways that the different units within a campus community interact with each other, both across the academic sector, and between academics and the support and operational units on campus. "Community engagement describes collaboration between institutions of higher education and their larger communities (local, regional/state, national, global) for the mutually beneficial exchange of knowledge and resources in a context of partnership and reciprocity."[18] A course of study that is guided by clear learning outcomes and that draws on and encourages reflection on all the ways that students learn and then use what they have learned—in the classroom or laboratory, on campus in cocurricular activities, in the community or at work—can lead to a meaningful degree. To design a sequence of this kind, faculty members need to develop a culture of collaboration based on a sense of shared responsibility for the outcomes of the educational experience. As Holland made clear, the things that a twenty-first-century college or university will be rewarded for are materially different from the aspirations and assumptions of the twentieth century. Institutions that were successful in gaining support and resources in the twentieth century offered a comprehensive array of disciplines; sought support for their scholarship from a few federal agencies; focused on grants, publications, and technology transfer as indicators of success; sought to educate only the most well-prepared students; and defined excellence largely in terms of the work of individual faculty. In those institutions, the core work of the institution was defined largely in terms of the teaching, research, and service activities of individual faculty members, and these three functions were seen as separate activities, with most institutions valuing individual scholarship over other forms of faculty contributions.[19]

A very different picture is emerging today across the diversity of higher education institutions in this country. Many institutions are now emphasizing a smaller number of signature themes or programs supported by a focused mix of disciplines, having concluded that the current financial model cannot support a desire to be "all things to all people." A growing number of institutions are working collaboratively with other universities and colleges, public K–12 schools, the nonprofit and business sectors, and communities and networks of organizations that span regional, national, or international scales. These new forms of cooperation and networking are meant to create a working environment for scholarship and learning that spans the boundaries of individual institutions and opens up access to the large, world-shaping "Big Questions." In this larger educational context, institutions seek to enrich the undergraduate experience and provide access to contexts in which students can practice advanced intellectual skills while applying what they know to pressing and "unscripted" problems.

These trends are shaping *who* is learning as well as *where*, *when*, and *how* they will learn. Growing concern about access and success in higher education as a "nation goes to college" has led to a growing interest in rethinking the pathways that students take as they seek advanced education and as they prepare themselves to be successful at the college level.[20] Important modifications are being made to developmental or remedial education to ensure that bringing students up to speed also accelerates their movement into a program of study. Innovative approaches to instruction and learning (technology-based and experiential) are being used to enhance student learning and completion.[21] These changing patterns of scholarship and learning are resulting in the inclusion of students as active participants and contributors to scholarship and community engagement. The convergence of faculty scholarly interests and student interests with the growing use of high-impact practices and a growing involvement of members of the broader community in the generation and application of knowledge is leading to new definitions of excellence. Excellence is now being created by the measurable impact of collaboration on quality of life, culture, health, economic stability, and the environment both locally and further afield. All these new trends are demanding new forms of collaboration both within the academy and in and across other sectors. As the twenty-first century continues to unfold, we shall see more examples of effective community formation on our campuses as well as between our institutions and the larger society that we all serve. As that trend unfolds, so will a growing appreciation for and support of a high-quality education.

What kinds of changes will be required in the culture and functions of a college or university to create these kinds of learning opportunities and to ensure that all students have access to them? In a recent essay, Frank Ardaiolo laid out a straightforward plan to promote the institutional cultural change necessary to create an engaging learning environment in which students can practice the art of responsible and informed citizenship, both on campus and beyond. In his view, the key is to engage the individual agency of everyone who is a member of a campus community.[22] I would add that we need to harness that individual agency in ways that will foster the kinds of collaborations that will be needed to achieve the flexibility, institutional adaptability, responsiveness to different situations, and balance of theory and practice, contemplation and action. These qualities of institutional life and culture will create a working democracy within the culture of the institution and experiences of associated living needed to prepare graduates who can contribute to the daily workings of a healthy democracy both in their communities and in the workplace.[23]

Notes

1. Commission on the Humanities and Social Sciences, *The Heart of the Matter* (Cambridge, MA: American Academy of Arts and Sciences, 2013).
2. Association of American Colleges and Universities, *Greater Expectations: A New Vision for Learning as a Nation Goes to College* (Washington, DC: AAC&U, 2002); Association of American Colleges and Universities, College Learning for the New Global Century (Washington, DC: Association of American Colleges and Universities, 2007).
3. Parker J. Palmer and Arthur Zajonc, *The Heart of Higher Education: A Call to Renewal* (San Francisco: Jossey-Bass, 2010), 2.
4. John Dewey, *Democracy and Education: An Introduction to the Philosophy of Education* (New York: Macmillan, 1916).

5.   Martha Nussbaum, *Cultivating Humanity: A Classical Defense of Reform in Liberal Education* (Cambridge, MA: Harvard University Press, 1997), 8, 83–84.

6.   William Cronon, "Only Connect": The Goals of a Liberal Education, *Liberal Education* 85, no. 1 (1999), 6–13.

7.   Judith Ramaley, "What Does It Mean to Be Educated?," in *Uses and Misuses of Data in Accountability Testing: 2005 Yearbook of The National Society for the Study of Education (NSSE)*, ed. Joan Herman and Ed Haertel (Washington, DC: NSSE, 2005).

8.   Kim Stafford, *The Muses among Us: Eloquent Listening and Other Pleasures of a Writer's Craft* (Athens: University of Georgia Press, 2003), 61, 77.

9.   Horst W. J. Rittel and Melvin M. Webber, "Dilemmas in a General Theory of Planning, Policy Sciences," *Policy Sciences* 4 (1973), 155–69.

10. John Camillus, "Strategy as a Wicked Problem," *Harvard Business Review*, May 2008, 100.

11. Ibid., 100, 99.

12. Millennium Project, *Global Futures Study and Research*, retrieved from *www.unmillenniumproject.org/goals/index.htm* on June 13, 2014.

13. Paul Lingenfelter, "Efficiency, Effectiveness, and Self-Regulation: An Impossible Dream for Educational Quality Assurance in the Digital Age?," *Middle States Commission on Higher Education*, December 6, 2012.

14. Association of American Colleges and Universities, "VALUE: Valid Assessment of Learning in Undergraduate Education," retrieved from *www.aacu.org/value/rubrics/index_p.cfm* on November 3, 2013.

15. George Kuh, *High Impact Educational Practices: What They Are, Who Has Access to Them, and Why They Matter* (Washington, DC: AAC&U, 2008).

16. Lumina Foundation, *Degree Qualifications Profile*, January 2011, *www.luminafoundation.org/1_no_parent_nav_bar_fix/publications/special_reports/degree_profile*.

17. Debra Humphreys, "What's Wrong with the Completion Agenda—And What We Can Do About It," *Liberal Education* 98, no. 1 (2012), *www.aacu.org/liberaleducation/le-wi12/humphreys.cfm*; Judith A. Ramaley, "Seeking More High Quality Undergraduate Degrees: Working with Policymakers," *Peer Review* 15, no. 1 (2013), *www.aacu.org/peerreview/pr-wi13/Ramaley.cfm*.

18. Carnegie Foundation for the Advancement of Teaching, "Classification Description: Community Engagement Elective Classification," *classifications.carnegiefoundation.org/descriptions/community_engagement.php*, retrieved on June 13, 2014.

19. Barbara Holland, "Advancing the Engagement Mission," Presentation to the Oregon State University Outreach and Engagement Strategic Conference, October 29, 2012.

20. Association of American Colleges and Universities, *Greater Expectations*.

21. Complete College America, "Core Principles for Transforming Remedial Education: A Joint Statement by the Charles A. Dana Center," Complete College America, Inc., Education Commission of the States and Jobs for the Future, *www.completecollege.org/docs/Remediation_Joint_Statement-Embargo.pdf*.

22. Frank P. Ardaiolo, "Changing Institutional Culture to Advance Civic Learning," *Diversity and Democracy* 6, no. 4 (2013), *www.aacy.org/diversitydemocracy/v0116n04.ardaiolo.cfm*.

23. Judith Ramaley, "Moving Mountains: Institutional Culture and Transformational Change," in *A Field Guide to Academic Leadership*, ed. Robert M. Diamond (San Francisco: Josie-Bass, 2002), 59–74.

8

PREPARING STUDENTS FOR WORK AS CITIZENS: REFLECTIONS OF A NEW COLLEGE PRESIDENT

Adam Weinberg

In the introduction to this volume, Harry Boyte argues for an expanded view of citizenship. Boyte's call rests on the assumption that we face a series of critical global issues that most Americans feel powerless to address, leading to a narrowing of citizenship as seen in voting and volunteerism. Boyte articulates a deep desire to revive and reinvent notions of citizenship in which people get off the sidelines and work with others to solve problems and create things of lasting social value.

The key concept for Boyte is public work, defined as "sustained, largely self-directed, collaborative effort, paid or unpaid, carried out by a diverse mix of people who create things of common value determined by deliberation. Public work is work by publics, for public purposes, in public."[1] Boyte expands on his early writings by calling on higher education leaders to contribute to the growing debate over jobs and to consider how we expand notions of citizenship and public work to include the sphere of work. As Boyte correctly notes, work and workplaces are too important to be left out of the debates over revitalizing citizenship. People's lives and identities are consumed by the world of work. Likewise, work and workplaces are vitally important to addressing most critical global issues.

As I have transitioned into the role of president of Denison University, I have been reflecting on Boyte's challenge. My thinking has been informed by my own personal experiences doing public work through my professional pursuits. First, I spent a decade as a faculty member and dean at Colgate University, working on a series of campus-community partnerships directed at economic development.[2] For the last eight years, I worked for a global organization called World Learning, often known as the Experiment in International Living or the School for International Training (SIT). Each year, World Learning works with about ten thousand young people from over 140 countries to address critical global issues.

In the course of my work, I came to believe that there is a growing gap between the possible and the likely. Let me explain.

First, we have what we need to address significant global challenges, so there is great potential in doing so. In the sociological sense, we have the technology (for example, knowledge, methods, processes, and physical tools) and the locally rooted assets to focus on climate change, human rights abuses, water shortages, joblessness, ethnic conflict, and other critical global issues. What we lack is the capacity to come together as human beings and socially organize ourselves to use our technology and assets to address these problems. While the potential is huge, the reality is daunting. Colleges can play a larger role in closing this gap by increasing the capacity and commitment of our students, faculty, staff, and alumni to engage in public work.

Second, the potential to act as a citizen-professional is increasing. Across the globe, the most interesting and meaningful forms of citizenship are coming from those who find ways to engage in public work through their professional careers. This is happening in a myriad of ways, including new kinds of social entrepreneurship and socially responsible businesses. It is also happening within large firms as a new generation of managers—more socially oriented than in the past—retool old business practices. And it is happening across the professions as lawyers, doctors, engineers, graphic designers, and other professionals use the new economy to "go it alone" and find ways to be citizen-professionals.

At the same time, there is growing anxiety over joblessness and increasing pressure on colleges to track students narrowly into careers and professions that bifurcate citizenship and work. Jobs matter. Colleges have an obligation to prepare people to thrive in their postcollege life. To do this correctly, we need to change the narrative and articulate how we will prepare students to succeed in their personal, professional, and civic pursuits by learning to design lives that connect these spheres in mutually reinforcing ways. That is the true promise of higher education.

Third, higher education has an expanding civic engagement tool kit, but we keep using the same limited tools. We need to broaden our approach. The usual calls for more service-learning classes and student volunteer groups have their natural limits in reaching our student body. We need to look for new places on our campuses to engage students in civic conversations and actions.

Narrowing the gap between the possible and the likely requires a nuanced understanding of how we increase the capacity and commitment of students to be citizens. It also requires exposing students to effective mentors and role models, while also helping them develop their interest and potential in various careers and professions.

Taking Capacity Development Seriously

If we want students to be effective citizens, we need to help them develop the capacity to engage in public work. This means knowing how to do the mundane stuff, including asset mapping, agenda setting, meeting facilitation, and evaluation. And it requires a grounding in the arts of the tougher stuff: how to listen and hear somebody who sees the world differently, how to persevere through repeated failure until you succeed, how to effectively manage constant change, and how to understand the ways in which local, regional, and global perspectives and issues are interconnected. There is a range of skills that good community organizers, nonprofit managers, and others know that enable them to organize diverse groups of people to get things done over sustained periods of time.

People learn the subtleties of public work by doing public work. It is an experiential process that requires coaching and training. Too often, we send students out into communities with little training. They sign up for some sort of campus volunteer organization. We send them an e-mail about when the van is leaving, and off they go. We do a great job of giving students opportunities to get off campus and take actions in the local community, but we do a poor job of using these actions to train students to be successful in the art of community engagement. We can start by making sure that every student engaged in the local community has the necessary coaching and training before they start to do work that matters.

But this alone will not get us very far. We need to look beyond community service and view our own campuses as sites for civic learning. For example, first-year residential halls are among the best places to teach the arts of public work, and almost nobody in the civic engagement community is paying attention to them. In the typical first-year residence hall, we pack a diverse group of people into small rooms. For many of them, it will be the first time that they have shared a room with another person. It's also the first time that many of them have bumped up against diversity. Over the last thirty years, our residential halls have become increasingly diverse, mixing students of different racial, ethnic, religious, and economic backgrounds; sexual orientations; mental and physical challenges; alcohol or drug issues; and a range of other characteristics or issues.

Students come to our residence halls with an array of needs, likes, dislikes, passions, and goals. As the reality of everyday living sets in with inevitable clashes, we have moments to coach students as they learn to build understandings and behavior patterns for the future. Instead, we often avoid conflict and professionalize problem solving. Before students have a chance to learn to work through their differences, we ask our professional staff to step in and mediate conflict, move roommates, or enforce rules. We would be better off training students to communicate more effectively, resolve conflict, and solve problems creatively.

Take the following two examples. A typical roommate conflict begins with students getting annoyed, but rather than deal with the problem directly, they often use cell phones to text their friends and/or call their parents. Eventually they talk to a resident advisor (RA) or a member of our staff. By the time they confront the roommate, they are angry and often voice the annoyance in an extremely negative way. Everyone gets upset. Friends take sides, and the hall becomes divided. Paid professionals then step in to solve the problem. Sometimes we move one of the students. Other times we create rules that allow for people to share space by minimizing social interaction.

Rather than seeking quick fixes to roommate problems, we should see them as moments to teach students the habits and skills of civil discourse. Roommate conflicts are opportunities for students to learn to voice opinions in a constructive fashion, hear different viewpoints, and reconcile competing views into an action or policy. In my experience, the largest problem faced by most public work projects is the inability of people to effectively work with people they don't understand or like. Roommate conflicts may be our best place to help young people develop this capacity.

A second example is the typical problem of late-night noise on a residence hall floor. Under the current model, students learn poor civic responses that mirror society at large. First, the individual usually approaches the group and asks if they could lower the noise level. When that doesn't work, students call the local authorities, often campus security or RAs. If this does not have the desired effect, they lump it by either finding another place to study or learning to live with it. Another approach would be for our students to be coached to organize their neighbors to solve the problem. In the process, students would learn to work in groups, develop the art of creative problem solving and project implementation, and acquire the skills of persistence, communication, and con-flict negotiation. They also would learn to hold their peers accountable—and be more accountable themselves.

Student organizations are another lost opportunity. If one treats the campus as community, then student organizations are our local associations. Imagine using the language of civic opportunity and public work to get student organiza-tions to understand themselves as community-based organizations. Too often, students involved in these groups are learning poor organizing skills. Meetings are poorly run. Programs are unsuccessful. Conflict is not negotiated. By com-mitting ourselves to well-run campus organizations, we would both improve campus dynamics and capture many educational moments to help students de-velop the arts of public work.

How do we capture these opportunities? We can start by exposing students to the liberal arts, especially during their initial years in college. Former Benning-ton College president Liz Coleman expressed this well when she wrote, "'Deep thought' matters when you're contemplating what to do about things that mat-ter."[3] The historian William Cronon articulates why the liberal arts are crucial to our ability to do this when he described the outcomes of a liberal arts education as fostering the capacity of students to listen and hear; read and understand; talk with anyone; write clearly and persuasively and movingly; solve a wide variety of puzzles and problems; respect rigor as a way of seeking truth; practice humility, tolerance, and self-criticism; understand how to get things done in the world; nurture and empower the people around them; and see connections that allow one to make sense of the world and act within it in creative ways.[4]

Whether our students are English majors or in nursing programs, we need to use the initial years of college to provide them with a broad-based curriculum that gives them the attributes of engaged citizens. We need to use what they are learning in the classroom so they can understand campus life as a design studio for translating the liberal arts into civic skills, values, habits, and knowledge.[5]

This will require a much deeper commitment to student mentorship and coaching. It also requires a more concerted effort to use the language of civic action. For example, we often use the concept of community when talking about campus life, but then we juxtapose the language of rules and processes. In effect, our campus nomenclature mixes frameworks of civic engagement with language of social control and bureaucratic management. There is a rich language used by people engaged in community work that is powerful, historic, and largely absent on our campuses.

As part of this shift, we need to focus on a different kind of training for both our staff and our student leaders. Very few people on our campuses have been trained to do community work. If we inventoried the different kinds of leadership training at our institutions, we might be surprised at how much goes on and how little of it involves the skills, values, and habits of community work. People trained to do public work know how to canvass a neighborhood and conduct one-on-one conversations with people who hold different views. And they are well-equipped to facilitate contentious meetings, set agendas, and keep people organized and aligned over time. They understand the art of framing an issue and are adept at seeking allies in unexpected places.

Finally, we need to embrace the messiness that comes with civic life. As a new president, I am keenly aware of how much easier my job is when the campus is free of conflict. This tends to lead to an overly professionalized or managerial view of the job. Quickly we slip into treating the campus as a residential facility, not a site for civic learning—a messy place filled with competing views, publicly contested issues, and engaged citizens. To transform our campuses into sites for civic learning, we need to take an experiential approach, giving students more space and time to learn by doing. This would lead to some messiness and, frequently, to some conflict. But we would see these as positive learning moments and not messy moments to be avoided.

Exposing Students to Mentors
Who Model Citizenship through Work

Many students have grown up in families and communities with poor civic role models. They have seen few people exert effective citizenship, either in private or public, or in their professional lives. We need to expose students to mentors and role models.

This starts on campus by supporting faculty and staff who want to engage in public work. There are many ways that administrators send out cultural signals and construct incentive structures that place tremendous obstacles in the ways of our faculty and staff who want to be citizen-professionals. Do we encourage junior faculty to get involved in public work projects? Do we free staff to attend civic meetings that take place during the workday? How do we treat staff when they take public stands that might not benefit the college? Changing practices that discourage public work requires tackling difficult and deep issues around how we define and reward different kinds of teaching and research. It means being willing to talk openly about what counts for promotion and tenure, and about incentive structures within our institutions that have mostly pushed faculty to be less engaged with our students and local communities.

But it goes well beyond role modeling on campus. Our students need mentors within local communities. In subtle and not so subtle ways, colleges shape the availability of these role models. Every day, colleges make a myriad of decisions about how to operate. In doing so, we shape the local environment in ways that either expand or constrict the ability of everybody in the local community to be citizens through work, and hence role models and mentors for our students. For example, as I have transitioned into my role at Denison, I have met people who are starting businesses and stores with an ecological bent; creating organic farms; engaging in social entrepreneurship; and working as independent professionals who have more time to participate in community-based endeavors.

As Denison makes daily decisions about how to operate, our actions either support this work or constrain it. As I serve in my first few months as president, I am keenly aware of how subtle the connections are and how easy it is to miss them. For example, we have told our new food vendor to purchase food from farmers who are trying to construct an innovative regional food system, allowing us to deepen relationships and help to stabilize a few farms that are connected to our environmental studies and first-year programs. We are exploring ways to get students off campus to support local stores run by citizen-professionals. In my initial talks to civic organizations, I talk openly about the need to protect the civic fabric of our community by more consciously supporting members of our community who are blending work and citizenship. As part of this, I am meeting with social entrepreneurs to open a dialogue on how the college affects their potential success.

These "ordinary" decisions have deep impacts. By role modeling, I am trying to implicitly give our faculty and staff more space to act in a similar way. I am also trying to consciously operate the college in ways that create room for more local community members to be the kinds of coaches and mentors our students need.

Helping Students Find Careers That Matter

Many students crave jobs that matter. Students are starting small-scale NGOs and seeking out firms that contribute to the social good. They are applying for positions at Teach for America and the Peace Corps by the droves. We can make progress by continuing our work to prepare students for jobs in nonprofits, education, and socially responsible businesses, and as social entrepreneurs.

At a deeper level, we need to prepare students to work in ways that transform the professions. We want to educate our students to be doctors, lawyers, financial investors, and others who approach their jobs as engaged citizens. It's one thing to prepare students to seek careers that have a positive social impact. It's even more exciting to nurture a generation to transform professions into jobs that have a social impact.

There are some complex shifts to this idea. Fundamentally, we need to transform how professionals see themselves in relation to others. How do professionals see their work in relation to their role as citizens? If compartmentalized, how do we break down barriers and let people work together as citizens? Are they professionals by day and citizens by night, or are they community members who seek to drive their businesses forward in ways that have social benefits? Further, when professionals act in the community, do they act for us or with us? How do we shift the professional mindset from someone who acts on us to somebody who acts with us?

This requires rethinking the career development process. The ramp into college needs to create a more intentional connection between the curriculum and career development, but not in the ways we usually articulate. We need to find ways early in students' college careers to frame large questions about their place in human history. The first-year experience should be filled with classes that explore the classic liberal arts issues. We then need to build on those classes during the sophomore and junior years to get students to draw connections between liberal arts frameworks and skills, and have real conversations about careers and professions. Imagine a preprofessional engineering program with a series of ethics, creative writing, and anthropology courses that help students explore what it means to be an engineer in the context of large historical sweeps of history. We need more thoughtful and intentional ways to connect classes to create an arc that helps students develop clear views about how civic lives are led through the professions—and this should be the main narrative, not just an addendum.

We also need to rethink the ways we launch students into their first jobs and ultimately into a profession. We need to expose them to alumni who can speak about jobs and about the ways people blend professions and public work. Too often we bring in alumni who work in the nonprofit sector and who speak to the civically minded students with a narrow focus on their notions of work. We then bring in alumni who work in the private sector and who often focus on more material goals in their talks with students. Why not blend the two? Why not use internships, externships, off-campus excursions, and campus programs to expose students to alumni who are working in a range of professions to build meaningful lives where public work is infused throughout their work lives. We need to give people permission and space to make the hidden visible to our students as part of a larger process of linking jobs to citizenship and public work.

At Denison, we are at the very beginning of a long conversation about how to move in this direction. We are taking a hard look at the first year to make sure we are effectively getting students to ask big questions as a way to unearth and upend assumptions, freeing their minds to explore and imagine. We are taking a hard look at the sophomore year to find places to get students to make better decisions about academic majors because this is another place where students start to form decisions about jobs that bifurcate work and citizenship. We are asking how we can use the time between semesters to connect students to alumni (and often parents of other students) through internships, externships, and profession-specific training. And we are examining new language and forms of mentorship that help students understand the career arc and the notion that the first few years out of college is the time to take some risk and explore.

Conclusion

Boyte's call to action has led me to consider a new perspective on my work that blends my professional practice with my civic passions in ways that are mutually reinforcing. I am also trying to lay out a blueprint for how higher education can better prepare our students to be effective and engaged citizens.

Boyte is correct in calling for a revived conversation about an expanded notion of citizenship. He is also right to connect it to the sphere of work. In my view, we have a generation of college students who crave this conversation. I also believe colleges and universities are uniquely positioned to lead the way in creating a new kind of exciting, citizen-led future.

Notes

1.   Harry Boyte, *Reinventing Citizenship as Public Work* (Dayton, OH: Kettering Foundation, 2013), 2.
2.   For more information on how to think about the campus as community, see Adam Weinberg, "Residential Education for Democracy," *Learning for Democracy* 1 (2005): 29–45; or Adam Weinberg, "Creating an Entrepreneurial Campus Culture," *Peer Review* 1 (Spring 2005): 24–26.
3.   Elizabeth Coleman, "Education: Agent and Architect of Democracy," *Teacher-Scholar* 2 (Fall 2010): 51.
4.   William Cronon, "Only Connect: The Goals of a Liberal Education," *American Scholar* 67 (1998): 73–80.
5.   The language of "design studios" is a wonderful way to conceptualize this work. See Rebecca Chopp, "Remaking, Renewing, Reimagining: The Liberal Arts College Takes Advantage of Change," in *Remaking College: Innovation and the Liberal Arts*, ed. Rebecca Chopp, Susan Frost, and Daniel Weiss (Baltimore: Johns Hopkins University Press, 2013), 13–24.

PART III

The Faculty Experience and Faculty as Agents of Change

I was once in a seminar on the theme of nonprofits and democracy, with one other person from academia. Others were from community groups, schools, and foundations. At the end of the three-day discussion, the other faculty member asked to have lunch. "I've been thinking about my behavior in this seminar," he said. "I gave my presentation and then have been quiet. I realize that I'm afraid to speak if I don't have 'the answer' and am not seen as a recognized expert." He added, "This is not simply my problem. I'm an endowed professor at an Ivy League university, which is recognized as one of the great institutions of the world. You would think I wouldn't suffer from such lack of confidence. But in fact we teach all our students to be experts in public, and to keep quiet if they're not."

My colleague was naming a pervasive and also hidden pattern—the sharply bounded identities of successful academics. Such long-developing identities make it very difficult to "break free," to join the open spaces of the public world. But a growing movement among faculty members is developing paths and strategies for doing so. This section highlights reflections of leaders and organizers long concerned with changing not only practices but also identities.

9

CAN A NEW CULTURE OF CIVIC PROFESSIONALISM FLOURISH?

Maria Avila

The separation of work from citizenship and its effect in democracy is at the center of the challenge that Harry Boyte poses to us in his essay "Reinventing Citizenship as Public Work." Here, I comment on Boyte's challenge from my perspective as a former community organizer, and from what I have learned by integrating organizing practices with civic engagement in higher education institutions. My comments are based primarily on my work at Occidental College, a small residential liberal arts undergraduate college in Northeast Los Angeles. In addition, I will also refer to my doctoral research at the National University of Ireland, Maynooth (NUIM)—a state research university with over eight thousand students, located forty-five minutes west of Dublin, the capital of Ireland—and to my postdoctoral research at the University of Southern California (USC)—a private research 1 university, near downtown in Los Angeles. In all three institutions my work has centered primarily on publically engaged faculty.

I began integrating community organizing practices at Occidental College in 2001, when I was hired as the founding director of the Center for Community Based Learning (CCBL). I left Occidental in 2011. I approached my work with CCBL from a set of assumptions, stemming mostly from my community organizing background, which include:

1. A concept of community includes the community within institutions of all kinds, not just the communities and neighborhoods outside academic institutions. Thus I saw the college campus as a community I needed to learn about and with, by involving faculty as cocreators and costrategists in the work of the CCBL.
2. All communities have existing and or potential leaders, and my job was to find those, primarily within faculty and community partners, since the CCBL was created to institutionalize community-based learning and community-based research.
3. Long-term, transformational, and reciprocal engagement must be cocreated and coassessed by faculty together with leaders from communities outside of the college.

4. Engagement should aim at transforming the college, partnering community organizations, and the community at large. For this assumption, understanding power dynamics within the campus, within each partnering organization, and in the region is essential.

These assumptions emerged in response to what I learned about the field of civic engagement nationally, during my early years at Occidental. At civic engagement conferences I remember talking with community-service and service-learning scholars and realizing then that their focus seemed to center on the disengagement of college students as politically active citizens of society.[1] Boyte illustrates my point here with his reference to Anne Colby and her colleagues in Educating for Democracy,[2] where they "point out that among the six hundred or so service-learning programs they studied, only 1 percent included 'a focus on specifically political concerns and solutions such as working with groups to represent the interests of a community,' while more than half provided direct service, such as serving food in shelters and tutoring." However, in my view, the topic of the civic and political disengagement of academic institutions and faculty members from their surrounding communities was not as widely discussed. And while many of those scholars were finding out about the lack of institutional support for publically engaged scholarship, not many seemed interested in doing something about transforming this aspect of the culture of higher education. In those conversations, two directors of centers of community service and service learning made their preference for working with students as opposed to working with faculty clear to me. They could not understand why I would be interested in institutional and societal cultural change, an uphill, unwinnable battle in their views.

With these four assumptions and this information about the state of civic engagement, I spent most of my first year at Occidental doing one-to-one meetings with Occidental faculty and thus found a small group of them who became coleaders with me in the creation of and in ongoing strategizing about the work of the CCBL. I eventually repeated this process with a number of community partners and created a regional network with neighboring schools and community leaders. Through these one-to-one meetings with faculty I heard stories about their interests, views, and experiences with community-based learning (CBL) and community-based research (CBR). I also learned that faculty members were often not comfortable crossing the college boundaries to engage with community leaders, but, though one confirmed this, not many would admit to it. From my one-to-ones with school and community leaders, though with some exceptions, I learned that they often saw the college as a source of superior knowledge, power, and resources compared to theirs and seemed happy to accept college students to do service even if this service did not build their organizational capacity or transform their communities.

I shared this information with my faculty and community coleaders, and we decided that it would make sense to create new spaces and opportunities for faculty and community leaders campus- and community-wide to engage in conversation, for instance, over lunch and in community-based learning workshops. We decided to frame these conversations, as well as invitations to these gatherings, by asking everyone to suspend expectations about working together (that is, through CBL or CBR projects) and, instead, use the opportunities to hear each other regarding interests and objectives of CBL/CBR for faculty, and interests and objectives of the services provided through their organizations for community leaders. We intentionally planned these gatherings in fairly unstructured ways, using most of the time for conversations, and then followed up as needed with those who were interested in partnering. As it turned out, a number of CBL and CBR partnerships emerged from these gatherings, but most important, faculty and their community partners began to understand the concept of reciprocity by cocreating, together, partnerships that took into account each other's interests, resources, and limitations.

In creating these new spaces for conversations between faculty and community leaders, we were intentional and strategic about allowing for relationships to emerge naturally, and in the process addressing barriers such as difference of cultures and calendars, power inequalities between the campus and the community, and the challenge of long-term sustainability of campus-community partnerships. Some of these barriers have been discussed by several authors writing about service, CBL and CBR.[3] But there is a larger context for this example of engagement, which is really about creating spaces and situations where democracy can be practiced, and where faculty can reconnect with their civic agency by cocreating their engaged classes and research with those with whom they partner in the community. This example of engagement also fits with Boyte's views in his essay about ways to sustain civic agency:[4]

> Civic agency movements are appearing with growing frequency and also disappearing quickly. What will create foundations for sustaining them? A molecular organizing process that weaves alternative civic and political concepts and their corresponding practices into everyday life is the key. These include democracy as a society, not simply elections; citizenship as work with public qualities, not simply voting and volunteering; citizens as cocreators and producers of democracy, not mainly consumers of democracy; and politics as the way we work across differences to solve problems and create a democratic way of life, not a polarized partisan spectacle.

The truth of Boyte's belief that the "realization that leaders won't save us" has generated a movement "in which citizens themselves reclaim responsibility for democracy" is evident in my example at Occidental, where faculty and school and organizational leaders from communities outside Occidental acted based on their civic agency and not on a mandate from their leaders.

There is, however, another side of this story. In recent conversations with a small group of faculty and community partners who cocreated the engagement work of CCBL with me, we reflected about what we accomplished in terms of transforming institutions where we each worked, as well as the communities surrounding the college. Our conversations were rich with stories of success, but also with questions that are still pending for us regarding the extent to which our

institutions were transformed. As one faculty member put it, speaking specifically about the college, "how far do we need to go to really transform our institutions?" Faculty members who were part of these conversations raised questions
about the limits of their civic agency in the face of the reality of the power (and
resources) that higher education presidents have, which, in institutions where
shared democratic governance is symbolic at best, can wear out even the most
committed civic faculty/professionals.

I encountered this same concern about shared, democratic governance (or
lack of it) from faculty who I interviewed for my doctoral research at NUIM
in Ireland, and most recently, from faculty I interviewed for my postdoctoral
research at USC. A faculty member from NUIM reflects about questions related
to faculty civic agency and power: "What is the meaning of the faculty? What do
we stand for? What are we trying to do? Or do we just meet once a month and
rubberstamp decisions? Where is the power? There doesn't seem to be much
power in the faculty; can we generate some power?"

One faculty member at USC reflected on a slightly different way of feeling
powerless:

> Well, I had hopes at one point of creating a center for civic engagement
> at USC . . . having links to people all over the university and outside the
> university. . . . When I came here it was highly decentralized. It was essentially
> a collection of professional schools with a very weak [College of Letters, Arts
> and Sciences]. And now they have strengthened the college a lot. A lot. But
> the professional schools are still there as powerful actors, so it is very hard to
> institutionalize anything university-wide here unless it comes from the provost,
> the president of the university, and even then it is difficult to do. . . . So, I have
> decided just to work within this school and with people that I have some
> common ground with.

What is peculiar to me is that all faculty members who expressed concerns (and
in many cases frustration) with the lack of democratic governance on their campuses think this is happening only in their institution, and in the case of NUIM,
that this "top-down leadership," as one faculty member called it, is happening
only in their country and not in the United States.

Community partners in my conversations and reflections about our work
at Occidental too expressed a concern about the concentration of power and
resources in the top leadership. In the case of school community partners, for instance, they endured the uncertainty of their jobs every time there was a change
of regional and district leadership of the Los Angeles Unified District. In fact
a few of them were transferred to other schools several times during our work
together, because of changes related to new leadership and budgetary decisions.
Their transfer to other schools often lead to weakening or shutting down the
spaces for democratic engagement they had helped create in their schools. One
school leader expressed this in regards to creating a network of schools in the
area surrounding the college: "I think that some of the things that we did that
were good things . . . we developed those relationships amongst the schools,

and it was disappointing that we weren't able to do that more within the district schools because the district was actively working against us, which is mind boggling."

Yet the stories of success are too powerful and real to be ignored. One Occidental faculty member said: "So it was the organizing as well as multiple ways that you brought people together and interacted [that] helped to create the possibility of new ways of doing things. New ways of thinking about the work and people . . . like myself, who really wanted to do this kind of work for a long time but didn't have the right kind of model for doing it. Did earlier attempts and didn't like the way that power felt on that. So I had to step back, and this gave me a new way of thinking about that." An Occidental Community partner from a surrounding school, but who was later transferred said this:

> I think that my practice as a professional was changed by what we were doing. . . . I think it's the relational thing . . . and the organizing lens. You know, I'll say, "Oh, we need to do a power analysis," so we will do a power analysis. . . . When I'm thinking about wanting to make some changes here at this school, I'm going to look at my faculty, I'm going to look at who my people are, I'm going to look at where everybody is, and I think about my leverage points. Or my tipping points. But I'm going to go about that very much in an organizing way. I'm going to have one-on-one conversations with people, I'm going to try to find out what their interests are, I'm going to try to find out if I can put people together around an interest and I can create something meaningful for them, so they can work forward from that place.

At Occidental, perhaps the biggest success of the work of the CCBL, and especially of the use of community organizing practices, is that the CCBL continues to exist, three years after I left, and even as we experienced a turnover of five presidents and five college deans in the ten years of my tenure as director. At NUIM, a group of faculty who emerged as civic engagement leaders through my research continue strategizing today, in conversation with others on campus and with their new university president, two years after my research ended. At USC, there are early signs of an emerging faculty leadership interested in creating spaces for conversations about possibilities for breaking through the disconnectedness and feelings of frustration, and creating opportunities for acting as a collective on their public scholarship.

So there is enough evidence from my account alone, but also from Boyte's examples of academic institutions where faculty members are acting on their civic agency to transform their institutions and their communities. But the question is how do we grow this movement in a way that has breadth, but also depth? Where do we start? The NUIM faculty member I quoted above reflects here on how the division of the university into various faculties makes it hard to connect with others on campus: "One of the other tragedies of the university is that the faculty system has evolved and we have become detached. My first year in Maynooth [NUIM] I interacted all the time. . . . I knew people in maths [mathematics], in physics, . . . but I don't know anyone now because we are divided into humanities, science, social science. . . . When I first came I think there was science and arts. . . . I don't know anybody anymore. . . . I think there is an obligation for people within every faculty to engage but how do you do that?"

I believe that revitalizing democratic practices in our institutions and in partnership with other institutions in ways that are long-term sustainable is the biggest challenge in transforming higher education, and society at large. I also believe that in order to do this we have an imperative mandate to take time to pause, reflect, and refocus our efforts as a collective of concerned "civic professionals," together, so that we can cocreate a unified strategy for action. This is hard to do, especially because the current culture in our institutions and in society tends to value quantity over quality. More activity is better. More articles, more books, more funding, more students, more examples of best practices, more programs. Some of it makes sense and cannot be helped because we have jobs to be accountable to, families to support, and mortgages to pay. But I wonder if some of our activity-driven work comes from our own preferences and habits, which, if this is the case, we can control and change, individually and collectively. In writing this essay my hope is to contribute to Boyte's efforts to build a collective of civic professionals that engage in cocreating a culture where our civic and professional lives merge, regardless of what our jobs require us to do. And I believe this can be done. But I also know this work takes strategic, slow, and careful collective work. I am hopeful, however, from what I have experienced at Occidental, at NUIM in Ireland, and now at USC, where I have seen evidence that there are enough faculty members who are interested in engaging in this type of cultural change within their institutions and in society.

Notes

1.   See Edward Zlotkowiski, *Successful Service-Learning Programs* (Bolton, MA: Ankler, 1998); Barbara Jacoby, *Building Partnerships for Service Learning* (San Francisco: Jossey-Bass 2003); and Thomas Ehrlich, *Civic Responsibility and Higher Education* (Phoenix, AZ: Oryx Press, 2000).

2.   Anne Colby, Elisabeth Beaumont, Thomas Ehrlich, and Josh Corngold, *Educating for Democracy: Preparing Undergraduates for Responsible Political Engagement* (Palo Alto: Carnegie Foundation for the Advancement of Teaching, 2007), 4–5.

3.   Including David J. Maurrasse, *Beyond the Campus: How Colleges and Universities Form Partnerships with Their Communities* (New York: Routledge, 2001); and Randy Stoecker and Elizabeth A. Tyron, *The Unheard Voices: Community Organizations and Service Learning* (Philadelphia: Temple University Press, 2009).

4.   Harry Boyte, "Reinventing Citizenship as Public Work," in *Democracy's Education: Public Work, Citizenship, and the Future of Colleges and Universities* (Vanderbilt University Press, 2015).

10

TRANSFORMATIONAL ECOTONES: THE CRAFTSPERSON ETHOS AND HIGHER EDUCATION

Romand Coles and Blase Scarnati

We live in a time when higher education is undergoing a severe assault—along with most public goods, the ecosystem, and democratic institutions and practices.[1] This attack advances in the name of neoliberalism, austerity, efficiency, corporate privatization, consumer preference, technocratic expertise, outcome-based metrics, performance standards and assessment, culture war, vocational education reduced to job training, liberal education shrunken to the needs of business, and democracy education eviscerated and presented as episodic bouts of service. If to no small degree higher education has been a space where, in Gerald Taylor's terms, "knowledge artisans" have enjoyed significant freedoms through which we have collectively shaped the conditions of our work, we now find ourselves in shrinking pressurized boxes increasingly governed by imperatives that have little to do with our craft.[2] In this context, many faculty members are sliding toward politically impotent modes of defensiveness and cynicism.

Yet, such exhaustion can be taken as an opportunity for reflection and a challenge to explore new transformative movements. Many at Northern Arizona University and elsewhere have been involved in efforts to reenvision and re-fashion pedagogical practices in ways that appear to be resonating with myriad faculty, students, members of diverse communities, and with numerous people in university administration, local government, nonprofits, social movements, and the business community. Indeed, there are important signs that these initiatives may be able to attract, engage, and reassemble a vast and powerful movement. Moreover, the lessons that are emerging from our experiences at NAU are akin to trends in the nationwide democracy education movement that are being explored in networks such as the Kettering Foundation, American Commonwealth Partnership, Imagining America, Center for Information and Research on Civic Learning and Engagement, the American Democracy Project, and the New Economy Institute.

In this chapter, we propose that what we call a "craftsperson ethos" can provide a highly illuminating frame for understanding this transformative movement in higher education for democratic purposes, pedagogies, knowledge, networks, publics, and power for a diverse and complex commonwealth. This claim may initially have a counterintuitive ring, as the purposes of liberal education, for example, have often been understood to be far loftier than—and perhaps even at odds with—those typically associated with craft. Moreover, there is a long tradition of opposing the richly pluralistic life of politics to what is often taken to be the drab and mundane activities of labor and work. Yet, rather than seeing craft contrasted with grand visions of higher education and democratic life, we believe an expansive recovery of the language of craft can draw together liberal education, democracy, and public work in ways that generate magnetic visions and intersecting interests that can contribute to profound cultural and institutional change in higher education.

Ecotone refers to the edges and overlaps between different ecosystems that are often extraordinarily fructiferous zones teeming with evolutionary potential. We reflect here on the ecotones that emerge between engaged democratic pedagogy, vocational formation, and the highest goals of liberal education when they are interpreted through the lens of a craftsperson ethos. We tend not only to the *fertility* of this intersection, but also to its *tone*, for ecotones are often sonorous ecological zones. Just as Martin Luther King Jr. and Dorothy Cotton understood that musicality was integral to the civil rights movement, there is a certain *musicality*—a chorus of *voices*, an *ecology* of *calls* and *responses*—that is no less important for efforts to reform higher education in ways that carry on the spirit and substance of their legacy.[3]

Recovering a Pedagogies, Politics, and Vocations of a "Craftsperson Ethos"

Through the lens of "craftsmanship," Richard Sennett offers a rich and transformative vision of epistemology, learning, vocational formation, and democratic citizenship.[4] Sennett advances the enlightenment philosophy articulated and displayed in the images in Denis Diderot's thirty-five-volume edited project, *The Encyclopedia, or Dictionary of Arts and Crafts*. The point is not that reflective reason and critical judgment are unimportant—far from it, but rather that *daily practices* and *engaged understanding* are integral to the development of both our intellects and our ability to change the world. With this claim, Sennett places himself in tension with a philosophical tradition dating back to ancient Greek understandings of *theoria*, which has linguistic kinship with "*theatron*, a theater, which means literally a 'place for seeing.'" For this tradition, "understanding [is] separated from doing, the 'mind's eye' [becomes] that of an observer rather than of a maker" (124). This is problematic, because it minimizes or discounts altogether the "continual dialogue with materials" that is integral to the arousal and development of human knowledge.[5]

For Sennett, "the craftsman represents the special human condition" of "being engaged" and illuminates how both "understanding and expression are impaired" when the "head is separated from the hand" (20).[6] By presenting us with resistance, incompleteness, and ambiguity, bodily experience provokes our imaginations to move, swerve, and evolve in order to improve our grasp of the world. People thus engaged with the world's specificities develop suppler capacities for self-criticism that can otherwise be easily avoided when thinking becomes too spectatorial and comfortable.[7]

People working with a craftsperson's ethos also cultivate greater capacities for "domain shifts." When faced with challenges, we create unexpected adjacencies that enable us to draw on tools, concepts, parables, principles, and insights from other realms of doing and knowing in order to open up new perspectives. We thereby develop a sense that myriad sources of knowledge and permeable boundaries are often necessary to respond to real-world challenges.[8] We learn patient discernment that enables us to pursue good work in relation to frustrating situations. We "befriend ambiguity" as a provocation and occasion for learning, as well as for replenishing modesty. We are drawn outside of ourselves as we "become the thing on which we are working"—experiencing what Merleau-Ponty calls "being as a thing" (Sennett, 174) and developing collaborative arts with others thus drawn to work on the world of challenges and opportunities. These are among the practiced virtues of the craftsperson ethos.

Thus the craftsperson ethos engenders conditions for *enhancing*—not diminishing—learning, teaching, and scholarship. It amplifies those aspects of *the liberal education tradition* that articulate the virtues of engagement. When disciplines are brought to engage the world and the myriad other sorts of knowledge that are also involved with it, they are deepened, reflectively examined, creatively developed, broadened, supplemented, and enlivened in ways that are far more difficult if not impossible when they are pursued as self-enclosed and compartmentalized disciplinary journeys. The craftsmanship ethos is integral to the movement from myopic blindness toward collaborative engagement with others in supple relationships through which we may understand things better and, thereby, hope to impact the world.

This brings us to a second insight, concerning the relationship between craftsmanship and *democratic political activity*. Hannah Arendt conceives of politics as a realm in which natality (new and unexpected political responsiveness and action) is solicited and performed with others under conditions of plurality.[9] She sharply divides political life from labor and work, arguing that the mundane repetitiousness of labor tends to suppress political imagination and action. In contrast, Sennett's account illuminates many ways in which natality, imagination, and judgment are animated by the repetitions of working engagement with the world. Indeed, from this vantage point, not only is such engagement a condition of the qualities that Arendt names as political; Sennett's writing also suggests why political thought and action that is *not* thus engaged has a pronounced tendency to magnify destructive tyrannies of unchecked abstraction, acquire strategic rigor mortis, and develop little resilience. If the pragmatists are right, both academic disciplines and politics become reified when disengaged from the work of confronting real-world challenges and opportunities with others. Even as there are always risks, theoretical vision, political natality, and pragmatic action are conditions of each other's possibility, when rightly conceived and practiced. Hence we might call these vital intersections and ecotones "visionary pragmatism": engaged work that opens horizons of possibility.

Finally, we believe that the craftsperson ethos suggests a mode of engagement through which students are most likely to become aroused to pursue a *vocational education* in the very richest sense of this word as *formation*—distinct from merely preparation for a "job" (originally a lump of coal, which accurately describes the treatment of people in the most disposable sectors of the labor market), or even a "career" (which shares a Latin root with "careen").[10] In relation to supple engagements with the marvelous abundance, profound complexities, and awful challenges of the world, we are stimulated to imagine our life as a distinct gift. We envision a lifetime of difficult, rewarding, and energetic involvement in response to problems and purposes bigger than ourselves.

Yet there is another sense of vocation that is, we believe, equally important for public work—which almost always involves *the work of forming publics*. Max Weber connected vocation with the German *Beruf*, which "contains two resonances: the gradual accumulation of knowledge and skills and the ever-stronger conviction that one was meant to do this one particular thing in one's life" (Sennett, 263). This term, which means occupation, is rooted in the term *Ruf*—to call or to cry—and thus Weber associates vocation and *Beruf* with a *calling* (which has profound religious resonances), in the sense of a deeply meaningful and coherent accord between one's work and one's life purposes. To accent calling is to give vocation an intonation that draws it close to its Latin roots and resonances, namely *vocatio*—a call—and *vocare*—to call. With these resonances we want to suggest that the vitality of nearly all vocations, and perhaps most especially the vocation of transformational democratic citizenship, is profoundly related to our capacity *to hear a call from the world and from others and, through an empowered voice, to call to others*.[11]

Vocation understood as a craftsperson ethos and care for the world hinge on this profound capacity to call out, to hear the calls of others, and to form relationships through which we become capable of discerning commonalities and differences, and engaging in mutual work and action for commonwealth. Vocations that neglect this expressive work will tend to be oblivious and technocratic (indifferent to and manipulative of others). *Vocare*, voice, is the indispensable capacity to be moved by and move each other in ways that enhance mutuality. Vocation, or good work thus understood, emerges from the resonances one finds between a deep listening to the gifts and passions within oneself, and the subtleties and surprises in the voices of others, and a sharp attentiveness to the specific textures of things, place, community, traditions, and broader contexts. Through this "meaningful conversation," we acquire the power to make differences that are more democratic and just.

John Paul Lederach, whose vocation has been to be a grassroots peacemaker and craftsman of democratic communities for decades, argues persuasively that such profound *listening* is the condition of "bringing to public expression what has been denied," for radical receptivity "requires a journey . . . a step toward and into the unknown . . . to live at the edge of known cartography."[12] When we dedicate ourselves to listening attentively to and working with intersecting voices we embark on a journey with our whole lives. Through such work, or what we might consider the metavocation that accompanies and lifts up all vocations when they are pursued in the deepest soils, we find our voices. Yet the essence of such discovery is to be discerned not merely in what we say or what we do—though these things are vitally important, but rather in "who [we] are and how [we] see [ourselves] in relation to others . . . finding a way to speak with our lives," and in so doing call and move each other to public work and political action.[13] This rich sense of responsive voicing has been integral to crafting change at Northern Arizona University.

Engaged Democratic Pedagogy at Northern Arizona University

In his introductory essay to this volume, Harry Boyte provides a very thoughtful critical typology of paradigms for citizenship, including liberal frames that foreground traditional civics; communitarian visions of citizen service volunteers; civil society models that emphasize advocacy, protest, and broad-based organizing; and a public work frame that embraces community-building, vocation and civic professionalism, and democratizing public work.[14] While Boyte acknowledges that each paradigm highlights important elements of citizenship, his writing has for decades sought to emphasize the solutions-oriented, productive, collaborative, and institutionally reconstructive aspects of everyday politics, while critiquing more disruptive and agonistic modes that involve political protest. Even as he acknowledges that such modes have been important in what he calls democratizing public work, he is rightly worried that they too often slide toward simplistic polarization, ideological sloganeering, impotent righteous moralizing, strategic rigor mortis, and an emphasis on episodic mobilizing over broad-based organizing. His work—like that of Bayard Rustin, whom he so admires—conveys a strong sense that it is time to move "*from* Protest *to* Politics [as broadly collaborative]" rather than cultivate elements both simultaneously.[15]

Our work to broaden and deepen cultural and institutional change for democratic pedagogy and scholarship at Northern Arizona University resonates with Boyte's critique of formulaic modes of polarizing politics, as well as his constructive vision of everyday political practice. In our work with faculty communities of practice, community partners, action research teams, and seminars, we accent themes of radical receptivity that pursue pathways toward abundance rather than assuming scarcity to create broad-based and unexpected collaborations, and assume the necessity and possibilities for transforming small and large institutions and systems of power. Our movement for democratic education is profoundly formed by a craftsperson ethos dedicated to resilient work and action in relation to the complex, ambiguous, and resistant character of the world in relationship with diverse communities.

Yet, the craftsperson ethos also informs our work in ways that lead us to embrace what is perhaps a more heterogeneous, tension-filled, and open-ended understanding of the political modes that are necessary to achieve democratic change in the face of today's dominant powers and unprecedented urgencies. Though profoundly dissatisfied with prevailing modes of polarizing politics, many of us suspect that inventing new forms of performative protest, disturbance, and creative dramatic staging—*while not getting lost and disconnected in these modes*—will likely be important aspects of the overall mix of tools required for opening doors and to cocreate and become the democratizing change that we seek. Thus, while our work is seated in democratic pedagogies and practices deeply indebted to traditions of broad-based organizing and patient public work, our pedagogies and practices are pluralistic and explore the possibilities, as well as the risks and dangers, of these other modes. As craftspersons with vocations for democracy, we remain attentive to ambiguity, the possibility of "domain shifts," "breakthroughs," and the wide array of pedagogical tools and strategies that help facilitate the arts of political midwifery.[16]

We are, in a sense, consummate *bricoleurs*. We seek to reuse and refashion the broadest range of available tools for new purposes—engendering experience, critical reflection, and a rich narrative memory of the promises, pitfalls, and possibilities we encounter as we do so. It is thus that we most profoundly teach, learn, and cultivate judgment about democratic practice; thus that democratic citizens and our polity become more responsive, supple, dynamic, powerful, and resilient; and thus that we may relearn how to give and receive the musicality of democracy, the improvisational interaction of call and response that is an elemental condition of democracy's emergence.

The understandings that we have sketched above have grown not merely out of theoretical considerations, but through our intimate relationship with an expansive movement of engaged democratic pedagogy at Northern Arizona University called CRAFTS (Community Reengagement for Arizona Families, Transitions, and Sustainability). Action Research Teams (ARTs) that have curricular connections with our First Year Seminar Program (FYSeminar) are an integral part of this initiative.[17] About half of the eighty sections of FYSeminar each year have ARTs integrated into the course curriculum. Real-world issues identified by myriad community organizations and students on sustainability, social justice, and grassroots democracy are collaboratively engaged to cultivate a more responsive and skilled citizenry and enhance commonwealth. Across the wide range of issues engaged by the ARTs—and often within each specific ART—students learn about, employ, and reflect on multiple modes of democratic engagement.[18]

Consider the Immigration ART. A significant portion of their work over the past several years has been in the domain of cocreating public work in collaboration with a local Industrial Areas Foundation affiliate, Northern Arizona Institutions for Community Leadership (NAICL). Working with NAICL, the Immigration ART has organized community conversations with law-enforcement leaders to identify and make improvements in issues concerning ethnic profiling and abuse, community safety, and the implications for law enforcement and crime prevention of Arizona's anti-immigrant legislation. This, in turn, caused the Flagstaff chief of police to broaden his sense of his public mission by speaking to the Flagstaff city council on the law-enforcement challenges posed by anti-immigration legislation. The chief's leadership on this issue also helped the city council to oppose the anti-immigration SB 1070 bill in the Arizona state legislature. The Immigration ART has also acted with community groups such as NAICL and the Repeal Coalition in civil society organizing and advocacy to oppose anti-immigrant legislation. Sometimes these efforts have been extremely broad based and collaborative, and at other times they have involved modes of dramatic protest to draw attention to labor abuses as well as the exclusions and severe suffering associated even with what passes as "moderate" immigration politics. Simultaneously, the Immigration ART has sponsored deliberative dialogues, performed more traditional service activities, and engaged in the politics of bearing witness.[19]

Since such diverse peoples and organizations collaborate in the Immigration ART, it employs a wide range of modes of democratic engagement that allow students a rich context for reflecting on the strengths, weaknesses, advantages, disadvantages, and potential interconnections of service, community organizing, advocacy, public work, civil discourse, agonistic confrontation, and educational outreach. The same is true of many of the other ARTs.

What are the impacts of the ARTs on NAU students as they engage with deeply political issues democratically developed with community partners? Many have stated that this work has simply changed their lives. In response to a question concerning their sense of agency in the face of challenges to their communities, a first-year student who had been a Public Achievement coach for elementary students in a low-income minority neighborhood lifted his forearm straight up at a right angle from the table on which his elbow rested and spoke: "You know, before this experience, all the problems in the world just seemed like walls that were impossible to move or get around." Then, gesturing toward his forearm now lowered to the table, he said, "But now, after seeing what a team of kids can do with a little coaching—they learn to work collaboratively together to identify, research, and act on an issue—everywhere I see challenges, I'm starting to see pathways." There is no more import thing that a student can say than this.

Moving through coursework and civic work, our students begin to open up into the richer idea of vocational formation. Students experience that work toward a vocation exceeds the narrow interests of career development. We believe that students' learning experiences in civic engagement will have direct purchase and value as they seek work as socially responsible business entrepreneurs, educators, grassroots leaders, workers in nonprofits, farmers, health care professionals, government employees, and become active citizens, giving voice, and living lives of rich significance. Growing numbers of students who have been involved in NAU's civic engagement initiatives for three or four years are selecting diverse vocational paths that demonstrate a sharp concern for commonwealth and democratic engagement.

Students in FYSeminars and ARTs pursuing civic agency and public work at NAU are excited about learning. The assessment results for the ARTs are impressive. The ARTs have been effective in increasing retention rates. Minority students who successfully complete FYSeminar-ARTs sections—those earning A, B, or C grades—is 16 percent higher than the retention rate for non-FYSeminar-ARTs minority students. Further, the retention rate for women who complete FYSeminar-ARTs sections is 9 percent higher than for non-FYSeminar-ARTs female students. We are currently redesigning our assessment research to study the impact of FYSeminar-ARTs on first generation students, but anecdotal evidence already suggests that engaged democratic pedagogy plays a vital role in acculturating these students to the pertinence of their curricular and cocurricular work in higher education. Students participating in FYSeminar-ARTs are also experiencing significantly increased engagement with NAU's liberal education learning outcomes. In particular, FYSeminar-ARTs sections are especially effective in promoting course-specific learning activities and outcomes involving diversity, cultural influences, and multiple perspectives.

How has a craftsperson ethos impacted faculty agency, empowerment, and rhizomatic collaborations? The reinvigoration of engaged democratic pedagogy at NAU appears to be shifting a growing number of faculty away from both a despairing sense of disenfranchisement and predominantly defensive and reactive postures. Faculty are moving toward modes of agency—in relation to the curriculum, cocurricular action research, and pedagogical practices—that are imaginatively proactive and cocreative, and that emphasizes collaborative transformations that engender better teaching, learning, scholarship, and relationships with broader communities.

Our craftsperson ethos is impacting principles and models of institutional collaborative governance among faculty, administrators, students, staff, and members of broader communities that work in tandem. Through this work higher education becomes more profoundly *public* in the sense that myriad communities play a more active, collaborative, and cocreative role in the life of the academy. Further, collaborative governance seeks to reclaim democracy and commonwealth by relinquishing our own enclosures, and by responding receptively to those reaching from other directions. This is the heart of the craftsperson ethos and democratic action research.

These forms of collaborative agency and empowerment, paradoxically, hold out the promise of generating productivities and efficiencies that are holistic and integrative, in contrast to the kinds of market-driven efficiencies that tend to undermine themselves through narrow vision and short-sightedness. By involving myriad constituencies in collaborative processes of response and cocreativity, we *generate* efficiencies through collaborative governance and democratic power. We find that faculty and students become intrinsically motivated in ways that are conducive to higher productivity and student success as multiple constituencies gather to work together in processes of holistic integrated problem solving; as actively engaged students, themselves, take on significant agency and responsibility in teaching each other; as the costs of administration and management decrease; and as students make rapid progress through their educational career paths.

Conclusion

A craftsperson ethos at Northern Arizona University is providing students, faculty, and community member myriad opportunities to develop rich, subtle, and collaborative cultures of teaching and learning. It drives us to deploy a wide range of democratic practices—a plural use of democratic strategies—that allow our students to cocreate their education through action research with community organizations to establish more just, democratic, and sustainable communities. The premise of our work is that grassroots democratic theory and practice can and should mutually inform each other, as should the scholarly and various other knowledges and traditions in the wider community. Our students engage in a deep and broad understanding of a career as a *vocation*, as we have been arguing, in which personal flourishing and broad public purposes are intertwined.[20]

We believe that a craftsperson ethos provides a useful frame in higher education for revitalizing democratic purposes, pedagogies, knowledge, networks, publics, and power to help form a more diverse and complex collaborative commonwealth. Through the ecotones that emerge between engaged democratic pedagogy, vocational formation, and the highest goals of liberal education as interpreted through the lens of a craftsperson ethos, we seek to voice, to sing, to open wildly creative spaces of democratic practice in these sonorous ecological zones.

Notes

1. We would like to thank the Kettering Foundation for providing support to develop some of the ideas presented in this chapter.
2. Gerald Taylor, "Prometheus Unbound: Populism, the Property Question, and Social Invention," *Good Society* 21, no. 2 (2012): 224.
3. See, for example, Robert Lischer, *The Preacher King: Martin Luther King Jr. and the Word That Moved America* (Oxford: Oxford University Press, 1997); and Dorothy F. Cotton, *If Your Back's Not Bent: The Role of the Citizenship Education Program in the Civil Rights Movement* (New York: Atria Books, 2012).
4. Richard Sennett, *The Craftsman* (New Haven, CT: Yale University Press, 2009). Hereafter cited in parentheses in the text.
5. Sennett notes, in passing, that great medieval sociologist Ibn Khaldun, who traveled extensively himself, witnessed that many crafts guilds owed their greatness to "travel and mobility." However, Sennett neglects to discuss the fact the Greek *theoria* refers not only to sight, but also to travel: the first theorists were those who traveled from polis to polis and were aroused to generate insight comparatively. See Peter Euben, "Creatures of a Day: Thought and Action in Thucydides," in *Political Theory and Practice: New Perspectives*, ed. Terence Ball (Minneapolis: University of Minnesota Press, 1977), 28–56. At stake in reclaiming a craftsperson ethos and epistemology

of engagement is a theory of how the mind is *moved* in corporeal and metaphorical travels to become educated dialogically.

While the Greeks rightly connected theory and bodily and imaginative travel, they undermined this possibility by separating observing from doing. Sennett notes that, by Aristotle's time, the theatrical actors had become professionalized and the audience—kept offstage—became mere speculative critics. In a profound sense, the pragmatist position that Sennett articulates seeks to reconnect the spectator and the performer by reclaiming the (pre-Aristotle) archaic theater in which spectators and performers repeatedly took each other's places. In thus connecting seeing, movement, and doing, our capacity for theory and practice are more powerfully and fully set in motion: "his or her arousal is more complete" (125). His point is not to dismiss the potential virtues of more distanced theoretical movement, but rather to supplement, correct, and animate it in relation to an epistemology and pedagogy emphasizing practices of engagement, for without the latter we easily become dogmatic—seeing what we already want to see no matter how much we move about.

6.   For "all skills, even the most abstract, begin as bodily practices," on the one hand, and "technical understanding develops through the powers of imagination," on the other (10). Our engagement with the world is indispensable because "materiality talks back, it continually corrects our projections" with experiences of complexity that resist, puncture, and spill beyond our simplifications (272).

7.   For Sennett, craftsmanship illuminates the discipline of sustained engagement that cultivates indispensable habits of mind, such as attentiveness to detail; learning from mistakes and thus diminishing our fear of them; developing a taste for "salutary failure" (97) and "generative crises" (113); developing a generative interaction between "honesty" (a tenacious sense of the "irregular" and "roughhewn" character of our world) and "fantasy"—the arousal of "intuitive leaps" from the sense that "what isn't yet, could be"—better understandings, tools, objects, relationships.

8.   We develop a facility to engage "tacit knowledge," both by questioning hidden assumptions and by drawing on latent understandings in order to make better use of them in new situations.

9.   So, too, it involves and cultivates what she called judgment, or the ability to "world travel" to other perspectives around the political table and broaden one's sense of the real in this process.

10. Sennett, *The Craftsman*, 265.

11. In this sense, vocation rightly understood has a profoundly embodied and expressive character that is intertwined with, yet exceeds, the epistemological and pedagogical links between the "head" and the "hand," insofar as it also involves the "heart." For a profound discussion of the interconnections of head, hands, and heart, see Marshall Ganz, "What Is Public Narrative?," *leadingchangenetwork.com/files/2012/05/What-is-Public-Narrative-Fall-2011.pdf*. For the relationship between radical receptivity and voice in grassroots democratic movements and broad based organizing, see Romand Coles, *Beyond Gated Politics: Reflections for the Possibility of Democracy* (Minneapolis: University of Minnesota Press, 2005); and Romand Coles and Stanley Hauerwas, *Christianity, Democracy, and the Radical Ordinary: Conversations between a Radical Democrat and a Christian* (Eugene: Wipf and Stock, 2007).

12. John Paul Lederach, *The Moral Imagination: The Art and Soul of Building Peace* (New York: Oxford University Press, 2010), 163.

13. Lederach, *Moral Imagination*, 165. This echoes the Quaker injunction to "let your life speak."

14. See Harry C. Boyte's opening essay to this volume, "Reinventing Citizenship as Public Work."

15. See also Bayard Rustin's essay, "From Protest to Politics: The Future of the Civil Rights Movement," *Commentary*, February 1965. In the numerous tables Boyte has provided to summarize and contrast his understanding of public work, dramatic forms of disruptive protest politics are always located in another column. See, for example, table 1, "Models of Democracy, Politics, and Citizenship," in Harry C. Boyte, *Everyday Politics: Reconnecting Citizens and Public Life* (Philadelphia: University of Pennsylvania Press, 2005), 93.

16. We use the concept of "breakthrough" similarly to that of both Theodor Adorno's Nietzscheian conception of breakthrough in late-period Beethoven and its adaptation by Thomas Mann in his novel *Doctor Faustus: The Life of the German Composer Adrian Leverkühn as Told by a Friend*, translated by H. T. Lowe-Porter (New York: Alfred A. Knopf, 1948). For a further explanation of the Mann-Adorno concept of breakthrough, see Rose Rosengard Subotnik, "Adorno's Diagnosis of Beethoven's Late Style: Early Symptom of a Fatal Condition," in *Developing Variations: Style and Ideology in Western Music* (Minneapolis: University of Minnesota Press, 1991), 15–41.

17. For more on CRAFTS and the ARTs at Northern Arizona University, please go to *www.nau.edu/CRAFTS* or *www.nau.ed/fyseminar*. See also Romand Coles and Blase Scarnati, "Supporting Students through Community Connections," *Diversity and Democracy: Civic Learning for Shared Futures* (American Association of Colleges and Universities)14, no. 3 (Fall 2011): 15; Harry C. Boyte and Blase Scarnati, "Building Democracy Colleges: A Different Kind of Politics," The Blog: Harry Boyte (blog), *Huffington Post*, May 3, 2012, *www.huffingtonpost.com/harry-boyte/ building-democracy-colleg_b_1471717.html*; and Harry C. Boyte and Blase Scarnati, "Transforming Higher Education in a Larger Context: The Civic Politics of Public Work," in *Civic Studies*, ed. Peter L. Levin and Karol E. Soltan (Washington, DC: Bringing Theory to Practice, 2014), 77–89.

18. There are currently sixteen ARTs at NAU, addressing issues as diverse as democracy education in K–12 schools (Public Achievement), sustainable food systems, energy, climate change, immigration, indigenous environmental issues, community-based enterprise and cooperative economic development, health, gender and sexuality, water conservation and rights, civil deliberation, and more.

19. The Immigration ART has sponsored speakers, debates, films, and deliberations. The Hot Topics ART, in collaboration with the Immigration ART, has sponsored forums for civil discourse on issues that seek to engage people and their views across the wide political spectrum found in Arizona. Others in the Immigration ART have collaborated with the group No Más Muertes (No More Deaths) in humanitarian aid initiatives to place water, food, and clothing at key outposts in the desert where many migrants lose their lives trying to cross the US-Mexico border. In collaboration with the Dreamers, the Immigration ART has drawn dramatic connections between the suffering and struggles of undocumented and queer people.

20. Going forward, we have established a new minor in civic engagement at NAU, which will begin enrolling students in the fall semester of 2014. In the civic engagement minor, students will explore the relationships between the discipline they study and a comprehensive knowledge of civic engagement history, theories, practices, and experiences. For more information on the civic engagement minor at NAU, see *www. nau.edu/CRAFTS* or *nau.edu/fyseminar*.

11

DISMANTLING INEQUALITY REGARDING SCHOLARSHIP

KerryAnn O'Meara

Despite significant efforts by some leading research and doctoral universities to disrupt the status quo,[1] status, legitimacy, and resources still tend to favor scholars and scholarship that add knowledge to disciplines over knowledge that is aimed at improving contemporary public problems. Though many colleges and universities have become Carnegie engaged, their "regard systems" lag behind their intentions to integrate public scholarship into institutional missions and faculty roles and rewards.[2] As a result, public scholars whom I have interviewed feel as if they have to "disappear for a while" from their public scholarship, or "shut themselves in a back room" in order to publish more traditional scholarship in their fields.[3] A complex system of higher regard for traditional scholarship, and neglect of or disregard for public scholarship, permeates most aspects of how faculty are recruited, socialized, evaluated, retained, and advanced on the tenure track in doctoral and research universities. Priorities and incentives within disciplinary associations and world and national ranking systems also contribute to this system that sustains traditional scholarship over public scholarship.[4]

The organizational systems that devalue public scholarship are very similar to what Joan Acker identified as "inequality regimes."[5] Although Acker's work refers primarily to how organizations, such as universities, maintain inequality for women, people of color, and other marginalized groups, I think the concept of inequality regimes as "interlocked practices and processes that result in continuing inequalities in all work organizations" (441) is instructive for understanding what needs to change in faculty roles and rewards to support engaged scholarship.[6]

Take for example two very self-motivated scholars. Emory and Eileen arrive at their institution, Research University, at about the same time. Emory is involved in interdisciplinary, translational research on health equity for Latino/Latina communities in the School of Public Health; Eileen studies string theory in the physics department. The university immediately sets up Eileen with a huge research lab and equipment totaling over a million dollars, while Emory is encouraged to seek funding from state grants and foundations for his work on race differences in awareness of health issues and heart and diabetes screenings. Eileen is asked to teach one class a year while Emory teaches four. Not surprisingly, after five years the investment made in Eileen pays off in federal research grants. She is heralded as one of the promising "star" scientists on banners that fly near the entrance to campus. Emory has found a way to partner with state governments to develop five community-run health screening centers, which have resulted in over ten thousand people being screened for diabetes, who would not have had this possibility. Emory's research, in partnership with a local health-related nonprofit organization, has reached the attention of the American Medical Association, is highlighted in a recent NIH report, and is regularly cited in local policy and op-ed discussions on health issues. However, Emory's colleagues are concerned about his chances for tenure. Emory's scholarship has not resulted in as many peer-reviewed articles as department colleagues deem appropriate or as many publications as his peer Eileen across campus, who will likely sail through the tenure process. Also, he often publishes papers and reports with partners from off-campus, which casts doubt as to whether he is really doing "research" or "service."

Several years later, Eileen is recruited for a faculty position by Stanford and provided a hefty retention offer. Emory on the other hand, who just squeaked through the tenure process, has linked his research to the local area and therefore does not pursue or respond to outside offers. As a result his salary is forever less than Eileen's despite stellar teaching evaluations and receiving the president's medal for service. Ten more years pass, and Eileen and Emory both serve on many campus committees together. Eileen's research receives awards from her disciplinary association and field, which improves her department and institutional rankings. She is given the title of "distinguished professor." When she participates in key committees and taskforces on campus, her views are taken very seriously by colleagues. Eileen knows she is a valued member of her institution and has achieved every bit of legitimacy, status, power, and resources it is possible to obtain at her institution, simply by doing the intellectual work she wanted to do and was good at.

Emory has not had the same experience. He has been an associate professor now for twelve years because his colleagues feel his research does not have enough citations in the Web of Science and do not value the local and regional impact of his work as much as international reputation and status. He has been an excellent university citizen, serving on many committees related to community engagement. However, he has noticed that he tends not to get appointed to some of the more important committees—those that distribute resources and convey status (such as committees that make decisions about faculty research grants, annual faculty awards for research, and promotion and tenure). When he is appointed to university committees, he has observed his opinion is not listened to or weighed as heavily as opinions of colleagues like Eileen or others from more traditional science, technology, engineering, and math (STEM) fields. He continues to love his work, and to maintain strong relationships with regional health organizations and health policy leaders. These colleagues and relationships allow him continuous feedback on the impact of his work on health disparity in his state. However, he knows that to advance at his university, he will need to shut himself away from these relationships for a while so he can do more theoretical work his department favors. Emory questions his value to his institution. There is a disconnect between the scholarship he loves and does so well and what his institution regards and rewards.

I want to make three observations about Emory and Eileen, who are both composite characters in institutional contexts threaded together from engaged and traditional researchers I have interviewed and learned from as colleagues in doctoral and research universities. First, although many scholars, including myself, have drawn attention to the bigger barriers and structures facing engaged scholars, such as graduate school socialization, the promotion and tenure process, and access to funding and faculty development,[7] systems of regard, as I have called them, are also an accumulation of smaller moments of affirmation or disregard.[8] Many engaged scholars receive awards from colleagues in the community engagement movement or from the community for their work. Yet on their own campuses they receive messages, similar to those described in gender studies as "little cuts" and/or microaggressions. Such messages send signals that public scholarship and those who do it are "less than" or not as good as those who do more theoretical bench science. Such messages are everywhere; they occur when public scholars are invited to serve on some committees and not others, when they receive annual merit reviews, when they see what is highlighted from the president's office or what is lauded as the most important kinds of faculty scholarship by offices of research. Similar to Acker's work on inequality regimes, the issue is not always how their work is discriminated against, as much as how much more others' work is valued. Thus, supporting public scholarship and public scholars means addressing the big barriers as well as the smaller but nonetheless pernicious inequalities described above.

Second, I intentionally positioned the traditional scholar as a female faculty member and did not note the race of either scholar to make the point that such inequality can occur among engaged scholars and traditional scholars regardless of faculty gender and race identities. However, many studies have shown women faculty and faculty of color are drawn to work that has relevance to contemporary public problems. Women and underrepresented faculty face established inequalities in research and doctoral universities based on their social identities, which are only compounded when they are also engaged in public scholarship. Such contexts are further complicated when we bring discipline and field into the picture, as many studies have shown STEM fields with significant federal and industry funding tend to have more power and legitimacy on campus than professional schools, social science disciplines, and the arts and humanities, where many public scholars reside.[9] Thus, reengineering research and doctoral universities to better support engaged scholarship cannot be separated from reengineering these spaces to have greater equality for women and underrepresented minorities, and greater equality in resources, prestige and voice among the disciplines on campus.

Third, imagine for a minute that department colleagues told Eileen that she could pursue string theory research if she wanted to, but she was unlikely to receive resources, status, legitimacy, or support from her institution to do so. Most people would see this as an issue of academic freedom. Why, therefore, is it not an issue of academic freedom for Emory to try to understand, and then impact, health disparity between Latina/o communities and white communities? I think part of the reason goes back to how these different research areas are valued by their institution.

There is an underlying assumption operating in the regard system described above, that Eileen is doing "real science" that is more complex, rigorous, and thus deserving of institutional support and stature. Interestingly this is not an assumption shared by the Bill and Melinda Gates Foundation, which committed $100 million to encourage scientists worldwide to fight our greatest health challenges—such as finding ways to provide vaccines in single doses for families that will not be able to travel back and forth to receive them, or developing low-cost nets to lessen the impact of insects in spreading diseases such as malaria and dengue fever. Likewise the National Academy of Engineering has adopted a set of twelve grand challenges, such as providing access to clean water, and restoring and improving urban infrastructure. Organizations that are hard at work trying to solve contemporary public problems have much evidence to suggest this work requires systematic, deep thinking, along with collaborations and partnerships, and is every bit as intellectually rigorous as the bench science developing cures for cancer, and theories related to how matter is organized in the universe. Such work, and the scholars doing it, deserve better. I believe the American Association of University Professors (AAUP) could play an important, reimagined role in supporting faculty careers and the public good mission of higher education institutions by publicly calling out universities that discriminate against scholars engaged in public scholarship, as an infringement on academic freedom.

It is true that the kinds of systematic disadvantages I have described present real barriers for engaged scholars and the work they are doing. However, there are also signs of hope. Disciplinary associations, national academies, NSF, and NIH, as well as many leading research universities, have taken steps to push for reform in academic reward systems; to provide funding, faculty development and mentoring for engaged scholarship; and to include community engagement in accreditation of academic programs. There are entrepreneurial, engaged faculty leaders who have found innovative ways to craft careers with one foot in the world of practice and one in academe, and do their best work because they hold both perspectives.

In conclusion, we are in a waiting period in many ways. As we wait for reforms to become the "new normal" it is critical to help engaged scholars navigate their academic homes, and find ways to thrive despite the existence of stated inequalities. Just as many doctoral and research universities have tried to alter the representation of women and minority faculty through affirmative action, cluster hires, and dual and career hiring, doctoral and research universities can take similar efforts to attract more public scholars to their campuses. Institutional leaders can recruit engaged scholars into their graduate programs, celebrate engaged departments on banners, and recognize the impact of such faculty members' work in addressing grand challenges and local public problems.

Research and doctoral universities are large, complex organizations with many subcultures and ways in which status, power, and information is transferred. There is not one thing that can be done to give public scholarship equal status. However, if we study, and try to dismantle the many organizational practices where implicit and explicit bias against public scholarship exists, our institutions will be better able to serve the public good, and to appropriately regard public scholars for their contributions to knowledge and our democracy.

Notes

1. Syracuse University, Tulane University, and University of North Carolina Greensboro for example, have all made efforts to revise academic reward systems.

2. John Saltmarsh, Dwight E. Giles Jr., KerryAnn O'Meara, Lorilee Sandmann, Elaine Ward, and Suzanne M. Buglione, "Community Engagement and Institutional Culture in Higher Education: An Investigation of Faculty Reward Policies at Engaged Campuses," in *Creating Our Identities in Service-Learning and Community Engagement*, ed. Barbara E. Moely, Shelley H. Billig, and Barbara A. Holland (Charlotte, NC: Information Age Publishing, 2009), 3–29.

3. KerryAnn O'Meara, *Because I Can: Exploring Faculty Civic Agency*, Kettering Foundation report (Dayton, OH: Kettering Foundation, 2010), *kettering.org/publications/because-i-can-exploring-faculty-civic-agency/*.

4. KerryAnn O'Meara, "Inside the Panopticon: Studying Academic Reward Systems," in *Higher Education: Handbook of Theory and Research*, ed. John C. Smart and Michael B. Paulsen, vol. 26 (New York: Springer, 2011), 161–220.

5. Joan Acker, "Hierarchies, Jobs, Bodies: A Theory of Gendered Organizations," *Gender and Society* 4, no. 2 (1990), 139–58.

6. Joan Acker, "Inequality Regimes, Gender, Class and Race in Organizations," *Gender and Society* 20, no. 4 (2006), 441.

7. KerryAnn O'Meara, "Faculty Civic Engagement: New Training, Assumptions, and Markets Needed for the Engaged American Scholar," in *To Serve a Larger Purpose: Engagement for Democracy and the Transformation of Higher Education*, ed. John Saltmarsh and Matthew Hartley (Philadelphia: Temple University Press 2011), 177–98.

8. O'Meara, "Inside the Panopticon."

9. Gary Rhoades and Sheila Slaughter, *Academic Capitalism and the New Economy: Markets, State, and Higher Education* (Baltimore: Johns Hopkins University Press, 2009).

12

THE EMERGING CITIZENRY OF ACADEME

Timothy K. Eatman

> Increasingly I find that the University
> is no place for humanity.
> —Humanities doctoral student

A Powerful Message about Graduate Education

As an educational sociologist, I am interested in the myriad issues of democratic equity and inclusion in higher education, and most especially in questions of the cultural dynamics associated with institutional transformation. This includes work with students, the full range of academic professionals and university leaders, community partners, and higher education associations, networks, and foundations. My aspiration is quite simply stated: to evoke, explore, enact, and expand the democratic potential of humanity through educational enterprises. And I believe that academe is a ripe milieu for such work. So when I received the message in my e-mail inbox from which the epigraph for this chapter is excerpted, it struck me powerfully; indeed it almost broke my academic heart.[1]

The message is one of the clearest expressions I have ever seen of frustration over the chasm between the actual functioning and the potential possibilities of higher education as a force for true democratic engagement in society. The young humanist whom I quote questions if the university should even be considered a place where humanistic concerns and ideals can be realized. It is a single voice from among the emerging citizenry of academe, but one I fear represents a pervasive and unfortunate attitude. One can only imagine the experiences and interactions that brought this young scholar to such a dismal place. But we in academe do not have to work very hard to imagine it.

We know the practices and rhythms of our work lives. We observe so many graduate students who are socialized to embrace (still in the twenty-first century) an Ivory Tower Academy (ITA) ideology that privileges a solipsistic frame for scholarly work. We feel the energy and sense of wholeness dissipate from those who initially entered the academy desiring to use the life of the mind to make positive change in the world. How often do we stand by as colleagues reject applicants for graduate work because their aspirations, which include community-engaged work, do not strike us as "scholarly enough," or how often do we fail to mentor students who struggle to assimilate into the normative flow of traditional knowledge production often because of the inequities embedded within our consciousness and structures about authority and knowledge?

We hear of emerging scholars who are persuaded to turn away from or "back burner" publicly engaged scholarly work that does not fit the traditional academic model. We shake our heads as early-career scholars become absorbed in community-based work only to learn that the available policies and evaluative models are still not sophisticated enough to appropriately consider and register the innovations and artifacts of their knowledge making and scholarly endeavor. Unfortunately this is often the case even when institutions have established policies that value engaged scholarship. And as a result their tenure and promotion is often thwarted. We know the deleterious impact that this has on their lives, their families, and our communities and institutions.

The Promise of Publicly Engaged Scholarship for Democracy

Lest I am perceived as overly dramatic or fatalistic I hasten to affirm my sense of hope. To be sure there exists a persisting cultural logjam characterized by Saltmarsh et al., who astutely observed that the civic engagement agenda runs against the institutionally normalized ways of knowing within academe; nonetheless I am encouraged about the future.[2] Indeed I have argued elsewhere that the arc of academic career bends toward publicly engaged scholarship, buttressed by evidence from a mixed-methods research study that I am conducting on the aspirations and decisions of graduate students and early-career publicly engaged scholars.[3] This chapter draws on some of these findings toward the promise of Publicly Engaged Scholarship (PES) for democratic engagement.

Higher education forms part of a broad-based movement that is uniquely positioned to bring concerted energy to bear on social equality. The history of the role that American higher education institutions have played in this regard, albeit in fits and starts with great variances of intensity, is substantial. Finding ways to value the true diversity of knowledge making is an important key to this work. PES makes possible a fluid, hybrid mix of socially responsive scholarly forms that emerge from and nourish the practices of students and professionals on and off campus who are academically inclined, civically conscious, and action oriented. It encompasses intellectual work that seeks to balance the need to know with the need for public problem solving, employing an integrated view of scholarly activity where research, teaching, service, and professional practice overlap and are mutually reinforcing; this is engaged scholarship across the faculty roles. And yet questions about the extent to which PES can be understood as a vehicle for catalyzing civic work identity warrants systematic inquiry.

Boyte's framing essay for this volume sets forward a challenge to appropriate the power within higher education to reflect and act. Urging an appreciation of his observation that "civic agency movements are appearing with growing frequency and also disappearing quickly," he asks and then quickly answers, "What will create foundations for sustaining them? A molecular organizing process that weaves alternative civic and political concepts and their corresponding practices into everyday life is the key." If it is viable to see higher education as "moving from objects of change to agents of change," as Boyte suggests, I believe that it requires organizing work on the front of institutional culture change. The essential elements of cultural change include understanding and relationship building. The socialization and nurturance of the pipeline of publicly engaged scholars warrants focused attention and analysis, leading to structural change. There is a need for much deeper knowledge about the emerging citizenry of academe. We need to know so much more about the full range of publicly engaged scholars from community-based professionals, graduate students, and contingent faculty to assistant, associate, and full professors, given their aspirations and decisions for career pathways and work.

So how do graduate students and early-career publicly engaged scholars see their status and prospects for publicly engaged work in and beyond institutions of higher education? The perspective represented by the emerging humanist at the beginning of this chapter notwithstanding, there is a strong current of emerging scholars who express civic engagement as an important dimension of their work. A letter to the editor of the *Chronicle of Higher Education* by Syracuse University graduate students,[4] and under the signature of publicly engaged graduate students from around the nation,[5] has the flavor of a molecular organizing process and the sense of hope that we would do well to catalyze. The graduate students were writing in response to an article in the *Chronicle* titled "Syracuse's Slide: As Chancellor Focuses on the 'Public Good,' Syracuse's Reputation Slides,"[6] which presented the disparaging view of a few selected faculty members who took issue with the emphasis that Syracuse University has placed on publicly engaged scholarship and full participation.[7] These young people do not mince words:

> We write to share our stories of engaged research, teaching, learning, and civic life as citizens of Syracuse, N.Y., and students of the university. Far from experiencing or perceiving a decrease in the rigor of our educational experience, we acknowledge what a privilege it is to grow in our disciplines through sharing and co-creating knowledge with diverse and valuable communities. In response to your article, one graduate student within our network posted the article on Facebook expressing outrage and dismay that work with, by, and for publics could be labeled as a "lack of commitment to significant scholarly work. " This may have been the spark out of which an alliance grew with the collective sense to speak back and express our belief that engaged scholarship powerfully adds to our academic experience, combats the out-of-date "Ivory Tower" metaphor, and rigorously contributes to our academic community.

The phrase "as citizens of Syracuse " and similar references in the letter of these emerging scholars evoking citizenship as identity particularly strike me. The coauthors articulate a bold connection between academic and civic identity; clearly they are pushing back against ITA ideology, something that rarely surfaces among their ranks within the academy. I also see in their letter an agentic posture that is consistent with the highest ideals associated with the life of the mind as pursued within the university context. There seems to be at least some space for humanity here. We turn to data from the aforementioned study for additional evidence of this ethos. But first it will be useful to evoke some historical context with an eye toward critical but unfortunate omissions that challenge the narrative and epistemology of engaged scholarship.

Forgotten Historical Roots of PES in Higher Education

This volume grows out of the American Commonwealth Partnership led by Harry Boyte at the invitation of the White House and launched in 2011 as part of a national organizing effort that pivoted on the sesquicentennial of the first Morrill Land-Grant Act in 2012.[8] Both Morrill I and II are public policies that are by nature intricately political and deeply consequential.[9] Unpacking this complexity goes beyond the scope this chapter. However, it is important to note here that the gravity of this legislative pair—offered by Senator Justin Morrill from Vermont—as it relates to the historical significance of democratic engagement has been grossly overlooked and understated. This is especially true as concerning the nexus of community engagement and access, diversity, and inclusion or full participation.

I maintain that it is not possible to grasp the fullest context of publicly engaged scholarship in the American context without examining the impact and implications of the Morrill Acts, including both contributions and challenges. We should not ignore the profound paradoxes that characterize them. For example, at the same time these acts can be understood as making an immeasurable contribution to the democratic underpinnings of society through higher education, they also serve as a powerful indicator of how deeply segregation was embedded in the prevailing social order of the times. Further, because of the divisive outcomes of the Morrill Acts they can be seen as a major structural support for the antithesis of democratic engagement especially regarding access and equity for women and people of color. The vestiges are apparent almost two centuries later.

There is much to be said for and celebrated about the contributions of the brilliant thinkers, theorists, and activists who have helped advance the discourse and practice about democratic engagement within the academy. Their names and work are cited often. However, as Stephanie Evans points out in her book *African Americans and Community Engagement in Higher Education: Community Service, Service-Learning, and Community-Based Research*,[10] we are fractured by what is seemingly a systematic failure to include the theoretical constructs and praxis of harbingers of publicly engaged scholarship who are outside of the mainstream of American institutions of higher education. W. E. B. DuBois, Septima Clark, George Washington Carver, Ella Baker and many others represent these omitted voices. This again calls the question, Is the university a place for humanity?

The nexus between engagement and full participation is palpable, but the structural realities of the formation and development of US higher education unfortunately serve to exclude important stories and perspectives that have the potential of contributing substantively to both the theory and practice of PES. For example historically black colleges and universities (HBCUs), many established under Morrill II, were and still are some of the best examples of democratically engaged institutions. These are places where the principles of civic duty can be seen in many aspects of the institution from curriculum to student and faculty and staff development. It may be argued that this is in part necessitated by the conditions of their founding. It may be that with respect to democratic engagement in American institutions of higher education HBCUs are like the catalyzing fungi of mycorrhizal symbiosis essential for the absorption of nutrients in the roots of a plant but little known. These institutions have played an essential role in preparing the minds and serving as a launching place for some of the most impactful and transformative leaders of the civil rights movement and generally in American society. Perhaps one way to address Boyte's challenge of molecular organizing is to remember what we have forgotten about the important role of these institutions as cultural incubators for civic professionals.

Ella Baker's life and work provide one shining example among many of effective but unsung civic professionals. After a robust baccalaureate experience she began work as a community organizer. Deeply engaged in communities with the focus of using her "work site as a civic site," Ella worked through many organizations to empower citizens for democratic participation.[11] Her particular methodology centered on broad-based leadership development to activate a core of individuals within communities to support civic amelioration. This represented a departure from hierarchical models, which pivot on the charisma and personality of what most often turn out to be male-dominated leadership spaces. Even as it is important to remember Ella and the type of civic professional that she represents it is useful to note the admonitions of Harold Cruse to the growing number of black scholars who succumbed to the assimilationist seductions of the ITA.[12] There are lessons to be learned from this history and especially from leaders of the South African black consciousness movement (see Mangcu in this collection), who advanced a cultural stance on the human condition that challenged the "Enlightenment rationality" that has been a dominant current in high-status institutions. In the United States as in Africa, it is crucial to expand awareness of these forgotten institutions and the individuals who were their creators and their stories and practices as an organizing resource for transformation.

Some of the Things We Know about Civic Professionalism and Publicly Engaged Scholars

When self-described publicly engaged scholars (N=509) were asked about their aspirations as it relates to ITA-connected careers, several important messages registered.[13] Four patterns that contain special relevance for the development of civic professionals from the findings follow:

1. Playing a role in enacting civic leadership, engagement and responsibility matter.
2. Expanding knowledge methods and/or scholarship in the discipline is as highly regarded as expanding the same in the public.
3. Early-career publicly engaged scholars hold low expectations for ITA, placing much value on PES in the future.
4. Institutions that value PES are seen as ideal places for work for those who aspire to academe.

In full disclosure I note that while the study of the aspirations and decision of graduate students and early-career publicly engaged scholars from whom I have drawn these findings speak to civic professionalism, it was not designed with civic professionalism as its primary focus. Rather the study sought to distill perspectives about graduate school experiences, career pathways, and contexts. We are using the research to establish profiles of self-identified publicly engaged scholars to learn about their educational and career aspirations, including reflections on their identity development, professional evolution, and motivations. Through the survey we first explore the degree to which mentoring and postsecondary experiences influence their interest in PES. Another section asks questions about the practice of PES as regards methodology and knowledge creation in the context of graduate school. The final section on aspirations probes what they see as viable career pathways. Focus distinctions notwithstanding, the research team has been struck by the importance of these findings to deepening understandings about how emerging scholars see their work connected to democratic engagement.

For example, when asked, "what do you hope to accomplish through your engaged scholarship?" approximately 68 percent of the respondents indicated "Enact or support civic engagement and responsibility." Forty percent of the respondents emphasized civic leadership in this regard. This suggests awareness about intersections among their scholarly work and democratic engagement. Although the awareness of these intersections registers high, respondents indicate that graduate school preparation is lacking. Respondents were asked, "Through your courses, mentoring, and advising, how much training did you get in engaged research methods (Community-Based Research, Participatory Action Research, public scholarship, community-engaged research)?" Almost 70 percent indicate less than average training. This represents an important area of focus for democratically engaged academic professionals. Dzur posits the importance of the role that pedagogy can play in graduate and professional preparation for careers in this regard.[14] Further, it is unfortunate that more than 50 percent of the respondents view the evolution of engaged scholarship over the next five to ten years as "a niche commitment among a few engaged faculty." Yet less than 1 percent believes that PES "will no longer be a topic area of interest in higher education." I am encouraged that there seems at least among this pool of respondents a permanence to the ethos of a democratically engaged academy.

Perhaps the clearest message concerning the work life of publicly engaged scholars from the data is that they have a great desire for positions at institutions that value publicly engaged scholarship, as 73 percent indicate it is important to extremely important. Dewey's ideal of professors being trained "to think in terms of their public function" may represent an important opportunity for the molecular organizing needed to advance civic professionalism, moving the Ivory tower academy to a more progressive stage of development.

Data from sixty semistructured phone interviewees also illuminate important patterns. One respondent reflects on the role that citizenship plays in her professional identity in a way that represents expressions from others. She says: "I cast myself as a citizen and I think that citizen whether it's in their professional work or in their free time it should in some sense be involved in public dialogue and . . . there's this other element to my publicly engaged scholarship that I call knowledge democracy. I believe academics, to the extent that we can, should be trying to institutionalize ways for knowledge to be diffused more widely and for more people to participate in knowledge." This quote reminds us that as Boyte has observed, "the commonwealth of knowledge is not a zero-sum dynamic." Building on the expressed inclination of publicly engaged scholars to help socialize them into greater sensitivity toward broadening participation in knowledge production through their work is one strategic way to advance actionable knowledge.[15] There are many impulses that drag academics away from the identity of citizen-scholar, but early findings from research suggest it is possible to rekindle this ethos.

If the university is a place for humanity, and I believe that it is, then it must rise to its ideals. First this means that we have to understand the role that institutions of higher education like community colleges, not just universities, play in the cultivation of democratically engaged scholars. We need to remember what we have forgotten about available resources including models and strategies from among HBCUs and philosophical approaches from engaged scholars who may be less frequently evoked in the discourse on publicly engaged scholarship. It also behooves us to systematically examine the aspirations and decisions of graduate students and early-career scholars. These constitute the emerging citizenry of academe.

Notes

1. The full sentence reads: "I am working on a dissertation in Modernist literature and American philosophy, teaching classes like 'Love in World Literature,' and 'American Identity in the World.' I know that such classes, as well as my own project speak to all of us on a human level, but increasingly I find that the University is no place for humanity."

2. John Saltmarsh, Matthew Hartley, and Patti Clayton, *Democratic Engagement White Paper* (Boston: New England Resource Center for Higher Education, 2009).

3. Timothy Kenneth Eatman, "The Arc of the Academic Career Bends toward Publicly Engaged Scholarship," in *Collaborative Futures: Critical Reflections on Publicly Active Graduate Education*, ed. Amanda Gilvin, Craig Martin, Georgia M. Roberts (Syracuse, NY: Graduate School Press, Syracuse University, 2012), 25–48.

4. Syracuse University Graduate Students, "Syracuse Graduate Students Embrace Change, *Chronicle of Higher Education*, October 23, 2011, *chronicle.com/article/ Syracuse-Graduate-Students/129497.*

5. Graduate students from the Publicly Active Graduate Education (PAGE) program sponsored by Imagining America: Artists and Scholars in Public Life played a leadership role in coauthoring this letter.

6. Robin Wilson, "Syracuse's Slide: As Chancellor Focuses on the 'Public Good,' Syracuse's Reputation Slides," *Chronicle of Higher Education*, October 2, 2011.

7. Susan Sturm, Timothy Eatman, John Saltmarsh, and Adam Bush, *Full Participation: Building the Architecture for Diversity and Public Engagement in Higher Education White Paper* (New York: Columbia University Center for Institutional and Social Change, 2011).

8. Morrill Land-Grant Act–I. (1862) 12 Stat. 503, 7 U.S.C. 301 et seq.

9. Morrill Land-Grant Act–II. (1890) ch. 841, 26 Stat. 417, 7 U.S.C. 322 et seq.

10. Stephanie Y. Evans, *African Americans and Community Engagement in Higher Education: Community Service, Service-Learning, and Community-Based Research* (Albany: State University of New York Press, 2009).

11. Barbara Ransby, *Ella Baker and the Black freedom Movement: A Radical Democratic Vision* (Chapel Hill: University of North Carolina Press, 2003).

12. Harold Cruse, *The Crisis of the Negro Intellectual* (New York: Morrow, 1967).

13. Tim Eatman, Staci Weber, Adam Bush, and Wendy Nastasi, *Study of Publicly-Engaged Scholars: Career Aspirations and Decisions of Graduate Students and Early Career Professionals and Practitioners*, research study (Syracuse, NY: Imagining America: Artists and Scholars in Public Life, 2013).

14. Albert W. Dzur, *Democratic Professionalism: Citizen Participation and the Reconstruction of Professional Ethics, Identity, and Practice* (University Park: Pennsylvania State University Press, 2008).

15. Edward P. St. John, *Research, Actionable Knowledge, and Social Change: Reclaiming Social Responsibility through Research Partnerships* (Sterling, VA: Stylus, 2013).

PART IV

From Citizen-Student to Citizen-Alumni: Students and Alumni as Agents of Change

How can today's college students and recent graduates—a more diverse population than ever before in the nation's history—become agents of constructive civic change, building a viable world, which they will inherit? This question is at the heart of this collection of voices and experiences on "citizen-students" and "citizen-alumni." This section includes a diverse group of organizers and thinkers who are at the cutting edge of developing a new story of the meaning of "student" and "alumni."

13

BECOMING A CIVIC ARTIST

Jamie Haft

It was one of those classes that always had a long waiting list—in this case, a class packed with theater students who, for one reason or another, had given up on their dream of starring on Broadway. Here, students didn't have to hide their cultural identities, their feelings for their home communities, or their concerns about social justice. There was hope in this classroom, but also an undercurrent of shame about leaving the professional performing arts' dominant paradigm. This feeling was compounded by stress about student loans and the notoriously high unemployment rate among artists. Here's a skit we improvised:

PROSPECTIVE ARTS STUDENT: Excuse me, are you an artist?

GRADUATE 1: I use the arts in the public school classes I teach helping middle school students learn to express themselves and understand the material from their other subjects in new ways. No, I'm not an artist.

PROSPECTIVE ARTS STUDENT: Are you an artist?

GRADUATE 2: I use art to facilitate community dialogues, with the goal of encouraging civic participation and changing local policy. No, I'm not an artist.

PROSPECTIVE ARTS STUDENT: Are you an artist?

GRADUATE 3: No, I use the arts to help people with spinal cord injuries find the will to go on. I'm not an artist.

PROSPECTIVE ARTS STUDENT: What about you—are you an artist?

GRADUATE 4: Yes, I am! I have a Bachelor's of Fine Arts, and now I'm temping by day and bartending by night—waiting for my big break on Broadway or in Hollywood!! I'm an artist!

If livelihoods weren't enough for arts students to worry about, many are feeling the tremors of escalating social problems just beyond their hermetic training studios. These include stark income disparity, environmental degradation, mass incarceration (a nation inside), and immigration issues—for starters. Hope for a reasonable collective future for my generation depends on beginning to solve such problems, and a democratic approach to the arts has the potential to help us do that. Unfortunately, in traditional arts training programs across the country, there are typically no courses about the history of democratic arts or about the possibilities of the citizen-artist; about the relationship of culture, power, and public policy; or about the ethical responsibilities of the nonprofit sector in a free-market economy.

The premise of this essay is that art, a devised expression of culture, is fundamental to individuals and communities becoming civic actors. Harry Boyte's essay argues that higher education has significant power to shape the civic identities and career plans of students. As it describes and analyzes a model curriculum for developing citizen-artists, my essay explores the opportunities and obstacles for students in arts training programs to embrace a broader conception of what an artist is and the role artists can play in advancing the ideals of democracy.

A Curricular Model: The Appalshop Immersion

One of the country's flagship community-based arts organizations is Appalshop in Whitesburg, Kentucky. Started in 1969 as part of Lyndon Johnson's War on Poverty, the Office of Economic Opportunity seeded job training programs in film for young people in a dozen communities with high rates of poverty. When the program was discontinued less than two years later, the young people at Appalshop, excited about the possibilities of telling the region's stories in the voices of the people who lived there, found the means to continue the work. They responded to the social and economic injustices around them through a full range of artistic forms, including the creation of scores of community-centered plays, the production of more than two hundred documentary films, the creation of hundreds of community-initiated radio documentaries and music recordings, and the founding of leadership programs to stimulate citizen participation in social reform and policy change. Appalshop's full- and part-time staff of thirty, most of whom have multigenerational roots in the Appalachian region, see themselves as citizen-artists.

In 2005, Dudley Cocke, artistic director of Appalshop's Roadside Theater, and Jan Cohen-Cruz, professor at New York University, developed a weeklong immersion in the theory and practice of community-based arts for the Scholars Program at New York University's Tisch School of the Arts. Taking place at Appalshop during New York University's spring break, the program was structured as an exchange between the Appalshop artists and Tisch students, faculty, and staff from departments including drama, musical theater, film, photography and imaging, and dramatic writing.

As part of the extensive preparation for the immersion, the Tisch contingent formulated inquiry questions for their hosts: "What is it like to be part of an intimate, creative environment so far from the mainstream of urban artistic activity? Can community-based work become too insular? How do people see Appalshop's place in the national arts community?"[1]

To answer these and many other questions, students, staff, and faculty engaged in an array of experiences: an intense twenty-four-hour production period in collaboration with Appalshop artists and their community partners making an original play, short film, set of photographs, music recording, or radio documentary; touring coal mining operations and learning about the history of the tightly-packed coal camps where the miners lived; discussing Appalshop's documentary films with their makers; listening to and talking with old-time musicians; appearing on Appalshop's 24/7 radio station, which streams live on the Internet and broadcasts to parts of five states; discussing the history and national policy environment of the community arts field; eating soup beans and cornbread; and square-dancing with local people—young, old, and in-between—at the Cowan Creek Community Center. It was an exhausting and exhilarating week.

Daily story circles were the glue that held all the activity together. They were facilitated using a particular methodology that Roadside Theater has developed for creating new plays and holding community dialogues. The concept of a story circle is inspired by traditional Appalachian and Scotch Irish storytelling, as well as practices used in community organizing and popular education, both of which were prominent in the US civil rights movement to which Appalshop owes a debt for its start. Roadside Theater's methodology has strict guidelines meant to give equal value to each individual's personal story and to deepen the collective story of the circle.

The Appalshop Immersion exposed students, faculty, and staff to principles for effective community work: that those with the most direct experience of a problem must lead the design and implementation of the solution; that constant attention, to all parts of the community, is a necessity; that sustainability depends on a transparent and iterative critical discourse to build and sharpen each participant and the group. It was emphasized that these principles rested on the fundamental concept of cultural equity: that all people everywhere have the right to inherit and develop their intellectual, emotional, material, and spiritual traditions. We all learned that the Universal Declaration of Human Rights (article 27, section 1) affirms this principle: "Everyone has the right freely to participate in the cultural life of the community, to enjoy the arts and to share in scientific advancement and its benefits."[2] It was our pledge of allegiance.

The most powerful aspect of the immersion for students was their experience of how community-based art reinforces their own cultural identity, something the Tisch training program was intent on stripping them of so they could be marketable in the mass popular culture. As one student confessed to all of us, "I put this pressure on myself when I'm at school to reject my community and my home. When I have the chance to write about it, I think, oh, it's not good enough for this class."[3] Another student elaborated: "Everyone thinks identity is an individual thing, and if you're not blazing your own path, tearing down traditions and creating something new, then it's not worthwhile. Even people who have influences try to like, claim it as their own. It's this shameful thing to be a part of something, especially at Tisch. It's nice to see artists who are just naturally following in the tradition and in others' footsteps."[4]

During the Immersion, Tisch students, who are typically pitted against each other vying for limited parts in main stage productions or a few slots in a talent agent showcase, rejoiced in having their peers as collaborators instead of competitors. Hierarchies dissolved as students, staff, and faculty worked together on equal footing. As one Tisch staff member admitted in the closing reflection circle: "It's been an amazing surprise to work with each of you students in story circles and projects, and just being in the van together. I have so much respect for all of you, and I'm going to take that back with me."[5]

The program was mutually beneficial for Appalshop participants. In addition to financially compensating the practitioners for their teaching, the exchange proved invigorating—as one Appalshop founder shared: "When you're hosting visitors, you see your community through their eyes, and, for me, that was part of what happened this week. In an organization we can take each other and our work for granted, and this was a way to reconnect."[6]

The weeklong Appalshop Immersion modeled a balance of three elements important to becoming a citizen-artist: community engagement; training in both aesthetics and community organizing; and scholarship about the history, animating ideas, and policy and economic environments of the community-based arts field. This triangulation for an exemplar curriculum was endorsed by Imagining America's 2008 national research study, "The Curriculum Project: Culture and Community Development in Higher Education." The study was based on twenty-eight in-depth interviews and 231 online survey responses. It valorized the hands-on community engagement that the Immersion represented, noting "that there is no substitute for placing one's body, mind, and spirit in the crucible of community work."[7]

Becoming a Citizen-Artist: Obstacles and Opportunities

A narrow conception of what it means to be an artist dominates the culture of arts departments, where many faculty are trained to believe in the imperative of individual genius, and therefore have little interest in the citizen-artist's high regard for amateur expression—for what folklorist Alan Lomax called the inherent genius of every cultural community.[8] In Harry Boyte's phrase, such arts departments need to transition from the cult of the expert to a community of experts. This pronounced bias for the individual expert reinforces major inequities in the professional arts industry, where the majority of arts funding goes to institutions focusing on the elite Western European canon and serving audiences that are predominantly white and wealthy.[9]

While each year's Appalshop Immersion had a profound impact on the visiting students, staff, and faculty, it had no effect on the structure of New York University. For Tisch School of the Arts, the program was regarded as extracurricular, offered no credits for students, and was financially possible only because of investments by the Scholars Program and a private foundation interested in the intersection of art and social justice.

As the opening skit playfully illustrated, the prospect for finding work as a citizen-artist is better than the prospect for those in the professional arts industry; however, the talent and training of citizen-artists is still woefully underemployed. As Goldbard noted in the Curriculum Project report: "In other regions of the world, public entities are the major sponsors of community cultural development work: throughout Europe, for instance, municipalities and neighborhoods employ community arts officers whose task it is to plan and coordinate program offerings for that area. In the developing world, educational and aid agencies employ community artists to engage people in envisioning and directing local community development efforts, or to take part in public campaigns such as health promotion."[10]

Unfortunately, the grassroots arts and humanities field itself is in a deep crisis. As Dudley Cocke documents in his 2011 essay, "The Unreported Arts Recession of 1997," community-based arts and public humanities institutions of any significant scale are in danger of becoming extinct.[11] The Immersion and the Curriculum Project study confirmed that such organizations are critical to advancing higher education's capacity to train a generation of citizen-artists. This issue is a major concern for the organization where I work, Imagining America: Artists and Scholars in Public Life, a national consortium of more than one hundred colleges working at the nexus of publicly engaged scholarship and the arts, humanities, and design.

Harry Boyte emphatically states in his essay, "Today, across the political spectrum, Americans feel powerless to navigate the changes and challenges of our time, from climate change to school reform, from immigration to joblessness and growing poverty." Community-based arts and the public humanities offer a store of resources to empower individuals and communities to be agents of change. Transforming the paradigm of professional arts training programs to prepare citizen-artists is an exciting direction for reinventing citizenship as public work.

Notes

1. Questions from NYU students participating in the March 2006 Appalshop Immersion, provided by Appalshop to the author.
2. The Universal Declaration of Human Rights, accessed November 27, 2013, at *www.un.org/en/documents/udhr*.
3. Quotes from the March 2006 Appalshop Immersion with NYU, transcribed by the author.
4. Ibid.
5. Ibid.
6. Ibid.
7. Arlene Goldbard, "The Curriculum Project Report: Culture and Community Development in Higher Education" (Imagining America: Artists and Scholars in Public Life, 2008), 18, accessed December 2, 2013, at *imaginingamerica.org/fg-item/the-curriculum-project-report-culture-and-community-development-in-higher-education/?parent=442*.
8. See Alan Lomax, "An Appeal for Cultural Equity" (1972), accessed December 5, 2013, at *www.culturalequity.org/ace/ce_ace_appeal.php*. From the Program of the Festival of American Folklife, ed. Thomas Vennum Jr., Smithsonian Institution, 1985. First published in *World of Music* 14, no. 2 (1972).
9. Holly Sidford, *Fusing Arts, Culture, and Social Change: High Impact Strategies for Philanthropy* (National Committee for Responsive Philanthropy, 2011), 1, accessed November 27, 2013, at *www.ncrp.org/files/publications/Fusing_Arts_Culture_Social_Change.pdf*.

10. Arlene Goldbard, "The Curriculum Project Report: Culture and Community Development in Higher Education" (Imagining America: Artists and Scholars in Public Life, 2008), 45, accessed December 2, 2013, at *imaginingamerica.org/fg-item/ the-curriculum-project-report-culture-and-community-development-in-higher-education/?parent=442.*

11. Dudley Cocke, "The Unreported Arts Recession of 1997" in *Research in Drama Education: The Journal of Applied Theatre and Performance* 16, no. 1, (Routledge, February 2011), 93–96, and accessed November 27, 2013, at *roadside.org/asset/ unreported-arts-recession-1997.*

14

WHAT'S DOCTORAL EDUCATION GOT TO DO WITH IT?: GRADUATE SCHOOL SOCIALIZATION AND THE ESSENTIAL DEMOCRATIC WORK OF THE ACADEMY

Cecilia M. Orphan

> Many experience their position in higher education as a
> very real struggle in which they are asked, for the sake of
> professional advancement, to set aside central convictions. . . .
> With the dangling carrot of professional stability and the
> stick of threatened banishment as incentives, scholars are
> asked to delay doing the work they're passionate about.
> —Kevin Bott

I will never forget what George Mehaffy told me when I started my doctoral program. "You are about to embark on the most powerful socialization process you will likely ever experience. Don't lose sight of why you're doing this." I nodded and listened with the perfunctory respect due my mentor and boss of five years, without fully letting his words permeate. Little did I know that George was trying to prepare me for a culture that was very different than any I had experienced up until that point. I went to graduate school to study higher education because I believe in public colleges and universities. Specifically, I believe in the power and potential of public higher education to build a stronger democracy. I have maintained this focus, though as George predicted, I have experienced a socialization process that has called many of my values and convictions into question. So just what happens in doctoral programs? And what does this have to do with public work?[1]

There has been sparse attention paid to the role of graduate school in the civic engagement movement,[2] with much of the literature focused on strategies for helping undergraduate students develop civic skills and efficacies.[3] Yet, many doctoral students become professors, and those professors become administrators who are ultimately responsible for the institutionalization and maintenance of civic engagement efforts.[4] These doctoral students undergo socialization processes within graduate school that prepare them for academic life, and just as George cautioned, this is a particularly powerful experience that warrants our attention.

Socialization refers to "ritualized processes that involve the transmission of culture,"[5] and these processes are both anticipatory and organizational.[6] Within higher education, the anticipatory component concerns the early messages sent to doctoral students about what academic life will be like. Organizational socialization occurs when graduates commence with academic careers.[7] For the purposes of this paper, I focus specifically on how well graduate programs act as anticipatory socialization processes in preparing doctoral students for academic public work. Academic public work is defined as: "Scholarly or creative activity integral to a faculty member's academic area. It encompasses different forms of making knowledge about, for, and with diverse publics and communities. Through a coherent purposeful sequence of activities, it contributes to the public good and yields artifacts of public and intellectual value."[8] We should be concerned with doctoral socialization because it is in part responsible for determining how receptive early-career faculty are to notions of academic public work and the essential democratic engagement of the academy. It is my belief that graduate programs fail to incorporate public work as a core value of academic life. Indeed, graduate socialization processes may actually detract from the formation of the public identities of doctoral students.

When I was deciding which graduate school to attend, I was invited to applicants weekends hosted by the universities I was applying to. These weekends allow universities to test-drive prospective admits and impress them with doctoral programs so these students choose to attend if they are selected. I applied to three public and two private universities. All of the universities I applied to have the designation of being "very high research," as determined by the Carnegie Classifications. This is not unusual as doctoral-granting institutions tend to have high research output. I suppose it is no surprise, then, that at one of these institutions, the dean, in his welcoming remarks, told students that if they came to this university, they would be trained as researchers. He specified that they would be trained to be researchers at *research 1 institutions*, and then in a conspiratorial tone he said, "and there are universities on that list we don't want you going to." The dean's remarks were met with laughter and knowing nods from the audience of applicants. Thus one of the first messages sent by the dean to prospective students was clear: what matters is research and employment at research-intensive universities. This is an example of what I believe to be the dominant socialization norms of graduate programs at work—the messages that are sent to prospective students about what is expected of them. While this is a blatant example of how doctoral socialization processes manifest themselves, there are subtle messages sent to doctoral students on a daily basis that are pervasive and often at odds with academic public work. Minding George's admonition to remember why I was applying to graduate school, I made clear my desire to be a publicly engaged scholar through my applications and interviews. I subsequently selected an institution and academic advisor that I knew would support my development in this way. Though I have a supportive advisor who measures my success in public work terms, I believe he is an exception to the dominant cultures within doctoral programs.

Students report that doctoral programs are primarily concerned with professional development with emphasis on career preparation.[9] There is often a lack of attention to helping doctoral students form identities around being public intellectuals. Upon acceptance into doctoral programs, students begin receiving messages about what constitutes "service," and this service is defined in terms of national service and service to academic disciplines. This initial eschewing of local engagement and public work for national service sets important precedents that are often carried throughout the lives of professors. Doctoral students are further encouraged to cultivate specificity and expertise in narrowly defined research topics, and to be the sole author of journal articles.[10] Students are also encouraged to become academic entrepreneurs through the pursuit of grant-funded research. The rise of this form of academic capitalism has coincided with a narrowing of the public mission of higher education and an expansion of its private purposes.[11] A manifestation of this shift in higher education has been the transformation of professors into academic entrepreneurs. The core message communicated by this rise in academic capitalism is that knowledge produced in the academy is proprietary—not public—and graduate students often internalize this norm.

Socialization operates formally and informally,[12] and in graduate school it is communicated by faculty members, student peers, and the institution.[13] Informal messages are sent to doctoral students that define success as employment at research-intensive universities with light teaching loads and large research budgets.[14] This message is sent most powerfully by doctoral advisors. Faculty often report being deeply satisfied with their lives within the academy,[15] and most have been employed by their institutions for several years. Many faculty are unfamiliar with other tracks outside of a research-intensive faculty life so it is not surprising that they would encourage their advisees to pursue similar pathways. Doctoral students also receive socialization through observing the rewards and incentives given to faculty, with more weight in evaluation processes given to research than teaching and service. Yet many graduate students report being uneasy about the publish or perish mentality that is dominant in tenure-track jobs.[16] I have spent time with doctoral friends across the country who are torn between wanting to fulfill the expectations of advisors of their becoming tenured faculty members immersed in research, and their own desire to live academic lives that embody public work. For all these reasons, doctoral students feel "that they must adjust or sacrifice their own interests and goals (often the very interests and questions that led them to graduate school) to fit the expectations and interests of their advisors."[17]

Fellow students are also a powerful vehicle of doctoral socialization. These messages are transmitted by what other graduate students respect and are impressed by. Doctoral students are often impressed by degrees from elite institutions, presentations at disciplinary conferences, publication in peer-reviewed journals, and research that is considered "cutting edge."[18] Presentation at practi-

tioner conferences and activist research is not given as much respect and attention. It is my belief that these messages often originate from faculty members and
are then relayed through fellow graduate students. Regardless of their source, the
effect of these peer messages is powerful and can discourage doctoral students
from pursuing public aspirations.

The final domain of graduate student socialization is delivered by the institution and often operates formally through program goals, admissions decisions,
and the isolation students experience from outside influences including other
disciplines, program models, and career paths.[19] Doctoral life is demanding and
can seem all-consuming. Gardner found that the formal commitments placed
on graduate students can create an isolating effect that reinforces the socialization process.[20] The primacy of research is also communicated through the formal
expectations placed on doctoral students. Many are expected to produce a great
deal of research and then teach, but the most emphasis is placed on building
a researcher portfolio and identity. Another formal message concerning what
it takes to be successful in academic life is who is competitive in application
processes. Applicants are advantaged if they already hold degrees from research-
intensive institutions and have identified specific, narrowly focused research interests that are disciplinary based.

Despite these dominant socialization processes there exists evidence that not
all doctoral students aspire to follow traditional academic pathways.[21] There are
many doctoral students and early-career faculty who desire lives of meaningful
public work. Indeed many report public goals as the primary driver for attending graduate school.[22] So what might graduate school socialization look like that
has the goal of developing students as public academics? Imagining America
(IA) has been a leader in conceptualizing faculty life as publicly engaged, and
two reports from IA are particularly instructive. These reports are focused on
faculty life; however I think graduate programs can glean lessons from their
findings. The first is *Full Participation*, which describes the desire felt by many
faculty, especially those in the early stages of their careers, to be publicly active.[23]
Full participation refers to institutional support for faculty who wish to integrate the three primary dimensions of academic life—research, teaching, and
service—under the banner of public work. In a related study about publicly engaged scholarship, Eatman made several recommendations for reshaping faculty
life in support of fostering full participation including developing peer review
processes that include nonacademics, the production of diverse scholarly products, encouragement to pursue nonacademic career paths, and interdisciplinary
approaches to scholarship (as opposed to the narrowly focused norms of doctoral programs).[24] In light of these two reports, the question becomes how might
we incorporate norms around full participation and academic public work in
graduate school?

I believe doctoral socialization processes could be reshaped to embrace public academic work and full participation in the following ways. The first would
be to change formal policies so that doctoral students are required to complete
public service as part of their programs. Doctoral programs could also encourage interdisciplinary scholarship that integrates a variety of theoretical and

disciplinary approaches, and doctoral students could be encouraged to select research and dissertation topics that embody public work. Informal and formal messages should be intentionally communicated that honor the multiplicity of career pathways available to doctoral students after graduation, one of which is that of being a public intellectual. Doctoral programs that embrace public work would also encourage doctoral students to produce scholarship that is publicly available, and is written in an accessible format so that lay audiences can understand the findings. The overarching goal of such scholarship would be to leverage knowledge to build a stronger democratic society. Last, and perhaps most important, established faculty members are pivotal to reimagining doctoral programs. Mentoring is a key component of doctoral programs, and Eatman advocates for the mentoring of graduate students by other public intellectuals through the encouragement of scholarly products that are shared with the public.[25] Faculty modeling should also communicate the importance of public engagement. The faculty within my program act as public intellectuals—they are highly productive researchers and they also speak on National Public Radio, write opinion pieces for local and national media outlets, and volunteer in their communities. This sends important signals to my fellow doctoral students about what faculty life should look like—life that is not spent solely within the walls of an ivory tower but also spent producing public knowledge and laboring in public spaces.

A year into my doctoral program, George told me that he was glad that I was resisting the dominant socialization processes. I told him that I was lucky to have a good advisor. He responded that this was true—I did have a good advisor—but that public work is part of who I am, and the doctoral socialization process, no matter how powerful and convincing, was not going to change that. When George said this, I was reminded of what often happened when he and I made presentations to faculty audiences about the American Democracy Project (ADP), a national civic engagement initiative we co-led that is focused on helping universities and colleges institutionalize public engagement. Inevitably there would be at least one senior professor who would approach us at the end of our presentation and say something to the effect of, "This is why I became a professor. I wanted to make the world a better place, I wanted to be publicly engaged. Somewhere along the way through graduate school and tenure and promotion, I lost sight of that. Thank you for reminding me of why I got into this." The "losing sight" of public aspirations these faculty members shared speaks to the effects of academic socialization processes that fail to advance public work and engagement. I wonder what happens to those doctoral students who have not been socialized to the democratic role for higher education. Will they also "lose sight" of nascent public aspirations and have similar regrets later in life?

Socialization is a powerful mechanism for perpetuating cultural norms and practices and determines organizational operations and values.[26] If we are serious about reclaiming academia's essential public work as an animating theme of university life, we must attend to the powerful socialization process that occurs during graduate school. Ultimately graduate schools should socialize future faculty and administrators to value higher education's role in democracy. During my years at ADP, we spent ample time helping universities reshape faculty socialization processes, our recommendations being to reform faculty rewards and tenure requirements, and convocation and orientation events so that they advance public work. We also reminded administrators to use their bully pulpits to advocate for civic engagement. These same strategies need to be used in doctoral programs if we are truly going to transform higher education into an engine of democracy.

Notes

1. The epigraph for this chapter is from Kevin Bott, foreword to *Collaborative Futures: Critical Reflections on Publicly Active Graduate Education*, ed. Amanda Gilvin, Georgia M. Roberts, and Craig Martin (Syracuse, NY: Graduate School of Syracuse University, 2012), iv.

2. Amanda Gilvin, Georgia Roberts, and Craig Martin, *Collaborative Futures: Critical Reflections on Publicly Active Graduate Education* (Syracuse, NY: Graduate School of Syracuse University, 2012).

3. Elizabeth Beaumont, Thomas Ehrlich, and Josh Corngold, *Educating for Democracy: Preparing Undergraduates for Responsible Political Engagement* (San Francisco: Jossey-Bass, 2007); Dan Butin, *Service-Learning in Theory and Practice: The Future of Community Engagement in Higher Education* (New York: Palgrave MacMillan, 2010); Peter Levine, *The Future of Democracy: Developing the Next Generation of American Citizens*, (Lebanon, NH: University Press of New England, 2007).

4. Stephen Percy, Nancy Zimpher, and Mary Jane Brukardt, *Creating a New Kind of University: Institutionalizing Community-University Engagement* (Boston: Anker, 2006).

5. William Tierney and Robert Rhoads, *Enhancing Promotion, Tenure and Beyond: Faculty Socialization as a Cultural Process* (San Francisco: Jossey-Bass, 1993), 21.

6. Pilar Mendoza, "Academic Capitalism and Doctoral Student Socialization: A Case Study," *Journal of Higher Education* 78, no. 1 (2007), 71–96.

7. Ibid.

8. Julie Ellison and Timothy Eatman, *Scholarship in Public: Knowledge Creation and Tenure in the Engaged University* (Syracuse, NY: Imagining America, 2008), iv.

9. Susan Gardner and Benita Barnes, "Graduate Student Involvement: Socialization for the Professional Role," *Journal of College Student Development* 48, no. 4 (2007), 1–19.

10. Mendoza, "Academic Capitalism."

11. Elizabeth Berman, *Creating the Market University: How Academic Science Became an Economic Engine* (Princeton, NY: Princeton University Press, 2012).

12. Edgar H. Scheid, *Organizational Culture and Leadership*, 3rd ed. (San Francisco: Jossey-Bass, 2010).

13. Ann K. Bragg, *The Socialization Process in Higher Education* (Washington, DC: George Washington University, 1976).

14. Ann E. Austin, "Preparing the Next Generation of Faculty: Graduate School as Socialization to the Academic Career," *Journal of Higher Education* 73, no. 1 (2002), 94–122.

15. Collaborative on Academic Careers in Higher Education, *Selected Results from the COACHE Tenure-Track Faculty Job Satisfaction Survey* (Cambridge, MA: Harvard University Graduate School of Education, 2010).

16. Austin, "Preparing the Next Generation."

17. Ibid., 98.

18. Gardner and Barnes, "Graduate Student."

19. Bragg, *The Socialization Process.*

20. Susan Gardner, "Faculty Perspectives on Doctoral Socialization in Five Disciplines," *International Journal of Doctoral Studies* 5 (2010), 39–53.

21. Gilvin et al.

22. Ibid.; Gardner and Barnes.

23. Susan Sturm, Timothy Eatman, John Saltmarsh, and Adam Bush, *Full Participation: Building the Architecture for Diversity and Public Engagement in Higher Education (White Paper)* (Columbia University Law School: Center for Institutional and Social Change, 2011).

24. Timothy Eatman, *Collaborative Futures: Critical Reflections on Publicly Active Graduate Education* (Syracuse, NY: Graduate School of Syracuse University, 2012).

25. Ibid.

26. Scheid, *Organizational Culture.*

15

FOSTERING CIVIC AGENCY BY MAKING EDUCATION (AND OURSELVES) "REAL"

David Hoffman

What Does Democracy Feel Like?

What does democracy feel like? More specifically, what is it like to be a college student discovering the capacity to work with others to produce positive social change? These questions are rarely asked, but their answers have enormous implications. If higher education is to respond effectively to Harry Boyte's call for a new synthesis between workforce preparation and democratic engagement, Rom Coles and Blase Scarnati's vision of a renewed ethos of craft, or Adam Weinberg's call to coach and train students in the art of public work, its strategies should emerge from insights about students' lived experiences of achieving civic agency.

At the University of Maryland, Baltimore County (UMBC), we are in the thick of a broadly inclusive campus-wide organizing process built in part on insights and contributions from undergraduates who had experienced extraordinary growth as civic agents. The early results are inspiring. Students, faculty, and members of the campus administration are working hand-in-hand to deepen our democratic culture and practices, and they are succeeding.

Undergraduates Becoming "Real"

UMBC is a midsized public research university with an emerging national reputation for innovation. Led for more than twenty years by President Freeman A. Hrabowski III, who participated as a twelve-year-old in the in the 1963 Children's Crusade for civil rights in Birmingham, Alabama, and now chairs President Obama's Advisory Commission on Educational Excellence for African-Americans, UMBC has achieved distinctive success in preparing underrepresented minorities for graduate school, especially in the STEM disciplines (science, technology, engineering, and mathematics). For the past six years running, *U.S. News and World Report* has ranked UMBC number 1 on its list of national universities "making the most promising and innovative changes in the areas of academics, faculty and student life."[1] UMBC's longstanding commitment to democratic values is embodied in the Shriver Center (named in honor of Sargent and Eunice Kennedy Shriver), a hub of service learning and community engagement, and in a robust tradition of shared campus governance.

In order to gain insights about UMBC undergraduates' civic agency journeys, I conducted a study involving a small number of students who had been active and effective agents of change on campus and in communities beyond the campus.[2] In a series of one-on-one interviews and focus groups sessions, I worked closely with the students to explore how they had developed the inspiration, critical awareness, and sense of self-efficacy needed to make civic contributions—beyond participation in mass rituals such as voting—which they regarded as profoundly meaningful and authentic expressions of their free will, and which they perceived as transforming their own lives by expanding the scope of their free will. I wanted to learn how they were making sense of their experiences and environments as they "read the world" for evidence of the liberating potential of civic involvement and their capacity to govern and change their communities.[3] My research methodology—hermeneutical phenomenology—involved storytelling and collaborative meaning making.

My initial interviews with the five students with whom I worked most extensively lasted a total of 221 minutes.[4] In those interviews I used the words "real" and "really" a total of seven times, often in the context of expressing that I "really" appreciated their volunteering to participate. The students, on the other hand, used the words "real" and "really" 314 times. Often they used those words in order to express the strength of a conviction or emotion. But as I transcribed the interviews, reflected on the students' stories, and engaged them in subsequent conversations, it became clear that the words carried other meanings as well. For those students, civic agency and the experiences that gave rise to it *felt real* in a way that many of their previous experiences had not. In its original usages in medieval Britain and France, the word "real" referenced the objective, concrete existence of a thing outside of people's imaginations and the beauty and majesty of royalty.[5] Many of the students' invocations of the term seemed to carry resonances of both of these definitions: of genuineness and tangibility that was also special, rich, and noble. "Real" people and communications were honest, open and humane rather than phony, manipulative, and mechanical. "Real" situations were organic and fluid rather than manufactured and predetermined.

The students had spent much of their lives immersed in everyday worlds they had experienced as fundamentally unreal: structured around falsehoods, hidden agendas, or scripts. At UMBC, their sense of unreality had been greatest in courses in which the content had felt disconnected from practical applications and outcomes; in peer interactions in which others seemed to be going through the motions and playing games rather than communicating from the heart; and in conversations with some faculty and staff members who subtly objectified them, sometimes simply by lavishing them with praise they did not feel they deserved. The students also described occasionally discouraging encounters with administrators in the context of advocating for changes on campus, the most typical of which involved what they perceived as disingenuous, bureaucratic, conflict-suppressing, "what a nice idea!" brush-offs.

Against the backdrop of these unreal-seeming experiences and encounters, the students achieved most of their civic agency gains in two ways. One was by causing visible, meaningful changes in people and situations. Among their transformative experiences were participating in program and budget decisions and then seeing their consequences; launching a new organization and having it embraced by UMBC staff and students; and engaging in conversations with peers, faculty members, and administrators that altered the mindset or behavior of the other participants. Observing the changes they had made, the students drew the inference that they were actually present in a world that could be altered through their actions and experienced themselves as newly visible and alive. Inspired and empowered, they approached subsequent opportunities to make a meaningful difference with new eagerness and confidence, feeding what became a virtuous cycle of experience, reflection, and growth.

The students also drew profound inferences about their agency and capacity to make a difference from authentic interactions that departed from the usual scripts. Many of these conversations occurred outside the context of any experience designed to foster democratic engagement. For the students, simply being seen and appreciated when they did not expect to be, and transcending the constraints of agency-inhibiting roles to achieve a mutual and genuine presence with others, inspired a greatly expanded sense of efficacy. Having cocreated and experienced a fluid space of mutual authenticity (even in circumstances disconnected from nominally civic work), the participants experienced themselves anew as subjects rather than objects, human beings rather than actors on a stage, and potential agents of change in a world of real possibilities.

Some of the students' civic agency gains did occur in the context of activities designed for that purpose, but less frequently so than a university educator might hope. Designed activities are both useful and inevitable in higher education: they create occasions for learning and partition experiences into controllable increments of time, task, and topic; and they enable us to gauge progress, manage outcomes, and measure and acknowledge achievement. But the stories of the UMBC students with whom I worked suggest that *the very fact that activities had been designed* may have discouraged students accustomed to powerlessness in educational settings from perceiving them as real. When the students achieved civic agency gains through such activities, it appears to have been because the experiences felt real *despite* having been partitioned from everyday life, because the designers had found ways to foreground the participants' agency and so forestalled their reading the situations as completely artificial.

A part of the significance of calls like Harry Boyte's to foster convergences between education for workforce development and for democratic engagement is that doing so can help make learning *feel more real*, and so more likely to empower. One less partition means one less potentially agency-undermining symbol of educators' power to frame and constrain students' experiences. The challenge for educators pursuing any democratic engagement strategy, including Adam Weinberg's excellent suggestions to train students as organizers and expose them to civic mentors, is to avoid inadvertently signaling to students that they are involved in simulations designed for their educational benefit and not real life.

BreakingGround at UMBC

UMBC's BreakingGround initiative is an ongoing, institutionally supported organizing process led by a team of students, faculty, and staff, inspired in part by Harry Boyte's theoretical work on civic agency and by the American Democracy Project, American Commonwealth Partnership, National Task Force on Civic Learning and Democratic Engagement, Imagining America, and other higher education collaborations in which the contributors to this volume have participated. Formally launched in fall 2012, BreakingGround builds on many years of work at UMBC, including research by engaged scholars, courses with applied learning components, Shriver Center programs, and coaching and support for student leaders through the Division of Student Affairs. Some of Breaking-Ground's most important UMBC forerunners were student initiatives, including the intentional transformation of UMBC's Student Government Association (SGA) from a minimally empowered student legislature with a service delivery arm into a catalyst for all students' engagement as producers of the campus community. The SGA's signature initiative, Prove It!, challenges students to develop practical plans to solve problems and create new resources on campus and backs the winners with grants, stipends, and guidance through the implementation process. Winning projects have included the development of a Wi-Fi plaza above the campus pond, the production of biodiesel fuel out of waste oil from campus eateries, and the use of colorful, student-designed fiberglass statues of UMBC's retriever mascot to promote unity and a sense of affiliation.

Drawing in part on stories and insights shared by the students in my study, BreakingGround aims to promote civic agency primarily by nurturing and making visible an already robust campus culture and practices that help people experience themselves, their relationships, and their potential to produce social change as *real*. Two BreakingGround grant programs established by UMBC provost Philip Rous support curricular innovations and community projects with civic agency at their core. A BreakingGround website (*umbcbreakingground .wordpress.com*) features first-person narratives from UMBC change agents: students and nonstudents on equal footing. Often their stories involve breaking through traditional higher education partitions to find ideas, partners, and support across disciplines and divisions. The stories relate to individual initiatives and established campus programs; research, teaching, and service; activity on campus and beyond; the past, present, and future; one-time events and life-long commitments. With remarkable rapidity, BreakingGround has become a prominent cultural reference point, linking disparate people, programs, and events in a common narrative of civic possibility. The initiative's components are evolving organically as more people work with BreakingGround's diverse team of organizers to identify ways to deepen and express their own capacity and desire to shape our world together, and launch or connect with civic projects, many of which predate BreakingGround but had not previously been visibly linked.

The process at BreakingGround's heart is a series of real conversations. There is strategy and design behind them: the initiative's organizers have sought out people on campus who have seemed to embrace or demonstrate civic agency, or who have been in a position to help support its promotion on campus. But the conversations have been essentially free of maneuvering and salesmanship. Mostly we have asked students, faculty, and staff about their own experiences with civic agency (though typically not in those words) and have sought to make the road to BreakingGround's objectives by walking it with them.

Because our goal for BreakingGround is to foster an inclusive *culture* of civic agency, my colleagues and I have been very careful to avoid agency-dampening partitions wherever possible. The last thing we want is for BreakingGround to become confined in its own bureaucratic and cultural silo, with its own instructors or managers responsible for delivering a curriculum or set of experiences to student consumers, and the rest of the campus implicitly relieved of any responsibility for civic agency. We have been intentional about including people with different kinds of institutional affiliations as full partners in Breaking-Ground's development and implementation. The core organizing team includes undergraduate and graduate students, faculty, and staff members. Members of this working group coordinate an abundance of creative work going forward across the campus without directly controlling any of it, an arrangement that has worked remarkably well because of the enthusiasm and good will of participants inspired and bonded by the cocreative process.

One of the working group's most important strategic decisions has been to banish what we call "institutional voice" from all communications relating to BreakingGround. This is another refusal to erect an agency-dampening partition. We want people at UMBC to view BreakingGround as our collective work and culture, not as a separate entity with a mind of its own. If Breaking-Ground ever addressed them ("BreakingGround asks . . ."; "BreakingGround recommends . . ."), then symbolically it would be excluding them. So "Breaking-Ground" never takes action, hosts events, sends invitations, or sponsors programs; people and groups do. No story ever appears on the BreakingGround website without a named individual author (complete with a photograph). Partly as a result, BreakingGround has resonated across campus as a grassroots expression of our common values that is neither coercive nor manipulative. Breaking-Ground is simply, and increasingly, who we really are.

At times the work of developing, implementing, and extending Breaking-Ground has been messy. Real conversations take time. For many of the people who have contributed their talent and care to BreakingGround, the work has been at the periphery of their primary campus roles, although increasingly they are finding ways to move it to the core. As new components have generated interest on campus, we have struggled to focus attention on how BreakingGround emerges from, leverages, and links longstanding efforts and campus traditions. And we have wrestled with the usual tensions and ambiguities involved in developing community partnerships that serve and empower all participants, both on and off campus. BreakingGround has benefited enormously from support from UMBC's most senior leaders, but those leaders may depart in time, and take their enthusiasm with them. In a period of scarcity, it is possible that Breaking-Ground could come to be viewed as a secondary concern for the campus, a luxury we can no longer afford. But our progress to date has been promising. Harry Boyte has called BreakingGround:

> a window into a remarkable, ongoing process of engagement at UMBC, which has made the university a model for hundreds of colleges and universities across the country. . . . Students have been agents of constructive change. They have helped to co-create pioneering approaches to teaching and learning, public problem solving, and productive alliances with faculty, staff, and administrators. In the process, students and their partners in academic and student affairs with passion, energy, and talent have shown the powerful desire among young adults today to become part of the transformation of education, higher education, and the wider democracy: architects not objects of the changes sweeping our society.[6]

Rutgers University–Newark chancellor Nancy Cantor, another contributor to this volume, remarked that when it came to civic engagement, UMBC had "long ago leapt beyond 'let's pretend,' and the BreakingGround initiative testifies powerfully to that. . . . It's not just an activity, it's your identity."[7] Like democracy itself, BreakingGround is a journey rather than a destination, and only in its early stages. But it is a process through which many at UMBC are finding ways to enact their values and identities in collaborative work for the common good.

Conclusion

Both my research with UMBC students and our campus experience with BreakingGround point to the proposition that if higher education is to fulfill its potential as a forum for democratic renewal, students must be involved in the process as agents rather than objects. For faculty and staff, that means approaching teaching, learning, and democratic engagement initiatives with a kind of directness and humility: a willingness to share power and status, forego pretensions, avoid assertions of absolute mastery, and allow collaborative work to unfold without knowing exactly where it will lead. That kind of humility runs against a culture in much of American higher education that demands expertise, control, predictability, and efficiency. But as we are discovering at UMBC, it is possible to cultivate a new consciousness and commitment to fostering realness and agency, and to take care to avoid reinforcing the unreality (and consequent powerlessness) many of us, especially students, are likely to have experienced elsewhere in our lives. All of us, educators and students alike, have the potential to help each other in this process, and to build our collective power on the foundation of our common humanity. We do so in part by tempering our designs with appreciation for our mutual capacities as cocreators of our lives, institutions, and world, all of which we may yet make real together.

Notes

1. *U.S. News and World Report*, "Up-and-Coming Schools: National Universities" in *Best Colleges, 2014 Edition* (September 10), accessed online February 14, 2013, at *colleges.usnews.rankingsandreviews.com/best-colleges/rankings/national-universities/up-and-coming*.

2. The study, entitled "Becoming Real: Undergraduates' Civic Agency Journeys," constituted my dissertation research for UMBC's doctoral program in Language, Literacy and Culture.

3. Paulo Freire and Donaldo Macedo, *Literacy: Reading the Word and the World* (Westport, CT: Bergin and Garvey, 1987).

4. The students were Yasmin Karimian, Stefanie Mavronis, Richard Blissett, Kati Henry, and Jae Song (a pseudonym).

5. *OED Online* (Oxford: Oxford University Press, September 2013), accessed on line September 28, 2013, at *www.oed.com/view/Entry/158926*, s.v. "real, adj.2, n.2, and adv."; *OED Online* (Oxford: Oxford University Press, September 2013), accessed on line September 28, 2013, at *www.oed.com/view/Entry/158925*, s.v. "real, adj.1 and n.1."

6. Harry C. Boyte, e-mail message to author, July 26, 2013.

7. Nancy Cantor, *UMBC Spring 2013 Honorary Degree Speech*, video file (May 23, 2013), accessed online February 14, 2014, at *www.youtube.com/watch?v=YFXB1awvibc*.

16

THE CIVIC CREATIVITY OF ALUMNI

Julie Ellison

The energy of educated young people committed to working for the public good is a crucial force for change in every nation. Collectively, the many voices of this symposium urge us to work in fellowship with college students moving into lives in which they seek to thrive as active citizens. How, then, do we respond to the aspirations of publicly committed graduates? How can those of us who work in colleges and universities encourage the civic life choices of current students, while also building networks of former students? How can we see, value, and collaborate with public-minded alumni, while also crafting new ways for them to relate back to campus?

There is an emerging movement by, for, and with civically engaged alumni. Promising strategies form part of the larger work of "re-growing the everyday relationships" needed to reconnect colleges to their regions.[1] But if we think more expansively, the regional meaning of the college's public purpose can extend to the aggregated civic efforts of its graduates in their own communities, near *or* far from campus. Colleges and universities are beginning to view their region as encompassing the distributed agency of former students in the places where they live and work.[2]

Happy Graduation. Now What?

A collection of cards on display in June 2012 at a bookstore near Columbia University shows the depth of our intergenerational discomfort surrounding college graduation. The "voice" of the cards is that of a sardonic parent addressing a graduating daughter or son: "This diploma represents the completion of your degree. It also marks the beginning of your student loan repayment. *This is far from over.*" "Happy Graduation IOU. . . . *Void when you start contributing to society.*" "No, you can't move back in with your parents. . . . Yet. Congrats graduate!" "You now owe your parents $114,291.56. Plus books. Congratulations grad." Or, most succinctly, "Happy graduation. Now what?" Graduation, therefore, while it remains a ceremonious occasion of congratulation, has also become a matrix of intergenerational stress. The divorce of meanings and measures appears in the two tracks of our language: publicly singing, at commencement, the individual and collective achievements of new graduates over a discouraging counterpoint of rueful, ironic, or embittered truth telling about indebtedness and under- or unemployment.

New graduates, alums in the postgraduate gap years, and long-situated alumni can be forthright about the frustrations of publicly active alumni. Alumni associations and outreach programs come in for their share of criticism, which tends to focus on their practices of inclusion and exclusion as well as the unrelenting barrage of their electronic and hard-copy solicitations.

One recent graduate objected to the "clubhouse" culture of the alumni association, calling it tilted toward potential major donors, perpetuating social litmus tests. A graduate in his forties critiqued his experience of alumni involvement in student recruitment. He was frustrated in his desire for deeper levels of engagement:

> I was asked to make phone calls, ask students to come to the university, did this for a little bit, then I asked, please let me know, are any of these students actually coming to the university? No, we can't tell you. Now, I can look at the student directory. But that's not the point. You have a whole department doing this. Do you even care? I stopped doing this six or seven years ago. Just last week I got a recruitment packet. Nobody even cares enough to look at the list and say, "this guy's not doing it anymore and take him off the list."

But many recent graduates tell a more optimistic, though still critically observant, story. Though certainly anxious about finding work that pays and matters, they are motivated by experiences in college that encouraged them to see themselves as "democratic professionals" able to find the publicness in their work, whatever their work turns out to be.[3] This is particularly true of those who, as college students, were "presented with positive experiences of communities' civic agency as well as their own."[4]

From Citizen-Students to Citizen-Alums

We are getting better at graduating community-oriented students. Around the country, alumni are remembering their educational turning points, identifying points at which a new sense of being an agent or founder opened up. At the 2013 Imagining America conference, for example, Noelle Johnson, who was a Public Achievement (PA) democracy coach and PA program coordinator as an undergrad at Western Kentucky State University, recalled that "my big start" was working with a faculty mentor, Paul Markham (now at the Bill and Melinda Gates Foundation), who was proactive in inviting her into leadership roles. She responded by organizing the first national meeting of PA democracy coaches. Noelle is currently a graduate student in the Sustainable Communities program at Northern Arizona University. She coordinates Public Achievement at sites in Flagstaff while continuing her national effort to nurture a board of coordinators and a strong national network of Public Achievement coaches who meet each year at the American Democracy Project conference.

Peter Erkkila, a recent Minnesota graduate, talked about his decisive experience, made possible by a credit-bearing internship through his political science major, of joining a student organization, "a somewhat useless group" that became a vehicle for transformative legislative activism by students on behalf of higher education in Minnesota. It also became a pathway for Erkkila's current work—six months after graduation—as a founding member and lead organizer of a political action committee supportive of the university.

Delro Cornelius Harris, speaking on the panel with Johnson and Erkkila, generalized from his experience as an entertainment professional who started his Detroit-based business, Alter Ego Management, in the extended period between his third and fourth years of college. He introduced the notion of "enhancement." Undergraduate education is not a script for success ("graduate and make so much money"), but rather "something that enhanced my experience in terms of the work that I'm [already] doing." Going to college enriches rather than dictates an educational and career direction: "If you have something that you do . . . education becomes this thing that gives . . . more depth and more color to what it is you're already doing."

Erica Lehrer, now director of the Center for Ethnographic Research and Exhibition in the Aftermath of Violence at Concordia University in Montreal, recalls her own eagerness to sustain a conversation with her alma mater, Grinnell—a college that is notable for its past and present innovations in alumni relations: "What I had been looking for in my first post-college decade was a way to share my excitement about the professionalization experiences I was undergoing, and to share the wisdom I was gaining (and the challenges I was facing) on my path to becoming an anthropologist, documentarian, and 'culture broker'— and trying to forge a different kind of path through the academy as a 'publicly engaged scholar,' with current Grinnellians."[5]

Work

Graduates like Peter, Delro, and Erica are pioneering a new conversation between alumni and the colleges they attended. As Peter Erkkila puts it, there is a "gap between what [former students] are able, willing, and eager to do and what the institution says an alum is." The culture of donor-centered alumni relations is deeply embedded in the planning, budgeting, and communications processes of higher education institutions, as well as in many of their celebrations and ceremonies. And the equation of "graduate" with "donor" is starting to shape discussions about outreach to former students in universities on every continent.

Responding to our "Copernican moment" in higher education, contributors to this symposium explore the larger, systemic drama of reimagining the relationships among the institutions implicated in college, citizenship, and career.[6] The alumni nexus is one of the locations where learning and work intertwine because it is a system for connecting former students to the campus and to one another over the arc of their working lives. The mediating work of alumni relations is important for those who enter college as traditional-aged college students, and potentially even more important for those who do not. Thinking ahead to a future identity as a civically engaged alum is compelling for older students who are combining work, families, and study—the New Student Majority. They are writing the script for new kinds of "graduateness."

We live in a period of acute—and acutely felt—socioeconomic inequity. Inequality is experienced in the classroom, in students' residential options, in their paying jobs and unpaid internships, and—long before college—in their differential access to the mediating institutions that Deborah Brandt calls "sponsors of literacy."[7] Inequality operates in the domain of educational policy, too, as we know. Derek Barker's observation, cited by David Mathews in his contribution to this symposium, is that "the gorilla in the room" of higher education debates is the effort "to make colleges and universities more productive and efficient in a time of the rapidly growing costs of degree attainment."[8] Strategies of efficiency include a greater reliance on contingent faculty, tuition hikes, and staff layoffs, as well as a greater dependency on donors.[9] These conditions have generated both activism on campus and new networks of publicly engaged graduates.[10]

For those finishing college and graduate school during and in the aftermath of the 2008 recession, finding a job has been harrowing, as Paul Markham details in his essay in this volume. Frustrating job searches and high educational debt pinch recent graduates and their families. For people at every career stage, a growing sense of employment insecurity, combined with "declining opportunities for occupational inheritance" and a "growing public sense of hardening stratification" have fed into narrowly focused efforts to quantify the worth of a college degree.[11]

Both the aspirations and the worries of college graduates center on work. The challenges of a lousy job market, educational debt, and the question of what to do with their democratic and civic skills are not the exclusive purview of twenty-somethings. People of all ages seek socially responsive work lives, from the teens whose political lives are valued and documented by the Center for Information and Research on Civic Learning and Engagement (CIRCLE) to the constituency of *Encore.org*, "people over 60 who are changing the world," including those who are attending the forty community colleges of the Encore College Initiative.[12]

Some campus programs are resisting the temptation to reduce the "college-to-life" transition, with its latent civic dynamism, to a preordained match between students and anticipated job openings in a narrow range of fields. Those working to suffuse alumni relations with civic purpose also take seriously the agency of graduates in their working lives. Civically engaged alumni, and the staff, faculty, and students who seek out relationships with them, are part of the broader trend to understand "work as a civic site." As professionals who work the world in consequential ways, as David Hoffman, among others in this volume, describes, they are cocreators of a new model of multigenerational civic learning.

Publicly active graduates in particular are looking for new kinds of post-college identities, ones that resonate with their most salient experiences of collaborative agency as undergraduates or graduate students. This restlessness is beginning to yield results. People who connect with alumni—college and university presidents, deans, faculty members, department staff, alumni relations and advancement professionals—are starting to listen. It is possible to challenge the national obsession with the economic instrumentality of a college education while also honoring the widespread hunger for work that pays and matters. While alumni may tune out fund-raising appeals, many are looking for ways to sustain the civic activism they pursued as undergraduate, graduate, or professional school students.

Infrastructure for Change

Much of the infrastructure needed for such changes already exists. The first place to look for the architecture of alumni engagement is in curricular and cocurricular innovation. A number of the people participating in this symposium, along with many others working in the civic renewal movement in higher education, have spent the last two decades building the educational infrastructure for citizen-students: curricular programs (majors, minors, certificate programs, community residencies, internships) as well as an array of cocurricular options. The organizers of these programs—some are graduating their first cohorts, others their twentieth—have a lively interest in the impact of active, publicly purposeful learning opportunities on graduates.

A flurry of assessments of for-credit programs documents student civic engagement after college. These publications include studies of graduates of the Democracy Fellows Program at Wake Forest;[13] the Tisch Scholars Program at the Tisch College of Citizenship and Public Service at Tufts; and (in a three-way comparative study) the Public and Community Service Studies Program at Providence College, the Citizen Scholars Program at the University of Massachusetts–Amherst, and Stanford's Public Service Scholars Program. These evaluations are already teaching us much about the value of sustained, developmental, cohort-based, programs through which students practice democratic skills while responding to new roles, contexts, and relationships, as other contributors to this symposium demonstrate at length.

Interviews and surveys are also underway, with an intentional focus on "citizen-alums," at other academic programs that reframe civic learning as co-created public agency. The Kettering Foundation's Beyond Service research working group aims to move student engagement beyond the service orientation to a concept of democratic politics understood as the work of "engaging people as active creators of stories."[14] These programs range from Living Democracy at Auburn, to the multiple sites of Public Achievement (a youth civic engagement program), and the minor in community action and social change and the Semester in Detroit at the University of Michigan, among others.

These curricula are producing graduates who like to stay connected, as faculty and staff are realizing once they undertake to learn about the political and professional lives of those graduates. The findings are encouraging. Yet even more important is the fact that these studies sustain or restore connections to former students. Networks and relationships, in this case, matter as much as research results. As a result of sustained innovation in civic learning, we now have models of feedback loops connecting citizen-alums to citizen-students in community-engaged learning programs. Faculty may, for example, invite graduates to participate actively in the learning of current students, presenting to the capstone course or sharing their experiences of navigating the college-to-life transition as early-career civic professionals, activists, or social entrepreneurs. For some programs, the first alumni cohort included the very students who lobbied for, then helped to design the program.

So the first place to find the infrastructure for building the civic capacity of college graduates is on campus, in academic and cocurricular programs. The second place to look for the infrastructure of postbaccalaureate civic engagement is in the field of alumni relations. Reichley, in his discussion of "the alumni movement," points to the post–World War II appearance of "a new kind of professional . . . in alumni, institutional relations, and development offices." Professionals in these roles, he notes, face "a difficult fight against impersonality in what was supposed to be a highly personal endeavor." As people who think of themselves as relationship builders above all, they find themselves responding to "ever greater demands for efficiency and evaluation," including an ever-greater emphasis on fund-raising.[15] Despite these pressures, however, the presence of alumni relations offices on campus, combined with networks of regional alumni association chapters, could be a civic resource. Alumni relations staff members can claim the role of civic professionals who serve the university's public mission. After all, they are experts on occasions of gathering. They both stimulate and respond to the hunger to reconnect with people and place. In this arena, also, pathways exist that can channel the flow of two-way relationships with publicly active alumni.

While we have both academic and alumni relations infrastructures in place, it is not easy to change institutional cultures so as to support student and alumni engagement over time. The professionalization of the development and advancement fields in universities is one form of what Xolela Mangcu calls "technocratic creep."[16] Capital campaigns can be an institutional survival tactic in the face of radically reduced public funding for large and small universities, as well as rallying points for committed alumni of means. Nonetheless, the "financialization" of the university reinforces the perception of postsecondary education as a private good partially supported by a minority of highly valued alumni.[17] The availability of only a handful of alumni identities—donor, sports fan, reunion attender, professional networker, mentor—blocks the full participation of alumni who hunger, not just for recognition, but for sustained working relationships with campus programs relating to issues and places that matter to them.

By working through this creative irritation, people with "a mix of interests" are gathering around a "common table," (as Boyte proposes), drawn together by the desire for a more capacious definition of "graduateness," as UNISA (University of South Africa) calls it. A practical first step for those coming to the table is to gather knowledge about those assembled. Who knows what about publicly engaged alumni? Who on campus owns this knowledge? The ability to locate and contact alumni is rightly understood as a form of capital in colleges and universities, especially those that have large alumni relations and development operations, with their respective commitments to maintaining networks and relationships and identifying potential donors. But the capacity to have the kind of sustained relationships with graduates that make it possible to follow their unfolding lives and work is typically located in the memories of faculty (rarely aggregated) and the files maintained by departmental staff. The initial challenge of how to gather, manage, and share information in a democratic fashion brings everyone into the process of building civil infrastructure right at the start.

Cultures of Commitment

There is a third resource available to those who value college graduates as active citizens: cultures of giving by black community members, including black alumni. The lessons of cultures of black giving lie in their civic, organizing, and associational energy. Because we cannot ignore the fact that civic action, including civic learning, sometimes includes raising money, we need to learn from and engage with traditions from civically engaged cultures of donation, even as we defy the equation between graduating and giving.[18] There are particular lessons to be learned from organizations that have generated a culture and politics of engaged college graduates.

Alumni traditions at HBCU's (such as Founders Day at Spelman College) and among networks of African American Greek letter, social, and civic organizations may serve as a generative resource for civically engaged alumni. These associational traditions inform scholarly work in alumni relations studies that explores the relationship of African Americans to "the college and university giving process." The principle of looking for models beyond the civic renewal movement in higher education applies broadly. It can take us to change-oriented philanthropy by other activist networks of, for example, women, LGBTQ, "First Gen," and Latino alumni, to name a few. There we are likely to find allied financial and nonfinancial modes of engagement and action. Attending to these examples can help us understand commitments, rooted in civic purpose, that are based on financial gifts, and how they resemble or differ from commitments that are not.

The proud, pragmatic tradition of black giving and the organizations through which it has been sustained have been strongly allied with political movements, from the abolition of slavery to civil rights, equity, and justice ("full participation"). Marybeth Gasman points out that organized giving has been central to the "role of blacks in shaping their own institutions" since the eighteenth century and is "rooted in efforts to overcome oppression." She argues that black Americans are most likely to be "motivated . . . [by] efforts that make a difference in the daily lives of other African Americans"—and here the phrase "daily lives" seems particularly salient to the "everyday politics" valued by Boyte and others.[19] Self-organized, historically aware, politically savvy, spiritually energized, and locally committed African American communities have used tithing, fund-raising fairs, family reunions, and organizations' pledges to address the "physical and social needs" of African Americans. Solicitation in this context, while certainly not exempt from elitism, was (and is) a form of what Boyte calls "cultural organizing."[20] Donation became part of a "tradition of mutual aid . . . which stressed . . . communalism and social solidarity" at the local level and nationally, through the state and local chapters of national associations.[21]

These practices are still emerging and changing, as Ange-Marie Hancock's discussion of "giving Black" in Los Angeles shows.[22] Hancock finds three donor profiles among African Americans in Los Angeles: the "building the black community" donor; the "issue impact" or millennial donor; and the donor who is "hardwired to give" across causes and groups. Hancock points to the energy being channeled into financial support for social justice causes, especially for younger cohorts, and the appeal of issue-oriented engagement that reaches across racial and ethnic identities.

Networks of alumni from historically underrepresented groups are likely to be at the leading edge of civically committed educational philanthropy. The example of black giving practices points to a counterculture of donation that resists the heroic individualism of mainstream approaches to development in colleges and universities. These countercultural practices have broader implications, too. Hancock's three donor profiles, translated as "builder of the community," "issue-oriented organizer," and "supporter of a broad spectrum of constituencies and causes," can be usefully applied in efforts to craft alumni identities that *do not* involve financial giving. In sum, these roles can clarify the terms of engagement for groups and individuals whose stance is either sympathetic or resistant to financial donation.

Citizen Alum: An Organizing Strategy

The effort to connect civically engaged students and civically engaged alumni is a significant addition to the democracy movement on campus and in communities, expanding that movement in time and space. In January 2012, as part of the linked initiatives of the American Commonwealth Partnership, Citizen Alum was launched at the White House meeting, "For Democracy's Future— Education Reclaims Our Public Mission." Its mission is to "counter the image of alumni as primarily 'donors' with a vision of them as also 'doers.'"[23] Citizen Alum grew out of two questions: How can colleges and universities empower more, and more diverse, graduates as in their workplaces and communities? And how can they do this through participatory relationships with alumni themselves? Conceived at a lively lunch table at the 2011 national meeting of the American Democracy Project, Citizen Alum supports campus efforts to deepen institutional cultures of engagement by involving graduates and those on campus who work with them. Citizen Alum is one of several programs and organizations, including the Sustained Dialogue Campus Network, that have joined together under the auspices of the Kettering Foundation's project on Civically Engaged Alumni.

As John Silvanus Wilson Jr. observed, speaking at Alcorn State University, change involves looking "back, around, inside, and ahead."[24] Citizen Alum had the advantage of being able to look around at (and learn from) well-established programs oriented to engaged college graduates. The Tufts University CASE Network (Connecting Alumni and Student Experiences) sustains the university's commitment to active citizenship by connecting students to alumni through a summer mentorship and networking program. A more independent approach was pioneered by the Princeton AlumniCorps, the 501(c)3 alumni network founded by Ralph Nader that offers a different model for supporting young civic professionals in the nonprofit sector. Syracuse University started a program for Engagement Fellows, fifth-year postbaccalaureate fellowships that allow publicly engaged graduates to continue their work with community organizations while pursuing a master's degree.

Based at the University of Michigan, Citizen Alum is now active at over twenty campuses. The organizing unit of Citizen Alum is the campus team, which brings together alumni, campus leaders, faculty, staff, and current students as "agents and architects of democracy."[25] The teams challenge institutional silos by creating an unconventional mix of university offices and departments, bringing together both the usual suspects—community-engaged faculty and staff—and people from units that are rarely at the table when the institution's public mission is addressed. This approach is a form of community organizing, as colleagues in alumni relations, development offices, advising, and career services along with those from academic and outreach programs, come together as committed professionals with civic purposes. The cross-cultural encounter between faculty members and alumni relations staff can be stressful. They are not likely to know one another; they probably have negative assumptions about each other; and they are in environments that construe civic engagement and community service in different ways. Participants' experience to date suggests that the first step in inventing civically engaged alumni relations consists of building relationships across campus.

At the inaugural Citizen Alum Summer Institute in June 2012, attendees met first in their campus teams, then in four "role groups" (faculty, deans, and academic affairs; alumni relations and development; community partnerships and community-based learning; university outreach, public engagement, and advocacy), then in teams again. The session organized around work identities decisively altered the self-understanding of participants when the campus teams reunited on the second day. The teams become spaces that offer, across the generational and identity divides of "student" and "working adult," "scholar" and "fund-raiser," opportunities to speak and to be heard as a "doer."

Citizen Alum teams around the country are showing remarkable creativity in building bridges between publicly engaged students and alumni networks. After forming an inclusive campus team, the sole requirement for Citizen Alum members is to undertake an "alumni listening project"—an effort to hear, learn from, and act in concert with publicly engaged alumni. Deliberative dialogue and digital media have provided platforms for intergenerational storytelling. Metropolitan State University in Minneapolis focused on an interview-based curricular module. The community arts practitioners in Ashé College Unbound held public reflective performances and are working on a collective book about their experience as that program's first graduating cohort. A workshop at Kennesaw State University focused on "turning public work into jobs" for unemployed and underemployed alumni. The University of La Verne's alumni listening project has put fifty vignettes of citizen-alums on the University website. Behind that web page is an archive of information-rich, transcribed interviews. Students in

Auburn's Living Democracy curriculum interview citizen-alums and write brief articles about them. At Metropolitan State, undergraduates in Professor Danielle Hinrichs' citizen-alum course module interview engaged alumni, transcribe the interviews, and write papers about the experience. This assignment enables students to do more than listen to stories told by alumni. It shows them how stories grow deeper and more complex and enables them to read those narratives' themes, plots, and metaphors. Citizen Alum has just launched a national task force on Intergenerational Learning for College Students, chaired by Professor Hinrichs.

Through these listening projects, campuses are gaining a new understanding of turning points in the public work of their graduates. They are also looking beyond listening to action, including curricular design, joint projects that connect alumni and campus programs around issues, and participatory action research about alumni with alumni.

Like my partners in this dialogic effort to imagine "democracy's education," I see in projects that strengthen the civic roles of college alumni an emphasis on building the agency of individuals and teams. People are working as "communities of experts" to change our understanding of "graduateness." Moving forward, colleges need to encourage the civic life choices of current students; to see and value their public-minded alums; and to strengthen communities by identifying ways to support the situated lives of publicly active graduates.

Notes

This essay is partially adapted from "Civically Engaged Alumni: A Framework for Collaborative Inquiry," written with the support of the Kettering Foundation and for the Kettering Workshop on Civically Engaged Alumni held November 20–21, 2013, at the foundation's center in Dayton, Ohio.

1.   Harry C. Boyte, "The Soul of Higher Education: Concluding Reflections."
2.   Julie Ellison and Timothy K. Eatman, "Reflections on *Building the Capacity for Publicly Engaged Scholarship: Community Engagement and ODL*" (unpublished report), University of South Africa (UNISA), August 2013, 1.
3.   Harry C. Boyte, *Reinventing Citizenship: Public Work, Civic Learning, and the Movement for a Citizen-Centered Democracy; A Study for the Kettering Foundation* (Dayton, OH: Kettering Foundation, 2013), 3, 12 15–17, 24.
4.   "Engaging Students as Citizens: Beyond Service Learning" Kettering Workshop Agenda, Dayton, OH., November 2012, 1.
5.   Blog post. *www.citizenalum.org/voices-of-citizen-alums-responses-to-one-professors-invitation*, accessed December 15, 2013.
6.   David Scobey, "Why Now? Because This is a Copernican Moment," in *Civic Provocations*, ed. Donald W. Harwood (Washington, DC: Bringing Theory to Practice, 2013).
7.   Deborah Brandt, *Literacy in American Lives* (Cambridge: Cambridge University Press, 2001), introduction and chs. 1, 4, and 6.
8.   David Mathews, "Har Megiddo: A Battle for the Soul of Higher Education."
9.   For a summary of these, see *Shaping Our Future: How Should Higher Education Help*

Us Create the Society We Want (Dayton, OH: National Issues Forum, 2012), *www.nifi.
org/issue_books/detail.aspx?catID=6&itemID=21640.*

10.   As I write, members of the Black Student Union at the University of Michigan—
acutely conscious of the history of black student organizing on this campus—are
demanding steps to address racial and economic inequality through the Twitter
campaign #BBUM (Being Black at the University of Michigan), demonstrations,
a planned Speak Out at the undergraduate library, and ongoing negotiations with
university leaders.

11.   Theresa Sullivan (president, University of Virginia), "The Liminal Role of the Research
University President," presentation at the Liberal Arts and Sciences in the Research
University Today: Histories, Challenges, Futures, May 22–24, 2013, University of
Michigan.

12.   *www.encore.org*, accessed December 15, 2013.

13.   Jill J. McMillan and Katy J. Harriger, *Speaking of Politics: Preparing College Students
for Democratic Citizenship through Deliberative Dialogue* (Dayton OH: Kettering
Foundation Press, 2007); Tania Mitchell, Virginia Visconti, Arthur Keene, and Richard
Battistoni, "Educating for Democratic Leadership at UMass, Providence College, and
Stanford University," in *Why Community Matters: Connecting Education with Civic
Life*, ed. Nicholas V. Longo (State University of New York Press, 2007), ch. 6, 115–48.

14.   Kettering Connections 2012, "Living Democracy," 22.

15.   R. A. Reichley, "The Alumni Movement: An Overview," *Handbook of Institutional
Advancement*, ed. A. Westley Rowland (San Francisco: Jossey-Bass, 1977), 275–76.

16.   Xolela Mangcu, "The Promise of Black Consciousness."

17.   Randy Martin, *The Financialization of Daily Life* (Philadelphia: Temple University
Press, 2002).

18.   I am grateful to my colleague, Phil Deloria, associate dean for Undergraduate
Education, College of Literature, Science, and the Arts, University of Michigan, for
sharing with me his unpublished essay, "Entrepreneurship: Toward a Definition,"
which has helped me to work through questions relating to university donors, and the
place of entrepreneurship and social entrepreneurship programs in the lives of our
students.

19.   Marybeth Gasman, "An Untapped Resource: Bringing African Americans into the
College and University Giving Process," *CASE International Journal of Educational
Advancement* 2, no. 3 (2002): 280, 282–83. See also Nicole Reaves, "African-American
Alumni Perceptions Regarding Giving to Historically Black Colleges and Universities,"
PhD diss., North Carolina State University, 2006. Marybeth Gasman, "An Untapped
Resource," 280. Thanks to Sarah Robbins for sharing her work on the history of
Spelman College Founders' Day, in author's possession.

20.   Harry C. Boyte, "Bringing Culture Back In," *Good Society* 21, no. 2 (2012): 300–19.

21.   Gasman, "An Untapped Resource," 282.

22.   Ange-Marie Hancock, *Giving Black in Los Angeles: Donor Profiles and Opportunities
for the Future* (Los Angeles: Liberty Hill Foundation, 2012).

23.   In addition to the Kettering Foundation, Citizen Alum partners with the American
Democracy Project, the Democracy Commitment, Imagining America, Association
of American Colleges and Universities, the Jandris Center for Innovative Higher
Education at the University of Minnesota, and the Center for Institutional and Social
Change at Columbia Law School.

24.   John Silvanus Wilson, "A Multidimensional Challenge for Black Colleges," *Chronicle*

of Higher Education, September 18, 2011. "Besides looking down, they can use at least four other angles to view and improve their collective fate. With renewal and excellence in mind, these diverse institutions should also look back, around, within, and ahead to gain compelling perspectives for reshaping the future."

25.   Harry Boyte and Elizabeth Hollander, Campus Compact: Providence, RI, 1999. *www. compact.org/initiatives/trucen/wingspread-declaration-on-the-civic-responsibilities-of-research-universities*. *Wingspread Declaration on the Civic Responsibilities of Research Universities.*

PART V

Community Organizers
Consider the Challenges

As Maria Avila describes in her earlier contribution, "community organizers" can organize in the communities of higher education, just as surely as in neighborhoods. This section, from the perspective of community organizers, begins with the contribution of one such organizer, Jenny Whitcher. Robert Woodson, longtime community organizer, describes his work with "ex's"—ex-convicts, ex-prostitutes, ex–gang members, ex–drug dealers. He gives a compelling challenge to higher education to rethink the nature of "service," from one-directional efforts to "fix" people, based on a deficit view of poor and minority communities, to work that is "on tap," not "on top." Finally, Sam Daley-Harris, founder of the world's most successful citizen antipoverty lobby, takes a look at higher education drawn from more than twenty years of successful citizen action.

17

BREAKING THE CIVIC SPIRIT: EXPERIENCES OF YOUNG ORGANIZERS

Jenny L. Whitcher

The Mobilizing-Nonprofit Complex

"What I am doing is not organizing. At least not how you taught us."[1] As these words came out of alumnus Felipe Vieyra Jr.'s mouth with uncharacteristic apprehension, I had two responses: (1) I was impressed that he so quickly identified and articulated the difference between mobilizing and organizing within a working environment right out of college—a student-teacher civic learning assessment moment; (2) I was concerned.

Too many recent graduates who are well versed in the community organizing model, who have developed a civic identity and purpose, and who have a vocational calling to civic work seem to experience bitterness and defeat within one to two years after college. This is the result of traumatic experiences within "organizing" nonprofits, less interested in relational meetings and more interested in turning out numbers. These are organizations sustained by constant turnover of burned-out young adults, which demonstrates a lack of interest in the personal and professional development of staff or community members. Those managing these mobilizing operations are also caught in the mobilizing mechanism, and their work is evaluated based on numbers-driven impact assessments. Managers often do not know alternative ways of making change or do not feel empowered or supported to use alternative methods. As Harry Boyte describes, this mobilizing culture of citizen powerlessness has spread beyond groups traditionally known for this work into a broader cultural problem. "The pattern of one-way, expert interventions, inattentive to the cultures and individual stories of communities . . . spread across the sweep of civic life."[2]

Bright, talented, and committed young adults are being trampled and thrown away like trash by the emergent mobilizing complex within the nonprofit sector, which conflates "community organizing" with what is actually a mobilizing model. The stories of recent graduates reveal a violent, spirit-breaking mobilizing operation that is not only brutal on individuals, but also threatens the civic capacity of this generation. Higher education has power to engage and impact this cultural dysfunction if we claim our power and choose to do so. In the process we may create new models and pathways toward a more democratic civic culture that values relationships, agency, and public skill development, a culture that respects diverse people and different ideas.

During his undergraduate degree, Felipe Vieyra Jr. was a Puksta Scholar, part of a four-year civic development program and intentionally diverse community that I previously managed. He is now a member of the Denver Mayor's Immigrant and Refugee Commission. Confident in his public skills, versed in community organizing training and practice, and experienced as a Public Achievement coach, Felipe took a job billed as "community organizer" right out of college. Over the next year and a half, he struggled through the mobilizing-nonprofit complex that many young social change agents experience as they embark on a civic vocation. Felipe describes the characteristic culture of disposability:

> There was so much turnover. Eight staff members left the organization while I was there. Not only did I become the veteran organizer, I was the second longest running staff member at the organization, and I had only been there for a year and a half. It was a frustrating experience because I saw so many people leave and we had to redo many of the things we were working on. The community saw what was happening, but there was not an action plan to handle the change or the [community] relationships.[3]

Imagine the individual level, where young civic leaders are treated as disposable resources, their skills, energy, and commitment extracted like the juice of a ripe fruit, leaving them to wonder if they will ever regain the sweetness and fullness—the calling—they felt before they took the job. Describing the human costs of the mobilizing-nonprofit complex, Felipe reflected:

> I was working sixty hours per week, doing everything I could. The expectation is that you will give everything to the organization, and you have no time for yourself. It is frustrating because as an organizer you need time to recover and time to develop yourself further. It was draining, and it made me question wanting to be [an organizer]. And this is something that I feel happens to a lot of organizers, or they experience something like this—they question whether or not they should even go back to the nonprofit world, to the service world. Towards the end of my time with the organization, after the campaign was over, my supervisor gave me two options, either you do a two-week probation, making certain [quantitative] goals to prove that you deserve to be here, or you start transitioning out. When I was given that ultimatum, it hurt more than anything else did, after all the work I that I had put in. I knew they did not truly value me, and it made me feel used.[4]

This is not just a typical first-job-out-of-college kind of experience, a collegiate rite of passage where the top-of-the-world senior year meets entry-level working world in one swift transition. While such first jobs have their challenges, the expectation is that the employer has some responsibility to the welfare and professional development of employees. What is happening in the mobilizing-nonprofit complex is the degradation of young civic leaders: toxic and traumatic work environments and management; demoralization; physical, mental, and emotional exhaustion; and ultimately burnout in one to two years.

Breaking the Civic Spirit

Young adults who go into community organizing or civic work do so for a larger purpose. They want to "reinvent citizenship as public work," because they know voting and extracurricular volunteerism are too limited and ultimately ineffective in addressing the problems of the day. They are often willing to make large initial sacrifices of time, health, and financial solvency in order to do something meaningful in the world. These are vocationally driven students who feel called to this work, as not simply a job, but as a way to be in the world. Young people with this calling want a way to live out their core values while holding them in tension with our collective democratic values and to use their gifts and talents for the betterment of self and society—or self-interest, richly understood, as the authentic organizing tradition teaches. This is to do something and to be someone that matters beyond the self, for the self and for the common good.

In my teaching experience, these kinds of students are driven by explicit values, and as a result, they expect ethical work environments where actions are consistent with beliefs for themselves, their coworkers, and the organization. When such authentic alignment starts to slide—when the true nature of mobilizing culture reveals itself—their civic spirit starts to tear, as those in official positions of power cause them to question their calling, talents, and worth, and ultimately their ability to follow their vocation.

Knowing Felipe for the past six years, as mentor, professor, program director, and now friend, I have absolute faith that he has what it takes to be an organizer. As I interviewed him for this piece, he recounted numerous stories where he did the right thing, in terms of ethical, relational organizing and public work, but was made to feel incapable and unsuccessful by his supervisors for operating outside of the mobilizing script and resisting unethical practices. Reflecting on the ultimatum he received from his supervisor, Felipe explains, "That is why I am a bit bitter towards organizations. It has made me doubt myself. I am doubtful of myself as a community organizer, whether or not I can actually do the work. It was not a good experience."[5]

It is poignant to see a young civic leader doubt his potential, particularly when he has a proven record of accomplishment for exceeding expectations. Felipe says he is in a good place now and is grateful for the time to reflect and to think critically about future opportunities where he will be able to thrive and grow.

Noelle Johnson is a first-year graduate student at Northern Arizona University studying sustainable communities, and a Public Achievement coordinator. During her undergraduate studies at Western Kentucky University, she was a Public Achievement coach and coordinator for almost four years. The summer between finishing her undergraduate degree and starting her graduate degree, Noelle took a "community organizer" job in Cincinnati, Ohio. It lasted one week.

I had to leave because I was told it was not okay to consider the demographics of the neighborhoods, to discuss the issue in depth—my task was only to solicit donations, and not to build any relationships with members and supporters. It was not a job that I felt comfortable with, and I started to consider that I might not find a similar organizing model outside of Public Achievement or the Industrial Areas Foundation (IAF).[6]

When it was my day to go door-to-door and have someone follow and watch me and then critique what I said, I introduced myself to the people and asked if they were familiar with the issue before I would do the script [which I had been handed by the group I was working for]. I was told by my supervisor that I was not allowed to do that. "You are supposed to just tell them the issue, just tell them the problem. Do not ask if they know anything, do not ask if they care, just go straight into telling them and asking for money." Like Harry Boyte said in a workshop, organizations will make it all about good versus bad, and that is it. That is what started making me think about the work that I did last summer.

For a while I was beating myself up because I thought I should have stuck with it, thinking, well, this is part of the experience. If this is organizing, I need this too, and maybe I would have continued thinking that until now, because now this discussion is not just me, there are other people in the same boat. I think [the mobilizing culture] is really causing damage. I was thinking that if I was more confident about finding a job in organizing, I might not have even gone to graduate school; I would just be out there organizing. But I almost feel safe within higher education, because at least at Northern Arizona University we have Public Achievement, and I can do that.

I am studying sustainable communities, and my program uses an organizing model, and we are reflecting on not only environmental sustainability, but also social and economic sustainability. I do not know what this degree will do for me if there are not many organizations out there that use the model that I am passionate about and trained in.[7]

It is problematic when students like Felipe and Noelle, who are skilled and capable civic agents, have difficulty finding work that practices a democratic, relational, broad-based organizing culture. While higher education is trying to respond to the "calls for revitalization of civic education and civic learning," a growing gap emerges as "concepts of work as a site of citizenship and workplaces as civic sites have largely disappeared."[8] In order for students to follow a civic vocation, there must be opportunities to meaningfully engage their civic talents with others.

Alison Wisneski, is a second-year graduate student in the master of arts in social change (MASC) degree program at Iliff School of Theology. I have known Alison as a student in classes that I teach and in my role as the director of the MASC program. Before she entered graduate school Alison worked at a reputable nonprofit that does important work, but relies on a small staff and is highly dependent on volunteers. She started out as a volunteer, fell in love with the organization, and decided she wanted to work there. Alison describes what is an emerging response to the mobilizing-nonprofit complex:

> I thought getting in the door was enough. I assumed they would see the value and importance of what I was doing, and my training, and they were going to really like what I was doing and move me up. After being there for a year, I still wasn't making enough money, to the point that I was on food stamps. The value of work is important no matter where you are, whether you are working in for-profit, nonprofit, or government. The value of work is the value of work, and you should be treated with the respect and monetary means to get you by. There is this assumption that if you are in a nonprofit then you should be scraping, and you should be used to having to do the grunt work, the canvassing, the cold calls, and a lot of times you can't move up from that, and there is the burnout that turns people off from nonprofits and organizing work.[9]

Over the last seven years, I have increasingly heard many students decry the lack of civic opportunities available after college that pay a living wage, and for many students it is important that they also be paid enough to cover monthly educational loan repayments.

It is well known that AmeriCorps Volunteers in Service to America (VISTA) and City Year members often survive using the Supplemental Nutrition Assistance Program (SNAP), a federal program that offers nutrition assistance to low-income individuals and families. The monthly stipend each yearlong volunteer receives is calibrated according to the federal poverty line for the region of service, making the program financially most accessible to middle and upper-class young adults who can afford to "live in poverty" with external financial support from family. For those young adults coming from lower-income backgrounds, such postgraduate opportunities are an unlikely option. Not only is the lack of meaningful civic work problematic, but the lack of appropriate compensation for civic work is an ethical problem that has the potential to end civic vocations before they even start.

These are just a few of the concerns of recent graduates searching for meaningful civic work, but faced with spirit-breaking mistreatment, devaluation, powerlessness, and polarizing politics that dismiss the value of the community. Perhaps, as you read their stories, something sounded familiar. The sickness present in mobilizing culture is pervasive, crossing sectors and cultures, suffocating democratic culture, and breaking the civic spirit. It is alarming to consider the long-term impact of engaging meaningful civic development work in higher education when students are met with such violent postgraduate experiences of professional praxis.

Higher Education's Power to Engage

While the disposability and human cost of the mobilizing-nonprofit complex threatens civic capacity, higher education is also uniquely situated to engage this issue as the preparatory site for professional employment. As we explore ways to create meaningful civic culture and identify developmental civic processes, they must include expectations for both formal education and postgraduate professional sites of civic learning and practice. Higher education can play a far more powerful role in both screening and guiding professional sites toward improved democratic civic cultures.

A few years ago, an impressive job recruitment flyer crossed my former desk at the University of Denver's Center for Community Engagement and Service Learning. It had all the right words and phrases: grassroots community organizing, democracy, power, relationships, social justice, and working toward the common good. These key terms formed lyrical sentences that painted a picture of authentic, relational, broad-based community organizing—directly contradicting the predominant mobilizing practice of the nonprofit-civic sector. With awareness of the kind of civic positions generally available to current or graduating students, I questioned the authenticity of such civic claims. Unfortunately, personal experience and the stories of students have taught me that in terms of entry-level civic positions, "If it seems too good to be true, it probably is."

The organization was seeking permission to recruit and hold interviews with students in the common space just outside of our office in the student center. The flyer came to me from the work-study student managing the front desk of our office who received the initial request. Intrigued, I asked the student to bring the guest to my office so I could learn more. Over the course of our conversation, I asked pointed questions about the type of work required for the position, their organizing practices, and intended outcomes of their efforts. The polished language of the flyer began to tarnish as the organizational representative described in detail a top-down mobilizing model, which offered no resemblance to their democratic civic claims.

Seeing a potential learning opportunity, I took the time to share my concerns with the organizational representative. I first pointed out that the claims of their written announcement did not match the job duties, methods, or intended outcomes. Such deception is not only unethical, it is ineffective as students waste their time starting jobs they do not want and therefore leave shortly after, resulting in high employee turnover. As a result, organizations must focus resources on constant recruitment and training of new short-term employees, which negatively affects larger organizational goals, reputation, and success.

This first point was followed by what I imagine is a less common message from higher education: These are not the kind of jobs that our students are interested in, because they know this is not meaningful civic work, nor an effective approach to social change. The civic skills, knowledge, and capacities of our students far exceed the opportunities of such positions. I told the representative I appreciate the eagerness to recruit on campus, but I will not approve use of this space to recruit and interview university students for these positions. It is not a good match. In the future, if they had opportunities that were a better fit, I would be happy to talk again.

Truth be told, I did not have official university authority to decide who could use the tables in the common space located within the student center and surrounded by not only the Center for Community Engagement and Service Learning, but also the offices of Academic and Career Development, Living and Learning Communities, Pioneer Leadership Program, and Religious and Spiritual Life. Instead, in that moment I drew my authority from the university community of students, staff, and faculty who work toward the education and development of students who deserve better opportunities after graduation.

I share this story to highlight higher education's power to engage the civic-nonprofit sector—to not only listen to what the community wants, but to be a truly collaborative, relational partner willing to also share our own hopes, needs, and expectations toward the development of a meaningful and ethical civic sector.

Higher education seems all too eager to appeal to potential employers with little critical evaluation of the kind of work and working environment we encourage students to seek after graduation. In the current economy, colleges and universities are primarily concerned with gainful employment, tracking job offers, full-time versus part-time work, and compensation without concern for quality or purpose of employment. Higher education courts employers of all sectors, inviting them to campus to set a table up in the student center or at internship and career fairs, to guest lecture in classrooms, and even hold adjunct faculty positions where they can teach and recruit simultaneously.

Higher education should absolutely engage in a diverse range of community-campus partnerships, and colleges and universities should encourage use of their facilities as public space for community-campus dialogue, collaboration, and public work. But what higher education should not do is sell out students to persistent courtiers without exercising any power to address the challenge of shaping meaningful civic workplaces and professions. Within these community-campus relationships, colleges and universities can challenge internship sites and employers to develop authentic civic opportunities and demand just and ethical treatment of civic professionals. The recurrent pattern of benign neglect demands that higher education levy the power it has to support broader cultural change, and stop ignoring the problematic mismatch between vocational preparedness and a lack of professional sites where young adults—or any adult for that matter—can practice and further develop civic agency. Otherwise, we risk graduating students into a diseased civic culture and a political system in which many have already lost faith, which may ultimately lead to a loss of civic vocation.[10]

It is an ambitious call to action, and there are various ways higher education can engage the problem. I will let the students speak about some opportunities of impact they identified and have the final word. Both Noelle and Felipe identified mentors as key to navigating postgraduation civic opportunities. As Noelle puts it: "For students like me who are about to graduate, we need to know what to look for. What nonprofits can we trust—if it is going to be a nonprofit? Which ones are actually going to use the community organizing model [versus mobilizing]? Higher education as a whole does a poor job with the screening process, but mentors make a difference—somebody who can help with the screening process, someone we can go talk to and say: this is what I'm looking at, what do you think?"[11] Higher education mentors who help students think through options, decipher the glossy words and job descriptions, and have community relationships and engage in public work are able to teach students how to identify meaningful opportunities for civic work.

For Felipe, mentorship necessarily includes considerations for structural racism and includes the development of mentors within nonprofits and the broader community—something higher education could engage in a more meaningful way as part of alumni engagement, internships, long-term community-engaged research, or public work:

> When it comes to being a person of color, there needs to be an emphasis put on mentorship. Coming out of college, I would have loved to have someone to support me when I was organizing. Someone who understands organizing, is a person of color, and is willing to push me to develop my abilities further. Latino males need more mentors. Those Latinos already at the table need to put more effort into mentoring young Latinos who are trying to succeed. When people of color make it to the table, they have worked hard to get a place at the table, and they often feel strongly about protecting that position. They do not always work to bring other people of color to the table, because they feel like . . . places at the table are [so] sparse to begin with, why should they compete for so few seats at the table? This is something that needs to be addressed.[12]

Felipe's insight about the value of mentorship is reflective of the lack of racial diversity within nonprofit leadership—an issue mirrored in higher education that also continues to demand attention and action:

> As . . . Latino[s,] we were the face of the organization, but it did not seem like there was any opportunity to move up, or a willingness amongst organizational leaders to develop [us] into leadership positions. I was always looking for ways to develop myself, or to push myself to learn from others, but it did not bode well in that organization. It always seemed that I had to explain myself for wanting to learn and do new things, to develop myself—explain why I even would want something like that. The whole organizing team was Latino, but then there was the executive director, the communications director, and other staff director positions, and they were all white. [I] would notice subtleties of how we [the organizing team] were viewed by the administrative staff. There was a disconnect between the organizers and the staff, and there was a huge disconnect between the staff and the parent members that we worked with. Parent members would come over to the office, and it was unsettling to see how the rest of the staff would not even try to connect with the parents. I understand there was a language barrier [as the parents were mostly monolingual Spanish-speaking Latinos and the staff were all English speaking and white], but at least you can try. Say hello to these parents, try to make a connection with the members who are part of the organization.[13]

The final lesson for higher education is to teach students to value and develop grounded, realistic confidence in themselves and their work. This emerges from the community organizing concept of self-interest, which lies between selfishness and selflessness on a spectrum and is about self among others. It is also a component of theological Personal and Professional Formation at Iliff School of Theology. It would be absurd to graduate students with the title "Master of Social Change" if we did not also teach them to master self-care and self-worth. Alison Wisneski shared this lesson that she learned while at Iliff:

> I am not doing anybody any favors if I am going to a workplace where I do not feel valued, and then I go home and relay that information over and over to my partner, who in turn says: just get out. But then it turns into conversations of: I love this organization, I love this work, I love organizing, and I know I'm doing a good job, and maybe one day they will be able to pay me. You will see a lot of people sticking around such workplaces, but I have learned that it is okay to place value on yourself. If you cannot do these things like self-care, and you do not have self-worth, then you are not going to be of any value to anybody else. Realizing that you can be selfless while putting yourself first was a really big realization for me, which brought a lot of things home and is giving me a lot more civic agency.[14]

We are not doing anyone any favors by pretending we do not have power to change the mobilizing culture that threatens our civic capacity. After all, we as a society created it, and higher education plays an important, if often unselfconscious role in the process.

We are the ones to help create a new civic culture.

Notes

1. Felipe Vieyra Jr. (University of Denver alum) in discussion with the author March 20, 2013. Quote approval granted February 3, 2014.
2. Harry C. Boyte, "Reinventing Citizenship as Public Work," in *Democracy's Education: Public Work, Citizenship, and the Future of Colleges and Universities*, ed. Harry C. Boyte. Nashville: Vanderbilt University Press, 2015.
3. Felipe Vieyra Jr., telephone interview by Jenny L. Whitcher, February 1, 2014. Quote approval granted February 3, 2014.
4. Ibid.
5. Ibid.
6. Noelle Johnson (Northern Arizona University graduate student and Western Kentucky University alum), e-mail message to author, February 2, 2014. Quote approval granted February 2, 2014.
7. Noelle Johnson, telephone interview by Jenny L. Whitcher, February 2, 2014. Quote approval granted February 3, 2014.
8. Boyte, "Reinventing Citizenship as Public Work."
9. Alison Wisneski (Iliff School of Theology Master of Social Change graduate student), telephone interview by Jenny L. Whitcher, February 2, 2014. Quote approval granted February 3, 2014.

10. Harvard University Institute of Politics, "Survey of Young Americans' Attitudes toward Politics and Public Service: 24th Edition," 2013, *www.iop.harvard.edu/survey-young-americans%E2%80%99-attitude-toward-politics-and-public-service-24th-edition.*
11. Noelle Johnson, telephone interview.
12. Felipe Vieyra Jr., telephone interview.
13. Ibid.
14. Alison Wisneski, telephone interview by Jenny L. Whitcher, February 2, 2014. Quote approval granted February 3, 2014.

18

"ON TAP," NOT "ON TOP"

Robert L. Woodson Sr.

Throughout the past five decades, institutions of higher education have played a prominent role in the development of social-intervention strategies intended to address poverty and related dysfunctions. A large portion of the billions of dollars that have poured into the antipoverty effort has been spent on social science research in pursuit of solutions. Social planners have relied on the advice of academic institutions in the design and implementation of the War on Poverty, which expended in excess of $15 trillion over the past fifty years—only to see the conditions of the poor worsen.

Perhaps it is time to rethink the fundamental approach that academic institutions adopt as they interact with communities in crisis, both in its programmatic interventions and in the deployment of both paid and volunteer student participation. One of the first obstacles that must be addressed is what I call "intellectual imperialism."

Many people have gross misperceptions about low-income communities. Because of the widespread despair, high crime rates, proliferation of drug use, and increased incidence of out-of-wedlock births in impoverished communities, there is a tendency to make sweeping generalizations about all people that reside there. It is assumed that if people were sensible, intelligent, and morally sound, they would leave and live elsewhere.

The second assumption is that conditions of poverty make people not only frustrated and dispirited, but also stupid, lacking wisdom, and, therefore, incapable of making informed decisions about what is in their best interest. Perhaps it's this predisposition that explains why so many antipoverty intervention programs that are designed by academic "experts" and parachuted into low-income neighborhoods fail. When that happens, rather than analyzing the approach for flaws, the tendency is to assume that the fault lies with the programs' purported beneficiaries who are unresponsive to what is best for them. In spite of its ineffectiveness, the outside intervention is never challenged as being inappropriate or incompetent.

The third false assumption, closely linked to the second, is that a noble intention always leads to beneficial outcomes. This last assumption is one of the most difficult to overcome. As martyred theologian Dietrich Bonheoffer wrote in his essay On Folly—part of a collection in his Letters and Papers from Prison: "Folly is a more dangerous enemy to the good than malice. You can protest against malice, you can unmask it or prevent it by force. Malice always contains the seeds of its own destruction, for it always makes men uncomfortable, if nothing worse. There is no defense against folly. Neither protests nor force are of any avail against it, and it is never amenable to reason." Before pursuing the noble goal of integrating academic pursuit with public service, it's important to establish the groundwork of a clear understanding of the community that will be served. First of all, it is important to recognize the assets its residents possess, what its residents have already undertaken to address the problem, and what type of assistance is needed.

Typically, academics begin with "needs assessments," which often become surveys of pathology, tallying how many people are on drugs, are dropping out of school, or are incarcerated. These demographics become the foundation of proposals that are submitted for funding, with the bulk of money going to professional outsiders to conduct interventions intended to "cure" people by establishing programs of incentives and sanctions that are intended to compel improvement in their behavior.

Whether we are talking about aid to third-world countries, government programs for the poor, or student services in disadvantaged communities, good intentions are not enough. Providing the right type of assistance channeled through right vehicles is a crucial component of effective service. In the conventional approach of antipoverty experts, when interventions fail to correct a pathology or dysfunction, the nature of the intervention is seldom brought into question. Instead the failure of the approach is viewed as evidence that the problem is worse than was originally anticipated, and more resources are collected and directed for the intervention—only to result in continuing failure.

Some years ago, sociologists Don Warren and Rachael Warren of the University of Michigan were among the first academics to approach low-income communities by first pursuing their strengths. They surveyed residents, asking where they turned to in times of stress and crisis. They answered that the first resources they turned to in times of trouble were family members, local churches, ethnic associations, and institutions that were all within their geographic zip code. Their last resort was a professional outsider. In sum, the conventional antipoverty approach tends to employ institutions that are last choice of those who are in need as the primary means of providing assistance to the poor.

The trailblazing academic "godfather" of recognizing and building on the capacities and the strengths of low-income people is my friend John McKnight, emeritus professor of education and social policy and codirector of the Asset-Based Community Development Institute at Northwestern University. Other scholars highlighting the strengths of low-income communities include Robert B. Hill—former director of research at Morgan State University and the author of *The Strengths of Black Families* and *The Strengths of African American Families: Twenty-Five Years Later*[1]—and John Sibley Butler—director of the Herb Kelleher Center for Entrepreneurship and the Institute for Innovation, Creativity and Capital at the University of Texas at Austin.

The university can play a meaningful and a constructive role in assisting those who are in need if it can learn to be "on tap" but not necessarily "on top."

What does this mean? What is the proper "outside/inside" relationship dynamic? The model that I have in mind comes from the book of Genesis in the Old Testament in the story of a Hebrew young man, Joseph.

Joseph was one of twelve brothers and the favorite son of his father, Jacob. His ability to interpret dreams and the gift from his father of a resplendent coat of many colors caused him to fall into disfavor with his envious brothers. In a jealous rage, they faked Joseph's death and sold him to slave traders journeying to Egypt. They then brought his blood-soaked cloak to their father, telling him that Joseph had been killed by a wild animal.

During the years of his captivity, Joseph maintained his integrity. He was a good steward and dutifully executed his responsibilities, yet he remained steadfast in his faith to his God. While he was in prison he correctly interpreted the dreams of the pharaoh's servant. When the pharaoh was troubled by a dream that none of his soothsayers could interpret, upon the advice of this servant, Joseph was brought before him. Joseph warned the pharaoh that a famine was coming and advised him to store up grain to survive. When Joseph's predictions came true and Egypt, alone, was prepared for the famine, he was appointed to a position of leadership second only to the pharaoh.

This is a powerful metaphor: a wealthy man in the most powerful position placed the interest of the nation's future ahead of all the conventional wisdom. He looked beyond race, class, and ethnic differences to follow the guidance of an uneducated Hebrew shepherd and appoint him to a position of great authority.

Modern-Day Josephs

Throughout the past thirty-three years the Center of Neighborhood Enterprise has found effective solutions to some of the most intractable problems facing low-income people and disadvantaged communities. From youth violence, teen pregnancy, and drug addition to finding homes for abandoned and neglected children, the solutions were abiding in the same neighborhoods that suffered the problems.

The grassroots leaders who have engendered community uplift and personal transformations against the greatest odds are our nation's modern-day "Josephs." Whether they serve in disadvantaged urban neighborhoods or impoverished rural areas, the grassroots leaders who are the agents of change and renewal have identifying characteristics in common.

They tend to live in both the geographic and cultural zip code of those they serve and most are available on a 24/7 basis. Their programs predate funding and did not originate as a result of a grant, and nearly all operate on a shoestring budget. They are impassioned about serving those who are in need and view their work as a calling rather than a job. If their funds are temporarily diminished they seldom give up the cause. Most have made a lifetime commitment to those they serve. In their community, they have established a reputation for honesty and integrity. Very seldom are they at the forefront of any protest or demonstration. They are not seeking to bring attention to themselves but are constantly promoting the welfare of others. They are humble about their accomplishments and avoid celebrity. Though they are proven experts in the arenas in which they serve, they welcome and value assistance and advice on practical matters.

These grassroots leaders are America's innovative "social entrepreneurs." Like their counterparts in the market economy who create 60 percent of new jobs, they have an ability to turn problems into opportunities. Just as venture capitalists provide resources to bring entrepreneurial ideas to fruition, our nation's social entrepreneurs need support and resources to continue and expand the solutions they develop based on firsthand experience of the problems they address. This is where the university and the skills, knowledge, and expertise of its students can play a critical role.

These street-savvy social entrepreneurs tend to be poor bookkeepers and may need assistance in accounting. Though they have a critical need for access to capital, they may not be the best at writing a grant application. And while they are thoroughly invested in working on a personal level with those they serve, they may lack the time, expertise, and skills needed to document their success and evaluate their impact. The universities and student volunteers can play a crucial role in meeting all these needs and more, using their talents and knowledge in the service of indigenous community leaders.

Whether assistance is given to grassroots efforts in a rural African village or an inner-city neighborhood, the principles of effective support and assistance are the same. One example is the collaboration embodied in the national Violence-Free Zone initiative launched eight years ago by the Center for Neighborhood in some of the most trouble-plagued schools in our nation. The initiative is typically coordinated through a grassroots community organization. It includes roles for representatives of the school administration and staff and local police department, but its most critical element—and the key to its effectiveness—is enlisting young adults who grew up in the same neighborhoods and attended the same schools as hall monitors, mediators, and character coaches. These peer mentors have earned the trust, confidence, and respect of the students, and, being attuned to the "buzz" of youth communication, they are able to identify and avert potential conflict.

The most prominent site of this initiative is the Violence-Free Zone (VFZ) in Milwaukee. For the past five years, Professor Byron Johnson and his research team at Baylor University have been conducting a comparative analysis tracking incidents of violence, truancy, and academic achievement in VFZ schools and in schools that do not participate in the initiative. This study has recently been accepted for academic review.

Three evaluations produced to date reported that the VFZ had measurable impact in improved safety, reduction in suspensions and truancies, and increased academic performance. In addition, "climate surveys" of the initiative's impact on the incidence of crime in surrounding communities and a cost-benefit analysis are also being conducted.

In their analyses, Johnson's staff worked closely with the local youth advisor in the schools. They listened to their accounts and were able to capture and document the innovative interaction between the peer mentors and the students as well as how they interacted with law enforcement and professional school staff. This objective independent evaluation documented the measurable impact of the VFZ approach with regard to improved safety, reduction in suspensions and truancies, and increased academic performance. The role played by the Baylor team provides a threshold for additional support and can serve as a model of how to provide effective assistance in addressing a critical problem of a low-income community.

In sum, to avoid injuring with the helping hand and to most effectively serve disadvantaged communities, universities and student volunteers should follow these simple guidelines:

1. Provide assistance to strengthen and support the efforts of indigenous grassroots initiatives and neighborhood leaders. An outsider should never inadvertently become competitive with an informal indigenous provider of service.

2. Offer one's most valuable skills, talents, and expertise in service to local community leaders who, uniquely, have the capacity to engender personal transformation and empower individuals to become agents of their own elevation and community uplift. (Helping the poor should not mean ladling soup in a shelter, especially for college-educated students who can offer critical support in areas ranging from grant applications to documentation and evaluation of success.)

3. Do not come in with a preconceived of what help is needed. Listen to neighborhood leaders who are serving their communities to find out what type of assistance would be most beneficial to their efforts.

Only when volunteers offer their assistance in a way that respects the indigenous culture, recognizes community capacity, and works in partnership with local leaders can each side be enriched, to the benefit of all.

Note

1. Robert Hill, *The Strengths of Black Families* (New York: Emerson Hall, 1972); Robert Hill, *The Strengths of African American Families Twenty-Five Years Later* (New York: University Press of America, 1997).

19

HOW CAN HIGHER EDUCATION RECLAIM ITS POWER?

Sam Daley-Harris

When Harry Boyte asked colleagues to write essays addressing this question—"How can higher education reclaim its power to reshape citizens in broad ways including through work?"—the following image came to mind. I saw my son, now fifteen, going through T-ball, and the various levels of Little League, and then on to travel teams and high school. We do a pretty good job of teaching baseball, but a terrible job of teaching the skills of democracy. The university, a culprit in this failure, can also be the focal point for its solution.

I first came face-to-face with our failure in civic education thirty-five years ago when I asked seven thousand high school students to name their member of Congress. I had just gotten over my hopelessness about ending global poverty and started speaking to high school students about the subject. Before going into the first classroom I read statements from a National Academy of Sciences Food and Nutrition Study calling for the "political will" to end hunger and asked the students to name their member of Congress. Out of seven thousand students asked only two hundred could answer correctly—fewer than 3 percent. I believe that if I had asked who knew what a fly ball was, or better yet, asked them to demonstrate catching a fly ball, the success rate would have been much greater than 3 percent.

This failure of civic education was reconfirmed in my most recent survey. Three-quarters of my lectures in the fall of 2013 were on college campuses, and once again, thirty-five years later, I asked students to name their member of Congress. Only 10 percent could do so. We cannot continue to ignore this breakdown in educating on one of the most basic tools of democracy.

As Boyte said, in "Reinventing Citizenship as Public Work," "We need to move beyond overly narrow views of citizenship as voting and voluntarism, and reinvent citizenship as *public work*. This means putting *education for work with public qualities* at the center of teaching and learning, for the sake of ourselves as educators, for our students, and for the democracy."

I might add to this list "and for the sake of the planet." While the examples in Boyte's essay include a series of inspiring innovations needed to revitalize crumbling institutions, none provided a way to equip students, faculty, and staff to deeply and powerfully reclaim their democracy as citizen-lobbyists.

In this essay I will discuss ways the university community can correct this failure to empower, providing instead a truly deep experience of citizenship. My work has been focused on creating structures of support within civil society organizations. Educators could use these support structures, which come from the best in education, to teach the tools of democracy in order to solve our greatest challenges: domestic and global poverty, climate change, creating a domestic and global culture of peace, campaign finance reform, and more. Let me begin with a demonstration of the need for a deep curriculum.

In the twentieth-anniversary edition of *Reclaiming Our Democracy*[1] I tell the story of Cheryl McNamara, a Citizens' Climate Lobby (CCL) volunteer. McNamara read Ronald Wright's *A Short History of Progress*,[2] which showed how civilizations like the Mayans and the Polynesian society on Easter Island rose and fell because they gobbled up the environment that sustained them. She had been deeply concerned about climate change previously but had put it to the back of her mind. McNamara relates how that would change this time: "When I lay down Ronald Wright's book I envisioned myself as an elderly woman on her death bed, ashamed that I could have done something about this problem but did nothing and now that I lay dying, I was powerless to do anything. But it was not too late. I was in my prime, perfectly capable of helping to solve this gargantuan and dangerous problem." McNamara worked with her spouse to dramatically reduce their family's carbon footprint but realized it was not enough. "We needed others to drastically reduce their personal footprints too," she recalled, "and only government policy could make that happen." Around that time she was volunteering with a climate rally on Parliament Hill in Ottawa, Canada, and was struck by several realizations including this one: "We spent a lot of time and effort on an event that was largely ignored outside of the few thousand people who made a lot of noise outside Parliament that day. I asked myself, what was preventing us from going inside and actually talking to policy and law makers about this pressing problem? Why weren't we doing that?" (264). McNamara's question reverberates through our mostly hollow lives as citizens. The sad answer to why we aren't going inside and actually talking to the lawmakers is that most people who want big change don't know how and cannot find an organization capable of empowering them at a level equal to their desire for change. Most organizations ask us for nothing more than a mouse click and a check. They see us as little children who are too busy with play, too distracted, too naive, and too incapable of doing the homework necessary to go really deep with our democracy. But when citizens find an organization that treats them as capable adults miracles can happen.

The following quote is often attributed to Mark Twain: "The two most important days in your life are the day you are born and the day you find out why." Actually asking and then finding answers to these "why questions" is essential to revitalizing the original purpose of citizens: "Why am I here? What am I here to do? What is my purpose?" That is what McNamara was doing when she pictured herself on her deathbed ashamed that she had done nothing about climate change and then realized it wasn't too late to make a difference.

McNamara connected with her life's purpose and her intention to live consistently with it. She eventually found Citizens' Climate Lobby, an organization that helped her fulfill that purpose. There would be a good deal of trial and error along the way, but the course was set. Isn't this part of what is required if higher education is to reclaim its power to shape citizens?

In a truly introspective moment I think everyone would agree that one of the answers to "why we are here?" is to contribute, to make a difference, to leave the campsite cleaner than we found it. But for most people there is little introspection, and, if there is, the desire to contribute is smothered under layers of hopelessness, cynicism, and despair. Most advocacy efforts see this despair and offer programs congruent with it. They offer a thin gruel of simple and simplistic actions—a mouse-click here, a contribution there—that leave their members in virtual kindergarten as citizen-activists. Instead, they should offer a rich curriculum that propels citizen-activists to third, ninth, and twelfth grade and then on to college.

In late 2013 a CBS poll asked, "How much say do you have in government?" Three out of four respondents answered "not much." Imagine how difficult it would be to get those respondents into action. Why bother if you believe you have little say?

This despair is compounded by the perception that big problems aren't solvable. During eighteen campus lectures in the fall of 2013 I asked students if the end of poverty or a stable climate were possible. "I know we're on a college campus," I would acknowledge, "and you want me to define 'the end of poverty' or 'a stable climate,' but I won't do that. Just use whatever information you currently have and tell me if you think the end of poverty or a stable climate is possible." I asked each question separately and each time half of the students said either one or the other was impossible. Again, why bother to work on ending global poverty or addressing climate change if it's an unsolvable problem?

A new chapter in *Reclaiming Our Democracy* outlines thirteen commitments I see as needed to succeed at citizen empowerment and transformation. This begins my direct answer to the question "How can higher education reclaim its power to shape citizens?" The excellence inherent in each of these commitments can be drawn from the best in our educational system. In this essay I will focus on just four of the commitments: (1) a deep structure of support, (2) group support, (3) focus, and (4) a rich curriculum. Every mention of organizations or volunteers below should also be read as a campuses and students.

A deep structure of support is the foundation. This what the learning communities on all campuses attempt to create for their students, but few organizations or campuses succeed in developing a deep structure of support in the area of advocacy. The notion that all volunteers need is a training session on meeting a member of Congress, a packet of materials, and a sense that their cause is just ignores the heavy layer of cynicism and despair found in each of us and throughout society. The structure of support includes inspiring (1) nationwide monthly conference calls for groups, (2) weekly coaching calls for group leaders, (3) monthly action sheets, and (4) packets for editorial writers. Without that, all the other commitments become interesting ideas that are seldom implemented.

But as with everything, a structure of support can have people "going through the motions" or "going for breakthroughs." For example, each of the components of a nationwide conference call can be done in a way that empowers or a way that doesn't.

One section of the monthly conference call is the guest speaker. If the speaker is given twenty-five minutes but there is no time for questions, the volunteers (or students) become "bumps on a log" and not as deeply engaged as they would with a ten-minute talk followed by fifteen minutes of discussion.

Another section of the monthly conference call has two or three volunteers share a recent victory. But if all volunteers say is, "We met with our member of Congress, it was exciting, and we can't wait to do it again," and they omit the fact that it took a dozen phone calls to get the appointment, they had to meet with the district director first, and they were really nervous as they walked into the meeting, it won't be as useful for the others listening in around the country. When a discussion of the struggle precedes the victory, those listening in can more easily see themselves in both.

A third section of the monthly conference call, something most organizations omit entirely, is practicing to be more articulate. This might be closest to an oral exam or preparing for a class presentation. If a volunteer does a terrible job role-playing a call to a congressional aide and the staff can say nothing more than, "Thank you for volunteering, you were so brave to volunteer," then this section of the call is disempowering and a waste of time.

But an organization on or off campus cannot just begin offering empowering conference calls and expect that people will automatically show up. There has to be an enrollment process that lays out a compelling vision that inspires those who had previously been discouraged.

This leads to another of the commitments mentioned above: group support. Campuses often encourage study groups and group projects because that is how people often do their tasks in the world of work. Certainly groups are capable of moving to the lowest common denominator, but when well coached, groups can bring out the best in people and support participants in having breakthroughs.

Another aspect of citizen empowerment and transformation is focus. This might best be compared to choosing one's major or area of focus. If you have empowered groups around the country and they are slotted into a compelling structure of support, but the issue focus changes every two or three months, the volunteers are not able to develop the confidence and competence to move out of their comfort zones and take action.

One other commitment is a deep curriculum. Of course this is what all educational institutions strive to provide. But when advocacy campaigns flit from issue to issue they may do so because a number of issues need a grassroots push, because they don't have the discipline to focus, or because they have embraced the conventional wisdom that mistakenly assumes that if you focus on one issue over the course of a year the volunteers will get bored. This is true only if the curriculum is shallow and the issue lacks vision. What the conventional wisdom doesn't understand is that gaining mastery on a topic over time—deeply understanding the legislation, players, arguments, and politics—is thrilling for volunteers and gives them a confidence that is exciting, not boring. Rejecting the conventional wisdom, CCL has focused on a carbon tax and dividend for three years, and yet, as I write this chapter, their volunteers in the United States and Canada had 1265 letters to the editor and 248 op-eds published in 2013, up from thirty-six letters and twenty op-eds in all 2010. Is that what boredom looks like? I don't think so.

In two dozen lectures during the fall of 2013 I described how volunteers in the antipoverty citizens lobby RESULTS arranged for twenty-eight editorial writers to join conference calls with Grameen Bank founder Muhammad Yunus in 1987, nineteen years before he received the Nobel Peace Prize. This was the question: "How were volunteers able to get twenty-eight editorial writers to join a call in 1987 with an unknown man, Muhammad Yunus, engaged in an unknown intervention, microfinance, who worked in rural areas of a little-known country, Bangladesh?"

I walked my audiences through a monthly conference call that included a guest speaker on microfinance legislation with a question-and-answer period, sharing of grassroots victories, a section focused on learning to be articulate on the issue (in this case legislation focused on microfinance for the very poor), and a written action that could be taken on the spot (a letter to a member of the House or Senate or to the president). With me playing the role of a volunteer, here is what I shared with my audience:

It's January 1987 and I take the call with my group of other volunteers. We have a conference call guest on the microfinance legislation, a question and answer (Q&A) period, we hear some grassroots victories, we learn a little talk on the microfinance legislation and then write letters to our Representative. The call is on Saturday, I am an inspired volunteer, but on Monday I forget about it and don't do anything.

It's February 1987. We have a conference call guest on the microfinance legislation who is even better than the month before, Q&A, we hear some grassroots victories, learn a brief talk on microfinance and write one of our US Senators. Now I'm really inspired. On Monday I call the editorial writer, I call again on Tuesday and then again on Wednesday, but he never calls me back.

Now it's March 1987. We have our new microfinance guest speaker, Q&A, hear some grassroots victories, learn a little talk on microfinance, and then write a letter to the other Senator. On Monday I call the editorial writer again and this time he picks up the phone—by mistake. He thought it was someone he was expecting a call from. He asks me if I can send him something. It's 1987, so I can't e-mail it. I drive it over and leave it with the receptionist.

It's now April 1987. We have a really good guest speaker, Q&A, grassroots victories, learn a little talk and then write letters to President Reagan. Inspired again, I call the editorial writer and ask if we can meet for 10 minutes, perhaps just for coffee. He says yes and at the end of the 10 minutes, which have now stretched to 25 minutes, he looks me in the eye and says, "I have to be honest with you, I'm not going to write about this. Why don't you write an op-ed for the paper?" So I do. I've heard all these microfinance guest speakers, practiced all these little talks, written all these letters. My op-ed is really good and it's published in early May.

Now it's the May 1987 conference call. We have a guest speaker on the microfinance legislation, Q&A, grassroots victories (this time I'm telling people about how I got my first op-ed published), we learn a little talk and then write a letter to the editor.

It's now the June 1987 conference call. We learn that Muhammad Yunus will do a conference call with editorial writers in August. I call my editorial writer. He's obviously heard of Muhammad Yunus from me many times, he feels a little guilty for not having done anything yet, he really liked my op-ed, and says he will join the call.

Do you see that if we had focused on microfinance in January and February and then switched to child and maternal health in March and April and then switched to basic education in May and June that I, the volunteer, would not have been able to succeed? I needed focus, in this case the microfinance legislation, and I needed a deep and inspiring curriculum, the conference call guests and question and answer sessions; I needed printed materials, the monthly action sheets and packet for editorial writers, and I needed the section that encouraged us to be articulate.

Between the mid-1980s and today RESULTS has been at the center of advocacy efforts that have led to global child mortality rates plummeting from forty-one thousand per day in 1984 to eighteen thousand per day today and microloans to the very poor jumping from one million reached in 1986 to 124 million today. You might say yes, but that was launched more than twenty-five years ago—what about today? Let me return to CCL, a group that turned six years old at the end of 2013 and shows how this focused approach is working today.

Elli Sparks is a CCL volunteer from the Richmond, Virginia, area. Think of Sparks as a student on campus who, like most, would need serious coaching and empowerment to become a community leader. Sparks often said that when she joined CCL she was suffering from what she called "climate trauma." She would read Bill McKibben's book *Eaarth: Making a Life on a Tough New Planet* and weep at home and at work.

When Sparks joined CCL she hadn't be on a lobbying visit in a dozen years and had never met with an editorial writer. But eighteen months after joining, she co-led a workshop on creating relationships with members of Congress and editorial writers.

Citizens' Climate Lobby provided the ingredients discussed above: a powerful structure of support, groups of local activists to work with, focus on one issue, and a rich curriculum, ingredients any campus could provide. Needing a model for building relationships with members of Congress and editorial writers, Sparks said, "I adore romantic relationships, so I use romance as my model."

That first meeting with the editorial writer . . . it's like a blind date, only you've decided beforehand you are going to marry this fellow. You are going to be sweet and interesting, but not too intense. . . . If it doesn't work out with the editor, you are going to marry one of his friends at the newspaper—the business editor, environmental writer, or city editor. Someone at this paper will find you interesting and compelling—it's just a matter of being persistent until you find the right connection.

. . . I see the relationship with a member of Congress as an arranged marriage. If you live in her district, the member's aide has to meet with you. That's what our Congressman's legislative director (LD) told us in January. Since then, we've met five times with the LD in 2012. We schedule 45-minute meetings with him. He keeps us for well over an hour. He doesn't want us to leave! Why? Because a good arranged marriage starts out cold and heats up over time. That's different than a love match, which starts out hot and slowly cools down.

. . . I see the editorial page writer as a painter. His canvas is the editorial pages. His pallet is filled with letters to the editor, op-eds, and editorials. I am his muse, model, and assistant. . . . I want him to fill his canvas with colors that I like, so I'll have my group send 3–5 letters to the editor whenever the opportunity arises. The more colors I put on his pallet, the better chance of having him pick one or two of my favorite colors.

And then she got to the essence of citizen empowerment and transformation—a deep example of revitalizing of the original meaning of citizen. "During our conference I met with 20 congressional offices. I met with many folks whose view of the world was very different than mine. Going into their offices was hard. I had to let go of a lot of emotional baggage. I could no longer judge them or hold hostility in my heart towards them. I had to let go of my fear of climate change and my fear that they wouldn't listen to me. I had to center myself in love. Releasing fear and centering in love . . . this is sacred and profound work." Most people invited to meet with twenty congressional offices would see it at hopeless work or dirty work. But Sparks, who started at "climate trauma," now sees it as sacred and profound work.

Is this not the true goal of education: empowering students, faculty, and alumni to be visionary leaders in healing the planet, able to climb over discouragement and live their highest aspirations? Is this not what education is called to do, perhaps now more than ever. The model that RESULTS, CCL, the Peace Alliance, and a growing number of advocacy organizations use was all developed by teachers, was taken from the best in education, and must be brought back to campus if higher education is to reclaim its power to reshape citizens.

Notes

Portions of this essay are taken from the twentieth anniversary edition of *Reclaiming Our Democracy: Healing the Break between People and Government*. Copyright 2013 by Sam Daley-Harris and published by Camino Books, Inc., Philadelphia, PA. Used by permission of the publisher. All rights reserved.

1.   Sam Daley-Harris, "The RESULTS Model Takes Aim at Climate Change," 20th anniversary edition, *Reclaiming Our Democracy: Healing the Break between People and Government*, (Philadelphia: Camino Books, 2013), 263–65.

2.   Ronald Wright, *A Short History of Progress* (Toronto: House of Anansi Press, 2004).

PART VI

Possible Futures

Confronting what Paul Markham calls
the coming "avalanche" of change, a
stellar group of public intellectuals and
leading civic agents of change consider the
possibilities.

20

ILLIBERAL EDUCATION

Benjamin R. Barber

Like everything else in our society from digital media to public health, education continues to be privatized, commercialized, virtualized, instrumentalized, and trivialized. Almost every trend in the education domain is moving away from the liberal arts—by which I mean not the study of literature in college but rather, in the classical sense, the arts of free women and men seeking to acquire the competences of citizenship necessary to living in a free society. The liberal arts understood this way are made up in equal parts of critical thinking, moral and political reasoning, and civic responsibility. They are rooted in a promise that every citizen of a free society will receive an education, and that all those wishing or claiming to be a citizen (which in an ideal world should be *all* people) will be educated—helped to acquire the capacity for deliberation, common thinking, and civic judgment; which is to say, the capacity to exercise the natural liberty that is their birthright but by no means guaranteed to them in its actual realization.

By these criteria, today's pedagogical policies and trends are better described as *illiberal* education. How quaint seems the once robust Society for Values in Higher Education, of which as a former Danforth Fellow I am still a rather too listless member. Responsibility for the disrepute in which values are now held goes in equal part to zealous religious fundamentalists on the right and their zealous postmodernist critics on the left. Either way, with values off the table for liberals, how can they continue to treat education as the foundation of citizenship or the sine qua non of critical thinking and agency? From online "remote" education to the radical decline of majors in the liberal arts at elite four-year institutions, from the careerism of students to the specialization of the professoriate, from the subordination of teaching to testing and of preschool and out-of-the-classroom education to K–12 standard learning, every recent development is driven by the marketplace and the private sector. Education itself is for the most part deemed an exercise in job and career preparation for positions in a privatized society its participants neither choose nor benefit from as citizens. Today's students are urged to become passive servants of commercial society, urged to ask only what they might do for the world that shapes them rather than what they can do to shape the world.

Yet before railing still again against the deficiencies of modern pedagogy (which is what we ardent but frustrated old liberals tend to do), it is important to grasp that we—educators, scholars, teachers, liberals—are no longer in a position to do very much about these disturbing changes by reforming education alone. We tend to be the unwilling victims rather than the shapers of the trends that are undermining liberal education. For as education, like culture, religion, and other once primary human endeavors, is subordinated to a commercial civilization that has persuaded the majority that private markets serve public interests far better than public democratic institutions, the real struggle for education has shifted from pedagogy and education theory to politics broadly conceived. It lies now first of all in the domain of *digital media* (and the politics of digital media); and in the consequences of a ubiquitous *neoliberal ideology* and the political assault on public interests and democratic institutions that ideology has inspired. Let me look then at these two seemingly ancillary but in fact primary domains, both profoundly political (or, better, antipolitical) for clues to what we can do to reclaim liberal education and its promise for liberal citizenship.

Digital media. There is nothing in digital technologies per se averse to education: they represent merely another tool. But in a world where technology is privatized and commercialized, and where young people are far more exposed to its ubiquitous screens and magical pixels than they are to teachers (or preachers or counselors or family members), it opens the gates to corrosive forms of informal education, soft influence, and blinkered prejudice that are deeply corrosive of formal education. And it risks making us (in Thoreau's phrase) tools of our tools. Students in K–12 today receive perhaps thirty hours a week of instruction (it drops to six to nine hours a week in college); compare that with the sixty to seventy hours a week kids from two to twenty (thirty?) are tethered virtually to their PDFs and computers and smart phones—their TV and movie screens—and it is clear that neither teachers nor parents can act any longer as gatekeepers to or liberators of young minds. Whether we focus on animated feature films, boy-teen video games, insipid social media, or mass television advertising and marketing, we confront a world whose aims—let us not vilify them—are *other* than liberal, critical, civic, or public in character.

The celebrated social media, widely regarded as at worst innocuous and more often as a foundation for a happy social life, are in fact often pernicious to liberal education and citizenship. Not that digital interactivity is per se or intrinsically insidious: on the contrary. Although hardly a cyber-zealot, I was one of the first observers to predict that the "interactive possibilities of video, computers, and information retrieval systems open up a new mode of human communication [and] . . . can be used either in civic and constructive ways or in manipulative and destructive ways."[1] Moreover, in emerging democracies, smart phones and the web have played a role in fomenting and directing revolutionary activity. The web can remove all limits from deliberation and common decision making. It is a horizontal and point-to-point medium like the telephone, rather than a vertical platform that enables top-down authority and control. It broadens the territory of the agora and democratic assembly infinitely and makes time a servant of rather than an obstacle to instant communication.

Yet in part because it is a wholly owned subsidiary of media corporations wedded to profit, digital (electronic) media life has tended to reinforce social ghettoization and group think (see Eli Pariser in his book called *The Filter Bubble*).[2] Indeed, the speed that is a virtue of the web's efficacy can run rough-shod over democratic deliberation and obliterate democratic judgment. "Big data," inundating our brains and overwhelming our filters, does little for knowledge and less for wisdom (the "knowledge society" is anything but the "wisdom society"). Facebook encourages friendship (however superficial) and ubiquitous liking, but ignores "others" and neglects diversity. Democracy is about learning to live with people we neither like nor agree with—finding common ground among people with whom we may have little in common. Amazon has ingenious algorithms that permit it to tell us, once we have bought a book or two, which other books we might like. A democratic algorithm, however, would survey our purchases in order to tell us "here are a few books you will not like, and certainly will not agree with, which however you need to read to understand the political landscape in which you are living as a citizen."

How then can educators and citizens look favorably on the new media, even as those media look back at us, watching us 24/7 with electronic "cookies" and information-collection programs and "push commerce" aimed at exploitation and control? Who will not feel anxious about the entailments of the late Steve Jobs's chillingly cheery Apple mantra: "It's not the consumers' job to know what they want." Because it *is* the task of citizens to know what they want, what the public goods are that define their communities. And if new media cannot help them answer such questions, they are part of the challenge liberal education faces rather than a key to its successful realization.

Neo-liberal ideology. Market ideology over the past forty years has prospered at the expense not only of government but of the very idea of democracy and a democratic public (made up of citizens). Starting in the early 1980s with President Reagan's claim that government is part of the problem rather than part of the solution and Prime Minister Thatcher's insistence there is no such thing as society or a public good (beyond aggregated private goods), what George Soros calls market fundamentalism has been systematically eroding the global public's confidence in its own capacity to govern itself through democratic institutions. It has fixed in our civic thinking the counterintuitive idea that private corporations driven by private profits are better guarantors of our liberty than public institutions we ourselves control.

Market ideology intersects with the new media in particularly dangerous ways. The Clinton administration's shocking Telecommunications Act of 1996, which superseded the 1934 Federal Communications Act, which first cast broadcast media as public utilities demanding government regulation, initiated an era in which electronic media were cut loose from government oversight. Rooted in the notion that spectrum abundance rendered regulation moot (plenty of room for every voice in the new digital world of boundless bandwidth and infinite cable channels), the market approach ignored the reality of global media monopolies. It pretended that your tweet and Google's search engine were more or less equivalent, that your blog and the *Huffington Post* carried the same weight in the marketplace, that Bill Gates and Steve Jobs and Marc Zuckerberg and Jeff Bezos are so many everymen with voices no louder than anyone else's.

But a little less than two decades after the 1996 communications law was passed, it turns out that along with still-powerful but fading also-rans such as IBM, AT&T and Microsoft, four commercial megacompanies dominate the media world and its impact on education. Whether you are shopping, researching, chatting with fiends, looking for partners, watching a movie, listening to music, searching for porn, calculating figures, seeking information, or trying to play or earn remotely and digitally, you are probably doing it on, with, or through products and platforms made by Google, Amazon, Facebook, or Apple. Their content, their hardware and software, are all you need to live, think, and breathe digitally. But nothing like what you need to live, think, and breathe civically or communally or democratically. And that is the problem. Whatever else it is, "Facebookistan" is not about liberal learning or civic education. Could be, but it is not.

There is perhaps no better example of the disastrous intersection of new media and privatization in the education domain than in the popularity of the "remote education" programs being pursued by for-profit companies or nonprofit traditional institutions looking for ways to monetize their presumed excellence. Using all the right tropes and memes—democratization, outreach, inclusion, elite instruction for everyman and woman, remote education for the most part makes nearly everything worse for its actual students, for while it is touted as a method to increase the compass of education and allow those who would never normally have access to elite professors to do so, it is in fact a way to reduce contact between teachers and students, reduce the number of professors, and "skim" the student population. Those who prosper (or merely survive) in the setting of remote education are those with strong motivation and natural intelligence that permit them to learn under any conditions. The extraordinary rate of drop-out and the frustration of those very poor learners or unprepared students who flock to the web suggest that it is precisely the least privileged and most needy—those without the resources or time even to go to community colleges or part-time residential programs, the ones who should theoretically benefit the most from inexpensive remote education curricula—for whom the approach fails. Profits grow fast; liberal education grinds to a halt.

Even where it succeeds, remote education lends itself to empirical learning and memorization but is ill suited to cultivating judgment, discrimination, and discernment. The cultivation of these faculties calls for a live faculty, present and engaged with students, ideally one-on-one in the tutorial setting. Remote education also reduces peer learning by making interaction among students under the guidance of a teacher difficult, and leaving individual students in silos with little but pixels to rely on. Remote education makes good on only one facet of its name: it is remote from education.

The combination then of a market ideology that privileges the private over the public and treats citizens as political consumers (and political spectators— politics as something we watch on TV), with information and communication systems dominated by commerce, profit, and privatism, leaves educators out in the cold and puts citizens in a deep freeze. It is not that new point-to-point technologies might not be developed to meet civic and learning needs. It is that there is little incentive to do so in a society that no longer has much faith in government or democracy and has succumbed to the seduction of manipulative technologies.

Once these critical background conditions are understood, the debates about remote education, careerism, the professionalization of liberal education, and the substitution of testing for civic and moral development can be better appreciated. Even more important, we can see why it is so difficult to remedy the grievances of liberal education gone astray. Which is like trying to change the tires on a racecar while it is careening around the track or trying to reverse the course of a titanic ocean liner by turning around its deckchairs and pointing its passengers toward the stern. What we need to do is get the politics right: reclaim our democratic prerogatives, reassert the primacy of education as a public and civic good, and reimpose the criteria of democratic citizenship on pedagogy. The rest will follow.

Notes

1. Benjamin Barber, *Strong Democracy: Participatory Politics for a New Age* (Berkeley: University of California Press, 1984), 274.
2. Eli Pariser, *The Filter Bubble: What the Internet Is Hiding from You* (New York: Penguin Press, 2011).

21

JOBS, JOBS, JOBS: THE ECONOMIC IMPACT OF PUBLIC WORK

Peter Levine

America has struggled economically since the turn of this century. In the first decade of the 2000s, the US economy created about one million private-sector jobs, even though the population grew by thirty-three million.[1] College remains a path to employment, but it is an increasingly uncertain path and one open mainly to privileged young people. Eighty percent of young adults who grow up in the top quarter of the income distribution enter higher education, but only 17 percent who come from the bottom quarter even matriculate, let alone graduate.[2] College is expensive: a financial burden for those who can afford it and a barrier to attendance for those who cannot.

Under these circumstances, politicians predictably demand that colleges and universities produce more job-ready graduates at lower cost. Wisconsin governor Scott Walker has proposed to tie state funding to "performance," which "means not only degrees, but are young people getting degrees in jobs that are open and needed today?"[3] North Carolina governor Pat McCrory proposed to charge more tuition for majors that do not lead directly to jobs.[4] In Syracuse, New York, in August 2013, President Barack Obama announced a "new ratings system for colleges that will score colleges on opportunity—whether they're helping students from all kinds of backgrounds succeed; and on outcomes—[including] whether they have strong career potential when they graduate."[5]

These leaders do not spell out the implications, but we know that of all the majors in the United States, the ten with the best earning potential are various specialties within engineering, computer science, and pharmacy, all of which offer average starting salaries above $80,000. Meanwhile, the lowest-paying majors are counseling psychology, early childhood education, theology/religious vocations, and human services/community organization.[6] Studio and performing arts also fall in the bottom tier. Students who pursue these least lucrative and least secure majors often hope to work in community agencies, churches and other religious congregations, and arts organizations: pillars of American civil society. So politicians like Walker, McCrory, and Obama are—probably inadvertently—proposing that we significantly deemphasize the development of civic leaders.

That is a shortsighted strategy. Not only does it neglect democracy and the civic mission of higher education, but it also overlooks the economic benefits of civic engagement.

In a study for the National Conference on Citizenship, Kei Kawashima-Ginsberg, Chaeyoon Lim, and I considered two measures of civic engagement. One was the number of associations in any community that engage citizens, per population. For instance, we included churches and nonprofit service agencies. The other measure was the rate at which residents report working together and socializing with their neighbors. We found that these two measures of civic engagement predicted how well counties, cities, and states had recovered from the recession of 2008. We also considered levels of education and income, racial demographics, the role of the oil and gas industries, housing-price inflation, mobility, and many other factors, but civic engagement was a stronger predictor of communities' resilience against unemployment than any of these other factors.[7]

We have proposed several explanations, all of which are mutually compatible. First, participating in civic activities teaches skills that are also useful in the job market. After all, so-called "soft skills," like building consensus and solving problems in groups, are increasingly valuable in the twenty-first-century workplace, and you can learn them by participating as a citizen.[8] Higher rates of civic engagement may produce citizens who are more employable.

Young people also gain the motivation to stay in school and college and to pursue challenging academic work when they are involved in working with other people on social issues. A study for CIRCLE (the Center for Information and Research on Civic Learning and Engagement) by Alberto Davila and Marie T. Mora found that high school students who performed required service in courses were much more likely to graduate than peers who were similar except for their service experience.[9] According to our own rigorous longitudinal data, Tufts University students who become involved in sustained and demanding civic work tend to flourish better as students; they also report better mental health and success.

By working together on public problems, people develop trust for their fellow citizens.[10] When we trust one another, we are also more likely to undertake business partnerships: to buy, invest, and hire. Around the world, "social trust" (trust in fellow citizens) is a predictor of economic success.

A thriving civil society probably strengthens citizens' affection and loyalty to their own communities so that they choose to spend and invest locally.[11] If you have some discretionary money and you could hire a local contractor to renovate your kitchen, or else buy a flat-screen TV made in China, you may be more likely to hire the contractor if you are fond of and involved in your town.

Finally, a strong set of independent organizations and active citizens can hold governments accountable and improve their performance, cutting waste and corruption.[12]

More sophisticated and elaborate studies have revealed similar results. Robert Sampson led a massive study of Chicago neighborhoods that tracked individuals' well-being over many years and also examined the civic infrastructure of their communities. He found that a strong network of civic organizations boosted what he calls "collective efficacy," or the feeling that people can solve local problems by working together. In turn, higher collective efficacy was a powerful predictor of better education, less crime, and healthier economies.

Sampson observes, "It is the totality of the institutional infrastructure that seems to matter in promoting civic health and extending to unexpected economic vitality, whether in the form of rebuilding New Orleans or in rehabilitating vacant houses in economically depressed neighborhoods in cities around the country."[13]

Sampson's observation about two low-to-moderate-income, predominantly African American Chicago neighborhoods with strong collective efficacy has lessons for the whole United States: "There may be no great wealth to transmit in Chatham and Avalon Park, but by cultivating a sense of ownership and cultural commitment to the neighborhood, residents produce a social resource that feeds on itself and serves as a kind of independent protective factor and durable character that encourages action in the face of adversity."[14]

Using a very different method, Sean Safford looked closely at the economic trajectories of Youngstown, Ohio, and Allentown, Pennsylvania.[15] These two old manufacturing cities were economically and demographically similar when the crises of global competition and automation hit American manufacturing in the 1970s. Youngstown never recovered. It now has a median household income of $25,000 and a median home value of $52,000. Meanwhile, Allentown has turned into a successful postindustrial economic center with a median household income more than one-third higher than in Youngstown, homes worth almost three times more, just one-third as many murders per capita, and a substantially higher life expectancy.[16]

Safford traces the cities' starkly different trajectories to their different civic infrastructures. In their heyday as manufacturing centers, both had economic networks dominated by the interlocking boards of their local businesses. Both had social networks composed of private clubs. And both had civic organizations, which Safford defines as "those for which the primary goal is to improve the community in some way." But only Allentown had a separate, robust civic *network* composed of many linked civic organizations. When the economic crisis killed Youngstown's businesses and left the local elite competing for scarce financial resources, they had no place to gather, plan, and collaborate. But in Allentown, local leaders talked and cooperated in their overlapping civic organizations.

Lehigh University emerges in Safford's analysis as a significant civic hub. Its board included both activists and businesses. I presume that board members attended meetings to discuss Lehigh's affairs, but they also found time (perhaps over coffee), to talk about Allentown. As a result, the university itself started various economic development programs, while business and labor leaders developed broader economic strategies for their region.

All this research suggests that colleges and universities can help the economy if they produce graduates who do civic work, whether in explicitly civic professions like nonprofit management or else in private-sector jobs that allow them to collaborate with fellow citizens on shared concerns.

Further, colleges and universities can strengthen the economy if they act as good institutional citizens, participating in networks that enable discussion and collaboration about the welfare of their communities.

These are causal, empirical theories. My colleagues and I argue that investment in civic education and civic partnerships will yield economic benefits. Like all causal theories, our claims are uncertain and contingent. The economic payoffs will inevitably vary, depending on the context. We might find, for instance, that civic education creates jobs in recession-struck Las Vegas but not in booming Silicon Valley.

Uncomfortable exceptions may also arise. For example, Sampson finds that most associations boost "collective efficacy" in Chicago, but churches do not—a finding that would weaken the case for religious vocations if it turned up in other studies. Doug McAdam finds that the Freedom Summer volunteers who registered voters in Mississippi in 1964 had less success in their chosen careers compared to similar classmates who didn't go to Mississippi. In that case, civic engagement lowered the participants' professional success.[17]

Also, we might find that although civic education and engagement pay economic dividends, something else works even better: for example, distance learning, educational video games, or installing surveillance cameras in schools.

Thus we must be careful about how we generate, interpret, and use empirical findings. Often, social scientists presume that their job is to study a real-world practice that is already fully developed to learn whether—and why—it "works." Usually they define success in terms of the objectives of the practitioners or their funders. In this case, we would ask whether college-level civic education and engagement generate what governors and presidents demand: jobs.

But nothing simply "works." Success always requires experimentation, assessment, adjustment, reflection, and new experimentation, in an iterative cycle. By the same token, many things *can* work if they are developed properly. One could start with civic engagement or with surveillance cameras in schools and improve either one until it enhanced students' employment prospects.

In the best cases, the researchers who study a given practice are part of the reason that it works. They contribute to its development by offering their data and insights. They choose to work on this practice rather than something else because of a more fundamental commitment. I, for example, have studied deliberation in high schools. I *want* deliberation to work, and I hope that the research that I produce will contribute to its success. I have no such commitment to surveillance cameras. I would not study them or strive to improve their impact.

The reason for my hope in deliberation is fundamentally moral. I think a world in which people reason and work together is better than one in which they achieve the same levels of security, income, or welfare without freely collaborating. Deeper down, I believe in a theory that the good life is a life of freedom, reflection, and mutual commitment.

Thus I hope that civic education and civic engagement boost employment because I am fundamentally committed to civic values. My colleagues and I seek evidence of economic benefit to persuade policy makers to support what they should support anyway. If the economic evidence is favorable, we will use it strategically to expand support. If not, our values and commitments should encourage us to *improve* civic education until it enhances democracy and also produces jobs. Regardless of the empirical results we find, we owe a public explanation of our core values.

A public defense of our values also yields criteria by which to assess the practices that we have been studying empirically. For instance, this chapter is about college-level civic engagement (an input) and jobs (an output). I have discussed the empirical link between the input and the output, as they exist today. But both are subject to criticism and change.

Today, many civic programs basically take the form of volunteering. In the study cited above, Kawashima-Ginsberg, Lim, and I did not find any connection between volunteering rates at the community level and economic outcomes. I do not see a theoretical reason why volunteering per se should improve the economy.

But civic education can be reconceived so that it is less about volunteer service than about working on public concerns, where "working" implies serious commitment and accountability for results. "*Public* work," in the phrase championed by Harry Boyte and colleagues, means work that is done in public, by diverse citizens, on common issues. Reconfiguring civic education at the college level to look more like public work would satisfy core values that Boyte and colleagues have defended well.[18] It might also strengthen the impact of civic education on jobs and careers. Students would be more likely to learn skills useful for employment if their civic experiences in college were more like paid work.

Meanwhile, jobs could become more public. A given job *might* serve only the interests of the employer and deny the worker any scope to address community problems in public with diverse other citizens. But even if the employer is a for-profit firm, the job *can* promote and encourage public work. For example, I presume that the corporate executives, government officials, and labor leaders who attended meetings of the Lehigh University board contributed insights from their daily work to the conversations about Lehigh and Allentown. They then brought ideas from those discussions back to their jobs. If that is true, they were doing "public work" in the Lehigh boardroom and in their own offices. Public work is obviously harder for low-paid service workers and low-ranking bureaucrats, but within many industries and professions, a struggle is underway to recover their public and democratic traditions.[19]

If we made civic education into public work and also created jobs of greater public value, then the alignment between civic education and employment would be stronger and we would find more impressive evidence of economic impact. The data would then satisfy governors and presidents who want to see colleges produce jobs. More importantly, we would be building a better society and the educational system to support it.

Notes

1. Floyd Norris, "Job Growth Lacking in the Private Sector," *New York Times*, August 7, 2009, *www.nytimes.com/2009/08/08/business/economy/08charts.html?_r=0.*

2. M. J., Bailey and S. M. Dynarski, "Inequality in Postsecondary Education," in *Whither Opportunity? Rising Inequality, Schools, and Children's Life Chances*, ed. G. J. Duncan and R. J. Murnane (New York: Russell Sage, 2011), 120.

3. Dee J. Hall and Samara Kalk Derby, "Gov. Scott Walker Unveils Agenda for Wisconsin during Speech in California," *Wisconsin State Journal*, November 19, 2012.

4. Kevin Kiley, "Another Liberal Arts Critic," *Insider Higher Education*, January 30, 2013.

5. "Remarks by the President on College Affordability, Syracuse NY," August 22, 2013, White House, *www.whitehouse.gov/photos-and-video/video/2013/08/22/president-obama-speaks-college-affordability-0#transcript.*

6. Anthony P. Carnevale, Jeff Strohl, and Michelle Melton, *What's It Worth? The Economic Value of College Majors* (Washington, DC: Georgetown University Center on Education and the Workforce, 2013).

7. Kei Kawashima-Ginsberg, Chaeyoon Lim, and Peter Levine, Civic Health and Unemployment II: The Case Builds, National Conference on Citizenship: Washington, DC, 2012, *ncoc.net/unemployment2.*

8. JoAnn Jastrzab et al. "Serving Country and Community: A Longitudinal Study of Service in AmeriCorps," (Washington, DC: Corporation for National and Community Service, 2004), *www.abtassociates.com/reports/COMSRVS.pdf.*

9. Alberto Dávila and Marie T. Mora, *An Assessment of Civic Engagement and Educational Attainment* (Medford, MA: Center for Information and Research on Civic Learning and Engagement, 2007), *www.civicyouth.org.*

10. On trust, see K. M. Sønderskov, "Does Generalized Social Trust Lead to Associational Membership? Unravelling a Bowl of Well-Tossed Spaghetti," *European Sociological Review*, published online, 2010, doi:10.1093/esr/jcq017; and Francis Fukuyama, *Trust: Social Virtues and the Creation of Prosperity* (New York: Free Press, 1995).

11. On affection for communities and its connection to civic engagement and economic growth, see Gallup, Inc., *Knight Soul of the Community* 2010, 5, *www.soulofthecommunity.org.*

12. Robert D. Putnam, "Community-Based Social Capital and Educational Performance," in *Making Good Citizens: Education and Civil Society*, ed. Diane Ravitch and Joseph P. Viteritti (New Haven, CT: Yale University Press, 2001), 58–95; Robert D. Putnam, *Making Democracy Work: Civic Traditions in Modern Italy* (Princeton: Princeton University Press, 1993); Jeffrey M. Berry, Kent E. Portney, and Kenneth Thomson, *The Rebirth of Urban Democracy* (Washington, DC: Brookings Institution, 1993); Kent E. Portney and Jeffrey M. Berry, "Participation and the Pursuit of Sustainability in U.S. Cities," *Urban Affairs Review* 46, no. 1 (2010): 119–39.

13. Robert J. Sampson, *Great American City: Chicago and the Enduring Neighborhood Effect* (Chicago: University of Chicago Press, 2012), 372.

14. Sampson, *Great American City*, 398.

15. Safford, *Why the Garden Club Couldn't Save Youngstown* (Cambridge, MA: Harvard University Press, 2009).

16. The statistics on Youngstown and Allentown are not in Safford but come from Peter Levine, *We Are the Ones We Have Been Waiting For: The Promise of Civic Renewal in America* (New York: Oxford University Press, 2013), 16.

17. Doug McAdam, *Freedom Summer* (New York: Oxford University Press, 1988), 199–232.

18. See, e.g., Harry C. Boyte and Blase Scarnati "Transforming Higher Education in a Larger Context: The Civic Politics of Public Work," in *Civic Studies: Approaches to the Emerging Field*, ed. Peter Levine and Karol Edward Sołtan (Washington, DC; Bringing Theory to Practice, 2013), xx.

19. Albert W. Dzur, *Democratic Professionalism: Citizen Participation and the Reconstruction of Professional Ethics, Identity, and Practice* (University Park: Pennsylvania State University Press, 2008), 175–79.

22

REFLECTIONS OF A CIVIC SCIENTIST

John P. Spencer

> Isn't that what you do, Sonia . . . don't you take your net and
> throw it out into these far out places of quantum physics and
> systems theory, and don't you find that the only thing you ever
> catch is your own self back again? Like a fish trapped inside
> the wind. Where are the other people in your system, Sonia?
> The ones you love . . . the real people with their qualities,
> longings and weaknesses . . . where are you inside there,
> Sonia?. . . . Life is infinitely more than yours or mine obtuse
> theories about it. Healing the universe is an inside job.
> —From *Mindwalk*, Bernt Capra (director)

Harry Boyte's lead essay seeks to reinvigorate a sense of public work in higher education. This reflects a savvy understanding of how the world works—people are motivated to create change when change is integral to their self-interests. And if there's one truth in academia, it's that academics are *deeply self-interested* in their work. If we could make scholarly work civically engaged, then the energy, spark, and creativity of academia would be unleashed in the world. Rather than focusing our efforts on disciplinary endeavors or the betterment of a college or department, we could focus our work on the betterment of humanity.

Boyte's essay also highlights the importance of understanding knowledge and power. To create the world as it should be, you have to understand the world as it is. In our world, knowledge can bring power. Nowhere is this more apparent than in the world of science. Science infuses our daily lives and has a transformative effect on society in the form of medical advances, technological innovation, and tools to enhance our efficiency. Science is clearly a major source of knowledge and power in today's world.

Given that much of science in the United States takes place at research universities, it is critical that science be a central part of any discussion that seeks to reinvent or reinvigorate higher education. In my essay, I offer some reflections on the current state of science in society and point toward a new concept—civic science—that might impact public work in the sciences. These reflections include a particular civic science endeavor on school readiness that my colleagues and I began in 2012 with community partners in Iowa. The project—called "Get Ready Iowa"—shows an example of civic science in action.

The Knowledge War

Science is a great source of knowledge and power in the world today, and also a lightning rod for societal conflict. Today, societies face multiplying global crises—from economic collapse to global warming to crises in education and health care. This has led people to question the relationships among science, expert knowledge, democratic governance, and lay citizens. At the center of this questioning is an ideological battle—a knowledge war—that presents a fierce obstacle to public problem solving. This war exacerbates the polarization in our national civic and political life.

Harry Boyte, Scott Peters, Gwen Ottinger, Sherburne Abbott, and I recently articulated the multiple sides of this knowledge war. On one side is the cult of the expert.[1] This side represents a detached and technocratic approach to engaging science in society, championing the authority of "objective" scientific and disciplinary knowledge, while delegitimizing the authority and knowledge of lay citizens. Here, elite experts communicate the results of scientific research to the masses, who are viewed as passive clients and consumers of expert help and knowledge. If the masses fail to accept the authority of science for practice and policy, the remedy is to seek better messaging strategies, scientific literacy campaigns, and more energetic efforts to communicate scientific knowledge to citizens.

A second perspective can be characterized as an anti-intellectual "know-nothing" stance of victimhood and grievance, deeply hostile to scientists and science en masse. Know-nothing politics disparages and demonizes academic knowledge, science, and professional practices in the name of commonsense values and personal experience. This view is, arguably, a backlash against a technocratic stance that has lost the public's trust by claiming to know everything while simultaneously failing to provide solutions to global crises. Further, lay citizens whose skills and knowledge go unrecognized by the scientific elite may assert their common sense as a means of preserving their social identities.[2] Critically, the "know-nothing" stance is no more helpful in solving real-world problems than the technocratic approach.

The knowledge war's third side involves the production of claims and counterclaims by competing groups on different sides of a controversial issue, who recruit and fund their own experts and scientists to produce studies that favor their own positions. Although some such groups can be fairly accused of outright manipulation and misrepresentation of the scientific data,[3] others struggle over legitimate but divergent ways of framing questions, collecting data, and interpreting evidence.[4] The trend toward counterexpertise plays into larger dynamics of polarizing methods of political action and the erosion of spaces where diverse people interact in a productive, face-to-face fashion. The result is a Tower of Babel that hinders rather than enriches our public life.

Civic Science Offers a New Path Forward

Transcending the knowledge war calls for an approach that simultaneously values science and respects the knowledge, experience, and identities of people without scientific credentials to help build shared understandings and solutions rather than reinforcing factions. My colleagues and I have been working to reframe one approach—civic science—by emphasizing the "civic agency" of diverse participants in creating a sustainable, democratic way of life.[5] As summarized by Bäckstrand, "Civic science alludes to a changing relationship between science, expert knowledge and citizens in democratic societies. In this perspective, citizens and the public have a stake in the science-politics interface, which can no longer be viewed as an exclusive domain for scientific experts and policy-makers only."[6]

The desire to bridge the gap between scientists and nonscientists comes, in part, from philosophical arguments that are deeply critical of the "objectivist" stance of mainstream science. The objectivist stance asserts that science contains transcultural, socially neutral theories, models, and methods that enable scientists to "detect the facts about the order of the universe that are everywhere and always the same."[7] But this ideal is rarely the case in practice. Although controlled laboratory methods and reductive science have produced great insights, these insights only rarely translate directly into real-world solutions for the complex problems we face.

A key innovation of civic science is its *democratic* frame, part of a call for "strong democracy," extending normative values of participation into the scientific enterprise. In our view, the democratic frame is important but requires refining what it means for science to play a role in a healthy, functioning democracy. This requires explicitly acknowledging two things: that science is *political* and needs to shift from simply providing technical information to assisting in the process of governance and that science must be conceptualized within a *civic agency* framework.

Reframing Civic Science

Civic science builds on a rich history of efforts to translate scientific findings to real-world settings, full of complexity, ambiguity, and open-endedness, where science cannot be "applied" in any linear or straightforward way. But it frames these efforts with a new premise: that science is an essential part of politics, and, therefore, should assist in the process of governance, as well as provide input into policy. In these terms, "politics" is the interaction, negotiation, and integration of different interests and vantages to solve common problems and to create a shared way of life.

Civic science sees science as a resource for action *in* the world, more than simply a description *of* the world. As a living, dynamic practice rather than just a body of knowledge, science offers a powerful means of evidence-based learning and knowing that can be adopted and practiced by lay citizens as well as scientists. As such, it is a key tool of human and community empowerment. In this context, there is no clean divide between "basic" and "applied" sciences; rather, all forms of science—and all types of scientists—have the potential to directly contribute to discussions about the state of knowledge and how humans interact with one another and with the world around us. Indeed, using science effectively to solve real-world challenges, develop effective policies, and create a shared way of life requires the production of knowledge that strikes a balance between scientific and other forms of knowledge. This requires developing the capacities for working together, across partisan and other political divides.

Civic science also builds on a second central concept—*agency*. A sustained conversation has taken place over the last seven years between dynamical systems theorists who are generating an agent-based understanding of humans and human development, and political theorists and their partners who have placed agency at the center of a new "civic studies" field that extends beyond the liberal-communitarian arguments in political theory.[8] The result is a framework emphasizing individual and collective *agency* where scientists are understood to be *citizens*, working with fellow citizens, to solve real-world problems and develop new individual and collective civic identities in the process of such work. This frame holds potential to take the discussion of civic science to another level of usefulness in addressing a range of challenges. Thus, a key goal of civic science is to tap the vast potential for scientists to act with citizens—as citizens—to change the world.

Civic Science in Action: Get Ready Iowa

To illustrate a civic science approach, I turn to a specific example—the Get Ready Iowa (GRI)[9] school readiness initiative funded by the Delta Center and the Obermann Center for Advanced Studies at the University of Iowa.

The motivation for this project comes from recent data on the state of school readiness in the United States: between 35 and 45 percent of first-time kindergarteners are ill prepared to succeed in school.[10] It is widely recognized that early environments that provide consistent, stimulating, and emotionally stable care for both toddlers and preschool age children have a lasting impact on academic success and promote long-term benefits to the well-being of children. Three long-running studies—the High Scope/Perry project, the Abecedarian project, and the Chicago Longitudinal Study—demonstrate the potential payoff. For instance, the High Scope/Perry project calculated a lifetime benefit of $284,000 from a cost of $17,600 per child—a return on investment of 16:1.[11] Critically, this project lifted individual children out of poverty, reduced rates of criminality, and resulted in higher life satisfaction into adulthood.

Efforts to build on long-running intervention studies have shown more modest success. The challenges are numerous: the most at-risk children come from stressed family situations, with parents who experience high rates of economic and social stress and depression; teachers of at-risk children often do not possess adequate preparation, earn low wages, and experience high rates of depression.

One promising direction of recent readiness efforts is to build on advances in the science of individual development. The idea is simple: if we understand the processes that underlie growth and change in cognitive abilities in the critical window before children enter kindergarten, we can target those processes to promote readiness. Efforts in this direction have focused on how multiple components come together in the form of higher-level "executive" skills.[12] Data show that enhancing so-called executive functions can promote dramatic gains, but there is concern about whether skills generalize beyond the training context.

One insight from recent intervention efforts is that fostering school readiness is most effective when researchers intervene in multiple ways in the child's context. This suggests that school readiness requires "buy in" from multiple partners: *parents* must be educated about how children learn and how to prepare children for kindergarten; preschool and pre-K *teachers* must be trained about how to foster basic readiness skills in center-based daycare and in the classroom; and *communities* must be educated about the importance of early readiness and the basic science that underlies efforts to foster cognitive and self-regulatory skills in young children.

The goal of the Get Ready Iowa partnership is to work toward a statewide effort to foster school readiness by harnessing the processes that underlie basic changes in cognitive skills from birth to five years. This requires translating basic science into the real-world and partnering with colleagues from both within and outside the university community. We must tap the rich knowledge that parents, teachers, community partners, and researchers in education bring to bear on school readiness. Get Ready Iowa, therefore, pursues a view of "civic science" where citizen-scientists, citizen-teachers, citizen-parents, and other citizens come together to share knowledge, work together, and develop solutions to real-world challenges.

Get Ready Iowa Projects

GRI launched in the summer of 2012 at a summer workshop sponsored by the Obermann Center for Advanced Studies at the University of Iowa. Since that time, the larger group has been building relationships through one-on-one discussions that focus on each person's self-interest: why is each person part of the GRI community; what motivates each person to create change; what resources does each person bring to the table? In the process of forging these personal ties, concrete projects emerged. I describe a few examples below and then turn to some reflections.

Week of the Young Child. Each spring, families in Iowa City and surrounding communities come to the Iowa Children's Museum to learn more about resources available to them and their children. Families learn about local childcare options, how libraries and other community resources benefit children, and activities and programs available to our youngest citizens. Last year, over fifteen hundred people participated in this event, including state legislators, who participated in a legislative breakfast.

Playing Is Learning (*www.playingislearning.org*). This project implemented by the Iowa Children's Museum is serving over 175,000 children and adults annually. "Playing Is Learning" infuses the museum with simple, direct messaging within each exhibit, helping parents to understand how play shapes the brain for healthy child development. And the fun doesn't stop at the museum: children collect "Game of Games" cards that they can take home. Each "Game of Games" card has a "Did you know?" section with basic information about early development, and a "Try this at home" mini-game using simple materials that can be found in most households. This initiative is creating a deeper understanding about the connections between playing and learning and encouraging parents and children to experience the power of play firsthand.

Child Care Happy Hours. On Friday evenings at pick-up time, GRI team members go to local child care centers to meet with parents, eat pizza, and chat about topics related to development. While the children play mini-games with GRI staff, parents participate in a discussion about learning and school readiness with a researcher from the Delta Center. After the discussion, parents reunite with their children to play mini-games together. This gives parents an opportunity to observe how playing and learning are connected. Parents leave with a take-home gift: a "Game of Games" card deck designed to promote playing and learning at home.

Civic Science: Reflections from Community Partners

The GRI initiative has achieved several successes "on the ground," but it has also had a transformative effect by forming relationships among the many stakeholders involved in school readiness. Below are reflections from several GRI community partners that describe this impact.

> Prior to the Get Ready Iowa initiative, our community included many individuals each making a small difference. Researchers were discovering how children learn, what skills are important for later life, and how those skills build upon each other. Professors were teaching college students about the latest research and best practices. Elementary schools were identifying children entering kindergarten who weren't "ready" for school and labeling the missing skills. Head Starts and other early educators were working to teach early skills for children to be ready for kindergarten. Home visitors were striving to enhance the home environment to promote school readiness and strengthen the parent-child relationship. Parents were working to understand what they needed to do at home to get their 4-year-old ready for school. All of those pieces reflect our community's wealth of information ranging from theory to research to practice.
>
> However, there was little coordination between the efforts and we were missing the whole picture and the wisdom of our community partners. What good is it to know that children who live in language rich environments have

greater vocabularies at age 3 if it doesn't impact our practice? What does this research mean for parents and other caregivers?

With the efforts of GRI, we have developed a symbiotic relationship between the research community and the direct care community. Today, we are moving toward a shared definition, and a shared understanding, of what it means to be "school ready. " The exciting part is that we are exploring what "school readiness" means not only for children, but for schools, child care programs, families, and the community.

—Laurie Nash, Johnson County Empowerment

Before the creation of GRI, the early childhood community had a silo approach. My agency supports professional development of child care providers and as such we would get local teachers and AEA [Area Education Agency] staff to provide presentations and our staff provided presentations and consultations to agencies and child care programs. We had connections and we had partners, but I think we lacked the conviction that together we were going to create change.

GRI made us consider the process of change, and our part in it. This took time to meet, to talk, to get to know one another and to develop a sense of trust to the point that people felt comfortable sharing ideas. GRI provides us with a unique opportunity to combine the academic talents that the University of Iowa has to offer with community commitment and understanding of local conditions to create practical projects to improve school readiness for all children in our community.

—Susan Gray, director of 4C's—Community Coordinated Child Care

Imagine a community where children are valued so much that valuable resources are purposefully dedicated to insuring that every child enters kindergarten ready to learn. Imagine every child walking into the classroom that first day of school with the skills needed to be successful and the incredible impact that would make on our future.

"Get Ready Iowa" is working to realize this vision, and the movement is gaining momentum. What began as a small group of like-minded individuals determined to make early childhood research accessible to families has gained dozens of partners that represent broad community perspectives committed to the needs of children.

"Get Ready Iowa" has created an awareness in this community regarding the absolute need for high quality early childhood development, both inside and outside the home, and is creating opportunities for children and their families that will shape the future of the next generation.

—Deb Dunkhase, director of the Iowa Children's Museum

Civic Science: Reflections from a Scientist

As I reflect on civic science and GRI, I return to the theme of Boyte's essay—citizenship as public work. How can I create a sense of public work in my science?

One sense of public work I have explored connected my *teaching* to civic engagement. In the spring of 2013, I taught a graduate-level service-learning course called "Public Theories of Development." In this course, PhD students in psychology joined forces with graduate students in design studio and with play-ologists at the Iowa Children's Museum. The goal was to bring the science of development to the museum through a student project designed to communicate the science of play and learning to museum visitors. The students learned about modern theories of development, critically examined the scientific literature on play, and evaluated how these concepts might resonate with children, parents, and grandparents. The result was the Playing Is Learning initiative described above.

Overall, the course project was a rousing success. But evaluation of the course itself was mixed. The students felt the real-world project took over the class content as the project evolved, and the science suffered. Thus, when I think about service learning in the sciences, there are some real challenges: scientists need to find the right balance between teaching scientific content and practicing civic science.

Beyond the classroom, I also pursued a *public scholarship* perspective. I was hoping to connect my research to the GRI initiative. This tapped my self-interest (I deeply care about my research), and I was open to a democratic view of science: maybe this project would give me new insights in the lab, shift my research questions, and so on.

That hasn't happened, and that's an important admission. I am a basic scientist. My research questions are in the lab; my work is deeply rooted in the experimental method, experimental control, and laboratory science.

These experiences have left me with several major questions. I am convinced that basic science is relevant to civic life. But what's the path forward for the basic scientist? If scientists are already working sixty hours a week given the modern pressures of "big science," can we realistically incorporate a "civic science" approach?

This is where my thinking returns to the knowledge war. Whether it's realistic or not, scientists need to carve out time for civic science *because science and scientific freedom is under attack*. If we're going to win this war, we need basic scientists to get off the sidelines. We need to actively change mindsets about science to protect the freedoms we currently enjoy. Dzur states this motivation in his excellent essay.[13] I modify his comments slightly here: the question to each basic scientist must be, "what have I done with my scientific freedom to promote the freedom of others?"

Placing the knowledge war at the feet of individual scientists seems like a losing battle. How can one scientist make a difference? This can lead to a sense of powerlessness—a theme repeatedly expressed in this volume. My response is in the form of an experience that did something remarkable—it made me realize my work was relevant, *that I was relevant*.

I was at a local conference on child development, education, and intervention research feeling oddly out of place, on a different planet. The world of application and translation was completely removed from my world of laboratory science. There was no discussion of how children learn, about the big picture concepts of development. It was all just about different intervention programs and which worked—most didn't.

After listening to talks all day, I found myself talking to a parent during one of the breaks. He was representing his local parent group. He had a special needs child at home. I asked him my burning question from the day: *how do you think children develop?* He said, "No one has ever asked me that. I'm not really sure." We had a great discussion. He told me wonderful stories about his daily interactions with his special-needs daughter and his sense that development was made from these accumulated experiences. I told him about the discoveries researchers have made about how those daily, moment-by-moment interactions create development. In this exchange, a civic scientist was born; I realized I could be relevant.

I'm still discovering what "civic science" means to me. And I'm fortunate to have colleagues at the Delta Center who are joining in the discovery process. Although I'm not sure where this path will lead, I'm convinced that it's time to unleash the relevance of science, and direct engagement with other citizens—as citizens—is a critical first step.

This brings me to the movie *Mindwalk*. In the movie, Sonia, a quantum physicist, is talking to a poet, Thomas Harriman. After a day of exploring quantum physics and complex systems theory, Thomas stands on the sands of Mont Saint-Michel as the tide comes in, eloquently reciting Pablo Neruda's poem, and delivers his synthesis: "Where are the other people in your system, Sonia? . . . the real people with their qualities, longings and weaknesses . . . where are you inside there, Sonia? . . . Life is infinitely more than yours or mine obtuse theories about it. Healing the universe is an inside job." The new people in my system are the community of partners in GRI. I've discovered through this partnership that there's a lot more to "healing the universe" than my own obtuse theories. And these partners have taught me that it's OK to take this "civic science" experiment step-by-step. Each step can matter. I am not powerless.

I don't know how to win the knowledge war. But I know we won't win if scientists don't get involved. Similarly, I doubt we can transform higher education if science isn't in the mix. So I conclude with a call to action to scientists in higher education: it's time to realize your agency, form relationships in your community, and start asking, "what can I do to change the world?"

After all, healing the universe is an inside job.

Notes

Get Ready Iowa was launched at the 2012 Obermann Summer Seminar. This initiative is supported by the Spelman-Rockefeller Fund at the University of Iowa through a partnership between the Delta Center and the Obermann Center for Advanced Studies. I would like to acknowledge Harry Boyte, Scott Peters, Gwen Ottinger and Sherburne Abbott for collaboratively shaping the civic science concept, my colleagues at the Delta Center for exploring civic science in action, and Laurie Nash, Susan Gray, and Deb Dunkhase for sharing their perspectives. Supported by NSF BCS 1029082.

1. See Harry C. Boyte, *Civic Agency and the Cult of the Expert* (Dayton, OH: Kettering Foundation, 2009).

2. Brian Wynne, "Misunderstood Misunderstandings: Social Identities and Public Uptake of Science." In *Misunderstanding Science? The Public Reconstruction of Science and Technology*, eds. Alan Irwin and Brian Wynne (Cambridge: Cambridge University Press, 1996), 19–46; Mike Michael, "Ignoring Science: Discourses of Ignorance in the Public Understanding of Science." In *Misunderstanding Science?*, 107–25.

3. David Michaels, *Doubt Is Their Product: How Industry's Assault on Science Threatens Your Health* (Oxford: Oxford University Press, 2008); Naomi Oreskes and Erik M. Conway, *Merchants of Doubt: How a Handful of Scientists Obscured the Truth on Issues from Tobacco Smoke to Global Warming* (New York: Bloomsbury Press, 2010).

4. Daniel Sarewitz, "How Science Makes Environmental Controversies Worse." *Environmental Science and Policy* 7 (2004): 385–403; Phil Brown, "Popular Epidemiology and Toxic Waste Contamination: Lay and Professional Ways of Knowing." *Journal of Health and Social Behavior* 33 (1992): 267–81.

5. Brown, "Popular Epidemiology," 267–81.

6. Karin Bäckstrand, "Civic Science for Sustainability: Reframing the Role of Experts, Policy-Makers and Citizens in Environmental Governance." *Global Environmental Politics* 3, no. 4 (2003): 24.

7. Sandra Harding, "Should Philosophies of Science Encode Democratic Ideals?" In *Science, Technology, and Democracy*, ed. Daniel Lee Kleinman (Albany: State University of New York Press, 2000), 122.

8. Peter Levine, "The Case for Civic Studies." *Civic Studies*, ed. Peter Levine and Karol Soltan (Washington, DC: Bringing Theory to Practice/Association of American Colleges and Universities, 2014), 3–8.

9. Get Ready Iowa's website is *www.getreadyiowa.org*.

10. Elizabeth Hair, Tamara Halle, Elizabeth Terry-Humen, Bridget Lavelle, and Julia Calkins, "Children's School Readiness in the ECLS-K: Predictions to Academic, Health, and Social Outcomes in the First Grade." *Early Childhood Research Quarterly* 21 (2006): 431–54.

11. Jeffrey Mervis, "Past Successes Shape Effort to Expand Early Intervention." *Science* 333, no. 6045 (2011): 952–56.

12. Adele Diamond, and Kathleen Lee, "Interventions Shown to Aid Executive Function Development in Children 4 to 12 Years Old." *Science* 333, no. 6045 (2011): 959–64.

13. Albert Dzur, "The Democratic Roots of Academic Professionalism." In *Democracy's Education: Public Work, Citizenship, and the Future of Colleges and Universities*, ed. Harry C. Boyte (Nashville: Vanderbilt University Press, 2015).

23

HIGHER EDUCATION AND POLITICAL CITIZENSHIP: THE JAPANESE CASE

Shigeo Kodama

Background

In Japan, after WWII the American education system was introduced as a reform to the existing education system. The underlying principles of higher education were based on educating democratic citizens through general education.

However, this idea lost its substance because of these two factors. First, the Japanese education system was under bureaucratic control. Second, the political culture was dominated by an ideological dichotomy in the context of cold war politics. Therefore, politically oriented education was considered unfavorably.

After the 1990s, the situation changed, to become receptive of a politically oriented citizenship education. In this chapter, I will identify the mechanism by which this occurred and clarify the condition of political citizenship education.

Social Structure of Education in Post-WWII Japan

Figure 1 indicates enrollment and advancement rates in post-WWII Japan. For example, enrollment in upper secondary schools (high school for fifteen- to eighteen-year-olds in Japan) has risen from 50 percent in 1960 to over 80 percent in 1970, and to over 95 percent after the 1990s. Thus as Japan prospered economically, public upper secondary schools accommodated nearly all potential students in Japan. In the post–Cold War era, the social structure of education in Japan attained maturity. I believe the time is now ripe for citizenship education.

Let us consider the structural changes in school curriculums in post-WWII Japan. The era of progressivism (1945–1958) saw the predominance of problem-solving curriculums and waning of government regulation. From 1958 to 1992, systematic principles and discipline-centered curriculums were dominant, and government regulation was enforced. During the "pressure-free education" (*yutori*) period (1992–2008), the Japanese government reintroduced a problem-solving curriculum, and government regulation was partly relaxed. The "post-pressure-free education" period, from 2009 to the present, is of particular interest, because citizenship education through curriculum innovation is required to overcome the dichotomy between the discipline-centered curricu-

Figure 1. Enrollment and advancement rate of students in Japan

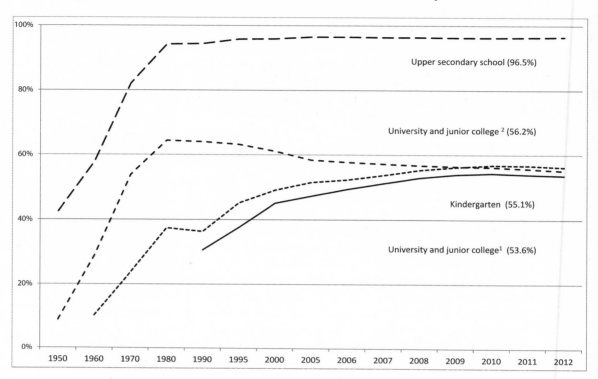

1. New entrants to university and junior college, as a percentage of the eighteen-year-old age cohort.

2. New graduates from upper secondary school who advanced to university and junior college upon graduation, as a percentage of the total upper secondary school graduates for each year. Figures include new graduates of upper division of secondary schools.
SOURCE: MEXT, 2012 School Basic Survey. *www.mext.go.jp/english/statistics.*

lums of the development era and the problem-solving curriculums of the current pressure-free education era.

The *White Paper on Education in 2009 Japan* indicates that after the mid-1990s, a majority of eighteen-year-olds enrolled for higher education, and the enrollment ratios at universities and junior colleges have risen each year, exceeding 50 percent in 2005 (*www.mext.go.jp/b_menu/hakusho/html/hpab200901/detail/1305857.htm*). This structural change created the possibility of introducing the notion of educating citizens as a principle of general education.

Specific Structural Changes in the Post–Cold War Era

Factors influencing social change in the post–Cold War era are globalization and postindustrialization, wherein public education faces two social pressures. These include the preeminence of the market initiated by neoliberalism, and the rise of technocratic and bureaucratic control, defended by the older form of social democracy. It is at this point that a new kind of citizenship education is needed to break down the dichotomy of neoliberalism and old-style social democracy.[1]

Two kinds of citizenship are to be considered in this context; the first is "citizenship as a volunteer," and the second is "political citizenship," or "citizenship as a civic producer." Harry Boyte explains the distinction between these two kinds of citizenship clearly. "The idea of the citizen as a volunteer, associated with communitarian theory, leads to the modern service movement, where the dominant focus is on individual helping, the concepts like power, politics, and self-interests are normally missing, and real world civic products are seldom discussed. The concept of the citizen as a civic producer or co-creator of the commonwealth leads to public work and everyday politics."[2] Both these two kinds of citizenship constitute a controversial issue in Japan and other countries like the United States and the UK. For example, Harry Boyte comments that the charter schools movement in the United States has been renewing lively cultures of civic innovation involving parents and sometimes other community members, as well as teachers and students, in creating education.[3]

Additionally, in Japan, a new type of public school, the "community school," was introduced in 2004. In 2010, the Japanese national government issued its policy, entitled *Vision for Children and Young People*. According to the policy, citizenship education involving political education is encouraged. "Education related to social development and social participation (citizenship education) will be promoted in order for children and young people to become independent as members of society and for them to adopt an attitude of becoming actively involved in society through the exercise of rights and obligations. Specifically, efforts will be made for schooling which enriches political education."[4]

In the UK, the *Crick Report*, a national report of England issued in 1998, also promotes two essential kinds of citizenship: community involvement and political literacy.[5] In all these countries, the key versions of new citizenship education can be categorized as citizenship as a volunteer or political citizenship.

The "Ignorant Citizen"

In the final part of this chapter, I focus on the significance of political citizenship as a key component of citizenship education in the post–Cold War era.

In volunteer activities, young individuals do not process the political meaning and implications of their activities and have been found to lack political judgment and political action skills, which are indispensable factors of citizenship. To address this issue, Bernard Crick and Harry Boyte focus on the significant importance of political citizenship in public education reform in the United States, the UK, and Japan. This political character of citizenship appears to be key to obtaining material for developing a curriculum for educating citizens that should be included within general education.

For the effectiveness of political citizenship in higher education, early exposure is crucial. In Japan, students have been sheltered from broader social and political movements and circumstances and, therefore, have not had sufficient opportunity to be active participants in the experiment of democracy. However, universities and colleges are now trying to implement an early exposure system. For example, the University of Tokyo is introducing a late specialization and early exposure system on a trial basis.

"The University of Tokyo is famed for the high stress it puts on extended (two years of junior course) liberal arts education, which is obligatory to all the freshmen. This system provides for delay for students to choose and focus on their specialized studies (*late specialization*). To make this unique system effective, giving opportunity for junior students to have views of specialized research fields and professional worlds (*early exposure*), would be fruitful."[6]

The definition and characteristics of exposure, and the nature and extent of early exposure required, need to be understood and outlined. Gert Biesta, an educational philosopher from the University of Luxembourg, emphasizes this by introducing the category of ignorant citizen. "The ignorant citizen is the one who is ignorant of a particular definition of what he or she is supposed to be as a "good citizen." The ignorant citizen is the one who, in a sense, refuses this knowledge and, through this, refuses to be domesticated, refuses to be pinned down in a predetermined civic identity. This does not mean that the ignorant citizen is completely "out of order."[7]

Biesta challenges the traditional idea that it is possible to have a model for a good citizen. Rather citizenship education must draw from various sources, especially practical experience, to effectively influence young individuals in becoming active citizens. According to Biesta, the ignorant citizen is a key category to break through the traditional idea of citizenship. "Learning here is not about the acquisition of knowledge, skills, competencies or dispositions but has to do with an 'exposure' to and engagement with the experiment of democracy. It is this very engagement that is subjectifying."[8] It seems that Biesta's "ignorant citizen" is like citizen as cocreator, which Harry Boyte states above, or Hannah Arendt's natality, that means a beginning that conserves the world as new, and prevents it from being ruined.[9]

Conclusion

An analysis of the post–Cold War context in Japan produced two factors for developing a curriculum for young "citizens" that could be included within general education.

First it involves restoring political citizenship education, which cannot be reduced to citizenship as volunteer, as part of general education. Second it involves providing the student with more opportunities for political and social exposure to engage with the experiment of democracy.

This is an important amendment not only to the Japanese higher education system, but globally. Such political citizenship also points beyond state-centered (social democratic) technocracy and neoliberal market politics.

Notes

1.   Shigeo Kodama, review of *Citizenship: A Very Short Introduction*, by Richard Bellamy, in *Citizenship Teaching and Learning* 6, no. 1 (2010): 110–11.

2.   Harry Boyte, *Everyday Politics* (Philadelphia: University of Pennsylvania Press, 2004), 92.

3.   Shigeo Kodama, "Citizenship Education and Politics in the U.S.A. and Japan: Preface to the interviews with Carrie Bakken, Walter Enloe, and Harry Boyte," in *Bulletin Report of Grant-in-Aid for Scientific Research (B)Research Project Number 18830176*. Principal Investigator of this research project: Teruyuki Hirota) (Tokyo: University of Tokyo, 2009), 226–27.

4.   Headquarters for Promotion of Development and Support for Children and Young People in Japan, *Vision for Children and Young People*, *www8.cao.go.jp/youth/suisin/pdf/vision_english.pdf*, 2010.

5.   Bernard Crick, *Essays on Citizenship* (London: Continuum, 2000). For the background of Crick's political philosophy, see Bernard Crick, *In Defence of Politics* (London: Continuum, 2005).

6.   University of Tokyo, "Activities of Junior Scholars Collaboration Initiative," 2010, *jsci.c.u-tokyo.ac.jp/en/about.html*.

7.   Gert Biesta, "The Ignorant Citizen: Mouffe, Rancière, and the Subject of Democratic Education," *Studies in Philosophy and Education* 30, no. 2 (2011): 152.

8.   Ibid., 152.

9.   Hannah Arendt, *The Human Condition* (Chicago: University of Chicago Press, 1958); also, Shigeo Kodama, "Rethinking Hannah Arendt in the Context of Politics in 1990's Japan: Focusing on Arendt's Critique of Karl Marx," in *Research Monograph: Studies of Human Development from Birth to Death* (Tokyo: Ochanomizu University 21st COE Program, 2006).

24

THE PROMISE OF BLACK CONSCIOUSNESS

Xolela Mangcu

Breaking through the Enlightenment Cage

Over the past year the University of Cape Town, South Africa, Africa's top-ranked university, has been caught up in a public debate about the use of race as the basis of affirmative action. Unfortunately, the debate has been on the margins of what I think are the real epistemological challenges facing South African universities—the need for new social consciousness among our students and new content in our curriculum. I believe that the black consciousness movement and its philosophy can offer ways forward for rethinking South African universities, especially as this relates to the issue of race. Both opponents and proponents of affirmative action do not address these epistemological issues at all in the debate. And thus we are likely to find that even if the complexion of the student body changes, they are still locked within paradigms that do very little to address the challenges of the present or the questions they seek to answer about South Africa and their place in its reimagination. As Michael Burawoy correctly pointed out in his 2004 presidential address to the American Sociological Association, our students are not "empty vessels into which we pour our mature wine, nor blank slates upon which to inscribe our profound knowledge. Rather we must think of them as carriers of a rich lived experience that we elaborate into a deeper self-understanding of the historical and social contexts that have made them who they are."[1]

I have entered the debate with the aims of transcending both the economistic conception of race shared by opponents of race-based affirmative action in the university and the mere reduction of race to skin color. The economistic approach is shared by left-wing Marxists, liberals, and conservatives, who, for different reasons, deny the validity of race as a social category. What this also means is that issues of culture are bracketed out of the educational experience. Put differently, only one culture is universalized in the form of the "canon." As Benjamin Barber notes, institutional arrangements and values that arose out of particular historical and cultural periods were consequently universalized and generalized for all time: "That Eton in the 19th century had one science master, one math master, one modern languages master and twenty seven classics masters teaching Latin and Greek is seen as a product of the canon, rather than seen as a force conditioning its modern incarnation."[2] In my field of sociology this canon has deep roots in Enlightenment thought and the rise of positivism in the nineteenth century. And thus, in my social theory class I teach my students the classical sociologists—Karl Marx, Emile Durkheim, Max Weber, even though the more pressing challenge may be to teach them about Steve Biko and what he had to say on a variety of sociological topics. I am slowly breaking out of the Enlightenment cage by teaching the sociology of African intellectuals.

The dominance of rationalist Enlightenment thought came out in a debate between me and the head of the university. Given that the university is predominantly white I asked whether white professors were best placed to vote on this issue in a way that would best serve the interests of black students. The head of the university argued that I was insulting the senate with my "presumption that intelligent, educated people cannot make ethical and rational decisions because they are interested in serving the interests of those of the same colour."[3] I tried to explain myself in a subsequent article by again asking whether it was really possible for my white colleagues "to check their social identities at the door as they decide on racial redress at UCT. Are they merely rational actors (and are we all?) with no 'background presumptions' or biases that may affect their approach to the matter?"

I further argued that race was a social identity that consists of worldviews that are often taken for granted: "by problematizing the prerogative of white professors to decide on racial redress in higher education I do not seek to insult them but to highlight a profound sociological dilemma—to what extent can they divorce their background presumptions from the decisions they are entrusted to make. Are they indeed, identity-less, rational actors, unencumbered by their social identities?"[4]

Ironically, the failure to look at race as a social identity is shared by proponents of affirmative action, who see race as no more than skin color. This can easily lead to a racial nativism and a dangerous sense of entitlement in the context of the scramble for resources among different groups. And yet, as Steve Biko unequivocally put it, "being black is not a matter of pigmentation—being black is a reflection of a mental attitude." Thus he defined blacks as "all those who are by law or tradition politically, economically and socially discriminated against as a group in South African society and identify themselves as a unit in the struggle towards the realization of their aspirations."[5] What this means is that the presence of black bodies does not tell us much about their potential contribution to the cultural reimagination of the university. We could just as well end up with a cohort of Enlightenment scholars in black skin, to paraphrase Frantz Fanon's *Black Skin, White Masks*.[6] "While skin colour and poverty intersect in crucial ways with race, they do not exhaust race as social consciousness of a particular historical experience."[7]

To begin a serious consideration of race as a form of social consciousness would require overall modification of the epistemological frame that I have elsewhere described as "technocratic creep," which is the Enlightenment idea that social problems require technical solutions.[8] This idea is so embedded in the self-conception of the university that there is hardly any conception of university education as cultural power. The university privileges certain ways of knowing and thinking about the world, which in turn puts in a stronger political and economic position those who possess such cultural knowledge. An example from my social theory exam should illustrate the advantages and disadvantages of cultural power. Black students who were battling with Marx, Durkheim, and Weber did much better on the section on Biko, Sobukwe, and Mandela.

The vision of the university as a space for the cultivation of social consciousness runs against two very strong traditions in the history of universities: the ivory tower and the vocational education models. The "ivory tower" model has ancient roots in Aristotle's Lyceum, which was one of the earliest examples of the university as a place for a select group of people whose intellectual faculties and cultural tastes are above the rest of the toiling masses. Thorstein Veblen traced the origins of higher learning to the ancient idea that there was a special class of people whose source of authority and prestige came from their "knowledge of the unknowable." This knowledge, Veblen further argued, "owes its serviceability for the sacerdotal purpose to its recondite character." It was possession of this recondite-esoteric quality that elevated the intellectual above the rest of society: "as a priestly servitor of the inscrutable powers that move in the external world." Veblen might as well have had in mind the contemporary rat race for rankings among universities when he described institutions of higher learning as "great sticklers for form, precedent, gradations of rank, ritual, ceremonial vestments and learned paraphernalia generally." He concludes that this is to be expected precisely because "the higher learning is, in its incipient phase, a leisure class occupation."[9]

The vocational model of higher education is essentially the flip side of education as a leisure-class activity. If higher education was originally conceived as a leisure-class occupation, the history of its development was within the context of the construction of the modern state in the post-sixteenth-century Enlightenment. The emerging nation-states felt they needed educated men who would bring discipline and expertise to the organization of the new entity. According to Zygmunt Bauman, "the robe of the political class was, so to speak, put to auction, and open to competitive bids."[10] The bids were invariably won by the newly educated expert class. However, the role of the expert took different forms. On the one hand the French played a leading role in the spread of rationalism and positivism under the leadership of positivist philosophers such as Auguste Comte. On the other hand were the Germans, the originators of the Romantic movement and Idealist philosophy. Max Weber tried to find a synthesis between these traditions with his invention of the concept of the Ideal Type, and his Protestant Ethic was an illustration of how a Romantic concept such as religion could be put to the use of a rationalized modern economy.

The practical view of education took hold as the emerging United States entered the nineteenth century with a new frontier of unparalleled bounty in a strange but vast land. According to Tocqueville, this "singularly concurred to fix the mind of the American upon purely practical objects." New systems of production in the wake of the Industrial Revolution hastened and intensified the demand for new technological capacities, skills, and energies. The response to industrialism was twofold—with the scientific empiricism of Enlightenment again having to contend with the Romantic thrust of people's movements. Woodrow Wilson, generally regarded as the father of American Progressivism (with a capital *P*) observed that in the early life of the American republic there had understandably been no great need for administration because the functions of government were simple and life itself was simple: "the functions of government were simple because life itself was simple; . . . populations were of manageable numbers, property was of simple sorts. There were plenty of farms but no stocks and bonds: more cattle than vested interests." Five years later, Wilson was getting even more exasperated: "A new era has come upon us like a sudden vision of things unprophesied, and for which no polity has been prepared."[11] Harry Boyte noted that "even John Dewey, who argued for democracy as a society, not a state, acquiesced in relocating politics to the state under the pretext of scientific expertise."[12] The role of the expert in straightening the affairs of government reached its high-water mark with the policy sciences of the 1950s—with the development of fields such as artificial intelligence, game theory, and various engineering and statistical models of society.

The emergence of what has sometimes been called the "second industrial divide,"[13] with its emphasis on flexible specialization and high quality competition, intensified the need for collaboration between business and the university. Businesses poured money into engineering and business schools to produce applied knowledge. The invention and popularity of the MBA is testament to this growing intrusion of the business world into the academic world. Another example is the master of science degree offered by Georgia Tech in partnership with AT&T. Within universities power rested with those departments and faculties that had the backing of powerful corporations and thus were the financial lifeline of the university. The university risked becoming "a kindergarten for corporate society where the young are socialized, bullied, and blackmailed into usefulness."[14]

Prospects for a Romantic Renaissance:
Examples from South Africa and the United States

The Romantic thrust of ordinary people's movements in the United States culminated in the populist movement in the late nineteenth century. The populists emerged as a response to the displacement of small farmers by big industrialists and large-scale farmers. Their displacement was not a merely economic affair but a cultural one. Karl Polanyi's description of the impact of colonialism on developing countries also easily captures the cultural dimension of this displacement even if the scale of the impact is not the same:

> Not economic exploitation as often assumed, but the disintegration of the cultural environment of the victim is then the cause of the degradation. The economic process may, naturally supply the vehicle of the destruction, and

almost invariably economic inferiority will make the weaker yield, but the immediate cause of his undoing is not for that reason economic; it lies in the lethal injury to the institutions in which his existence is embodied. The result is a loss of self-respect, and standards, whether the unit is a people or a class.[15]

The Romantic spirit was revived during the New Deal in the 1930s. The New Deal's Art for the Millions program gave new opportunities to artists by having them create new murals and public art, fusing both official and vernacular memory. Thousands upon thousands of artists were put on the government payroll to produce new works of art and craft, sculpture and paintings—resulting in just as many, if not more, paintings. More than a hundred art centers were established throughout the country, and sometimes in places where there was hardly any organized artistic activity By the end of the 1930s the Federal Music Project had also sponsored a quarter of a million performances drawing in millions of listeners. The music teaching program employed six thousand teachers and gave instruction to seventeen million students. The revival of folk music saw the emergence of eight thousand discs, which were subsequently lodged with the Archive of American Folk Song in the Library of Congress. Commenting on the Federal Writers Project, the writer Robert Cantwell noted how "American history has never before been written in terms of communities—it has been written in terms of its leading actors, and of its dominant economic movements, but never in terms of the ups and downs of the towns from which the actors emerged and in which the economic movements had their play."[16]

This "creative outpouring" came up against the exigencies of World War II and the onset of the Cold War. Suddenly the arts project was seen more as a waste of money on radicals who could not entirely be relied on to support the United States than as the grandiose schemes of government planners. But there was really no stopping of people's movements, as the civil rights and black nationalist movements not only gathered steam but also changed the academy. In the field of city planning, for example, Paul Davidoff introduced "advocacy planning" to question the role of the experts that were serving in planning commissions at the bidding of the business elite in American cities. He argued that planning departments ought to align themselves with the poor and the weak. An even more radical planning education emerged in the 1980s—the leading examples of publications in this radical tradition would be Pierre Clavel's *Progressive City* and Norman Krumholz and Clavel's *Equity Planners Tell Their Stories*. The much-celebrated department of economic development in Harold Washington's administration in Chicago consisted of former planning students from Cornell and MIT The head of that department, Rob Mier, also wrote a seminal book, *Social Justice and Local Development Policy*.[17]

But analyses of the Harold Washington administration contained hardly a word about the cultural power that accrued to African Americans and all the other formerly marginalized groups in the city. This ignored the reality that had it not been for the rebellion in the streets, African American, Latino, and women administrators might still be struggling to set foot in city hall, and Barack Obama might not have become the first African American president of the United States.[18] According to David Remnick, Harold Washington was "a political role model for Obama": "there is no telling how Obama might have developed had he answered an ad to work in some other city, but it is clear that the history of African Americans in Chicago—and the unique political history of Chicago, culminating in Washington's attempt to form a multiracial coalition—provided Obama with a rich legacy to learn from."[19] The writer Lewis Nkosi has described how Romanticism and its themes became useful for black people in South Africa: "The instruments which lay at hand were no different for the black writer than those which the Western artist, in his accumulating frustrations with the proprieties of Western bourgeois society, had fashioned out of a conglomeration of ideas and techniques, from Marxist economic theories to Freudian interpretation of dreams, from free association to verbal non-sequiturs or surrealist techniques."[20] In South Africa the best example of a Romantic movement would be the black consciousness movement, which also emerged in the late 1960s and dominated black politics through the 1970s. The movement was race based in the sense of race as a political identity outlined by Biko above, and it was culturally inspired to the extent that it made poetry, music, folklore, and all the arts a central component of its praxis. The students who founded the movement had read some of the great theorists of self-reliant development, from Frantz Fanon to Julius Nyerere and Paolo Freire. But they were also concerned about being lost in philosophical speculation. The movement's cofounder Barney Pityana cautioned against such a possibility: "It is essential for the black students to strive to elevate the level of consciousness of the black community by promoting awareness, pride and capabilities."[21]

The students extended themselves beyond the university and fanned out all over the country to make their skills available to communities in the areas of education, health, job creation, the arts, media, and community research. I was something of a participant observer in some of these activities—although more of an observer than a participant because of my age. As a little boy in Biko's hometown I went along with him to some of the projects he had started when he worked as a fieldworker for the Black Community Programs, whose most prominent project was the Zanempilo Health Clinic. As senior medical students, they were also somewhat qualified to staff the clinic, under the leadership of Mamphela Ramphele, who later became the first female and black vice chancellor of the University of Cape Town, then a managing director at the World Bank, and now a leader of one of the opposition parties, Agang. The students built several clinics and schools in different parts of the country. The other prominent example of public work was at Njwaxa Industries, which was a community-based employment creation project in the deep rural villages that surround the historic university of Fort Hare. Here villagers were brought together to utilize their own skills in bead making, upholstery, and the making of leather belts, hand bags, purses, and cloth garments. Focused mainly on women, Njwaxa was also known for its labor-intensive brick making and poultry farming.

What was distinctive about this new movement was the extent to which it put public work at the center of its organizing activities. Over and above these physical activities, the movement created a "culture of critical discourse" in the black community—nothing went unquestioned, particularly the actions of those in leadership positions. This bequeathed to South Africa a deliberative culture that continues to this day. In 1975, the movement's mouthpiece, *Black Review*, noted that the projects had gone beyond the provision of jobs to training people in basic production and management skills. The publication also noted that through its projects Black Community Programs created spaces for collective reflection throughout the country. Under the cover of "development" they were able to conscientize—a concept they had borrowed from Paolo Freire—communities to protect their assets. The idea was that people would be more willing to defend community assets if they had built them, and they would be more willing to defend their land if they had tilled it or had some farming going on. Biko explained the political rationale behind the projects: "We believe that black people as they rub shoulders with the particular project, as they benefit from that project, with their perception of it, they begin to ask themselves questions, and we surely believe they are going to give themselves answers, and they understand . . . this kind of lesson, has been a lesson for me: I must have hope. In most of the projects we tend to pass over maintenance of the project to the community."[22]

Affirmative Action as Civic Education

Like Biko, I believe that the more our students rub shoulders with the real world of race in South Africa, the greater will their capacity to play leadership roles in the future. This would mean an understanding of how race has shaped—and continues to shape—the life chances of the majority of the population. Thus if you are studying medicine you should understand the social conditions of disease or if you are a lawyer you should understand the criminological dimensions of the law, and so on. Barber sums up the challenge of civic education as if he was writing about the University of Cape Town: "lawyers and doctors are no more likely to make good citizens than dropouts if their training is limited to the narrow and self-interested world defined by vocational preparation and professional instruction. Youngsters preparing to turn their schooling to the purposes of economic competition with Japan and Germany must also be able to turn their schooling to the purposes of civic cooperation with their fellow Americans in making democracy work."[23] It hardly needs saying that in South Africa this civic education is made especially difficult by the refusal to talk about the reality of race. The measure of greatness for the University of Cape Town will not be in the number of academic papers published by its staff nor in the number of black bodies on campus. Those papers and those black bodies must reflect a consciousness that will give the university a certain cultural edge over other universities in South Africa. That edge could come from a bold conception of the university as a site of "cultural critical discourse" (CCD). Our students would not be mere technocrats locked away in their little specialized and even racialized cocoons. Instead they would be public workers able to move back and forth between different racial spaces. To use a distinction made by Richard Hofstader, our students would be not only intelligent but also possessors of intellect. While the former "is a manipulative, adjustive, unfailingly practical quality," the latter is "the critical, creative and contemplative side of mind." While intelligence will "seize the meaning in a situation and evaluate it" in order to come up with practical solutions, "intellect evaluates evaluations, and looks for the meaning of situation as a whole."[24]While intelligence enables practical problem solving possible within a given situation, intellect makes it possible to understand the situation as a whole. The former may indeed be the basis for excellent scholarship, but the latter is the stuff out of which great visions are built. Regrettably, none of the protagonists of affirmative action are addressing themselves to the potential contribution of black consciousness to a Romantic renaissance in our universities. But this is a task of historical retrieval that goes beyond South African universities to reclamation of cultural themes in higher education globally.

Notes

1. Michael Burawoy, "For Public Sociology," Presidential Address, American Sociological Association, 2004, published in *British Journal of Sociology* 56, no. 2 (2005): 259–94.
2. Benjamin Barber, *A Passion for Democracy* (Princeton, NJ: Princeton University Press, 1998), 180.
3. Max Price, "Dr. Mangcu Has Insulted Senate with His Presumption," *Cape Times*, South Africa, February 25, 2013.
4. Xolela Mangcu, "Race is the Keystone of Our Society," *Cape Times*, South Africa, February 27, 2013.
5. Steve Biko, *I Write What I Like* (Johannesburg: Picador Africa, 2004), 52.
6. Frantz Fanon, *Black Skin, White Masks* (New York: Grove Press, 1952)
7. Xolela Mangcu, "Attitude Not Skin Colour Shapes Race," *Cape Times*, South Africa, October 21, 2013.
8. Xolela Mangcu, "Johannesburg in Flight from Itself," in *Emerging Johannesburg*, ed. Richard Tomlinson, Robert Beauregard, Lindsay Bremner, and Xolela Mangcu (New York: Routledge, 2003), 286.
9. Thorstein Veblen, *The Theory of the Leisure Class* (New York: Penguin Books, 1994), 365–67.
10. Zygmunt Bauman, *Legislators and Interpreters* (Ithaca, NY: Cornell University Press, 1987), 25.
11. Woodrow Wilson cited in Dwight Waldo, *The Administrative State: A Study of the Political Theory of American Public Administration* (New Brunswick, NJ: Transaction Publishers, 1948), 20.
12. Harry Boyte, "A Different Kind of Politics," Dewey Lecture, University of Michigan, November 1, 2002, *www.ucdenver.edu/academics/colleges/CLAS/Centers/publichumanities/Documents/BoyteDeweyLecture.pdf.*
13. Michael Piore and Charles Sabel, *The Second Industrial Divide* (Cambridge, MA: MIT Press, 1984).
14. Benjamin Barber, *A Passion for Democracy*, 180.
15. Karl Polanyi, *The Great Transformation: The Political and Economic Origin of Our Time* (Boston: Beacon Press, 1944), 157–58.
16. Alan Lawson, "Brief Renaissance: A Depression Memory," *New Arcadia Review* 3 (2005): 118.
17. See Pierre Clavel's books *The Progressive City: Planning and Participation, 1969–1984*

(New Brunswick, NJ: Rutgers University Press, 1986) and *Harold Washington and the Neighbourhoods* (Princeton, NJ: Princeton University Press, 1991), and Norman Krumholz and Pierre Clavel's *Equity Planners Tell Their Stories* (Philadelphia: Temple University Press, 1994) and Rob Mier's *Social Justice and Local Development Policy* (New York: Sage Publications, 1993).

18. My PhD dissertation, "Harold Washington and the Cultural Transformation of Local Government in Chicago, 1983–1987," Cornell University, offers an alternative interpretation to the economistic and technocratic evaluations of Washington's impact on Chicago.

19. David Remnick, *The Bridge: The Life and Rise of Barack Obama* (New York: Alfred Knopf, 2010), 143.

20. Lewis Nkosi, "Negritude: Old and New Perspectives," in *Still Beating the Drum: Critical Perspectives on Lewis Nkosi*, ed. Lindy Stiebel and Liz Gunner (Johannesburg: Wits University Press, 2006), 284.

21. Robert Fatton, *Black Consciousness in South Africa: The Dialectics of Ideological Resistance to White Supremacy* (Albany: State University of New York Press, 1986), 68.

22. Millard Arnold, *The Testimony of Steve Biko* (London: Maurice Temple Smith Publishers, 1979), 94.

23. Benjamin Barber, *A Passion for Democracy*, 230.

24. Richard Hofstader, *Anti-Intellectualism in American Life* (New York: Vintage, 1963), 25.

25

TEACHING AS PUBLIC WORK

Lisa Clarke

How Did We Get Here?

Airwaves, Twitter feeds, and op-ed pages are filled with stories of failed schools, incompetent teachers, and miseducated kids. There is a sense of national crisis in many of these stories. But this crisis narrative is not new; some suggest it is a continuation of a twenty-year rallying call stemming from the 1983 report by the National Commission on Excellence in Education entitled *A Nation at Risk: The Imperative For Educational Reform*. One of the thirty-eight recommendations in the report was the need to create "more rigorous and measurable standards" to improve student learning.[1] We have seen many different waves in this standards movement; currently cresting is the Common Core or Career-and-College Ready Standards.

In 1986, the Task Force on Teaching as a Profession released a report suggesting that we could only improve learning for students if we provided better support for the teaching profession.[2] The report called for strengthening teacher preparation, improving teacher salaries and career opportunities, creating a professional culture that held teachers accountable for student progress, and giving teachers autonomy so that they could meet these standards. Over the last two decades, we have developed important standards for students and have developed accompanying accountability systems for teachers and principals, too. But after twenty years of work, there is still "a sense of urgency in politics, in the teaching profession, and also among the public about the need to get more high quality teachers . . . and it's putting teaching at the forefront of change."[3]

The authors of *Teaching 2030: What We Must Do for Our Students and Our Public: Schools Now and in the Future* tell us that the history of teaching in the United States has been shaped by control "by laypersons, a lack of clarity and rigor in the process of becoming a teacher, and limited prestige and income. These historical imperatives have constrained teaching and its professional possibilities. And the profession is still undermined by many of these same factors, although we are now in the second decade of the 21st century."[4] We can't ignore that a history of sexism also shaped the profession; for much of our past, male administrators handed down mandates to a predominately female teaching force. This history shaped the profession, but it doesn't have to dictate our future.

Making the Case for Remodeling the Profession

Our current national narrative explains teachers' inertia as a symptom of their unwavering commitment to the status quo. I must admit that I'd been swayed by that myth until I had the opportunity to travel around the country and meet with thousands of teachers. In contrast to this national narrative of sluggish teachers who resist change, the educators I've met *want* high standards for their students as well as meaningful evaluation systems that support the continuous growth of teachers individually as well as of teaching as a profession. However, for that accountability to be truly embraced, many teachers are demanding more support, respect, and autonomy. It only makes sense; if teacher evaluations are emphasized, teachers should have more control to shape the context in which they are evaluated. Thus, if we want to get public education right we need to not only reimagine what and how students should learn, but also what it means to be a public school teacher.

We have the power to remodel our profession and to transform our public education systems. Surely a first step toward success includes getting more high-quality teachers in our schools. But perhaps equally important is a willingness to profoundly change how we see teachers and the work we do. Some research suggests that our top 20 percent most effective teachers can generate five to six months more of student growth in a year than a teacher who is in the least effective category.[5] That said, we need to acknowledge that many of our students come to school with needs that our educators and schools are not designed to meet. In a remodeled teaching profession, educators collaborate with other citizens (parents, organizers, business leaders, military leaders, and policy makers) to meet the needs of their students. Schools become places where we wrap our collective minds, hearts, and resources around our children.

Yet many decisions are being made about the work teachers should and should not do, can and cannot do, without including teachers at the table. Seventy percent of teachers nationwide say they are not included in their districts' decision-making process.[6] And when they are at the table, teachers feel like they are "voting or volunteering," to use Boyte's formulation. For example, second grade teacher Justin Minkel explains, "sometimes the people who wrote the originals are just looking for a rubber stamp; other times they genuinely want our insights to inform their revisions. But either way, there's a big difference between helping to build something and just giving it a thumbs-up or thumbs-down once it's built."[7] While there is much discussion about teachers in the public and policy spheres, teaching as a profession should not only be publicly discussed by citizens. Instead, we must empower and support teachers to shape and participate in those conversations.

Teachers also reflect the larger trend of being excluded from important conversations about collective questions that matter. Boyte demonstrates that most Americans feel powerless in their role as citizens, and teachers feel similarly about their role in shaping our schools. Could there be a correlation between how we treat our teachers and how our citizens view their own power? Is the loss of civic knowledge and absence of civic engagement in our schools an un-intended consequence of the standards movement, the compliance culture that permeates teaching, or both?

Remodeling Teaching as Public Work: Why and When

The current changes sweeping our educational landscape provide an opening to respond to Boyte's call to "revitalize education as a great civic vocation, a vital form of public work."[8] Boyte suggests that one essential element of see-ing the work of teaching as a form of public work is to build the capacity of professionals in that field "to work *with* citizens, rather than acting *on* them."[9] To do this work in public education, we must reconceptualize teaching; we must see it as public work, and we must build the capacity of teachers to be teacher citizens.

If teaching were public work, we would understand that teachers "constantly make and remake," and teachers would understand "ourselves to be productive, creative people, who make and build things." Teaching is not a static job. Effective teachers constantly respond to contextual messages we receive from our students' behavior and work. While we need to be held accountable to high standards that ensure all students are engaged in relevant rigorous curricula, we also need to be supported in our individual and collective evolution as teacher citizens.

In order for our schools to be sites of academic, social, and civic engagement, educators need greater autonomy. Following Peter Levine's recent comments on citizenship, the core of teacher citizenship is "a combination of deliberation, col-laboration, and civic relationships."[10] Teacher citizenship is exercised not only in how teachers teach skills and content, but also in how they solve problems or innovate daily in our classrooms, schools, districts, and states. We need to see teaching as a profession where the work *itself* is an act of citizenship, where teacher citizens "seek to build, sustain, reform, and improve the communities to which they belong, deliberate with peers to define public problems and then collaborate with peers to address those problems."[11] Daniel Pink's theory, "con-trol leads to compliance; autonomy leads to engagement," provides an important insight into the rationale for teacher citizens.[12]

I have been using the language of remodeling the profession because I don't believe we have to build a whole new profession; there are many teachers who engage with their communities and participate in decision-making processes at the school, district, state, and federal levels. But we need to ensure that teacher engagement is not the exception or a token. As explained by eighth grade En-glish teacher Ariel Sacks, "there's nothing wrong with enlisting teachers to help implement a particular vision, but the teacher leaders have to retain the power to think critically, question the process, and contribute new ideas when applicable. At the same time, we need more teacher-driven initiatives; so ideally, teacher-leadership roles have built-in opportunities for collaboration and discussion."[13] My hope is that in remodeling our profession by making teaching a form of public work enacted by teacher citizens, we can move away from both the exceptionalism and tokenism of teacher engagement and toward supporting teachers as teachers not only of content, but of active and participatory citizenship.

Now Is the Time to Act

The remodeling of the teaching profession to a form of public work enacted by autonomous teacher citizens should not be seen as a new initiative but as the linchpin on which the success of our current improvement efforts rest. To date, forty-six states, the District of Columbia, and the US Department of Defense schools have adopted the Common Core State Standards; that represents close to 90 percent of US students.[14] We need to hold true to the promise of equity that formed the heart of the civil rights movement so *all* our young people receive an education worthy of their dreams. As we make this transition to Career-and-College standards we need to remember that education is both a means to the end of college and career preparation, but also the end itself. If the new standards are implemented with fidelity, all students will have more opportunities to participate in rigorous learning environments that foster collaboration, critical thinking, creativity, solving real-world problems, and communicating effectively. The issue, of course, is that it seems folly to suggest that our students will develop these skills if we don't develop these skills in our educators.

Important, we can't expect our students to evaluate differing perspectives, engage in civil discourse, collaborate, and solve real-world problems if we don't expect the same of our teachers. As Hillary Greene, a middle school teacher, noted: "If we want our public schools to create the next generation of thoughtful, engaged Americans, we need to support the people whose job it is to make an impact, and we need to work especially hard to retain the types of teachers who question the status quo and speak up even at the risk of being politically incorrect."[15] Doing this requires schools and districts to support teachers, which moves them from compliant subordinates to crucial partners in solving the challenges our schools—and nation—face.

Teacher Citizens and Collaboration

An essential duty that accompanies our autonomy as professional citizens engaged in public work is the *collective* responsibility to deliberate, collaborate, and build relationships with our students, our colleagues, and our communities. As my colleague Maddie Fennell suggests, "Teachers must share responsibility for the professional practice of every teacher in their school."[16] This suggests that, in order for teachers to become autonomous, we must be invested in each other *as well as* in our students. Teaching as a profession now feels like a single-player sport—some fail and some succeed, and each person is individually responsible for his or her performance. I am suggesting that we need to think of teaching as more of a team sport, where the rookies are given support and guidance, while the veterans are given leeway to shape and evaluate the newcomers. For that to happen, we need to build bridges across hallways, and these bridges need not detour to the principal's office.

In a recent study of strategies to enable students to assume more responsibility for their own learning, Carpenter and Pease discovered that:

> When students and teachers share responsibility for learning, students understand content more deeply and learn skills that will serve them well in a variety of endeavors. For this to happen, educators need to support learners as they experience greater autonomy and face new, inevitable challenges. Success in school and life demands a non-curricular skill set that provides a foundation for deep learning and personal growth. Educators who promote and teach skills in the areas of self-regulation, collaboration, and academic mindsets will help learners develop and thrive in school and beyond.[17]

Carpenter and Pease's claim fits well with my argument here; education is both a means and the end itself. It is important not only to prepare our students for their future, but also to engage them to show up in the present moment. That is, if we only train students for the future, we are training them to be passive and obedient, waiting to act until they are "done" with their education. If, on the other hand, we are working with them to be engaged citizens right now, we are giving them a space to be agents in their own learning. However, we can't ask our students to take risks we are not willing to take ourselves.

In moving from compliance to collective responsibility we need to tear down the walls that separate schools from the communities they serve. With the continuous dismantling of educational funding, it is imperative that schools partner with community groups. In a recent blog, educator Chris Crouch echoed this sentiment, when he noted that since schools and community groups are often "striving for a common goal, community activists could become the teeth in the gears to help communities improve and prosper."[18]

It is our *collective* responsibility to shape our students so that they can meet the challenges of the present and future. But to accomplish this requires an autonomous *and* collaborative teaching corps.

How Do We Get There?

This change won't happen overnight. As Hargreaves and Fullan remind us: "you can't fundamentally change the teacher without changing the person the teacher is, either. Thus, meaningful or lasting change will almost inevitably be slower than nonteachers want it to be. Human growth is not like producing hydroponic tomatoes. It can be nurtured and encouraged, but it cannot be forced."[19] So how do we remodel this profession for current and future citizen-teachers?

We have approximately 3,700,000 K–12 teachers; imagine what we could do if those teachers were supported as teacher citizens, if they saw themselves as enabling and modeling critical thought and action for the entire community? What can we do to make that happen? The most urgent task is to build the capacity of our teachers to do this work. The first step in that process is to think about professional development differently; too often our professional development is a one-size-fits-all deficit model of professional development. This "deficit model" focuses on weaknesses rather than strengths and is pitched at the level of our least effective educators. Instead, professional development should be aligned with what we know about how adults learn. Research demonstrates that adults learn best in the following situations: when they can bring their life experiences and knowledge to learning, when they are solving problems, when their learning is germane to the task at hand, and when learning is self-directed.[20] That is, instead of a model that tries to prevent failure, we need to think about how to enable success. We should be asking what we can do to change professional development so that it supports teachers to collaborate and solve problems with other educators *as well as* the larger public.

The second important step in building teacher capacity is to help school administrators learn to cultivate teacher citizens. Administrators don't have to carry the burden of problem solving; they can engage and empower teachers in that work. Not only will this take time to build as the supervisor/supervisee model is revamped, but we also need to build time into teachers' work days to do this work—collaborating with other teachers and engaging with the larger community should cease to be "volunteer" work that teachers do on their own time. This requires schools, districts, and unions to reevaluate the criterion that drives decision making.

In writing about developing teacher leaders, Larry Ferlazzo reminds us of the importance of experiential learning through problem solving. He writes, "Organizers look at community problems as opportunities to build individuals' leadership. In this view of things, the struggle is not just about the issue at hand—housing or childcare or unemployment—it's about building the skills, sensitivities, and relationships needed to sustain community progress."[21] With the right support, the problems we face as educators can be turned into opportunities that strengthen our individual and collective capacities as teacher citizens.

This also has significant implications for those who prepare teachers and principals. Teacher preparation programs need to continue to prepare students to lesson plan, assess, analyze data, and apply knowledge of best practices. But they also need to encourage their students to think critically, explore differing perspectives, and collaborate with each other and the community. Future teachers need to know how to work with others who have differing perspectives, dive into solving real-world problems, deliberate, and develop culturally and linguistically relevant relationships with students, teachers, parents, and community members.

During a recent visit to Metropolitan State University in Minnesota, I met with a diverse group of preservice teachers who spoke of their commitments to their community. When I asked if they could explain their level of engagement, one student replied, "our professors model the instructional strategies and community engagement they teach us about." Another place doing this well is the Teacher Leader program at Charleston College, where their teacher educators provide their students with "tools to traverse this landscape as effective communicators, problem solvers, and innovators."[22] One more place is Elon University, which offers a leadership development seminar sequence for teacher candidates through their participation in a virtual professional learning community, or VPLC. This VPLC helps develop teacher candidates' leadership and collaboration skills and prepares them to be change agents both in their classrooms and at the school level or beyond.

Our preservice teachers need more and better opportunities to engage in experiential learning: they should be in schools early and often. The University of Louisville offers some of its courses at local public schools. In doing so, they build the bridge from theory to praxis for preservice teachers and help professors remain engaged and relevant. Also promising are residency programs where new teachers are provided with full-year medical-style residencies where they teach alongside a highly trained master/mentor teacher. Last year, I met with students in the teacher residency program at Virginia Commonwealth University and was inspired by their ability to collaborate to solve problems and foster relationships with their community. Another residency program developed by the Center for Inspired Teaching prepares teachers to help students reach their full potential. Lamont Shipley, a 2012 Inspired Teaching Fellow, shared that this program prepared him for his "roles inside and outside of the classroom . . . [as] a changemaker and a leader." Students of these teachers "are not told what to think, they learn how to think, thereby developing critical skills needed to succeed in school today and in college and careers tomorrow."[23] There are places already developing teacher citizens. However, this must become the norm rather than the exception for a lucky few.

Broad Benefits

Too often our discussions are filled with a crisis narrative about the state or direction of public education and teaching in the United States. That couldn't be further from the truth. Our schools are filled with teachers who want more from their students and themselves, but we can't do it alone. The benefits of this new model include better-educated students, teachers as models for civic participation, and schools as sites of embedded participatory democracy. Remodeling teaching will improve our schools, communities, and democracy, but we must do this public work together. In *Redefining the Role of the Teacher: It's a Multifaceted Profession*, Lanier suggests that "politicians and parents, superintendents and school board members, employers and education school faculty . . . must also be willing to rethink our roles in education to give teachers the support, freedom, and trust they need to do the essential job of educating our children."[24]

To conclude, as teachers we need to recognize that shaping our profession is not simply about being seated at a table set by others; it is our table, and we don't need an invitation. As Jessica Cuthbertson, a teacher-citizen I admire, wrote, "it is our collective responsibility and opportunity to advocate for our profession and for our students."[25] Just like the civil rights song Boyte references, "we are the ones we've been waiting for." This is all true, but let's remember to engage with others and remember to bring others along with us as we build a teacher citizenry. In the aptly titled *You Can't Do It Alone*, Johnson offers some sage advice for collaboration: don't assume they know, don't assume they don't care, don't assume their minds are shut, and remember—civil, honest "dialogue always moves the needle."[26]

Notes

1. US Department of Education, National Commission on Excellence in Education, *A Nation at Risk: The Imperative for Educational Reform* (Washington DC, 1983), 29.

2. Carnegie Corporation of New York, *A Nation Prepared: Teachers for the 21st Century. The Report of the Task Force on Teaching as a Profession* (New York: Carnegie Forum on Education and the Economy, 1986).

3. Andy Hargreaves and Michael Fullan, *Professional Capital: Transforming Teaching in Every School* (Toronto: Teachers College Press, 2012), xii.

4. Barnett Berry and the TeacherSolutions Team 2030, *Teaching 2030: What We Must Do for Our Students and Our Public Schools: Now and in the Future* (New York: Teachers College Press, 2011), 167.

5. *"The Irreplaceables: Understanding the Real Retention Crisis in America's Urban Schools* (Brooklyn: TNTP, 2012).

6. Anne Duffe, Steve Farkas, Andrew Rotherham, and Elena Silva, *Waiting to Be Won Over: Teachers Speak on the Profession, Unions, and Reform* (Washington, DC: Education Sector, 2008), *www.educationsector.org/sites/default/files/publications/WaitingToBeWonOver_0.pdf*.

7. Justin Minkel, "Follow-Up: Teacher Voice Matters in Education Policy," Teaching Ahead: A Roundtable (blog), *Education Week*, July 23, 2012, accessed December 1, 2013, *blogs.edweek.org/teachers/teaching_ahead/2012/07/heres_a_troubling_riddle_what.htm*.

8. Harry C. Boyte, "Reinventing Citizenship as Public Work." In *Democracy's Education: Public Work, Citizenship, and the Future of Colleges and Universities* (Nashville: Vanderbilt University Press, 2015).

9. Harry C. Boyte, *The Citizen Solution: How You Can Make a Difference* (St. Paul: Minnesota Historical Society Press, 2008), 144.

10. "What Makes a Good Citizen?" *Academic Minute*, WAMC Northeast Public Radio (Albany, NY: WAMC, July 4, 2013), *wamc.org/post/dr-peter-levine-tufts-university-what-makes-good-citizen*.

11. Peter Levine, "What Is the Definition of Civic Engagement?" *A Blog for Civic Renewal*, December 11, 2012, accessed December 3, 2013, *peterlevine.ws/?p=10357*.

12. Daniel H. Pink, *Drive: The Surprising Truth about What Motivates Us* (New York: Riverhead Books, 2009).

13. Ariel Sacks, "Beyond Tokenism: Toward the Next Stage of Teacher Leadership," First Person (blog) *Education Week*, October 17, 2012, accessed December 1, 2013, *www.edweek.org/tm/articles/2012/10/17/tl_sacks.html*.

14. Alliance for Excellent Education, "Common Core State Standards," accessed November 15, 2013, *a114ed.org/issues/common-core-state-standards/*.

15. Hillary Greene, "The Coffee Crisis in Schools: Do Teachers Have to Feel So Alone?," First Person (blog), *Education Week*, June 11, 2013, accessed December 1, 2013, *www.edweek.org/tm/articles/2013/06/11/fp_greene_coffee.html*.

16. Maddie Fennell, "How Do We Measure and Value Effectiveness?" Rick Hess Straight

Up (blog), *Education Week*, July 25, 2012, accessed December 2, 2013, *blogs.edweek. org/edweek/rick_hess_straight_up/2012/07/how_do_we_measure_and_value_ effectiveness.html*.

17.   Jeffrey Carpenter and Jennifer Pease, "Preparing Students to Take Responsibility for Learning: The Role of Non-curricular Learning Strategies," *Journal of Curriculum and Instruction* 7, no. 2 (2013): 48.

18.   Chris Crouch, "3 Ways Community Activists Could Make Education Better," The Blog (blog), *Huffington Post*, November 26, 2013, accessed November 28, 2013, *www.huffingtonpost.com/chris-crouch/community-activists-can-improve-education_b_4330817.html*.

19.   Andy Hargreaves and Michael Fullan, *Professional Capital: Transforming Teaching in Every School* (Toronto: Teachers College Press, 2012), xii.

20.   If teachers' professional learning was self-directed they could identify their learning needs, formulate learning goals, identify resources, choose and implement appropriate learning strategies, and evaluate learning outcomes. Adapted from Malcolm Knowles, *Self-Directed Learning: A Guide for Learners and Teachers* (Chicago: Association Press, 1975).

21.   Larry Ferlazzo, "Developing Teacher Leadership for the Long Haul," CTQ Collaboratory (blog), *Education Week*, October 29, 2013, accessed November 27, 2013, *www.edweek.org/tm/articles/2013/10/28/ctq_ferlazzo_leadership.html*.

22.   For more information, visit *ehhp.cofc.edu/student-resources/Teacher%20Leader*.

23.   For information about the Center on Inspired Teaching, visit *www.inspiredteaching. org*.

24.   Judith Taack Lanier, "Redefining the Role of the Teacher: It's a Multifaceted Profession," *Edutopia*, July 1, 1997, accessed November 26, 2013, *www.edutopia.org/ redefining-role-teacher*.

25.   Jessica Cuthbertson, "Follow-Up: Teacher Leaders' Responsibility to Advocate," Teaching Ahead: A Roundtable (blog), *Education Week*, July 24, 2012, accessed November 12, 2013, *blogs.edweek.org/teachers/teaching_ahead/2012/07/follow_up_ action_advocacy.html*.

26.   Jean Johnson, You *Can't Do It Alone: A Communications and Engagement Manual for School Leaders Committed to Reform* (Lanham, MD: Rowman and Littlefield Education, 2012), 44–45.

PART VII

Summing Up

In discussions with students in the spring of 2014, background for the forthcoming National Issues Forum conversation on communities, higher education, and the changing world of work, Matt Filner, a political science professor at Metropolitan State University in Minnesota, found a pattern. When he asked students in his class about their concerns about higher education today, they voiced many worries—student debt, cost of college, uncertain job prospects, and the like. But as they discussed these questions, they realized they had concerns in common. They became aware that higher education's challenges are collective questions, not simply individual ones. They need collective redress. Put differently, students shifted from a "me" consciousness to a "we" consciousness.

Revitalizing the democratic purposes and stories of higher education will involve a shift from me to we.

26

ORGANIZING HIGHER EDUCATION BETWEEN THE TIMES

Paul N. Markham

> Historical change is like an avalanche. The starting point is
> a snow-covered mountainside that looks solid. All changes
> take place under the surface and are rather invisible. But
> something is coming. What is impossible is to say when.
> —Norman Davies

As I imagine what higher education will be for my young children, I am much less sure than I was even a few years ago.[1] The present opportunities and challenges facing American higher education have created an interesting dynamic of living between the times—a time of perceived threat to higher education and a time of great need to reform our postsecondary systems and institutions. Whatever the outcome, my children's higher education experience is sure to be different from mine.

The perspectives brought by the authors of this volume are diverse; yet they hit a harmonious tone regarding their call for higher education to address the most pressing issues of our day. We all agree what is at stake is no less than the state of our democracy and our collective ability to create a healthy society for all who live in it. What is less clear is how we achieve this end. The multifaceted and decentralized nature of higher education institutions makes culture change difficult. There seems no end to well-meaning programs designed to address important societal issues, but few acknowledge the fundamental issues of higher education such as access, cost, retention, and the changing demands of career preparation. The very serious challenge ahead for higher education professionals is to bring innovation to our postsecondary systems while at the same time navigating the delicate political cultures of traditional higher education institutions.

Living between the Times

The UK's Institute for Public Policy Research recently released a comprehensive study of issues in higher education. The report, entitled *An Avalanche Is Coming: Higher Education and the Revolution Ahead* is a sobering account of pressing issues facing higher education systems, institutions, and professionals.[2] The authors argue that a deep and radical transformation must occur in higher education. They use the "avalanche" metaphor to stress the urgency of the issue— "the one certainty for anyone in the path of an avalanche is that standing still is not an option."[3] Their central message to higher education leaders and policy professionals is that "the certainties of the past are no longer certainties. The models of higher education that marched triumphantly across the globe in the second half of the 20th century are broken. Just as globalization and technology have transformed other huge sectors of the economy in the past 20 years, in the next 20 years universities face transformation."[4] The report lays out three fundamental challenges facing higher education systems across the globe. Institutions must offer sustainable solutions to: (1) how universities will ensure education for employability, (2) how the link between cost and quality can be broken through the creation of new university ranking systems, and (3) how the entire learning ecosystem needs to change because of new technologies available to current and future college students.

As the epigraph suggests, the quiet, snow-covered mountain appears immovable; however, the severe and rapidly occurring results of an avalanche begin with much more subtle movements beneath the surface of the snow. The everyday academic and administrative work of maintaining a higher education institution often lacks serious attention to issues of the global economy and how radical changes at this scale affect the business of our colleges and universities. For instance, as economic power shifts toward the east, Pacific Asia's contribution to global GDP has risen from 9.1 percent to 22.8 percent over the past five decades.[5] At the current pace, by 2020, China alone will account for 29 percent of the world's college graduates ages twenty-five to thirty-four. Put flatly, this means there will be as many Chinese graduates in this age group as in the entire US workforce, so global competition is quickly entering the realm of higher education.[6]

This change in the global economy and the significant investments in education it entails create a heightened competition for students and talented graduates. This is all taking place in an economic context of recession and reprioritization. As before the great recession, those without a strong education struggle to remain economically viable, but today an alarming number of college graduates go unemployed. In 2011, the United States had almost three hundred thousand master's degree graduates dependent on food stamp benefits. A deeper concern arises given that in the face of record unemployment of college graduates, there are thousands of jobs going unfilled because of the lack of qualified applicants. In the November 2012 issue of the *Economist*, Dominic Barton described research showing that almost 45 percent of employers struggle to find people with the skills for entry-level positions, and 70 percent blame this shortfall on the lack of adequate skills graduates bring to the position.[7] The traditional tendency of higher education to press for specialization while employers demand interdisciplinary analysis and synthesis further complicates any agile attempt to address this shortcoming.

Meanwhile, the costs of a degree are increasing and the economic benefits of having it are decreasing. Recent data from the National Center for Education Statistics indicate that between 2000 and 2010 the cost of undergraduate tuition plus room and board at public institutions rose 42 percent.[8] The result is skyrocketing student debt, which has increased 51 percent in the years 2008 to 2012 and now stacks up to nearly $1 trillion.[9] But, isn't higher education an investment? Surely the increased earnings brought by the completion of a post-secondary credential make up for this immediate financial sacrifice.

Among the most common recruiting pitches for higher education is the promise of earning exponentially more income over the course of one's career. Although it is generally true those with more education earn more over their lifetime, the trend has now reversed. The average earnings for students with a bachelor's degree fell 14.7 percent between 2000 and 2012 despite the notable increase in the cost to attain the degree. While this trend does not hold for all degree programs (notably STEM—science, technology, engineering, and mathematics), the quip that "college pays" is less convincing than it was a decade ago.

These challenges do not fully describe the time in which we find ourselves. In addition to these imperatives, there are essential cultural concerns to bear in mind. As Rom Coles and Blase Scarnati thoughtfully describe in the introduction to their chapter, we live in a time when higher education is under close scrutiny and liberal education in particular is struggling to demonstrate its value in the job market. In this context, many faculty members are sliding toward politically impotent modes of defensiveness and cynicism as the core of their work seems threatened in the name of efficiency and productivity.

When the widely read blog the *Daily Beast* posted its story "13 Most Useless Majors, from Philosophy to Journalism" in April 2012, a conversation debating the merits of liberal education went viral. Understandably, faculty, administrators, and graduates of liberal arts institutions assumed a defensive posture in their response to the devaluing of traditional humanities programs. A Google query of the phrase "value of a liberal arts education" yielded as many stories in the year following the *Daily Beast* post as in the decade prior to the list being published. Faculty, who largely see their role as furthering student learning and/or conducting valuable research in their respective disciplines, are often critical of efforts directed toward efficiency, workforce training, and other efforts that potentially interfere with learning as an end in itself. In an effort to cultivate a conversation about the complexity of higher education, Imagining America co-directors Scott Peters and Tim Eatman warn against embracing a "single story" about higher education's public purpose.[10] They stress that higher education is about *both* educating students for prosperous careers *and* educating them for effective citizenship in a diverse world. Any viable solution to challenges in higher education will respect both of these public purposes.

Between the time of the coming avalanche and the severe assault on higher education itself rests a complex and delicate political environment where the deep work of education reform must take place. This is an environment where neither "big data" nor pure ideology will triumph. Living between these times requires a commitment to strategies that honor data and evidence as well as the diverse narratives that shape the higher education landscape. Restructuring higher education is like K–12 reform efforts in terms of complexity, but dramatically dissimilar in terms of systemic structure. Postsecondary institutions themselves are decentralized and operate with academic freedom and unit-level autonomy as a central feature. In this environment, it is critically important to locate what Coles and Scarnati refer to as *ecotones*—overlaps between organizational systems that are rich with shared self-interests and opportunities for common work—and capitalize on these in strategic ways.

A significant part of my work in higher education has been building infrastructures for public engagement. In this role, I have learned that pure ideological stances rarely result in solutions—at least in solutions that avoid collateral damage in the form of broken relationships and trust. I have had to understand and appreciate the concerns of faculty, students, and administrators inside the institution as well as the concerns of the multiple sectors that make up the communities in which the university resides. In this context, skills of *translation* are indispensable. Ecotones exist far more often than they are embraced and nurtured. We need public-work-minded professionals at the institutional and policy-making levels with the ability to create partnerships, surface self-interests, and build on shared self-interests to create viable solutions for the critical issues churning beneath the snow-covered mountain.

While this brief concluding chapter is not the place to provide a detailed list of suggestions for higher education reform, I will offer one modest proposal for addressing the challenges we face.

Introducing the Eight-Hundred-Pound Gorilla

In his chapter on the "soul of higher education," David Mathews begins with a story recounted by Derek Barker, a member of the National Task Force on Civic Learning and Democratic Engagement. This task force authored the widely read *A Crucible Moment* report released at the White House in January 2012. Barker noted that while the committee convened to discuss the role of civic learning in higher education, a silent "eight-hundred-pound gorilla" had been in the room. No one introduced the gorilla, but everyone knew he was there. According to Barker, this gorilla was the objective to make colleges and universities more productive and efficient in a time of rapidly growing costs of degree attainment.

This account helps to highlight an important area of opportunity for higher education institutions. In many ways, the service-learning and civic engagement movement has been successful. Most four-year institutions have a coordinating staff position or office dedicated to community-based learning. The Campus Compact, a national coalition of college and university presidents, has more than eleven hundred member campuses and represents approximately six million students. The compact advances the public purposes of higher education by deepening institution's ability to improve community life and to educate students for civic and social responsibility. There are also many other membership organizations focused on supporting institutional priorities related to community and civic engagement—this is true for both academic and student affairs organizations. All this points to nearly ubiquitous awareness of community-engaged learning across our nation's campuses.

Despite the widespread presence of civic engagement programs, these efforts have failed to fully realize the promises of the civic engagement movement. A 2011 study conducted by John Saltmarsh and Matthew Hartley brought together a number of scholars and practitioners to reflect on the current state of civic learning in higher education. Saltmarsh and Hartley note the abundance of efforts on campuses that seek to place students in service to their surrounding communities; however, they argue that, "without the intentionality of process and purpose, there is a diminution of democratic potential. Students may learn, and important service may be rendered. But rarely does such an approach to engagement result in actively contesting a problematic status quo or engender concerted action to challenge and change it by every democratic means possible."[11] While there are reasons to believe that the now traditional work of campus-based civic engagement centers has plateaued, the infrastructures—space, staffing, and operating resources—have remained largely intact.

Priority (*mis*)alignment between these centers and the universities and colleges that house them is in many ways indicative of our life between the times. Senior administrators are increasingly pressed to deal with issues such as affordability, access, retention, and alignment with job markets while engagement center leaders continue the laudable work of building programs and partnerships for social justice, civic learning, and community impact. Both roles are necessary to fulfill the public purposes of higher education, but if there is indeed an avalanche coming, its target will be the *whole* institution, so it is in our collective self-interest to leverage all the resources available to us in order to find a way forward. The current state of higher education in America serves as evidence that easy solutions will not be forthcoming. Given the abundance of intellectual resources within our institutions, "low-hanging fruit" has long been harvested, so new approaches must be adopted.

My modest proposal for moving forward begins by introducing the eight-hundred-pound gorilla. Specifically, introducing the gorilla within the context of our institution's commitment to civic and community engagement. Many colleges and universities have, within close reach, infrastructures and engagement professionals, which can be tremendous resources for averting—or at least properly bracing for—the coming avalanche. Effective university centers for community engagement have dedicated significant time to developing cross-sector partnerships and building bridges to address issues of community and campus concern. When engagement professionals understand that the avalanche is not about "numbers," but about the well-being of our society, they can bring significant insights and actionable strategies to the table. As Bruininks, Furco, Jones, Sommers, and Konkle brilliantly articulate elsewhere in this volume, this means that campus leaders from all areas see public engagement not as a program, but as a central *strategy* for addressing key institutional priorities.

In the Spirit of Public Work

Regardless of the formal title I carry, I fundamentally think of myself as an organizer of higher education. I owe this primary identity to a mentor, who helped me during a critical juncture of my life. I had been trained as a community organizer, which in essence is about being an effective connector, strategist, and facilitator of collective action. Specifically, I was shaped in the *cultural* organizing tradition, which is less about "winning" issues (elections, for example) and more about building capacity for sustainable change. During a particularly volatile moment, I expressed significant consternation over the decision whether to be an organizer or work in higher education, which I had the academic and administrative credentials to pursue. My mentor was able to see past these as competing desires and simply replied, "You need to be an organizer *in* higher ed." I've lived by this advice ever since.

Public work is what cultural organizers strive to cultivate. We work to create environments where diverse individuals and groups talk together, plan together, work together, and evaluate together. I've written elsewhere about how public work allows our imaginations to be shaped for possibilities that are otherwise inaccessible.[12] We need the spirit of public work to animate our efforts to address the coming avalanche in higher education. In terms of my own modest proposal, we need a public work effort to align engagement centers and programs with institutional priorities to address our most central challenges. As with any complex issue, I cannot make recommendations on how we end—because the destination is always determined by each step toward the solution—but I can confidently propose how we begin.

Public engagement professionals: Do your homework. In addition to managing a number of engagement programs, learn how to be effective organizers able to leverage public engagement as a *strategy*. Learn how to be a translator of public values—for example: How does or can your work address the coming avalanche? How is the avalanche a social justice issue as well as an issue of public policy? Understand what organizers refer to as the "self-interests" of all the stakeholders involved. This does not mean capitulate to *selfish* demands. Simply put, it means understand what each stakeholder cares about the most. What are they trying to accomplish? What are they held accountable for achieving? The organizer must always understand and be able to "translate" these self-interests across a diverse group. Finally, be prepared to demonstrate what you bring to the table. When an invitation comes to weigh in on the challenges ahead, rise to the occasion.

Senior-level campus leaders: Do your homework. Understand that public engagement is far more than the "good stuff" we all know we should be doing. There is a burgeoning literature on the positive effects of community and civic engagement on areas including development and advancement, access, retention, well-being, alumni relations, career-readiness, student learning, and campus climate. If you have a robust public engagement program or center on your campus, it is likely led by someone who can bring strategic insight and practical leadership to your priorities. Put them to the test. Invite them to the table and listen to what they have to contribute. If they've done their homework, they'll impress you.

Notes

1.   The epigraph for this chapter is Norman Davies, "Lunch with the FT: Norman Davies," *Financial Times*, October 19, 2012. *www.ft.com*.

2.   Michael Barber, Katelyn Donnelly, Saad Rizvi, and Lawrence Summers, *An Avalanche Is Coming: Higher Education and the Revolution Ahead* (London: Institute for Public Policy Research, 2013).

3.   Ibid, 3.

4.   Ibid, 4.

5.   Michael Barber, Katelyn Donnelly, and Saad Rizvi, *Oceans of Innovation: The Atlantic, the Pacific, Global Leadership and the Future of Education* (London: Institute for Public Policy Research, 2012).

6.   Organisation for Economic Co-operation and Development, *Education Indicators in Focus*, 2012, *www.oecd.org/edu/50495363.pdf*.

7.   Dominic Barton, "Young, Gifted and Slack: The Skills Gap Must Be Bridged If the World Is to Avoid Dire Consequences," *Economist*, November 21, 2012. *www.economist.com*.

8.   National Center for Education Statistics, "Tuition Costs of Colleges and Universities," 2012, *nces.ed.gov/fastfacts/display.asp?id=76*.

9.   Ruth Simon and Rachel Ensign, "Student-Loan Delinquencies among the Young Soar," *Wall Street Journal*, February 28, 2013. *online.wsj.com*.

10. Scott Peters and Timothy Eatman, "Countering the Single Story about Higher Education's Public Purpose," *Huffington Post—College*, September 27, 2013. *www.huffingtonpost.com/college*.

11. John Saltmarsh and Matthew Hartley, eds., *"To Serve a Larger Purpose": Engagement for Democracy and the Transformation of Higher Education* (Philadelphia: Temple University Press, 2011), 17.

12. Paul N. Markham, "You Don't Know Where You're Going until You're on Your Way There: Why Public 'Work' Matters," *Journal for Civic Commitment* 17 (2011). *ccncce.org/articles/you-dont-know-where-youre-going-until-youre-on-the-way-there-why-public-work-matters*.

27

THE SOUL OF HIGHER EDUCATION: CONCLUDING REFLECTIONS

Harry C. Boyte

> We have frequently printed the word Democracy. Yet I cannot
> too often repeat that it is a word the real gist of which still
> sleeps, quite unawaken'd, notwithstanding the resonance and
> the many angry tempests out of which its syllables have come,
> from pen or tongue. It is a great word, whose history, I suppose,
> remains unwritten, because that history has yet to be enacted.
> —Walt Whitman, *Democratic Vistas*

What do twenty-first-century freedom movements look like?

Tyrannies still proliferate where battle lines are clearly drawn, with powerless groups struggling to break free of obvious structures of oppression. But the most pivotal freedom struggle of our time may well involve invisible patterns that thwart the collective powers of whole societies to address common challenges and wicked problems, from climate change to rising inequality. Here, the struggle for the soul of higher education, in David Mathews's evocative phrase, is linked to the fate of democracy in the nation.

One way to look at the linkage is through examining the role that higher education plays in generating increasing inequality. In *Capital in the Twenty-First Century* Thomas Piketty demonstrates the dynamic of inequality. He writes, "Since the 1970s, income inequality has increased significantly in the rich countries, especially the United States, where the concentration of income in the first decade of the twenty-first century regained—even slightly exceeded—the level attained in the second decade of the previous century [the previous high]. . . . Will the world in 2050 or 2100 be owned by traders, top managers, and the superrich, or will it belong to the oil-producing countries or the Bank of China? It would be absurd not to raise the question."[1] Piketty shows that "this spectacular increase in inequality largely reflects an unprecedented explosion of very elevated incomes . . . a veritable separation of the top managers of large firms from the rest of the population." He argues that it "may be possible to explain [this separation] in terms of the history of social and fiscal norms."[2]

This argument was made at length by *New York Times* columnist Paul Krugman, who contrasted current norms with the more democratic norms of the 1930s. "Much more than economists and free-market advocates like to imagine, wages—particularly at the top—are determined by social norms," Krugman said. "What happened during the 1930s and 1940s was that new norms of equality were established, largely through the political process. What happened in the 1980s and 1990s was that these norms unraveled, replaced by an ethos of 'anything goes.' And a result was an explosion of income at the top of the scale."[3]

Neither Piketty nor Krugman draws connections between norms that legitimize exploding executive salaries and higher education. But connections emerge in *Democracy's Education*.

The values and approaches teachers learn through teacher education are a case in point. Anthropologist Annette Lareau, in her study *Unequal Childhoods*, finds that educators, whether in suburbs or inner cities, are trained in a "dominant set of cultural repertoires about how children should be raised," including highly individualist, competitive, and achievement-oriented norms. In contrast, for working-class and poor families, there is an emphasis on sustaining relationships with family and friends.[4] In her phrase, there exists a sharp clash of "cultural logics" between educators and working-class and lower-income children.

Put differently, conventional wisdom assumes that the issue is "an achievement gap" whose remedy is giving poor people and racial minorities resources and remediation so that they can make it in a hypercompetitive, individualist, meritocratic educational system and society. But a vantage informed by egalitarian, cooperative, and democratic norms sees another problem: the hypercompetitive, individualist education system and society itself. The system stigmatizes those who don't play by the rules as failures. And it teaches the "winners" a very narrow understanding of what education is all about.

The story of individual, competitive achievement as the point of education, taught to K–12 teachers, is also communicated to the broader society through college recruitment approaches. For years, they have highlighted higher education as a ticket to individual advancement. Increasingly they emphasize simply "return on investment," or how much money students will make in their lifetimes if they attend and pursue degrees in particular fields. According to John Dedrick, who has worked with hundreds of institutions, even Jesuit colleges have begun to put "Return on Investment" calculators on their websites.[5]

The cultural logic of individual, competitive achievement also increases disparities through its messages to students who enroll. Thus, recent research by Nicole Stephens and others sponsored by the Kellogg School of Management at Northwestern, "Unseen Disadvantage," describes the ways in which individualist achievement norms widen inequality through their effects on undergraduates in colleges and universities. Thus norms such as "doing your own thing," "paving your own path," and "realizing your individual potential" are familiar to middle- and upper-class students. Such norms are experienced far differently by first generation students from working-class families. For the latter, "expectations for college center around interdependent motives such as working together, connecting to others, and giving back," Stephens reports. In a series of four studies, Stephens and her fellow researchers found that as working-class students were exposed to the message of individual success and independence, a strong social class performance gap emerged.[6]

Finally, it is useful to remember that higher education has trained those who lead "the veritable separation of the top managers of large firms from the rest of the population." In a similar vein, as Nancy Cantor and I previously observed, it was the graduates of our prestigious universities—not evildoers from another planet—who created financial instruments like derivatives that caused the financial meltdown, even though that was not their intention.[7]

Indeed, virtually all professionals in contemporary knowledge societies are shaped by higher education. This is the dynamic that makes colleges and universities *anchoring institutions of citizenship*, for good or ill. When public impacts and meanings of work are off the table, citizenship becomes an afterthought with little impact on institutional life and practice.

It is worth reemphasizing here that today's cultural logic that touts hyper-competitive individual achievement as the main purpose of education is a relatively new development. As David Mathews, Scott Peters, and Albert Dzur describe in detail in their essays, alternative understandings of the aims of education and higher education once animated colleges and universities of all kinds. In 1908 Harvard president Charles Eliot argued, "at bottom, most of the American institutions of higher education are filled with the democratic spirit. Teachers and students alike are profoundly moved by the desire to serve the democratic community."[8]

Middle-class young people know how to perform according to the dominant cultural logic because they have grown up immersed in its activities. These enhance certain skills and dimensions of cognitive development, but they also socialize them in individualized accomplishment and dependence on authority, with few opportunities to develop capacities for self-directed collective action, as our colleague, family social scientist William Doherty observes.[9] Doherty has long charted the erosion of children's unstructured play and its damaging consequences. He recounts a conversation with a YMCA camp director who reported that middle-class young people have anxiety attacks during "free time" at camps, even when they are given several options.[10] Moreover, "career advancement" is often simply a taken-for-granted end in itself. Nan Skelton, codirector of the Center for Democracy and Citizenship for a number of years and a founder of the Jane Addams School, our partnership with new immigrants, describes how perplexed native-born college students working with immigrants often become when questioned by immigrants about leaving behind their families and communities in pursuit of individual success. They have never before encountered the question.[11]

Yet there are multiplying signs of discontent about such norms, including among those who succeed by following them. As early as the late 1990s, when Edwin Fogelman, chair of the political science at the University of Minnesota, and I interviewed several dozen senior faculty members, many with distinguished reputations in different fields, about their work experiences, we found much hidden discontent with the increasingly hypercompetitive research culture of the university. Almost all we spoke with disliked the "star" system. They decried growing disparities among tenured and adjunct faculty members. They were dismayed about the erosion of cooperative and interdisciplinary work, and the devaluation of teaching. These findings are summarized in my report for the Kettering Foundation, *Public Engagement in a Civic Mission.*[12]

In this *Democracy's Education* symposium, both students and young faculty members voice similar discontents. "I find that the University is no place for humanity," one graduate student in humanities wrote to Tim Eatman, whose research is focused on graduate students and young professionals. Eatman documents both the individualist achievement norms of research cultures, and also desire, among both graduate students and young faculty, for something different—publicly engaged and collaborative work. Jamie Haft quotes fellow students in a leading fine arts program. "I put this pressure on myself when I'm at school to reject my community and my home." Another recounts that "everyone thinks identity is an individual thing, and if you're not blazing your own path, tearing down traditions, and creating something new then it's not worthwhile." Cecilia Orphan tells of her own struggle to maintain her public commitments in a high-pressure graduate program. David Hoffman conveys the voices of students "immersed in everyday worlds they had experienced as fundamentally unreal: structured around falsehoods, hidden agendas, or scripts . . . courses in which the content had felt disconnected from practical applications . . . conversations with some faculty and staff members who subtly objectified them, sometimes simply by lavishing them with praise they did not feel they deserved." Even peer interactions embody the pattern "in which others seemed to be going through the motions and playing games rather than communicating from the heart."

Discontent is one thing. Changing long-developing patterns is another. It is worth analyzing the social foundations of the cultural logic of education in more detail as a background to discussing strategies for change.

The Polar Night of Icy Darkness

In 1902, Jane Addams warned about the emerging class of professionals, "experts" as she described them, who saw themselves outside the people. In her view, detached expertise reinforced existing hierarchies based on wealth and power and created new forms of hierarchical power that threatened the everyday life of communities.[13] Her warnings anticipated what Xolela Mangcu calls "technocratic creep," the spreading control by outside experts in various forms, from mass mobilizing politics scripted by professionals that divides the world into innocents on the one side and evildoers on the other, to an assumption, rarely deeply interrogated but nonetheless pervasive in our time, that trustworthy knowledge is created by rational, distanced outsiders and delivered to those who are largely passive. Scientists "bring their message to citizens," as the journal *Nature* put it. They don't see themselves *as* citizens.

Technocratic creep was anticipated a century ago by Max Weber, who wrote about what he saw as the inevitable spread of bureaucracy and rationalization through modern societies, "the iron cage" (or according to recent translators, the "steel carapace") of technical rationality that holds ends as constant and focuses on efficiency of means. Even more evocatively in his lecture "The Profession and Vocation of Politics," Weber described this as "the polar night of icy darkness."[14] As ends became taken as a given, public concepts were dramatically narrowed. *Democracy became something delivered; politics became simply distributive;* and *citizens became mainly consumers.*

This symposium shows connections between the polar night, which has narrowed democracy, politics, and citizenship, and developments in higher education. Through the process higher education and its communities have lost a good deal of civic agency. A key driver has been the growing detachment of faculty cultures from experiences of students and the civic life of society.[15] As this occurred, education itself became *delivered* by specialists who reside outside a common civic culture. In 1950 Baker Brownell observed the effects, in overblown but vivid language in *The Human Community.* After years of work with communities through cooperative extension, Brownell had taken a position as a philosophy professor at Northwestern University, and he reacted sharply against the norms and assumptions he encountered. "Truth is more than a report," he said. "It is an organization of values. Efficiency is more than a machine; it is a human consequence." He argued that professional classes shaped by higher education, captivated by technique, method, specialization, and abstract modes of thought, had lost sight of face-to-face relations. "Professionals, professors, businessmen, generals, scientists, bureaucrats, publicists, politicians, etc. They may be capitalist or they may be Communist in their affiliations, Christian or Jew, American, English, German, Russian or French. But below these relatively superficial variations among 'the educated' there is a deeper affiliation. They are affiliated in the abstract, anonymous, vastly expensive culture of the modern city. . . . It is the persistent assumption of those who are influential . . . that large-scale organization and contemporary urban culture can somehow provide suitable substitutes for the values of the human communities that they destroy."[16]

Brownell's argument found parallel in the views of organizer Saul Alinsky two decades later. "Our alleged educational system," he declared, produces people who "have been trained to emphasize order, logic, rational thought, direction, and purpose. . . . It results in a structured, static, closed, rigid, mental makeup."[17]

The detachment feeds fatalism about work, work sites, and institutions voiced by theorists such as Hannah Arendt, Benjamin Barber, Jean Cohen, and Andrew Arato, by organizers such as Ernesto Cortes, and by participants in the Falcon Heights town meeting. Even the nonprofit sector, home of citizens according to civil society theory, has become "colonized" by the expert delivery paradigm, as political theorist Derek Barker has shown.[18] Jenny Whitcher's essay in this volume poignantly shows similar patterns among many groups that describe themselves as doing "community organizing."

These are global patterns. They appear in Xolela Mangcu's account of South African universities, tied to technocratic creep, which substitutes "intelligence" for "intellect," the ability to "look for the meaning of situations as a whole." Shigeo Kodama describes parallel patterns in technocratic and neoliberal education in Japan.

The spread of technocracy and an individualist, hypercompetitive story of education has come at high cost. As citizen-teachers, citizen-business owners, citizen-clergy, citizen-librarians, citizen-nurses, and even "civil" servants have become service providers, we have seen the erosion of civic power and the replacement of a productive culture of citizenship with a consumer culture of democracy. The result is the "illiberal education" that Benjamin Barber describes, fed by both market and technocratic dynamics. But the diverse voices, experiences, and insights of this symposium also show an emerging alternative, a movement for productive citizenship, civic innovation, and civic empowerment growing in and around colleges and universities, partly in response to what Paul Markham calls the "avalanche of changes." This fledgling movement has enormous implications.

In his recent book, *If Mayors Ruled the World*, Barber makes an outstanding contribution by calling attention to the qualities of cities that make them fertile grounds for pragmatic, democratic experimentation and civic engagement across ideological lines. If the democratic initiatives and ideas described in *Democracy's Education* spread on a significant scale, we will see an enormous growth of the movement for a stronger, deeper democracy that Barber champions.

Philosophies of the public and democratic purposes of higher education and how to prepare students to be productive citizens of a changing world is powerfully expressed in this symposium by Martha Kanter, undersecretary of education from 2009 to 2013; and by university presidents Nancy Cantor, Robert Bruininks, Judith Ramaley, and Adam Weinberg. Kanter was a leading voice in the Department of Education in the Obama administration for the democratic purposes of education. Nancy Cantor has long been the chief philosopher of a broadened vision of the land grant concept of "democracy colleges" for all of higher education. She played a key role in the development of the "Bollinger brief" before the Supreme Court which helped to sustain affirmative action by showing the links between diversity and education for democracy. Robert Bruininks developed a planning process for university-wide changes at the University of Minnesota which made public engagement a strategic priority and a question of institutional identity, not simply activities. Judith Ramaley has long been a leading philosopher of multi-dimensional liberal education and civic learning, central in the work of the Association of American Colleges and Universities (AAC&U), for which she now is a senior scholar. In 2012, AAC&U released the report, *A Crucible Moment*, coordinated by Caryn McTighe Musil in the same White House meeting which launched the American Commonwealth Partnership, and in this symposium Ramaley gives eloquent expression to its argument for civic learning and democratic engagement across every type of college and university. Adam Weinberg, who pioneered in organizing to change the consumer culture of student life while dean of students at Colgate College some years ago—a culture he dubbed "Club Med"—expands his vision in his essay here, describing multiple ways in which colleges and universities can prepare students, as well as faculty and staff, for public work.

Faculty are the key architects of curriculum, and in this symposium faculty members Rom Coles, Albert Dzur, Tim Eatman, Julie Ellison, Andrew Furco, Shigeo Kodama, Peter Levine, Xolela Mangcu, KerryAnn O'Meara, Scott Peters, Blase Scarnati, John Spencer, and Jenny Whitcher show how education for democratic citizenship can come alive in many different ways. Students are energizers of change, in ways demonstrated by Jamie Haft, Erin Konkle, Celica Orphan, and Jayne Sommers. Staff are often crucial, if sometimes invisible, organizers of democratic change, and staff members Peter Englot, David Hoffman, and Maria Avila during her years at Occidental College embody this principle. Sam Daley-Harris, David Mathews, and Bob Woodson show how philosophers, storytellers, and organizers outside of higher education can make important contributions to the effort of democratic revitalization within the field.

Finally, Lisa Clarke, one of the nation's outstanding teachers, issues a call for a new movement of "teacher-citizens" to reclaim the sense of education as a great civic vocation, as relevant to colleges and universities as it is to K–12.

All the writers in this collection advance resources for building a movement for civic change in higher education that can also help us to civically work our way out of the polar night as a whole society.[19] Here are six: developing work as a civic and democratic site; a new politics of knowledge which can be called "civic science"; a view of citizens as "co-workers in the kingdom of culture," in the phrase of African American intellectual W. E. B. DuBois; the "re-placing" of colleges as part of communities; the translation of community organizing into higher education; and a new political table.[20]

1. *Developing work as a civic and democratic site.* Aspirations for civic agency are appearing in many settings. They will acquire lasting power and impact and generate widespread civic identities of producer rather than mainly consumer when they become woven into the ongoing work practices and cultures of schools and colleges, congregations, businesses and union locals, government agencies, and nonprofits in ways that revitalize free spaces, places where people develop confidence, public sensibilities, and the skills and habits of an empowering everyday politics. Developing work as a civic site requires attention to the formation of college students' identities and practices. More broadly, it will also require and generate far ranging changes in professions of all kinds.

    Seeing work as a civic site is a strategy for deepening higher education's civic identity and practices. There are many ways this can be expressed. Rom Coles and Blase Scarnati describe the resonance of a "craftperson ethos" at Northern Arizona University, which holds potential to develop citizen faculty. David Hoffman at the University of Maryland, Baltimore County shows the sense of "realness" that emerges from students experiences of civic agency, as they work the world in consequential ways and develop a sense of themselves as cocreators, not simply consumers. Jenny Whitcher challenges the phony concept of "organizer" that groups advertise on college campuses. Albert Dzur points to the expanded view of freedom and the political agency that emerge when faculty think of their work in public ways and communicate a larger range of work possibilities. John Spencer pioneers a pathway for the civic scientist. Finally, Lisa Clarke issues the call for the revitalization of the civic qualities of a whole profession: teaching. Our own experiences with partners at Augsburg have shown the liberation of talents and energies that come from "making teaching more public." At Augsburg we have also seen the power of professional education that prepares students to be agents of change as "citizen teachers," "citizen nurses," "citizen artists," and "citizen scientists."

2. *A new politics of knowledge—toward a civic science.* As Peter Levine has shown, the new interdisciplinary community called "civic studies," focused on agency and citizens as cocreators, challenges the dominant ways we have come to think about knowledge, especially the divisions between fields concerned with "facts" like natural sciences and social sciences; those addressing "values," such as humanities; and those concerned with "strategies" for action, such as professions. In this symposium, Levine explores the problem by describing how the civic studies approach, holding in tension facts, values, and strategies, complicates any straightforward focus on "job placement." Many interventions might "work" for a specific outcome like job placement, including electronic surveillance, Levine observes, if enough attention is given to making it work. But the more important question is the larger context within which the intervention operates—and how the intervention might affect the context. His argument is much like Mangcu's, who calls attention to the replacement of intellect, or the ability to look at situations as a whole, with narrow "intelligence," or a focus on means to achieve a particular objective without regard for larger ends. John Spencer gives a detailed account of the new epistemology, best called civic science, illustrating with the Get Ready Iowa coalition, the theme of a National Science Foundation workshop in the fall of 2014. Nancy Cantor and Peter Englot describe the remarkable work in Syracuse and Syracuse University to democratize knowledge politics, creating a "community of experts" rather than detached expertise.

3. *A view of citizens as cultural coworkers.* "For more than 500 years," writes Charles Wilkinson in *Blood Struggle: The Rise of the Indian Nations*, "white society on this continent has discussed how long it would be before Indian people finally disappeared into the general society. Not if but when." He observes that "now we have data: five centuries of survival under the most excruciating pressure of killing diseases, wars, land expropriation, and official government policy—forced assimilation, then outright termination. Yet the tribes are now the strongest they have been in a century and a half. Never has this land seen such staying power."[21] I am convinced that Indians survived because they understand themselves as something like Du Bois's "co-workers in the kingdom of culture," owning and shaping their own stories, with ways of understanding themselves and the world at odds with

the dominant hypercompetitive, individualist, consumer culture of the larger society.[22]

Grounding education in the culture and life of Indian communities has been key to what Wilkinson calls the rise of the Indian nations. "In the 1950s, the landscape of Indian education displayed little but wreckage," Wilkinson describes. "The BIA [Bureau of Indian Affairs] ran a sprawling system of boarding schools and on-reservation day schools. . . . Despite some dedicated teachers who fought the system, [they] usually ignored Indian culture and often actively sought to rub it out." Since then, significant change has come through Indians' success in regaining power about education. It is not a finished process, and many problems remain. "Modern Indian leaders have accomplished reform, not revolution," reports Wilkinson. "Nevertheless high school graduation rates have steadily gone up. The number of Indian people in colleges has climbed from about 2000 in the 1950s . . . to 147,000 in 2000. These are not just numbers. They are doctors, biologists, engineers, business people, historians, lawyers, economists, poets, teachers and generalists."[23] A new group of tribal land grant colleges and universities, designated 1994 land grants, have been central to the process. Like older land grants, tribal land grants combine "practical and liberal arts." They have a strong commitment to revitalizing native culture and history.

In this symposium, Xolela Mangcu and Tim Eatman write about the deep resources for understanding people as cultural coworkers forged in black freedom struggles against oppression, in traditions such as the black consciousness movement in South Africa and the historically black cultures and universities in the United States. Both combined cultural consciousness and cultural pride with extensive popular education and many practical community building projects of public work. Their lessons have wide application.

4. *The "re-placing" of colleges.* In recent years a growing number of strategies and approaches seek to re-place colleges and universities, revitalizing the sense that campuses are "part of" communities, not simply "partners with" communities. These include the idea from the American Democracy Project of state colleges and universities as "stewards of place" and the concept, pioneered by Ira Harkavy, a longtime leader in stressing the centrality of local communities, and the Netter Center he directs at the University of Pennvania, who have championed colleges and universities as "anchor institutions." In this symposium, Robert Bruininks and his colleagues at the University of Minnesota describe efforts over more than a decade to create more reciprocal and two-way relations with Minnesota communities. Julie Ellison discusses Citizen Alum as a new and highly promising strategy for regrowing everyday relationships needed for deep reconnection of colleges with places where they are located.

5. *Community organizing methods in higher education.* What is called broad-based community organizing has incubated a politics of civic

empowerment over the last generation, described by Scott Peters as "deeply relational, attentive to self-interests, critical but also prophetic and hopeful in tone, highly strategic in ways that are based on a rigorous analysis and mapping of realities and dynamics of power, and grounded in productive public work." Beginning to appear in higher education, it represents a revival and deepening of the old extension tradition of public work politics. The stories in this symposium of Maria Avila, Rom Coles and Blase Scarnati, Shonda Craft, Bill Doherty, Dennis Donovan, David Hoffman, Nan Kari, Paul Markham, Susan O'Connor, and Adam Weinberg directly emerge from community organizing and show some of the many possibilities that flow from its translation into higher educational settings.

6. *A new political table.* The participants in this symposium reflect a mix of interests and positions. They include proponents of different paradigms of civic engagement—liberal, communitarian, and civic agency. They cross a wide partisan range, from long-term activists in progressive causes to architects of citizen-driven change like Sam Daley-Harris, founder of the largest poverty reduction group in the world, RESULTS, and conservatives like Bob Woodson, a former civil rights activist who is now a senior advisor to Representative Paul Ryan, Republican vice presidential candidate in 2012. These differences call to mind Hannah Arendt's concept of the common table that acknowledges differences while occasioning commonality. The common table is connected to "world-building," which allows people to shift beyond subjectivities, feelings about each other, to common tasks. Linda Zirelli emphasizes, "Foregrounded in Arendt's account of action is something less about the subject than about the world. . . . What Arendt calls the 'world' is not nature or the earth as such but is related to . . . the human artifact, the fabrication of human hands, as well as to affairs which go on among those who inhabit the man-made world together."[24]

Half a century ago, the civil rights movement served as a common table that captured the nation's imagination with images of everyday citizens risking lives and livelihoods to end racial segregation and advance the nation toward "liberty and justice for all," a dramatic story of productive citizenship. Today, while racial and other forms of bigotry remain and often take more subtle forms, we also face new challenges, including a widespread expectation that somehow solutions to our problems will be delivered by experts outside a common civic life. This expectation feeds growing inequality, as well as collective powerlessness.

In 2012 and 2013 more than 150 forums in communities across the country explored people's views about whether higher education should work with communities to address mounting public problems. There was widespread sentiment that it needs to. "Seeing the different levels of a university present in one group with community members truly provided unique input," said Laura Lake, a student at Winona State University who moderated an early discussion. "Seeing the differences between the views was extremely interesting. What was more exciting was seeing the areas they agreed upon—that higher education does indeed help us create the society we want."

We need a common table if we are to address today's public problems, to civically work our way out of the polar night, and to become a nation of civic producers, not simply democracy's consumers. This symposium suggests that renewing the public work of colleges and universities could well become one. Most importantly, this could contribute significantly to a renewed democratic story about education, that helps to reanimate democracy in the whole society.

Notes

Epigraph: Walt Whitman, *The Portable Walt Whitman* (New York: Penguin, 2003), 427.

1. Thomas Piketty, *Capital in the Twenty-First Century* (Cambridge, MA: Harvard University Press, 2014), 15.

2. Ibid., 24.

3. Paul Krugman, "Toward One-Party Rule," *New York Times*, June 27, 2003; and Krugman, "For Richer," *New York Times Magazine*, October 20, 2002, 2, 6.

4. Annette Lareau, *Unequal Childhoods: Class, Race and Family Life* (Berkeley: University of California Press, 2003), 4, 5.

5. The description of the dominant message used in recruiting students is detailed in Harry C. Boyte, *Everyday Politics: Reconnecting Citizens and Public Life* (Philadelphia: University of Pennsylvania Press, 2004), chapter 9.

6. Rebecca Covarrubias, Stephanie Fryberg, Camille S. Johnson, Hazel Rose Markus, and Nicole Stephens, "Unseen Disadvantage." See Kellogg School of Management blog, March 15, 2012, *www.kellogg.northwestern.edu/news/unseen_disadvantage.htm*, accessed December 22, 2013.

7. Harry C. Boyte and Nancy Cantor, "We Are the Ones We've Been Waiting For," *Huffington Post*, August 24, 2011.

8. Quoted from Harry C. Boyte and Elizabeth Hollander, *Wingspread Declaration: Renewing the Civic Mission of the American Research University* (Providence, RI: Campus Compact, 1999), 3, online at *www.compact.org/initiatives/trucen/wingspread-declaration-on-the-civic-responsibilities-of-research-universities*.

9. See William Doherty, *Take Back Your Kids: Confident Parenting in Turbulent Times* (Notre Dame, IN: Sorin Books, 2000).

10. Bill Doherty interview with Harry Boyte, January 19, 2014, St. Paul, Minnesota.

11. Interview with Nan Skelton, June 19, 2014, St. Paul, Minnesota.

12. See Harry C. Boyte, *Public Engagement in a Civic Mission* (Dayton, OH, Washington DC: Kettering Foundation, 2000), on web at *kettering.org/publications/pub-engagement-civic-mission*.

13. Jane Addams, *Democracy and Social Ethics* (New York: Macmillan, 1902), 270.

14. Weber in Peter Lassman and Ronald Speirs, *Weber: Political Writings* (Cambridge: Cambridge University Press, 1994), 368.

15. For instance, Thomas Bender and Carl Schorske, *American Academic Cultures in Transformation* (Princeton, NJ:: Princeton University Press 1998); KerryAnn O'Meara and Audrey J. Jaeger provide a detailed account of the forces that have drawn faculty away from community involvement and public purposes in "Community Engagement: Barriers, Facilitators, Models and Recommendations," *Journal of Higher Education Outreach and Engagement* 11, no. 4 (2006), 3–26; Richard Arum and

Josipa Roksa, *Academically Adrift: Limited Learning on College Campuses* (Chicago: University of Chicago Press, 2010).

16. Baker Brownell, *The Human Condition* (New York: Harper Brothers), 19–20.

17. Alinsky, *Rules for Radicals* (New York: Random House, 1972), 166.

18. Derek Barker, "The Colonization of Civil Society," *Kettering Review*, 2010, 8–18.

19. I am indebted to Mary Dietz for this description of the task we face. For Dietz's use of another of Weber's concepts, "the slow boring of hard boards," see her remarkable essay "The Slow Boring of Hard Boards": Methodical Thinking and the Work of Politics," *American Political Science Review* 88, no. 4 (1994), 873–86.

20. Dubois quoted from Jerald Podair, *Bayard Rustin: American Dreamer* (Lanthan, MD: Rowman & Littlefield Publishers, 2009), 4.

21. Charles Wilkinson, *Blood Struggle: The Rise of Modern Indian Nations* (New York: W. W. Norton, 2005), 383.

22. For an extended version of this argument, see Harry C. Boyte, *The Empowerment Gap: Rethinking Strategies for Poverty Reduction—A Study for the Northwest Area Foundation* (Minneapolis: Augsburg College, 2014). Dubois quoted from Podair, *Bayard Rustin*, 4.

23. Charles Wilkinson, *Blood Struggle: The Rise of Modern Indian Nations* (New York: W. W. Norton, 2005), 281, 288.

24. Linda M. G. Zerilli, *Feminism and the Abyss of Freedom* (Chicago: University of Chicago Press, 2005), 14.

CONTRIBUTORS

Maria Avila began her community organizing practice in northern Mexico in the 1970s and worked as a community organizer with the Industrial Areas Foundation in the 1990s in California. Avila pioneered bringing community organizing practices into higher education, directing the Center for Community Engagement at Occidental College and consulting widely with institutions in the United States and Northern Ireland. She is now assistant professor at California State University, Dominguez Hills in the Department of Social Work, MSW Program.

Benjamin R. Barber is a senior research fellow at the Graduate Center, City University of New York; Walt Whitman Professor Emeritus, Rutgers University; and the author of eighteen books including *Jihad vs. McWorld*, *Strong Democracy*, and most recently *If Mayors Ruled the World*. As founder and president of the Interdependence Movement, he is currently leading a project to establish a Global Parliament of Mayors, a pilot for which may convene as soon as autumn 2015.

Harry C. Boyte, Senior Scholar in Public Work Philosophy at the Center for Democracy and Citizenship at Augsburg College and a senior fellow at the University of Minnesota's Humphrey School of Public Affairs, is author and co-author of eight books including *Everyday Politics*, *The Citizen Solution*, and *The Wingspread Declaration on Renewing the Civic Mission of Research Universities* with Elizabeth Hollander. In 2012 Boyte coordinated the American Commonwealth Partnership, a coalition invited by the White House Office of Public Engagement to strengthen higher education as a public good.

Robert H. Bruininks is president emeritus of the University of Minnesota. Throughout his career, he has emphasized the civic mission and responsibilities of higher education through public scholarship and the design of strategies to enhance the public engagement and contribution of the University of Minnesota.

Nancy Cantor is chancellor of Rutgers University-Newark, after having served as chancellor of Syracuse University from 2004 to 2013. She is a social psychologist, a member of the Institute of Medicine of the National Academies, and a fellow of the American Academy of Arts and Sciences. Her educational leadership has centered on the role of higher education as a public good—a pathway to social mobility and democratic engagement.

Lisa Clarke has recently ended her term as team leader for the US Department of Education, Teaching Ambassador Fellows. She was on loan to the DOE from the Kent School District in Washington where she teaches social studies at Kent-Meridian High School. She came to teaching after six years at Rutgers University, where she studied gender and public policy and worked at the Center for Women's Global Leadership (CWGL). She is a National Board Certified Teacher and has held a variety of leadership positions in the Kent School District including, among others, serving on the Superintendent Professional Learning Community, assisting with curriculum development, and acting as a social studies curricular leader. In 2011 she was honored as the World Affairs Council 2011 World Educator and was chosen to be a World Affairs Council Fellow based on her work to promote and improve global education.

Rom Coles is the Frances B. McAllister Endowed Chair and Director of the Program for Community, Culture, and Environment at Northern Arizona University, where he is a leader in a civic engagement Action Research Team movement that involves nearly a thousand students and hundreds of community members each semester. He is the author of several books including *Visionary Pragmatism: Radical and Ecological Democracy*; *Radical Future Pasts: Untimely Political Theory* (edited with Mark Reinhardt and George Shulman); *Christianity, Democracy, and the Radical Ordinary: Conversations between a Radical Democrat and a Christian* (with Stanley Hauerwas); *Beyond Gated Politics: Reflections for the Possibility of Democracy*; *Rethinking Generosity: Political Theory and the Politics of Caritas*; and *Self/Power/Other: Political Theory and Dialogical Ethics*.

Sam Daley-Harris founded RESULTS (*www.results.org*), the international anti-poverty lobby, in 1980; founded the Microcredit Summit Campaign in 1995 (*www.microcreditsummit.org*); began coaching Citizens Climate Lobby in 2007 (*www.citizensclimatelobby.org*); and founded the Center for Citizen Empowerment and Transformation in 2012 (*www.citizenempowermentandtransformation.org*). He is author of *Reclaiming Our Democracy: Healing the Break between People and Government*.

Albert W. Dzur is professor of political science and philosophy at Bowling Green State University. He is the author of *Punishment, Participatory Democracy, and the Jury*, *Democratic Professionalism: Citizen Participation and the Reconstruction of Professional Ethics, Identity, and Practice*, and numerous articles on democratic theory and citizen participation. He posts regularly in the "Trench Democracy" series for the *Boston Review* and in "Conversations on Participatory Democracy" for the *Good Society* journal. His current book project is entitled *Democracy Inside: Participatory Innovation in Unlikely Places*.

Timothy K. Eatman serves as faculty codirector of Imagining America: Artists and Scholars in Public Life. An educational sociologist, Dr. Eatman focuses his scholarly work on equity issues and institutional policy in higher education. He is the recipient of the 2010 Early Career Research Award for the International Association for Research on Service Learning and

Community Engagement (IARSLCE). Among several boards Tim serves Mount Pleasant Christian Academy, a K–12 independent school founded by his parents over thirty years ago in Harlem, New York.

Julie Ellison, professor of American culture and English at the University of Michigan, served as founding director of Imagining America: Artists and Scholars in Public Life. She currently leads Citizen Alum, which is active on thirty campuses. Author of three books on United States and British literary history, Ellison is currently working on *Lyric Citizenship: The Public Project of the Humanities*.

Peter Englot is senior vice chancellor for public affairs and chief of staff at Rutgers University-Newark; from 2006 to 2013 he served as associate vice president for public affairs at Syracuse University. A linguist by training, during his career of more than twenty-five years as a higher education administrator he has focused on increasing access and opportunity.

Andy Furco is an associate professor of higher education in the Department of Organizational Leadership, Policy and Development at the University of Minnesota, where he also serves as associate vice president for public engagement and director of the International Center for Research on Community Engagement. His research focuses on exploring the ways in which community engagement practices in K–12 and higher education, both in the United States and abroad, impact participating students, faculty, institutions, and communities. Prior to arriving in Minnesota, he worked for fourteen years at UC Berkeley as the founding director of the Service-Learning Research and Development Center and as a faculty member in the Graduate School of Education.

Jamie Haft is assistant director of Imagining America: Artists and Scholars in Public Life, where she is organizing its Presidents' Council and creating programs that bridge higher education and grassroots arts and cultural organizations. She recently conceptualized and produced a documentary web series on student activism, and published in the peer-reviewed journal *Public* and in a national collection of trend papers commissioned by Americans for the Arts. Haft received an MS from Syracuse University's S. I. Newhouse School of Public Communications and a BFA from New York University's Tisch School of the Arts.

David Hoffman is assistant director of Student Life for Civic Agency at the University of Maryland, Baltimore County (UMBC) and an architect of UMBC's BreakingGround initiative. His work explores and supports students' development as civic agents, highlighting the crucial role of experiences, environments, and relationships students perceive as "real" rather than synthetic or scripted.

Robert J. Jones became president of the University at Albany in January 2013. He came to UAlbany following thirty-four and a half years at the University of Minnesota, where he began his career as a faculty member in agronomy and plant genetics and later assumed a number of key leadership positions including senior vice president for academic administration. Jones is nationally recognized for his work to advance university-community engagement, and at UAlbany he is deeply involved in building partnerships to strengthen communities.

Martha Kanter is New York University Distinguished Visiting Professor of Higher Education and served as Under Secretary of Education from June 2009 to December 2013. In that capacity, Kanter oversaw the US Department of Education's policies, programs, and activities related to postsecondary education, career-technical and adult education, and federal student aid. She has had extensive experience in both teaching and administration and has been a board member and advisor to a variety of national, state, and local organizations. Before joining the Department, Kanter served as chancellor of California's Foothill-De Anza Community College District.

Shigeo Kodama, professor in the Graduate School of Education at the University of Tokyo, received his PhD in education from the University of Tokyo in 1998. He is cofounder of the Japan Citizenship Education Forum.

Erin A. Konkle is a graduate student at the University of Minnesota whose research interests include assets-based approaches in education such as Appreciative Education and StrengthsQuest, organizational culture, and change management. She is a graduate assistant in the Jandris Center for Innovative Higher Education (J Center). Her professional experience includes consulting work for institutions integrating Appreciative Advising and StrengthQuest. Erin also worked for the Department of Student Life at the University of South Carolina and began her career as a social worker with Big Brothers Big Sisters Southeastern Pennsylvania coordinating University partnerships.

Peter Levine is the associate dean for research and Lincoln Filene Professor of Citizenship & Public Affairs in Tufts University's Jonathan Tisch College of Citizenship and Public Service. His most recent book is *We Are the Ones We Have Been Waiting For: The Promise of Civic Renewal in America*.

Xolela Mangcu is a fellow at the Hutchins Center for African and African American Research at Harvard University. He has previously held fellowships at the Brookings Institution, Harvard University, the Massachusetts Institute of Technology, and the Rockefeller Foundation. He took his PhD at Cornell. His latest book is *Biko: A Life*, and he is currently working on the legacy of Harold Washington in Chicago.

Paul N. Markham is Program Officer for Postsecondary Success at the Bill & Melinda Gates Foundation where his work focuses on building partnerships for student success in higher education. He has led a number of student and community engagement efforts as a faculty member and higher education administrator and is the recipient of the 2012 national John Saltmarsh Award for Leadership in Civic Engagement.

David Mathews, president of the Kettering Foundation, was Secretary of Health, Education, and Welfare in the Ford administration and, before that, president of the University of Alabama. Mathews has written extensively on Southern history, public policy, education, and international problem solving. His books include *Politics for People: Finding a Responsible Public Voice*, *Reclaiming Public Education by Reclaiming Our Democracy*, and *The Ecology of Democracy: Finding Ways to Have a Stronger Hand in Shaping Our Future*.

KerryAnn O'Meara is associate professor of higher education and codirector of the University of Maryland's NSF-funded ADVANCE grant for inclusive excellence. Her research and practice examines academic reward systems, faculty professional growth and careers, and faculty civic and community engagement to understand how actors can put organizational policies, structures, and cultures in place to support faculty professional growth, success, and inclusion.

Cecilia M. Orphan is a PhD candidate in the higher education division of the University of Pennsylvania's Graduate School of Education. Ms. Orphan studies the effects of neoliberal ideology on public higher education with special focus on open-access, regional comprehensive universities. Prior to coming to Penn, Ms. Orphan directed the American Democracy Project (ADP), a multi-campus initiative of the American Association of State Colleges and Universities (AASCU).

Scott J. Peters is faculty codirector of Imagining America: Artists and Scholars in Public Life. He is also a professor in the Department of Development Sociology at Cornell University. His latest book is *Democracy and Higher Education: Traditions and Stories of Civic Engagement.*

Judith Ramaley has been president and professor of biology at Portland State University (1990–1997), the University of Vermont (1997–2001), and Winona State University (MN) (2005–2012). She served as assistant director of Education and Human Resources (EHR) at the National Science Foundation from 2001 to 2004 and as a visiting senior scientist at the National Academy of Sciences during 2005. She is currently a senior scholar at the Association of American Colleges and Universities and Distinguished Professor of Public Service at Portland State University.

Blase Scarnati is director of First and Second Year Learning, which includes the First Year Seminar Program, and codirector of the First Year Learning Initiative at Northern Arizona University. He is also an associate professor of musicology in the School of Music.

Jayne K. Sommers is a graduate student at the University of Minnesota, whose research interests include access and affordability in higher education, student leadership, development of student affairs professionals, and college student mental health. She teaches in the Leadership in Student Affairs MA program at the University of St. Thomas in St. Paul, Minnesota, and serves on the Board of Directors for the Minnesota College Personnel Association. Sommers has a decade of experience working in student affairs, including residential life, orientation, and student activities.

John P. Spencer is a professor of psychology at the University of Iowa, the current director of the CHILDS Facility (CHild Imaging Laboratory in Developmental Science) and the founding director of the Delta Center (Development and Learning from Theory to Application). He received a ScB with Honors from Brown University in 1991 and a PhD in experimental psychology from Indiana University in 1998. He is the recipient of the Irving J. Saltzman and the J. R. Kantor Graduate Awards from Indiana University, the 2003 Early Research Contributions Award from the Society for Research in Child Development, and the 2006 Robert L. Fantz Memorial Award from the American Psychological Foundation.

Adam Weinberg is the president of Denison University. Prior to coming to Denison, he was the president of World Learning. Dr. Weinberg began his career at Colgate University where he was a member of the Department of Sociology and Anthropology and also served as Dean of the College. Dr. Weinberg has a long standing interest in the connection between higher education, civic engagement, and community vitality.

Jenny Whitcher is the director of the Master of Arts in Social Change degree program and of Service Learning at Iliff School of Theology in Denver, Colorado. Her focus areas include social change theory and practice, community organizing and democratic culture, and spiritual and civic development. She is currently organizing with others to develop a Denver/Colorado affiliate of the Industrial Areas Foundation (IAF). Whitcher served on the National Council of the American Commonwealth Partnership and the Puksta Foundation Advisory Council. Dr. Whitcher received her PhD in religious and theological studies from the Joint Doctoral Program at the Iliff School of Theology and the University of Denver, an MA in international human rights from the University of Denver, and a BA in journalism and politics from New York University.

Robert L. Woodson Sr. is founder and president of the Center for Neighborhood Enterprise, which promotes inner city empowerment. A former civil rights activist and an organizer with inner city communities for many years, working with public housing tenants, ex-convicts, ex-gang members, and others who challenge what he calls the "prison industrial complex," Woodson was a senior advisor on urban policy and poverty to Representative Paul Ryan, Republican vice presidential candidate in 2012.